Also published by
James Currey & Ohio University Press

Civil War, Civil Peace
Edited by Helen Yanacopulos & Joseph Hanlon
in association with The Open University

No Peace, No War
An Anthropology of Contemporary Armed Conflicts
Edited by Paul Richards

VIOLENCE, POLITICAL CULTURE & DEVELOPMENT IN AFRICA

VIOLENCE, POLITICAL CULTURE & DEVELOPMENT IN AFRICA

EDITED BY PREBEN KAARSHOLM
Associate Professor of International Development Studies
Roskilde University, Denmark

James Currey
OXFORD

Ohio University Press
ATHENS

University of KwaZulu-Natal Press
PIETERMARITZBURG

James Currey Ltd
73 Botley Road
Oxford OX2 0BS
www.jamescurrey.co.uk

Ohio University Press
19 Circle Drive, The Ridges,
Athens
Ohio 45701
www.ohioedu/oupress

University of KwaZulu-Natal Press
Private Bag X01
Scottsville, 3209
South Africa
www.ukznpress.co.za

© James Currey Ltd, 2006
First published 2006

1 2 3 4 5 10 09 08 07 06

ISBN 10: 0-85255-894-5 (James Currey paper)
ISBN 13: 978-085255-894-2 (James Currey paper)

ISBN 10: 0-89680-251-5 (Ohio University Press paper)
ISBN 13: 978-089680-251-3 (Ohio University Press paper)
Global & Comparative Series, No. 6

ISBN 10: 1-86914-116-4 (University of KwaZulu-Natal Press paper)
ISBN 13: 978-1-86914-116-5 (University of KwaZulu-Natal Press paper)

British Library Cataloguing in Publication Data
Violence, political culture & development in Africa
1. Political violence - Africa - Congresses 2. Africa -
Politics and government - 1960- - Congresses 3. Africa -
Social conditions - 1960- - Congresses
I. Kaarsholm, Preben, 1948-
960.3'29

Library of Congress Cataloging-in-Publication Data
available on request

Typeset in 10/11pt Photina
by Long House, Cumbria
Printed and bound in Great Britain by
Woolnough, Irthlingborough

Contents

Notes on Contributors

Jocelyn Alexander is Lecturer in Commonwealth Studies at the University of Oxford. She has been engaged in research on Zimbabwean social history for over fifteen years. She is co-author of *Violence and Memory: One Hundred Years in the 'Dark Forests' of Matabeleland* (James Currey, Oxford 2000), and author of a forthcoming book titled *The Unsettled Land: State-making and the Politics of Land in Zimbabwe* (2006). She is currently working on a history of policing and punishment in colonial Zimbabwe.

Nigel Eltringham is a Lecturer in the Department of Anthropology at the University of Sussex. He worked for three years with a conflict resolution NGO in Rwanda before conducting doctoral research in Rwanda and among the Rwandan diaspora in Europe. He is the author *of Accounting for Horror: Post-Genocide Debates in Rwanda* (Pluto Press, London 2004).

Douglas H. Johnson, St Antony's College, University of Oxford, is a historian of the Sudan and primarily the Southern Sudan in the nineteenth and twentieth centuries. He was a resource person at the Sudan peace talks in Kenya, and in 2005 a member of the Abyei Boundaries Commission. His main publications include *Nuer Prophets* (Clarendon Press, Oxford 1994), the Sudan volume of *British Documents on the End of Empire* (The Stationery Office, London 1998), and *The Root Causes of Sudan's Civil Wars* (James Currey, Oxford 2003, rev. edn. 2006).

Preben Kaarsholm is Associate Professor in International Development Studies, Roskilde University. He is the editor of *Cultural Struggles and Development in Southern Africa* (James Currey, Oxford 1991), *Inventions and Boundaries: Historical and Anthropological Approaches to the Study of Nationalism and Ethnicity* (with Jan Hultin, IDS, Roskilde 1994), and *City Flicks: Indian Cinema and the Urban Experience* (Seagull, Calcutta 2004). Recent publications on culture, politics and development in Southern Africa include 'Moral Panic and Cultural Mobilization: Responses to Transition, Crime and HIV/AIDS in KwaZulu-Natal' (*Development and Change* 36: 1, 2005).

William Reno is Associate Professor of Political Science and a member of the faculty of the Program of African Studies at Northwestern University. His research focuses on the factors that shape the behaviour of militias. His current project investigates why some militias adopt predatory strategies while others in similar circumstances protect the interests of communities under their control. His field research for this project takes him to Nigeria, Sierra Leone, Somalia and the North Caucasus region. He also is completing a book manuscript, *The Evolution of Warfare in Independent Africa.* Recent publications include 'Order and Commerce in Turbulent Areas: 19th Century Lessons, 21st Century Practice' (*Third World Quarterly* 25: 4, 2004). His previous books are *Corruption and State Politics in Sierra Leone* (Cambridge University Press, Cambridge 1995) and *Warlord Politics and African States* (Lynne Rienner, Boulder 1998).

Paul Richards is Professor of Technology and Agrarian Development at Wageningen University and Professor of Anthropology at University College London. His current research interests focus on agrotechnology and agrarian reform issues in West African countries affected by war, and practice-oriented approaches to human rights. Recent publications include the edited volume *No Peace, No War* (James Currey, Oxford 2005).

Alessandro Triulzi is Professor of African History at the Università 'L'Orientale' of Naples. His research interests are Ethiopian history of the nineteenth and twentieth century, colonial imageries and the relationship between violence and memory. Recent publications include: *Remapping Ethiopia: Socialism and After*, ed. with Wendy James, Donald Donham, Eisei Kurimoto (James Currey, Oxford 2002); *State, Power and New Political Actors in Postcolonial Africa*, ed. with Maria Cristina Ercolessi (Feltrinelli, Milan 2004), *Dopo la violenza. Costruzioni di memoria nel mondo contemporaneo* (ed., L'Ancora del Mediterraneo, Naples 2005).

Koen Vlassenroot is a Professor at the University of Ghent, where he coordinates the Conflict Research Group. Since 1997, he has conducted extensive field research in the Great Lakes Region. He completed his doctorate in 2002 on 'The Making of a New Order: Dynamics of Conflict and Dialectics of War in South Kivu (DRCongo)' and has published on early warning and conflict prevention, the social and political functions of ethnicity, and warlord politics in Uganda and the DRC. His current research interests include stateless societies and new forms of governance in war-torn societies.

Acknowledgements

The majority of the chapters in this volume originate in presentations made to an intensive researcher training workshop, which was held at Hotel Romantik at Allinge-Sandvig on the Danish island of Bornholm from 21 to 25 May 2002. They have all been substantially revised, following discussions at the workshop and after, as well as in the process of preparing and editing the collection. A number of additional contributions were also commissioned in order to include discussions of a greater range of African countries and thematic issues.

The Bornholm workshop was organised jointly by the Graduate School of International Development Studies, Roskilde University, and the Danish Centre for Holocaust and Genocide Studies – since 2003 the Department of Holocaust and Genocide Studies within the Danish Institute for International Studies at Copenhagen. Additional support for the publication was made available subsequently from the same two institutions.

Special thanks are due to Inge Jensen, who was the administrative anchor for the workshop, and to Tore Storstein, who worked as editorial assistant. The editor is grateful to Jens Rudbeck and Sandro Triulzi who commented on the introduction, to the anonymous reader who reviewed the manuscript for James Currey Publishers and to the lecturers and PhD students who contributed to the discussions at the Bornholm workshop.

1

States of Failure, Societies in Collapse?
Understandings of Violent Conflict in Africa

PREBEN KAARSHOLM

In recent years, Africa has witnessed a remarkable number of transitions to democracy in the form of the adoption of constitutions that centre on majority rule, multi-partyism, the separation of executive, legislative and judiciary powers, recurrent elections and the protection of human rights. This has been related to what Samuel Huntington called a global 'third wave' of democratisation which culminated in 1989 in the breakdown of the Soviet Union as the world's last formal 'empire' (Huntington, 1991: 13–26; cf. Diamond and Plattner, 1996; Diamond, Plattner, Chu and Tien, 1997; Diamond, 1999).[1] In Africa, the 'wave' continued to gather force in the early 1990s, when 'the number of African countries holding competitive legislative elections more than quadrupled [from nine] to 38 out of a total of 47 countries in the sub-Saharan region' (Bratton and van de Walle, 1997: 7; cf. Young, 1999; Sandbrook, 2000: 3f.). In one case – South Africa – this was accompanied by the introduction of a constitutional framework which in terms of democratic ambition is unusually comprehensive, making Nelson Mandela proclaim democracy to be 'our national soul' (Mandela, 1996; cf. Sisk, 1995; Johnson and Schlemmer, 1996).

At the same time – and sometimes interacting with this 'wave' – societies on the African continent have experienced major crises of violent conflict, war and genocide and the actual modes of conducted governance in individual countries have indicated serious difficulties in arriving at 'consolidated' forms of democracy or peaceful regulation of difference and contestation. Coinciding with the upsurge in democratic transitions, sub-Saharan Africa has provided the scene for spectacular experiences of social orders disintegrating, sometimes to the point of what has been described as 'state failure' or 'state collapse' (Zartman, 1995; Doornbos, 1994; Reno, 1998; Bayart, Ellis and Hibou, 1999; Chabal and Daloz, 1999; van de Walle, 2001; Milliken and Krause, 2002; Leonard and Straus, 2003; Young, 2004; Triulzi and Ercolessi, 2004).

In countries like Kenya and Zimbabwe where multi-party constitutions were agreed, power-holders resorted to destabilisation and violence to avoid or stall

---

[1] The 'third wave' followed an extended 'first' one which grew out of the American and French revolutions that carried on from 1828 to 1926, and a 'second', which was an outcome of World War Two and had the decolonisation and independence of Third World nations as an important ingredient.

concessions (Berman and Lonsdale, 1992; Cowen and Kanyinga, 2002; Catholic Commission for Justice and Peace/Legal Resources Foundation, 1997; Rafto-poulos, 2003). In Uganda, Ethiopia and Eritrea, experiments with particularly 'African' forms of democracy and of 'hierarchism from below' moved from impressive early achievements to difficulties in the handling of political competition and organisational rights, and to escalations of political crisis into violent conflict and war (Mamdani, 1994; Karlstrom, 1996; Kayunga, 2001; Negash and Tronvoll, 2000; Clapham, 2002a; Doornbos and Tesfai, 1999; Dorman, 2003). In the Sudan and the Congo, civil war and challenges to the legitimacy of central national government grew into near-permanent conditions of political life and for a while interventions from neighbouring states seemed to create the rare possibility of redrawing national boundaries (Hutchinson, 1996; Johnson, 1998; Young and Turner, 1985; Willame, 1992; Nzongola-Ntalaja, 1999). In Rwanda and Burundi, political contestation within a framework of democracy led to forms of violent exclusion, culminating in the 1994 genocide the repercussions of which continue to destabilise the Great Lakes region (Lemarchand, 1994, Prunier, 1995; Reyntjens, 1999 and 2004; Mamdani, 2001; Pottier, 2002; Eltringham, 2004). In Liberia, Sierra Leone and Somalia, the idea of a central national government almost disappeared in the face of economic deprivation and violent contestations from sub-national forms of 'warlord politics' and other 'peripheral' mobilisations (Ellis, 1998, 1999; Richards, 1996; Reno, 1998; Compagnon, 1998). In Nigeria, 'transition without end', alternations between military and civilian rule, and the interaction between varieties of communal mobilisation presented dynamic potentials for violent conflict (Diamond, Kirk-Greene and Oyediran, 1996; Ibrahim, 1999; Agbu, 2004). In Angola, after decades of civil war, the death of the country's most prominent warlord, Jonas Savimbi, brought about possibilities for peace but not any immediate prospect of change in a regime form shaped by one-partyism, confrontation with apartheid South Africa, and long-term violent conflicts over the control of oil and diamond resources (Cramer, 1996; Messiant, 1995 and 2001; Seleti, 1999).

The contributions to the present book enter into this landscape of debate on the contradictions of development in Africa – on its possibilities, stalemates and violent conflicts, and on different understandings of contradictions and capacities for change in African political cultures. A central concern for the contributors has been to place such understandings in a historical perspective, to see them in the light of earlier conceptions and to reflect on the impact of memory and notions of the past on contemporary politics and culture.

The Dark Continent and the African State

While violence, war and genocide in all the cases referred to above were embedded within complex scenarios of political development, the media representations in the enlightened worlds of the North were keen to see them rather as reconfirming habitual understandings of Africa as the 'dark continent' or the 'heart of dark-ness' (Stanley, 1878, 1890; Conrad, 1899; Achebe, 2000). Adventurous corres-pondents like Ryszard Kapuscinski sent gripping reports of atrocities, roadblock terror and chaos in Ethiopia and Angola, but at the same time – in the depiction of the breakdown in social and political orders – seemed to recycle legends of an

African cultural and political essence going back to the age of high imperialism (Kapuscinski, 1986, 1987). Ambitious and philosophically minded writers like Robert Kaplan would enter battlefields of Africa that international organisations and powers were avoiding and fill them with mythological significance as harbingers of a 'coming anarchy' and a decline of global civilisation (Kaplan, 1994). Thus, paradoxically, as the Cold War was being won, a 'decline of the west' was being foreshadowed in new forms of violent horrors and terrorism, indicating that basic Western 'values' could no longer be relied upon as a foundation for universalist consensus (cf. Spengler 1918–22). Television images from Sierra Leone or Liberia seemed to confirm the return of the repressed – of atavistic forms of witchcraft, cannibalism and barbarism, enhanced by the use of globalised synthetic drugs, rock music and Rambo videos – apocalyptic visions of 'a rundown, crowded planet of skinhead Cossacks and juju warriors, influenced by the worst refuse of Western pop culture and ancient tribal hatreds, and battling over scraps of overused earth in guerrilla conflicts that ripple across continents and intersect in no discernible pattern...' (Kaplan 2000 [1994]: 29f.). It was such an image of Africa as a universe of 'meaningless violence' that provided the point of critical take-off in Paul Richards' book, *Fighting for the Rain Forest* in 1996.

Popular imaginings of this nature had substantial backing in academic thinking and writing, and particularly perhaps in theories of 'the African state'. Indeed, the style of Robert Kaplan's essay on 'the coming anarchy' could be seen as striking a bridge between the discourse of modern political science and the ponderings of Victorian travellers and clubland magazines of the era of 'high' imperialism. Kaplan quoted the explorer Richard Burton on the health risks of Africa to conclude that the continent now seemed to be 'more dangerous in this regard than it was in 1862'. On the same note, he could mobilise Samuel Huntington to conjure up a forthcoming 'clash of civilisations' (Kaplan, 2000 [1994]: 16 and 26), and make reference to the Hobbesian quality of political life in Africa in a way that recalled the views of Robert Jackson and Carl Rosberg on *Personal Rule in Black Africa* (1982).

Indeed, a dimension of Afro-pessimism and moralistic prejudice or generalising seems to have been as pervasive in scholarly writings on the dynamics involved in the politics of African societies as it has in mass media and popular cultural representations. The 'backwardness' of Africa has been seen as rooted in its economic underdevelopment, but not simply as identical with this, and a focus for debate has been whether the nature of African politics is in itself to blame for the economic crisis and lagging behind of nations.

Politics and the state in Africa are understood to operate through rent seeking, personal rule and patrimonialism. This may be because 'social classes are not yet sufficiently developed and organised to play any dependent and decisive role' (Martinussen, 1997: 192). From such a perspective, the African 'problem' appears to be one of 'catching up', or of energetic intervention from outside – 'even in most European states, modern political institutions took hold only after powerful personal rulers had first established effective governments and associated their personal authority with the new institutions. Thus, personal rule in Africa must be regarded in a similar manner, as possibly the only adequate system of governance under the conditions prevailing – but also as a system that, in the longer term, has to be replaced' (Martinussen, 1997: 192f; cf. Jackson and

Rosberg, 1982: 266–7). Democracy, in this view, would not be an option: 'What is the best feasible alternative? Decent, responsive and largely even-handed personal rule. Although neo-patrimonialism is virtually the only workable mode of governance in tropical Africa, Houphouët-Boigny's neo-patrimonialism is infinitely preferable to that of Idi Amin. The point is obviously that there is personal rule and personal rule. And that citizens will be more likely to comply voluntarily with the decisions of strongmen who are willing to listen to their grievances and wishes' (Sandbrook, 1985: 157).

Gloomier assessments have prevailed in both a short- and longer-term perspective which see personal rule, clientelism and neo-patrimonialism as features of an at once 'weak' and 'despotic' form of state that is peculiar to Africa. To quote Sandbrook again – now adopting a less hopeful point of view – 'African tendencies toward a personalisation of power are rooted in history and a particular social structure', but are also kept in place by Western governments and 'imperialism': the 'weak legitimacy of African governments is... undermined by the manifest and abject dependence of various strongmen upon foreign patrons who play the tune to which these leaders dance' (Sandbrook, 1985: 111). Within a pessimist scenario, democratisation is not a way out or forward, but rather something that leads to violent conflict: 'the weight of the evidence – and it is, indeed, very weighty – suggests that democratic openings have often aggravated communal tensions in divided societies... Free, party-based competitive elections in heterogeneous societies... encourage leaders to manipulate latent regional, ethnic, or religious animosities as a way to mobilise electoral support' (Sandbrook, 2000: 7).

In a different perspective, with implications that are both moralistic and social Darwinist, the 'weak', 'illegitimate', 'predatory' or 'vampirical' nature of the African state can be seen to stem from the fact that it has never had to really fight for its life, neither in order to come into existence, nor to survive. In this view, the European nation state, which has become a model for the world, came into existence and attained sovereignty through a storm of war and fire, confirmed in the Peace of Westphalia of 1648 and consolidated through subsequent processes of nation building (Tilly, 1975). By contrast, the 'post-colonial states in Africa faced no serious external pressure' and from the outset in decolonisation 'were given the right to existence' despite 'a lack of substantial statehood' and a 'lack of cultural and political community. Independence meant independence for colonial territories, upholding colonial borders... There was a measure of success in a few countries, but in general the project was a huge failure... the communities that prevailed were the different ethnic sub-groups which competed for access to state power and resources... The predatory system was in place... life insurance sovereignty for ex-colonies became the basis for ineffective regimes based on patron-client relationships' (Sørensen, 1999: 399; cf. Sørensen, 1996: 906f. and 1998: 49-52; Jackson, 1990).

In a more naturally Hobbesian world system than the post-colonial one, states incapable of providing security for their citizens would have been brought to book by conquest or international intervention, or, if they had functioning democratic systems of internal accountability, would have been forced to bring about a change of regime. Instead, they have been allowed to continue to malfunction with impunity, mistreat their own citizens, or, as in the case of Mobutu's Zaire, even to disintegrate in their capacity to uphold any pretence of social order.

'Weak post-colonial states can collapse completely and still retain formal membership of the society of states. There is no external threat of mismanagement leading to termination of the state' (Sørensen, 1996: 907). Representations of a 'dark continent' which in their use of metaphor and over-generalisation carry similar moralistic associations are prominent in Jean-François Bayart's rich and detailed account of African political development as determined by the 'politics of the belly' and the 'criminalisation' of the state. This is in spite of the fact that a declared intention of Bayart's work is to 'de-orientalise' African societies by showing that 'they are ordinary, and (particularly) ordinary in their politics' (Bayart, 1993 [1989]: 1; cf. Bayart, Ellis and Hibou, 1999 [1997]: 33 and 114–16). Echoes of stereotypes also add to the drama in Achille Mbembe's interpretation of post-colonial politics in Africa as governed by the greed, gluttony and conspicuous consumption of leaders (Mbembe, 2001). In his later writings, the undermining of 'sovereignty' in a Carl Schmittian sense within the African post-colonial state is represented as a radical 'loss of monopoly on violence... and territorial boundaries' (Mbembe, 2003: 32). At the same time, however, the perspective of 'darkness' is globalised, as this represents just one instance – even if extreme – of 'necropolitical' governmentality within the context of 'contemporary forms of the subjugation of life to the power of death' (Mbembe, 2003: 39; cf. Hansen, 2003). Mbembe has claimed more recently that the counter-perspective to this is a 'critical humanism', offering hope 'in the midst of an unprecedented epidemic of death' (Mbembe and Posel, 2004: 2).

In a recent book, Nicholas van de Walle has re-examined the 'classical' notions of personal rule, clientelism and neo-patrimonialism as features of a weak form of state that is peculiar to Africa and responsible for a semi-permanent and worsening state of economic crisis as well as for chronic instability and violence. According to van de Walle, it is such characteristics that have prevented the success of structural adjustment since the 1980s and continue to hamper the reform of policies and prospects for development. The prevailing outlook has been that 'this pervasive clientelism reflects a fundamental absence of state autonomy. Clientelism is viewed as weakening the state by overwhelming it with particularistic demands and lessening its ability to act according to its own preferences, or to carry out a developmental project in the public good' (van de Walle, 2001: 53). Such a perspective would even apply to the heretical analysis of writers like Chabal and Daloz, who would argue Africa is in fact able to function through various forms of seeming disorder in which neo-patrimonialism can represent a social capital of redistribution and insurance precisely because the state was 'never significantly emancipated from society' (Chabal and Daloz, 1999: 4; cf. van de Walle, 2001: 53, 118f.).

In another view, however, it is not the 'weakness' of the state due to patterns of social structure which is the problem. Rather, the state takes precedence over society as an explanatory factor and is seen to possess a high level of autonomy within African social contexts. 'Political factors' provide the 'dummy variable' without which it is impossible to find explanations for Africa's poor economic performance: 'variables such as the level of corruption, the extent of ethnic fragmentation, the level of political violence, or the quality of government services help explain the growth differential between Africa and other regions' (van de Walle, 2001: 11). It is 'the nature of political institutions' which represents the most important development constraint and more fundamental changes of political institutions have been prevented by international aid assistance, which more than anything have helped to keep corrupt, clientelist and violent regimes and governments in place (van de Walle, 2001: 50; cf. Leonard and Straus, 2003: 18, 105).

Within this 'relative autonomy', where the role of politics is dominant, the habitus, orientations and moral qualities of leaders play a significant role. Clientelism, low state capacity and the ideological preferences of decision makers' are the central characteristics determining African policy making and implementation. Thus, 'political authority in Africa is based on the giving and granting [sic!] of favors, in an endless series of dyadic exchanges that go from the village to the highest reaches of the central state' (van de Walle, 2001: 50f.). The clientelism at stake, however, is primarily one of elite cronyism: 'ethnolinguistic or regional solidarities that cut across stratifications of power and wealth ... are not really constraining to state elites,' who have in themselves become 'relatively autonomous', and who both plunder the state and exploit 'public resources to paper over [their] own internal differences' (van de Walle, 2001: 55). The personal convictions and ideologies of leaders are important in shaping policy – hence the nationalist, Marxist, Keynesian or other outlooks of politicians in power must be taken seriously. 'The socialist orientation officially chosen by African regimes, their vocal attachment to planning, or their concern for equity issues' should not be dismissed as just 'anachronisms' and 'a posteriori uses of ideology for political purposes,' but recognised rather as 'the sincere affirmation of deeply held beliefs' that have helped to prevent structural adjustment reforms from taking effect, contributing to the 'politics of permanent crisis' (van de Walle, 2001: 57).

Contributors to the present volume take issue with such dynamics of state and societal development and provide detailed discussion of the balance between them in a variety of African contexts (see in particular the chapters by Reno, Vlassen-root, Johnson and Richards).

From Failure to Collapse

Within a conceptual universe as outlined above, the height of the crisis of the African state takes the form of 'state failure' or 'state collapse', with the former denoting a functional and the latter an institutional dimension (Milliken and Krause, 2002: 753–5, 764f.). The radical notion of 'state collapse' gained currency following the publication of a collection of essays in the mid-1990s, which focused not just on Africa but also on developments in Eastern Europe and the ex-Soviet Union. In Africa, however, 'contemporary ... history began in state collapse, in the famous events associated with the collapse of the colonial state in the Congo,' and it is Africa, with its weak, post-colonial states that offers the most frequent and exemplary cases. This is a field in which, 'in its misfortunes and malfunctions, Africa has much to teach the world' (Zartman, 1995: 2).

According to Zartman, two 'waves' of state collapse are identified in Africa, one around 1980, 'when regimes that had replaced the original nationalist generation were overthrown' and a second wave from around 1990. In 1993, a 'study characterised half the African states as being in serious or maximum danger of collapse, if not already gone' (Zartman, 1995: 2–3). In this process, coinciding with Huntington's third wave of democratisation as well as with Robert Kaplan's visions of 'the coming anarchy', Somalia and Liberia are highlighted as paradigm cases, but 'state collapse' was seen by Zartman to be also under way in Ethiopia, Angola, Mozambique, the Sudan, Rwanda, Burundi and Zaire. Thus, in Mobutu's state, a 'parallel government born of the democratic movement whines for power, impotent. Interestingly, the greatest barrier to anarchy is the restraining memory of the bloody disorders of three decades ago; but the state, as a national authority, collapsed' (Zartman, 1995: 4).

In 1994, some of these contradictions were demonstrated by the coinciding events of negotiated and 'pacted' transition in South Africa from apartheid state to majority rule alongside state collapse and mass genocidal violence and civil war in Rwanda. The state in South Africa was obviously transforming, albeit radically, rather than collapsing, but the notion of 'state collapse' in Rwanda has also been problematised. Although 'Rwanda has frequently been called a collapsed state by policy-makers and journalists, the genocidal war that took place in that country in 1994 was *not* enabled or produced by the Rwandan state disintegrating. Instead, the genocide was produced by "highly disciplined agents of the state [who] pursued the task of murdering many of its people with hideous efficiency"' (Milliken and Krause, 2002: 757, quoting Clapham, 2002b). Also, the reconstitution of the Rwandan state after the civil war victory by Paul Kagame and the RPF happened remarkably quickly, although the government's pretensions to be building a new type of inclusive 'African' democracy inspired by Uganda also soon gave way to modes of autocratic leadership that continued the weaknesses of the past (Reyntjens, 2004: 208).

Similarly, as William Reno has argued, the 'criminalisation of the state' in Africa need not be a symptom of its collapse, but could indicate rather a consolidation and expansion of resources – a process not dissimilar to the ways in which wars, piracy and gangsterism contributed to state building in early modern Europe (Tilly, 1990). Thus, 'the crisis of very weak states may eventually favor the growth of internal order and promote their insertion in the global economy on more favorable terms. Wars and illicit commercial activity may complement economic and political activities that are more acceptable in the international system of states' (Reno, 2000: 11f.). Contrasting Museveni's Uganda with Charles Taylor's Liberia, Reno concludes that 'unconventional uses of state sovereignty need not necessarily weaken the overall global framework and norms of state sovereignty. In fact, they may play a role in buttressing them in areas that are economically and strategically marginal to strong states' (Reno, 2000: 30).

Even in the case of such a dramatic 'collapse' as that of Zaire in 1996-7 into the Democratic Republic of the Congo, the solidity of the state persisted at least as far as its national boundaries are concerned, although the involvement of Uganda and Rwanda in the conflict for a short period seemed to indicate that the Kivu provinces and the Banyamulenge might become part of Uganda or Rwanda. This possibility receded quite quickly, raising again the question of why borders in post-colonial Africa are so resilient to change and why such changes are outside the rules of international conventions. It is often pointed out that an important 'weakness' of African nation states is the arbitrariness of their colonially 'invented' borders, cutting across unities and divisions of more 'authentic' community (see e.g. Jackson, 1990; Sørensen, 1999: 399). The real mystery concerning such 'quasi-states' is not why they collapse, but rather why they persist (Milliken and Krause, 2002: 763). Examples of postcolonial national borders being changed or modified in Africa, even following cases of violent conflict, are very rare. Where they have occurred, as in the case of Eritrea, they have drawn legitimacy from demarcations that came into effect within the period of colonial rule rather than before or after. The system of international institutions and recognition makes it extremely difficult for new national boundaries to emerge from the ruins of 'state failure'. An example is Somaliland, where, following the collapse of Siad Barre's Somalia, and within the boundaries of the earlier British Protectorate, a political unit has emerged which controls its territory, has developed national institutions of security and administration and has an articulated ideology of origin and cohesion. In this sense, Somaliland has achieved a high level of *de facto* sovereignty, but has failed to have this translated into a '*de jure* sovereignty which is provided by international recognition' (Brons, 2001: 244-5).

Another reason why the national boundaries established through decolonisation have held up so strongly in the face of political crisis may be found in the extent to which nationalism has been a 'civic religion' even among citizens of impoverished and malfunctioning African states (Milliken and Krause, 2002: 758). In a variety of ways, nationhood and modernity have been popularly identified, as illustrated in James Ferguson's account of responses to economic crisis and mass unemployment in Zambia, when copper prices plummeted. From being Zambian nationals within a cosmopolitan modernity, the people say 'we are just poor Africans now' (Ferguson, 1999: 245). This perspective provides an antidote to the frequently expressed assumption that the primary political and cultural identifications of Africans are localist and 'tribal' (see Sørensen 1998: 51f). It also explains some of the difficulties involved in actually utilising the 'collapse' of a bad and repressive state to create a more flexible and democratically workable political organisation; how notions of citizenship and the nation state have been woven together too closely for more flexible democratic federalisms to emerge. In this respect, sub-Saharan Africa cannot be said to be exhibiting particularly exotic anomalies but is struggling to find solutions to problems concerning the balancing of central and regional or 'local' nationalisms not dissimilar to those experienced by India, Canada or Spain (Milliken and Krause 2002: 760).

From Post-Colonialism to Democratisation

An alternative to discourses of the 'weak', 'quasi-', 'failed' or 'collapsed' state in Africa, and the moralising that accompanies them is a more serious approach to the complexity of the historical processes, out of which political development took place when the individual nation states became independent. Thus, on the basis of comparative studies of the colonial state and its legacy in different parts of Africa, Crawford Young has reiterated the extreme fragility of most post-colonial states following independence and the absurdity of expecting these to function smoothly and at a high level of service delivery (Young, 1994, 2004). While the 'robust authority' of colonial states in Africa was in some respects impressive, the states were also minimalist, funded from capitation taxes and through indirect rule. In this sense, as Mahmood Mamdani has also emphasised, African societies were made to pay for and implement their own subjection through indirect rule (Young, 2004: 28; cf. Mamdani, 1996: 62f.).

Only in the decades following the Second World War did a different type of 'developmentalist' colonial state begin to emerge with other dimensions and ambitions, particularly for increasing employment resulting from continued growth. Post-colonial states were faced with honouring these expectations. It is against the backdrop of the colonial history of political underdevelopment that subsequent 'failures' and 'collapses' of postcolonial states must be assessed. With such a history of fragility, it is illusory to believe that the problem of economic and political malfunction was one of 'adjustment' and 'policy reform', for it assumes an ideal point of balance and departure according to which things can be 'set right' but which was never the experience of these societies (Young, 2004: 37–41).

In this context, the 'third wave' of democratisation takes on an added significance in Africa from around 1990, because it represents a new stage of political development rather than being the outcome of political conditionalities. The promise of nationalism and the ways in which the postcolonial 'predicament' decided the political agenda had begun to wane and new concepts of the state came to the fore. Even if first-stage political transitions brought about a backlash, new civil society structures, human rights agendas and an upsurge of new critical, public media were emerging, appropriating demands for democracy into local discourse and 'making it improbable that an autocratic restoration could restore anything resembling the state ascendancy over the citizenry of the [post-colonial] integral state years' (Young, 2004: 42).

Thus, in Kenya, a local political development took root enabling the opposition to overcome – even if not definitively – its 'traditional' fragilities of tribalism and localist clientelism. In 2002, it brought about the resignation of the Daniel Arap Moi regime (Barkan, 2004; on ethnicity and citizenship, cf. Ndegwa, 1998; Berman, Eyoh and Kymlicka, 2004). In Uganda, while the Presidency and the NRM government has tried to slow down the prospect of pluralism, the challenge of multipartyism and an emerging legitimate opposition has helped to develop governance in a democratic direction and has transformed the agenda for political discussions (see Therkildsen, 2004).

In Zimbabwe, political development proceeded from independence in 1980 to the 'unity' agreement of 1987-8, which brought together the two major parties of nationalist rivalry and ended the Matabeleland killings, then to agendas of human rights and democratisation in the late 1990s, based to a significant extent on civil society mobilisation, critical media and the labour movement (Sylvester, 2003; Raftopoulos, 2003). A historical background is provided by Jocelyn Alexander in the present volume. The defeat by referendum in February 2000 of a revised constitution that would have given the President extended executive powers and the near-victory of the opposition Movement for Democratic Change in the elections of July 2000, establishing a new two-party parliamentary balance, led to a violent backlash. For the time being, this has undermined the opposition and its capacity to develop alternative policies on central issues such as land reform. It has made the Zimbabwe government increasingly corrupt and autocratic, rather than a more 'consolidated' democracy. As in the case of Rwanda in the mid-1990s, the common descriptions of Zimbabwe as a 'failed' or 'collapsing' state have been contradicted by the ruthlessly efficient violence of the ruling party and its government towards the challenges of the new democratic opposition (Hammar and Raftopolous, 2003: 27f.). However, such a set-back does not negate the experience of political development. Rather, it may indicate that such development is not of an evolutionary nature, but proceeds through struggles, leaps and set-backs, in the process establishing agendas and political experiences with longer-term impact, representing a developing 'quality' of opposition (Kaarsholm, 2005a).

The three cases mentioned above provide new material for the discussion on how democratisation relates to violent conflict in Africa – does it stimulate conflict, or does it bring about superior possibilities for peace-making and conflict resolution? For Richard Sandbrook, the outcome is not given: 'democratisation ... has seemingly contributed to forestalling vicious conflict in some societies, while it has exacerbated such conflict in others. Political liberalisation is a gamble. However, since the alternative is probably not a benign, albeit authoritarian, developmental state but a predatory and weak autocracy, this gamble is worth taking' (Sandbrook, 2000: 10). Similarly, for Jean-François Bayart, 'multi-party politics is a necessary but not sufficient condition for democracy ... multi-party politics [can be] nothing more than a fig leaf, covering up the continuation and even exacerbation of the politics of the belly from the prudish eye of the West,' with democratic groupings in civil society eventually swelling 'the ranks of the batallions of political entrepreneurs choosing to militarise the factional struggles' (Bayart, 1993 [1989]: xii–xiii). In John Lonsdale's terminology, moving politics into a democratic arena may transform the 'moral ethnicities' of pre-modern African societies into forms of 'political tribalism', involving much more radical possibilities for exclusion than previously known (Berman and Lonsdale, 1992; Lonsdale, 1994) .

Taking another view, we may accept that all the three cases mentioned – Kenya, Uganda, Zimbabwe – have involved social 'learning processes' which in spite of reversals leave behind actions and ideas that are irreversible and which represent elements in a transformation of 'political culture', understood as 'the attitudes of citizens towards democracy'. A significant change and contrast in such attitudes in three other African countries with different histories of political development and experience – Ghana, Zambia and South Africa – have been suggested in an *Afrobarometer Paper* by Michael Bratton and Robert Mattes. Here the 'intrinsic' appreciation of democratic procedures and institutions as 'political goods', characteristic of Ghana and Zambia – societies that have experienced both democratic transitions and post-colonial repression – is contrasted with the 'instrumental' evaluation of democracy predominant in South African responses. If strong-man leadership, authoritarian government and a suspension of elections led to more employment and an acceleration of economic redistribution, a majority of South African respondents would be in favour (Bratton and Mattes, 2000: 8).

The indications of this as to citizens' attitudes contrast dramatically with the democratic elaborateness of the post-apartheid South African constitution referred to above and may help to explain why the suspension of rights of citizenship in Zimbabwe since 1999 and 'Mugabeism' as an ideology appear in certain respects to have been more popular in South Africa than in Zimbabwe (cf. Ranger, 2004). In this sense, paradoxically, through the level of broad 'intrinsic' appreciation of democracy attained, the development of political culture in Zimbabwe – in spite of the violent backlash recently experienced – could be argued in certain respects to be higher than that of South Africa, because of the more elaborate experience of political development which Zimbabwe has been through since independence in 1980. This would mean that – in spite of reversals – Zimbabwe has a capital of political experience which may help consolidate a future return to democratisation, while South Africa – in spite of the beauties of its constitution – contain frailties within its political culture which may undermine or work against democratic consolidation in the future. (For a 'micropolitical' perspective, cf. Kaarsholm, 2005b and the contribution by Preben Kaarsholm to this volume).

Political Culture and Political Development

While it is not uncommon to have 'political culture' presented as the instance which decides whether violence or 'consolidation' will be the outcome of democratic transitions, the very notion of 'political culture' has been somewhat neglected in discussions, possibly because of the ideological hopes invested in the notion when it was introduced at the height of the Cold War. In its early forms (as developed by political scientists such as Almond and Verba and Lucien Pye in the 1960s) the concept of political culture was related to modernisation theory and the ways in which political and cultural development were conceived within this theoretical framework. On the one hand, certain characteristics were claimed to have been important historical preconditions for the particularity of European/ Western development (such as the Protestant ethic, individualism, the emergence of an early 'civic culture' and participation). On the other hand, some of these characteristics together with increasing socialisation towards individualism and empathy were also assumed to be features that would result more or less automatically from economic growth and social development ('all good things go together'). In this sense, 'modernisation' as a term came to replace notions of 'Westernisation' or 'Europeanisation' to describe a process of universalisation of values and dispositions which 'development' was taking over from the colonial administrations (Lerner, 1968).

In its early stages, political culture theory was characterised by a number of features: First, by broadly conceived designations of the boundaries or 'territories' to which particular political cultures would apply, which could be national ('German'), continental ('African', 'Asian'), or religious ('Islamic', 'Confucian'). Second, it was characterised by similarly vague behaviouristic, social psychological or macro-anthropological definitions of 'culture' as 'a people's way of life' or 'way of living' – 'a people's predominant beliefs, attitudes, values, ideals, sentiments and evaluations about the political system of its country, and the role of the self in that system' (Diamond, 1993: 7f.) In this respect, political culture theory continued an older anthropological interest in a comparative study of the principles of 'political systems' in 'primitive' and 'complex' societies (Fortes and Evans-Pritchard, 1940). Third, it focused on elites as those whose 'predominant beliefs, attitudes' are important, for example, in the historical development of preconditions for democracy, where a 'civic culture' of tolerance, respect and competition among elites prior to democratisation provides the 'trust' and the 'pact' through which a sustainable transition to democracy could be effected (Diamond, 1993: 2). The modes of struggles, political achievements and outlooks of 'masses' or popular movements on the other hand were largely ignored as being insignificant for the build-up and constitution of a society's political culture. Fourth, a certain level of economic growth was taken to be a pre-condition for the development of political culture. It would not make sense to think about possiblities for consolidating democracy in societies with high levels of poverty; therefore, by implication the people were condemned to live in either despotism or instability until growth rates improved (cf. Berg-Schlosser and Kersting, 2003: 1f.).

These are all areas where recent theoretical efforts have attempted to bring about a more critical and dialectical understanding of political culture. In respect of the uniformity and homogeneity of political culture, for instance, Larry Diamond has divided the concept into different constellations of 'political sub-cultures' (Diamond, 1993: 8). This leads to more complex and dynamic under-standings in which different political cultures may struggle for hegemony and where the outcome of such struggles is in itself the result of meta-political contestation. Diamond has also argued that in efforts to re-argue the relevance of political culture theory in the context of discussions of democratic consolidation in the 1990s, 'mass publics' must be seen as equally important as 'elites' in determining how frameworks of political culture function (Diamond, 1999: 68, 173). In the relationship between political cultural and economic development, there is a reciprocity: just as prosperity may promote the development of trust, participation and respect for procedures, the taking root of a democratic political culture depends on its capacity to develop legitimacy though economic efficiency and re-distribution (Diamond, 1999: 78f.). On the other hand, it would be wrong to assume that democracy and protection of citizenship and human rights are irrelevant in contexts of poverty. Democratic aspirations and the development of political cultural values can be shown to be integral parts of struggles of poor people, whose basic need of a better livelihood includes both economic security and protection from invasion of rights (Berg-Schlosser and Kersting, 2003: 188-93)

Because of the imprecision and the sermonising overtones that often come into political culture theory, writers like Michael Bratton and Nicolas van de Walle have circumvented the term and focused instead on developing a 'politico-institutional-approach' of understanding (Bratton and van de Walle, 1997: 20, 41f.). This approach is three-tiered and examines first 'political traditions' which are 'long-standing cultural legacies' (and may therefore correspond quite closely to 'political culture' or 'sub-cultures' in Diamond's sense). Such traditions are exemplified by Putnam's contrasting of north and south Italy as different in 'civic spirit', and in Africa by patrimonial and neo-patrimonial institutions, discourses and practices as discussed in Bayart's *The State in Africa* (1993 [1989]), but also by indigenous democratic traditions like the Botswanan *kgotla*. 'Political traditions' are not necessarily the only or dominating influence within a social order and are not necessarily united, but can themselves be internally antagonistic. Second, 'political regimes' may incorporate different degrees of competition and participation and are built as 'aggregate clusters of interlocking institutions' (Bratton and van de Walle, 1997: 38f.). Third, 'regimes' in their turn are constituted by 'political institutions' through which regimes 'articulate', and which reproduce the 'values and configurations of regimes and traditions' (Bratton and van de Walle, 1997: 40). How exactly, institutions may also interpret and develop the values of regimes and traditions is not entered into in detail, but would be essential for both empirical study and the further elaboration of theory. As it is, Bratton and van de Walle's rephrasing of political culture theory does not proceed very far beyond the generalities developed by earlier political science understandings of African politics and a rather vague notion of 'neo-patrimonialism' remains the overriding 'political tradition'.

Among 'political institutions' Bratton and de Walle include those of civil society and point to the important role these may play in building up pressures that precede democratic transitions and within such transitions themselves. In this respect, they are in agreement with more recent political culture theories that see civil society development as a necessary precondition for both democratic transition and consolidation (Diamond, 1999: 218–60; cf. the national studies collected in Diamond and Plattner, 1996, and in particular the investigations of Nigerian political development in Diamond, Kirk-Greene and Oyediran, 1996). Bratton and van de Walle mention South Africa as a prime example, but it is stated to be a more general feature of African transitions that civil society institutions tend to lose impact in the aftermath of transition: 'in general, the institutions of civil society perform less well in the early stages of democratic consolidation than they do during transition... If a pro-democracy movement wins power, civic leaders are drawn into official positions in government and party hierarchies, thereby weakening voluntary organisations... the conclusion of a political transition can have demobilising consequences for civil society' (Bratton and van de Walle, 1997: 255). It is therefore difficult to bring about the differentiation, balance, mutual recognition and interplay between state and civil society that would be necessary for a consolidation of democracy.

This touches on an extended discussion of whether a Habermasian notion of civil society linked to a public sphere of communication and interaction between individualised citizens makes sense at all in an African political setting – either as descriptive notion of existing dynamics or as normative notion of institutional forms to be strived for. It may represent a 'Eurocentric' imposition (cf. Comaroff and Comaroff, 1999; Kaarsholm and James, 2000). Mahmood Mamdani has argued that because of the colonial heritage of 'bifurcated' government and indirect rule in African states, the counterpoint to state power represented in a European context by a public sphere and civil society institutions in post-colonial Africa tends to assume instead forms of localised organisation directed towards 'inter-ethnic' and 'intra-ethnic' conflict, thus potentially providing an incitement to violence rather than democratic consolidation (Mamdani, 1996).

To develop this discussion further, studies are needed to map out and analyse the ways in which 'public cultures' in a broader and more neutral sense function and are structured within different African contexts (cf. Breckenridge, 1995). This will involve an appreciation of the fora and discourses through which political understandings and endeavours are constituted; how these fora and discourses relate to the state and to each other in different ways and how they change and develop over time. It will involve investigations of cultural genres and institutions which do not necessarily resemble the civic associations and types of organisation that are most commonly identified with civil society in a

European or Western context. This will include institutions whose articulations do not necessarily concern themselves with politics at the level of the national state. Their concern may be rather with the micropolitics of 'local' society as represented in debates over issues of 'traditional' or cultural authority; disputes over the proper or improper relations between generations and genders, between 'indigenes' and 'migrants', or between different cultural styles, spiritual beliefs and moral orientations. In this way, the concept of what constitutes 'politics' is opened up for reconsideration.

On such a basis, it becomes possible to develop a more meaningful notion of political culture that engages with the ways in which such 'micro-political' debates and contestations are conducted, in which strivings for and against democracy come to the fore within them and how they change their nature within different environments of economic and 'macro-political' possibility. This procedure involves the mapping out of specific public spheres and public cultures and their modes of functioning – in terms of identifying the patterns of interacting, dialoguing, dominating and silencing that structure them internally as 'fields of power' (Clarke, Hall, Jefferson and Roberts, 1975: 9-74; Bourdieu, 1996: 113–73). Mapping them out also requires designating their boundaries and investigating how the 'local' is constituted and changed historically and dynamically as a node of interactions with other levels of society – both nationally, regionally and beyond – and with overlaying structures of public culture (Appadurai, 1996; Hart 2002; Kaarsholm 2005b). Through a constructivist and institutionalist approach of this nature to the study of political cultures as fields of interaction, configurated as the outcome of particular historical struggles, new perspectives are opened up on the dynamics and contradictions of political development in Africa. In the present volume, the historical dimension features prominently, and several contributions – in particular those by Eltringham, Alexander, Triulzi and Richards – focus on the importance of interpretations of memory for the legitimacy of both regimes in power and the movements of opposition challenging them (cf. also Werbner, 1991, 1998).

Such refinements of focus help us to make better sense of both trajectories through which democratic procedures have taken root in response to local needs and of the violence that has occurred when such possibilities have been eroded and different priorities and objectives have gained the upper hand. It also makes it possible to understand better the cumulative and structural effects generated by such violence in itself and the ways in which violence and disorder – rather than signalling a collapse of state power – may be developed into highly efficient political instruments (see the studies in Richards, 2005).

Violence, Political Culture and Development in Context

The chapters in this volume engage with the theoretical situation outlined above, and try to establish new understandings of the ways in which violence, political culture and development have interacted in recent African history. They do this in a continuum that stretches from William Reno's discussion in Chapter One of how 'warlord politics' in Nigeria have spread from collapsing state institutions to incorporate also social movements and civil society, to the last Chapter Ten by Paul Richards in which attempts to explain violence in anthropological and

sociological terms and defines the 'new wars' in Africa as outcomes of fundamental changes in social solidarity.

In his chapter on 'Insurgencies in the Shadow of State Collapse', William Reno
takes issue with Paul Collier's explanation of violent conflict as the result of
'greed, not grievance' (Collier and Hoeffler, 1998, 2001 and 2004), and presents
'the looting model' of rebellion and internal war as the result rather than the
cause of the form that these upheavals have taken. Using Nigeria as his primary
example, he shows the process of 'state collapse' to include a breaking-down of
the boundaries between state and society, as 'strongmen' move from political to
market enterprise. This also means that the relative autonomy of civil society is
invaded and that the forces and initiatives that might in different circumstances
have led to social movements and mobilisation for an alternative system of
governance are co-opted into the shifting tactics of corrupt power elites. Thus,
the hopefulness that has sometimes been attached to the dynamics of civil society
in Nigeria as harbouring the potential in terms of political culture for a
resurgence of democracy and accountability (see e.g. Diamond, 1988; Diamond,
Kirk-Greene and Oyediran, 1996) is seen by Reno to be illusory. The rebellious
groupings investigated in this chapter, such as the Bakassi Boys and the Oodua
People's Congress, may set out to fight criminals, halt corrruption and establish
order from below, but eventually they align with the 'strongmen' and structures
of influence they oppose. They become adjuncts to their violence, their looting of
resources and ethnic patrimonialism, rather than developing alternatives of
vision and social organisation. 'Predation', then, is the outcome of a process of
'collapse' rather than the cause. It spreads from the state to erode also the critical
capacity of civil society to develop a counterpoint.

Violence and the political mobilisation of groups of young men is also the
focus of Koen Vlassenroot's essay on 'Conflict and Militia Formation in Eastern
Congo'. Based on unique and extensive resesarch in the Kivu provinces (cf. also
Vlassenroot, 2002), Vlassenroot examines the processes through which violence
escalated in the Congo in the late 1990s as the Mobutu regime lost control of
central government and an array of opposition groups emerged which, together
with the intervention from Uganda, Rwanda and other African states, brought
Kabila *père et fils* to power, together with the state of instability that persists.
Although the demise of Mobutu was spectacularly chaotic, Vlassenroot argues
that it does not represent 'state collapse', and that the term as developed by
Zartman and others is inadequate, because it ignores historical context, and is
most often tautological. (States 'collapse' because they no longer perform the
functions that states are required to fulfil.)

Vlassenroot is similarly unhappy with the 'very popular "greed" account' of
the foundations of violent conflict in Africa as represented in the analyses
produced by Paul Collier and others for the World Bank (cf. Collier and Hoeffler,
2001 and 2004). It cannot be doubted that the drive for diamonds, coltan and
other mineral and natural resources plays a prominent role in the Congolese
internal war and the regional patterns of conflict around it. But neither this nor
the recourse to standardised assumptions of ethnic prejudice can explain the
forms of violence and exclusion that have been characteristic. More insightful
historical and sociological accounts are needed to understand how reasons for
conflict emerge within local societies, and how violence takes root in everyday
life as the 'solution' to conflict. In his chapter, Vlassenroot provides such an

account in his analysis of the ambivalence of the Mayi-Mayi militias within the Eastern Congo conflict. This involves dimensions of generational politics and of the effects on these of the democratisation manoeuvres of the final years of Mobutu's 'soft state' rule, which – in the sense of Chabal and Daloz – used 'disorder as political instrument', upset patterns of patrimonial obligation and brought forth new forms of ethnic political campaigning between local groups. This process activated dynamics of struggle on the peripheral boundaries of the national state, which, however, did not represent a chaotic and anarchic development of collapse, but had their own 'inner logic' within the local 'social and political order', according to Vlassenroot.

Nigel Eltringham's chapter 'Debating the Rwandan Genocide' discusses local understandings of the historical background to the 1994 genocide in Rwanda and the importance of debate over history in the aftermath of the coming to power of Paul Kagame and the Rwanda Patriotic Front. Eltringham recently published a book which deals more broadly with post-genocidal debate (Eltringham, 2004). In his contribution to this volume, he discusses in particular the way in which interpretations of the 1948 United Nations Genocide Convention have been drawn upon for explanations and arguments. History has been widely mobilised to raise moral capital and provide explanation or justification for horrors committed both during the 1994 genocide and in the campaigns that followed. The Holocaust has been deployed to signal a unique level of violence and will to extermination, and the UN Convention's definitions of what constitutes 'genocide' have been similarly used by opposing parties to judge unsurpassable atrocities. Eltringham looks at the ways in which comparisons with the Holocaust and definitions of violence as 'genocide' have been used by spokesmen for Rwandan RPF Government on the one hand, and by groups of Rwandans living in exile on the other, investigating in particular how earlier episodes of collective violence in 1959, 1963 and 1972 have been discussed and categorised. He debates the usefulness and limitations of the UN Convention's definitions in the Rwandan context and points out how presentations of the Holocaust as 'archetypal' genocide have been misleading, blinding people to the dynamics through which processes of political and collective violence may escalate towards genocide in different contexts.

In his chapter on 'Darfur: Peace, Genocide and Crimes against Humanity in Sudan', Douglas Johnson continues discussion of the meaning of 'genocide' by looking at disagreements around what violence in Darfur is really about, and who are the main contending forces. Inspired by understandings developed in Richards (2005), Johnson brings out the complexity of conflicts in Darfur and the linkages between national and international power relations and local micro-politics. On this basis, he underlines the necessity of a contextual understanding of violence which does not simply decipher the immediate set of incidents, but takes into account the prehistory and escalation of violence as well as its aftermath. Rather than being generically different, 'low-intensity' types of violent conflict and 'genocidal' violence may thus be closely related. At the same time, the interest in designating violence as 'genocidal' may well serve a political rather than an analytical purpose – in the case of Darfur, one of American and international politics and of the politics of oil.

Jocelyn Alexander's essay deals with 'Legacies of Violence in Matabeleland, Zimbabwe' and updates the research presented in *Violence and Memory: One*

Hundred Years in the 'Dark Forests' of Matabeleland', which Alexander co-authored with JoAnn McGregor and Terence Ranger (Alexander, McGregor and Ranger, 2000). 'Official', state-sponsored commemoration of violence as it occurred from colonial conquest in the 1890s, through the land appropriations and forced evictions of the colonial period to the nationalist struggle and liberation war of the 1970s and the internal conflicts that followed independence in 1980, are counterposed with the ways in which memories are narrated and preserved from below and given form in religious and political discourse. The success of the new opposition that emerged in Zimbabwe from 1999 in the form of the Movement for Democratic Change is seen in the light of its 'recrafting of the nation's history'. It was able to establish moral and political legitimacy by proposing forms of governance that would represent an alternative to the ZANU-PF government's atrocities in the 1980s, replacing 'unity' with 'democracy' as a more popularly plausible agenda for peace. In response, the Zimbabwean state initiated a well-orchestrated campaign of violence against the opposition's challenge that has been able to draw in turn on its own rephrasing of historical memory. It claims to represent a return to the unfinished agendas and popular aspirations of the 1970s liberation war.

Struggles around memories of a violent colonial and post-colonial past are also at the centre of Alessandro Triulzi's chapter on 'The Past as Contested Terrain: Commemorating New Sites of Memory in War-Torn Ethiopia'. The immediate context for the essay is the 1998-2000 war between Ethiopia and Eritrea, which was presented in the world's media as yet another instance of particularly 'African' forms of state violence and political decay. At the same time it was a war that involved nations in which great hopes had been invested as representatives of a different, 'second-generation' stage of post-colonial governance, following Derg violence in Ethiopia and the thirty-year-long Eritrean war for national independence. Triulzi's essay attempts to make sense of this violence 'between brothers' in terms of the ways in which both the warring governments had come to depend on a culture of violence and emergency to sustain their power and be able to fend off oppositional challenges as 'nations-at-war'.

Focusing primarily on Ethiopia, he examines the ways in which state legitimations of the war reactivated debates over the different ways in which Ethiopia and Eritrea had experienced colonisation. Such debates had been dormant for a long time, as a shared memory of repression and violence under first the Emperor's and then Derg rule dominated within the victorious liberation movements of both Ethiopia and Eritrea. Following Eritrea's successful struggle for national independence, which, as mentioned above, represented a unique instance of a redrawing of post-colonial national boundaries in Africa, the debates concerning this older layer of memories resurfaced as a 'war of words' that carried on in parallel to the violence of the trenches and the aerial bombardments. Thus, in Ethiopia, the decisive battle against the Eritreans at Badme in 1999 was presented as a re-enactment of the victory at Adwa in 1896, when the Italians had been repulsed, and the unity of the Ethiopian nation confirmed – emphasising how the Eritreans of that time had behaved as collaborators vis-à-vis the Italian colonisers in their attempt to escape the building of the Ethiopian nation. Triulzi traces this 'war of words' through debates in newspapers and other media as well as on the internet and shows the central involvement of diaspora voices in the chorus of disagreement. He understands the verbal war – like the physical violence and the mutual expulsion of citizens – as testimony to the finality of the secession of Eritrea but also as containing the seeds of 'a divisive future'.

Preben Kaarsholm's essay on 'Violence as Signifier: Politics and Generational Struggle in KwaZulu-Natal' discusses the historical and micropolitical background to the political violence which accompanied the transition from apartheid in KwaZulu-Natal. While at one level this violence was driven by rivalry between the two different nationalisms of the Inkatha Freedom Party and the African National Congress, fuelled significantly by the 'third-force' intervention of the apartheid state, there were also complex patterns of locally internal dynamics involved in the escalation of conflict into violence. Using a peri-urban slum locality for a detailed case study, Kaarsholm looks particularly at oppositions between older and younger men, and at relationships between issues of generation, of moral outlook and of ethnicity. (On generational conflict and political violence in Africa, cf. Abbink and van Kessel, 2005.) Forms of violence continuing into the post-apartheid period are also discussed and the essay tries to establish the 'meaning' of more recent 'criminal' violence as compared to earlier, more explicitly 'political' forms of violence. Violence is interpreted as a manifestation of different cultural styles where the criminal violence of groups of young men represents an outcry against the disempowerment of unemployment and poverty, sometimes assuming forms that are self-destructive. The anti-criminal violence of groups under the control of elders, on the other hand, can be seen as a striving towards moral reordering and upholding of 'tradition' and 'respect', which represents a different strategy of protest and counter-initiative in what is experienced as a continued context of social crisis.

Consumption and interpretation of mass media products such as *gangsta rap* music and violent video films are important ingredients in the formation of cultural styles within the South African local arena, as Kaarsholm describes. In the chapter 'Beyond Violence: Media and Localised Ideoscapes of the Liberian Civil War' – Mats Utas concentrates specifically on the significance of videotapes in the context of violence in Liberia. As his point of departure, Utas discusses a particularly grisly instance of popular video culture in the film showing the interrogation and torture of President Samuel Doe in 1990. The film attained a wide circulation, both within Liberia and among diaspora audiences, and its imagery – together with the monster costumes, *juju* magic and drug use of Liberian youngster rebels, was screened internationally as an instance of the 'African barbarism' characteristic of the war in Liberia.

Utas attempts to establish how the video, a rather abrupt *montage* of different ingredients, was produced and discusses the inspiration from popular visual cultural genres available in the Liberian arena. These include American action, Bollywood and *kung fu* films as well as low-budget Nigerian and Ghanaian movies. All include generally high levels of violence, but with different moral contexts and implications, and appeals to different groups of audiences. Utas is particularly interested in the impact from the 'Pentecostalist plots' of Ghanaian movies in which magic and divine powers are confronted and violence appears as the outcome of evil as well as of the wrath of God. He looks more closely at the reception of the Samuel Doe video and describes the particular local settings such as video parlours, in which videos are 'consumed' and discussed, and interviews audience members to illustrate types of response and interpretation. Through this reconstruction of the film's context in terms of production, circulation and reception, Utas arrives at a more elaborate understanding of the video's significance. It has the structure and moral of a heroic folk tale in which the evil magic of the corrupt president is demolished by the powers of Prince Johnson, the rebellious protagonist. Thus its violence inscribes itself and attains its power as propaganda within the 'local ideoscapes' of West Africa.

In the book's final chapter – 'Forced Labour and Civil War: Agrarian Underpinnings of the Sierra Leone Conflict', Paul Richards continues his studies of conflict in Sierra Leone and criticises the focus on 'violence', rather than 'war', which he claims has been dominant in anthropological studies of recent global instability. This has obscured rather than helped in understanding the 'new wars' (cf. Richards, 2005: 1-21). To understand the case of low-intensity (and low budget) conflicts typical of contemporary Africa, he argues that more of a sociology of war is needed in order to explain the particular forms of mobilisation represented in these violent conflicts.

In the case of Sierra Leone, we need to understand why young people develop such a level of 'greed' for opportunities of employment and education that it becomes a 'grievance' for which they are willing to go to war – to organise themselves and die for – in order to redress it. This cannot be understood in straightforward terms of calculation and controlled self-interest but requires different efforts of conceptualising as forms of what the sociologist Emile Durkheim would call 'social pathology'. Richards discusses the stages of the Sierra Leone war and its mobilisations in terms of such a Durkheimian vocabulary, in particular notions of solidarity and of 'anomic' and 'forced' forms of division of labour. In parallel to suicide, civil war can be understood within such a framework as violence which society 'inflicts on itself'. Like suicide, it can be categorised within a Durkheimian mould into different types of 'altruistic', 'egoistic', 'anomic' and 'fatalistic' civil war. While early rebellion in Sierra Leone was 'altruistic' in the sense that young people mobilised to fight for their 'dreams of responsible government and a strong state', Richards suggests that the later stages can be seen as an instance of 'fatalistic' civil war, where desperation meant that 'the intended outcome [was] not escape, but group transcendence, via extreme, apocalyptical destructiveness.'

He compares this type of mobilisation to experiences of American slave revolts such as that of Nat Turner in 1831, where violence was deployed in forms that were apocalyptic and suicidal rather than redemptive. He argues that the history of slavery within the Mende-speaking areas, where the Sierra Leonean war was most violent, helps to explain the ways in which it unfolded. In this way, deeper levels of historical memory may have helped to frame responses to the extreme levels of marginalisation, exclusion and exploitation experienced by young men in particular in Sierra Leone during the 1980s. They were deprived of access to education, employment and the possibility of forming families – and at the same time kept without rights of citizenship which might have enabled them 'to encourage a more open division of labour' by different means.

The importance of developing adequate explanations for the development of a 'new war' is of course not simply a matter of getting the history right but also of providing a background for ideas of possibilities for the prevention of future atrocities. Malthusian and economistic explanations offer little perspective for this through other means than military intervention and policing (cf. Richards, 2005: 6-11). On the other hand, a sociological and historically informed understanding, as outlined by Richards, may suggest more complex and rewarding routes of political reform and interaction that take seriously and attempt to remedy the agendas of injustice and exclusion which brought about the war in the first place.

Having started out with an outline of prevailing 'Afro-pessimism' and resurgencies of an imagery of Africa as a 'dark continent' of barbarism, the volume does not conclude in an equally flat, generalised and contra-factual 'Afro-optimism'. It presents an understanding of the development of wars and violent conflicts in Africa as responses to economic emergencies and political problems that are real, have histories, and can be engaged with constructively through both intellectual and practical efforts.

References

Abbink, Jon and Ineke van Kessel (eds) (2005) *Vanguard or Vandals: Youth, Politics and Conflict in Africa*, Leiden: Brill.

Achebe, Chinua (2000) *Home and Exile*, Oxford: Oxford University Press.

Agbu, Osita (2004) *Ethnic Militias and the Threat to Democracy in Post-Transition Nigeria*, Uppsala: Nordiska Afrikainstitutet, Research Report No. 127.

Alexander, Jocelyn, JoAnn McGregor and Terence Ranger (2000) *Violence and Memory: One Hundred Years in the 'Dark Forests' of Matabeleland*, Oxford: James Currey.

Appadurai, Arjun (1996) 'The Production of Locality', in Arjun Appadurai, *Modernity at Large: Cultural Dimensions of Globalization*, Minneapolis: University of Minnesota Press, pp. 178-204.

Barkan, Joel (2004) 'Kenya after Moi', *Foreign Affairs* 83(1): 101-13.

Bayart, Jean-François (1993 [1989]) *The State in Africa: Politics of the Belly*, London: Longmans. First published as *L'État en Afrique: La Politique du ventre*, Paris: Fayard.

Bayart, Jean-François, Stephen Ellis and Béatrice Hibou (1999 [1997]) *The Criminalization of the State in Africa*, Oxford: James Currey. First published as *La criminalisation de l'état en Afrique*, Brussels: Éditions Complexe.

Berg-Schlosser, Dirk and Norbert Kersting (eds) (2003) *Poverty and Democracy: Self-Help and Political Participation in Third-World Cities*, London: Zed Books.

Berman, Bruce and John Lonsdale (1992) *Unhappy Valley. Vol. 2: Violence and Ethnicity*, Oxford: James Currey.

Berman, Bruce, Dickson Eyoh and Will Kymlicka (eds) (2004) *Ethnicity and Democracy in Africa*, Oxford: James Currey.

Bourdieu, Pierre (1996 [1992]) *The Rules of Art: Genesis and Structure of the Literary Field*, Stanford: Stanford University Press. First published as *Les Règles de l'art*, Paris: Edition du Seuil.

Bratton, Michael and Nicolas van de Walle (1997) *Democratic Experiments in Africa: Regime Transitions in Comparative Perspective*, Cambridge: Cambridge University Press.

Bratton, Michael and Robert Mattes (2000) 'Support for Democracy in Africa: Instrinsic or Instrumental?' *Afrobarometer Paper* No. 1, *MSU Papers on Political Reform in Africa*, East Lansing, Michigan: Michigan State University.

Breckenridge, Carol A. (ed.) (1995) *Consuming Modernity: Public Culture in a South Asian World*, Minneapolis: University of Minnesota Press.

Brons, Maria (2001) *Society, Security and the State in Somalia: From Statelessness to Statelessness?* Utrecht: International Books.

Catholic Commission for Justice and Peace/Legal Resources Foundation (1997) *Breaking the Silence, Building True Peace: A Report on the Disturbances in Matabeleland and the Midlands, 1980 to 1988*, Harare: CCJP/LRF.

Chabal, Patrick and Jean-Pascal Daloz (1999) *Africa Works: Disorder as Political Instrument*, Oxford: James Currey.

Clapham, Christopher (2002a) 'Controlling Space in Ethiopia', in Wendy James, Donald L. Donham, Eisei Kurimoto and Alessandro Triulzi (eds), *Remapping Ethiopia: Socialism and After*, Oxford: James Currey, pp. 9-31.

Clapham, Christopher (2002b) 'The Challenge to the State in a Globalized World', *Development and Change* 33(5): 775-95.

Clarke, John, Stuart Hall, Tony Jefferson and Brian Roberts (1975) 'Subcultures, Cultures and Class: A Theoretical Overview', *Cultural Studies* 7-8 (special issue on 'Resistance through Rituals'): 9-74.

Collier, Paul and Anke Hoeffler (1998) 'On the Economic Causes of Civil War', *Oxford Economic Papers. New Series* 50 (4): 563-73.

Collier, Paul and Anke Hoeffler (2001) *Greed and Grievance in Civil War*, Washington: The World Bank.

Collier, Paul and Anke Hoeffler (2004) 'The Challenge of Reducing the Global Incidence of Civil War', Copenhagen: Copenhagen Consensus Challenge Paper. http://www.copenhagenconsensus.com/Default.asp?ID=221

Compagnon, Daniel (1998) 'Somali Armed Units: The Interplay of Political Entrepreneurship and Clan-Based Factions', in Christopher Clapham (ed.) *African Guerrillas*, Oxford: James Currey, pp. 73-90.

Comaroff, John L. and Jean Comaroff (eds) (1999) *Civil Society and the Political Imagination in Africa: Critical Perspectives*, Chicago: The University of Chicago Press.

Conrad, Joseph (1899) 'Heart of Darkness', *Blackwood's Edinburgh Magazine*, February, March and April.

Cowen, Michael and Karuti Kanyinga (2002): 'The 1997 Elections in Kenya: The Politics of Communality and Locality', in Michael Cowen and Lisa Laakso (eds) *Multi-Party Elections in Africa*, Oxford: James Currey, pp. 128-71.

Cramer, Christopher (1996) 'War and Peace in Angola and Mozambique', *Journal of Southern African Studies* 22(3): 481-90.

Diamond, Larry (ed.) (1993) *Political Culture and Democracy in Developing Countries*, Boulder, CO.: Lynne Rienner.

Diamond, Larry (1988) 'Nigeria: Pluralism, Statism, and the Struggle for Democracy', in Larry Diamond, Juan J. Linz and Seymour Martin Lipset (eds) *Democracy in Developing Countries, Volume Two: Africa*, Boulder, CO.: Lynne Rienner, pp. 33-91.

Diamond, Larry (1999) *Developing Democracy: Towards Consolidation*, Baltimore: Johns Hopkins University Press.

Diamond, Larry, A. Kirk-Greene and Oyeleye Oyediran (eds) (1996) *Transition Without End: Nigerian Politics and Civil Society Under Babangida*, Ibadan: Vantage Publishers.

Diamond, Larry and Marc F. Plattner (eds) (1996) *The Global Resurgence of Democracy*, Baltimore: Johns Hopkins University Press, 2nd edn.

Diamond, Larry, Marc F. Plattner, Yun-han Chu and Hung-mao Tien (eds) (1997) *Consolidating the Third Wave Democracies*, Baltimore: Johns Hopkins University Press.

Doornbos, Martin (1994) 'State Formation and Collapse: Reflections on Identity and Power' in M. van Bakel, R. Hagesteijn and P. van de Welde (eds) *Pivot Politics: Changing Cultural Identities in Early State Formation Processes*, Amsterdam: Het Spinhuis, pp. 281-93.

Doornbos, Martin and Alemseged Tesfai (eds) (1999) *Post-Conflict Eritrea: Prospects for Reconstruction and Development*, Lawrenceville, New Jersey: Red Sea Press.

Dorman, Sara Rich (2003) 'Eritrea's Nation and State-Building: Re-Assessing the Impact of 'the Struggle', *Queen Elizabeth House Working Paper Series* 105.

Ellis, Stephen (1998) 'Liberia's Warlord Insurgency', in Christopher Clapham (ed.), *African Guerrillas*, Oxford: James Currey, pp. 155-71.

Ellis, Stephen (1999) *The Mask of Anarchy: The Destruction of Liberia and the Religious Dimension of an African Civil War*, London: Christopher Hurst.

Eltringham, Nigel (2004) *Accounting for Horror: Post-Genocide Debates in Rwanda*, London: Pluto Press.

Ferguson, James (1999) *Expectations of Modernity: Myths and Meanings of Urban Life on the Zambian Copperbelt*, Berkeley: University of California Press.

Fortes, Meyer and E. E. Evans-Pritchard (1940) 'Introduction', in M. Fortes and E. E. Evans-Pritchard (eds) *African Political Systems*, London: Oxford University Press for the International African Institute, pp. 1-23.

Hammar, Amanda and Brian Raftopoulos (2004) 'Zimbabwe's Unfinished Business: Rethinking Land, State and the Nation', in Amanda Hammar, Stig Jensen and Brian Raftopoulos (eds), *Zimbabwe's Unifinished Business: Rethinking Land, State and Nation in the Context of Crisis*, Harare: Weaver Press, pp. 1-47.

Hansen, Thomas Blom (2003) 'Sovereign Bodies: Citizens, Migrants and States in the Postcolonial World', paper presented to workshop on 'Bio-Politics, States of Exception and the Politics of Sovereignty', Wits Institute for Social and Economic Research, 6-7 February.

Hart, Gillian (2002) *Disabling Globalization: Places of Power in Post-Apartheid South Africa*, Pieter-maritzburg: University of Natal Press.

Huntington, Samuel (1991) *The Third Wave: Democratization in the Late Twentieth Century*, Norman: University of Oklahoma Press.

Hutchinson, Sharon E. (1996) *Nuer Dilemmas: Coping with Money, War and the State*, Berkeley: University of Calfornia Press.

Ibrahim, Jibrin (1999) 'Ethno-Religious Mobilisation and the Sapping of Democracy in Nigeria', in Jonathan Hyslop (ed.) *African Democracy in the Era of Globalisation*, Johannesburg: Witwatersrand University Press, pp. 93-111.

Jackson, Robert H. and Carl G. Rosberg (1982) *Personal Rule in Black Africa: Prince, Autocrat, Prophet, Tyrant*, Berkeley: University of California Press.

Jackson, Robert H. (1990) *Quasi-States: Sovereignty, International Relations and the Third World*, Cambridge: Cambridge University Press.

Johnson, Douglas H. (1998) 'The Sudan People's Liberation Army and the Problem of Factionalism', in Christopher Clapham (ed.) *African Guerrillas*, Oxford: James Currey, pp. 53-72.

Johnson, R. W. and Lawrence Schlemmer (eds) (1996) *Launching Democracy in South Africa: The First Open Election, April 1994*. New Haven: Yale University Press.

Kaarsholm, Preben (2005a) 'Coming to Terms with Violence: Literature and the Development of a Public Sphere in Zimbabwe', in Robert Muponde and Ranka Primorac (eds), *Versions of Zimbabwe: New Approaches to Literature and Culture*, Harare: Weaver Press, pp. 3-23.

Kaarsholm, Preben (2005b) 'Moral Panic and Cultural Mobilization: Responses to Transition, Crime and HIV/AIDS in a KwaZulu-Natal Peri-Urban Settlement', *Development and Change* 36(1): 133-56.

Kaarsholm, Preben and Deborah James (2000) 'Popular Culture and Democracy in Some Southern Contexts: An Introduction', *Journal of Southern African Studies* 26(2): 189-208.

Kaplan, Robert D. (2000 [1994]) *The Coming Anarchy: Shattering the Dreams of the Post Cold War*, Westminster, MD: Random House. First published in *Atlantic Monthly*, February 1994.

Kapuscinski, Ryszard (1986) *The Emperor*, London: Picador.

Kapuscinski, Ryszard (1987) *Another Day of Life*, London: Picador.

Karlstrom, Mikael (1996) 'Imagining Democracy: Political Culture and Democratisation in Buganda', *Africa* 66(4): 485-505.

Kayunga, Sallie Simba (2001) 'The No-Party System of Democracy and the Management of Ethnic Conflicts in Uganda', PhD dissertation, Roskilde: International Development Studies.

Lemarchand, René (1994) *Burundi: Ethnic Conflict and Genocide*, Cambridge: Cambridge University Press.

Leonard, David K. and Scott Straus (2003) *Africa's Stalled Development: International Causes and Cures*, Boulder, CO.: Lynne Rienner.

Lerner, Daniel (1968) 'Modernization: Social Aspects', in D. L. Sills (ed.) *International Encyclopedia of the Social Sciences*, New York: The Free Press, Vol. 9, pp. 386-95.

Lonsdale, John (1994) 'Moral Ethnicity and Political Tribalism', in Preben Kaarsholm and Jan Hultin (eds) *Inventions and Boundaries: Historical and Anthropological Approaches to the Study of Ethnicity and Nationalism*, Roskilde: International Development Studies, Occasional Paper no. 11, pp. 131-50.

Mamdani, Mahmood (1994) 'Pluralism and the Right of Association', in Mahmood Mamdani and Joe Oloka-Onyango (eds) *Uganda: Studies in Living Conditions, Popular Movements and Constitutionalism*, Vienna: JEP Book Series, pp. 519-63.

Mamdani, Mahmood (1996) *Citizen and Subject: Contemporary Africa and the Legacy of Late Colonialism*, Princeton, New Jersey: Princeton University Press.

Mamdani, Mahmood (2001) *When Victims Become Killers: Colonialism, Nativism, and the Genocide in Rwanda*, Princeton: Princeton University Press and Oxford: James Currey.

Mandela, Nelson (1996) Speech on the adoption of the new Constitution, Cape Town, 8 May.

Martinussen, John (1997) *Society, State and Market: A Guide to Competing Theories of Development*, London: Zed Books.

Mbembe, Achille (2001) *On the Post-Colony*, Berkeley: University of California Press.

Mbembe, Achille (2003) 'Necropolitics', *Public Culture* 15(1): 11-40.

Mbembe, Achille and Deborah Posel (2004) 'A Critical Humanism', *The WISER Review* 1: 2.

Messiant, Christine (1995) 'L'Angola dans la guerre', special issue of *Politique Africaine* 57: 3-111.

Messiant, Christine (2001) 'Angola: une victoire sans fin?', *Politique Africaine* 81: 143-61.

Milliken, Jennifer and Keith Krause (2002) 'State Failure, State Collapse, and State Reconstruction', *Development and Change* 33(5): 753-74.

Ndegwa, Stephen N. (1998) 'Citizenship amid Economic and Political Change in Kenya', *Africa Today*

45(3-4): 351-68.

Negash, Tekeste and Kjetil Tronvoll (2000) *Brothers at War: Making Sense of the Eritrean-Ethiopian War*, Oxford: James Currey.

Nzongola-Ntalaja, Georges (1999) 'The Democracy Movement in Congo-Kinshasa, 1956-1994', in Jonathan Hyslop (ed.) *African Democracy in the Era of Globalisation*, Johannesburg: Witwatersrand University Press, pp. 289-314.

Pottier, Johan (2002) *Re-Imagining Rwanda: Conflict, Survival and Disinformation in the Late Twentieth Century*, Cambridge: Cambridge University Press.

Prunier, Gérard (1995) *The Rwanda Crisis: History of a Genocide, 1959-1994*, London: Christopher Hurst.

Raftopoulos, Brian (2003) 'The State in Crisis: Authoritarian Nationalism, Selective Citizenship and Distortions of Democracy in Zimbabwe', in Amanda Hammar, Stig Jensen and Brian Raftopoulos (eds) *Zimbabwe's Unifinished Business: Rethinking Land, State and Nation in the Context of Crisis*, Harare: Weaver Press, pp. 217-41.

Ranger, Terence (2004) 'Nationalist Historiography, Patriotic History and the History of the Nation', *Journal of Southern African Studies*, 30(2): 215-34.

Reno, William (1998) *Warlord Politics and African States*, Boulder, CO.: Lynne Rienner.

Reyntjens, Filip (1999) *La guerre des grands lacs: Alliances mouvantes et conflits extraterritoriaux en Afrique centrale*, Paris: L'Harmattan.

Reyntjens, Filip (2004) 'Rwanda Ten Years On: From Genocide to Dictatorship', *African Affairs* 411: 177-210.

Richards, Paul (1996) *Fighting for the Rain Forest: War, Youth and Resources in Sierra Leone*, Oxford: James Currey.

Richards, Paul (ed.) (2005) *No Peace, No War: An Anthropology of Contemporary Armed Conflicts*, Oxford: James Currey.

Sandbrook, Richard (1985) *The Politics of Africa's Economic Stagnation*, Cambridge: Cambridge University Press.

Sandbrook, Richard (2000) *Closing the Circle: Democratization and Development in Africa*, London and New York: Zed Books.

Seleti, Yonah (1999) '"Scars of War and Dying Children": Challenges of Transition to Democracy in Angola', in Jonathan Hyslop (ed.) *African Democracy in the Era of Globalisation*, Johannesburg: Witwatersrand University Press, pp. 314-39.

Sisk, Tim (1995) *Democratization in South Africa: The Elusive Social Contract*, Princeton, New Jersey: Princeton University Press.

Sørensen, Georg (1996) 'Development as a Hobbesian Dilemma', *Third World Quarterly* 17(5): 903-16.

Sørensen, Georg (1998 [1993]) *Democracy and Democratization: Processes and Prospects in a Changing World*, Boulder, CO.: Westwood Press.

Sørensen, Georg (1999) 'Rethinking Sovereignty and Development', *Journal of International Relations and Development* 2(4): 391-402.

Spengler, Oswald (1918-22) *Untergang des Abendlandes*. Vol. 1: *Gestalt und Wirklichkeit*; Vol. 2: *Welthistorische Perspektiven*, Munich. English translation (1936-8): *The Decline of the West*, New York: Alfred Knopf.

Stanley, Henry Morton (1878) *Through the Dark Continent; or, The Sources of the Nile, around the Great Lakes of Equatorial Africa, and down the Livingstone River to the Atlantic Ocean*, 2 vols. New York: Harper and Brothers.

Stanley, Henry Morton (1890) *In Darkest Africa; or, The Quest, Rescue and Retreat of Emin, Governor of Equatoria*. New York: Charles Scribner's Sons.

Sylvester, Christine (2003) 'Remembering and Forgetting "Zimbabwe": Towards a Third Transition', in Paul Gready (ed.) *Political Transition: Politics and Cultures*, London: Pluto, pp. 29-52.

Therkildsen, Ole (2004) 'Direct Taxes, Prisons and Politics in Uganda', Seminar paper, Copenhagen: Danish Institute for International Studies.

Tilly, Charles (ed.) (1975) *The Formation of National States in Europe*, Princeton: Princeton University Press.

Tilly, Charles (1990) *Coercion, Capital, and European States, A. D. 990-1990*, Oxford: Basil Blackwell.

van de Walle, Nicolas (2001) *African Economies and the Politics of Permanent Crisis, 1979-1999*, Cambridge: Cambridge University Press.

Vlassenroot, Koen (2002) 'The Making of a New Order? Dynamics of Conflict and Dialectics of War in South Kivu (DR Congo)', PhD dissertation, Ghent: University of Ghent.

Werbner, Richard (1991) *Tears of the Dead: The Social Biography of an African Family*, Edinburgh:

Edinburgh University Press.

Werbner, Richard (ed.) (1998) *Memory and the Postcolony: African Anthropology and the Critique of Power*, London: Zed Books.

Willame, Jean-Claude (1992) *L'automne d'un despotisme: Pouvoir, argent et obéissance dans le Zaire des années quatre-vingt*, Paris: Karthala.

Young, Crawford (1994) *The Colonial State in Comparative Perspective*, New Haven: Yale University Press.

Young, Crawford (1999) 'The Third Wave of Democratization in Africa: Ambiguities and Contradictions', in Richard Joseph (ed.) *State, Conflict and Democracy in Africa*, Boulder, CO: Lynne Rienner pp. 15-38.

Young, Crawford (2004) 'The End of the Post-Colonial State in Africa? Reflections on Changing African Political Dynamics', *African Affairs* 103(410): 23-49.

Young, Crawford and Thomas Turner (1985) *The Rise and Decline of the Zairian State*, Madison, Wisconsin: University of Wisconsin Press.

Zartman, I. William (ed) (1995) 'Posing the Problem', in I. William Zartman (ed.) *Collapsed States: The Disintegration and Restoration of Legitimate Authority*, Boulder, CO.: Lynne Rienner, pp. 1-11.

2

Insurgencies
in the Shadow of State Collapse

WILLIAM RENO

Violent predation occurs in wars in 'collapsed states', whether in Africa or in places like Chechnya or Haiti. Looting for personal profit has been a constant feature throughout the history of warfare. What is new about internal wars and rebellions, especially in Africa, is the extent to which economic interests shape the organisations and guide the behaviour of those who participate in these conflicts. This shift is seen in the extent to which predatory groups crowd out ideologically oriented mass-based social movements for reform or revolution that shaped the nature of conflict in many countries during the Cold War's anti-colonial struggles. Some scholars use a 'looting model' of rebellion to explain this predatory behaviour of politicians and warlords, and attribute it to changes such as increasing state reliance on rent-seeking sources of revenue, low incomes and more opportunities for individuals to get rich through small arms proliferation and better access to global criminal networks (Collier, 2000; 2003).

This does not explain why people who receive few benefits from such arrangements – or those who suffer great harm from them – fail to support ideologues instead, or why political entrepreneurs do not try to attract this type of follower. Even self-interested actors might identify important benefits in mobilising large numbers of people around something other than violent predation. Some groups do defy the 'looting model' logic. In one year to September 2001, Afghanistan's Taleban rulers cut opium production in areas they controlled by ninety-six per cent, giving up an income of $100 million while still fighting for control of the country (UNDCP 2001: iii, 11). Likewise, while remittances pay for numerous contending militias in southern Somalia, authorities in northern parts of Somalia rely upon to remittances from overseas workers to run their administration. Diamond mining in some parts of Sierra Leone supported home guard militias in that country's 1991-2002 war, while these resources sustained predatory armed bands just a few kilometres away. Why do armed groups amidst similar situations in these conflicts vary so greatly in their organisation?

Variations in the organisation of groups in conflicts raise important questions: is it possible for indigenous societies to construct public authorities in contemporary collapsed states, or do changes in global economic structures or local politics preclude state-building in the world's worst off places? Why do social movements for reform seem so ineffective in these places when they do appear?

Under what conditions do they succeed? These questions address why social revolution is absent from Africa, despite considerable popular criticism and opposition. This chapter thus considers the nature of rebellion in collapsed states. It focuses on Nigeria to explain variations in the organisation of armed groups as a step to answering some of these questions. Nigerians share a legacy of economic decline, periods of serious civil violence and popular anger at official corruption. Nigeria also hosts many non-state armed groups, of which the differing behaviours of the Bakassi Boys and the Oodua People's Congress (OPC) are examined in detail below. But first, the next section provides a framework to explain these variations and give deeper insight into the nature of conflict in collapsing states.

Explaining Variation in Organisation

Greed and opportunity play important roles in motivating some individuals to fight. The argument here, however, is that these factors usually emerge as consequences of underlying factors that shape contemporary conflict in most African cases. Wars and rebellions in places that are distant from the concerns of global economic and diplomatic centres of power constitute a special category of conflict. They often follow the collapse of state institutions and integrate mechanisms of pre-war patronage-based authority into their organisations. This form of authority creates structural obstacles to building mass-based protest movements. The rent-seeking economies and close connections to criminal networks that many identify as primary causes of predation are not inherently primary causes of predatory conflict; rather, it is the context of authority in which these factors are integrated that plays the critical role in shaping the character of conflict. For example, countries experiencing devastating internal wars are not necessarily more corrupt than countries like Indonesia or South Korea. For example, Vietnam stands at 114 in a corruption survey while managing an average per capita economic growth of 5.9 per cent from 1990 to 2003. Congo-Brazzaville stood at the same rank in the corruption index yet saw multiple outbreaks of predatory violence as its economy contracted at a 5.7 per cent rate over the same period. Indonesia, also dependent on oil exports, was even more corrupt at 133 in the index, yet managing per capita growth of 2.1 per cent, despite the disruption of its 1998 currency crisis (World Bank, 2004: 260-1; Transparency International, 2004). Thus Africa is not unique for its rent-seeking and resource reliance. Instead, the distinctive feature of predatory conflicts lie in their prior organisation of corruption into a patronage system in which rulers fragmented their exercise of coercion and exhibited hostility to any formal institutional and informal authority that they believed would be capable of challenging their regime.

This observation does not reject the notion that people in such countries may wish to overturn a deeply corrupt political system. One scholar notes, for example, 'an attitude of defiance on the part of the young with regard to political, economic, social, and cultural institutions' while also observing that these same youths often are implicated in violent activities of the same officials who they criticise (Diouf, 2003: 7). This collaboration reflects the tendency of politicians to migrate into violent clandestine rackets and to use control over this realm of economic opportunity to build political networks and manage opposition. Violent gangs have long played a role in enforcing this political and commercial authority and have tended to occupy the social space in which armed opposition might otherwise be likely to develop. The sociological configuration of *these* networks, rather than the appearance of specific manifestations of state collapse or opportunities for predation, structures the social space of armed opposition.

Armed youth as a social category form part of the distinctive political economy associated with collapsing states and crises of patronage politics rather than elements of 'civil society' autonomous of (collapsing) states. Though they may view themselves as marginal and personally criticise rulers, they often serve elite interests. Rebellion on these terms does not represent independent collective action, or at least seems much more resistant to the forms of autonomous social organisation that one finds among social bandits and others who belong to marginalised or excluded groups, since ultimately it does not work to destroy the existing social structure of society (*contra* Wolf, 1999; Hobsbawm, 2000; Scott, 1987). Rather, these groups try to exploit existing structures of political authority, even when members' personal ideological convictions and critiques reject any notion of such accommodations. They and their backers manipulate interstices in this system to force their way into the social system from which they are excluded, not overthrow it. This is seen most clearly among the Bakassi Boys examined below.

Nonetheless, other groups such as the OPC systematically apply violence in ways designed to advance the interests of wider communities of supporters, sometimes at odds with existing political structures. Its members occasionally reject opportunities for predation, and leaders over time prove able to discipline individuals who violate this restraint. They show some consistency in their devotion to a political programme and pursue it against the interests of strongmen and politicians who could offer them greater rewards for compliance. Groups like OPC do not represent 'civil society' as many scholars understand the term, however. These groups limit membership to people of a certain ethnic group while preying upon people outside their definition of a community. In any event, they consistently provide at least some public goods to communities, usually security, redistribution of commandeered resources and some enhanced level of order and predictability in everyday life. This distinguishes them from the exclusive pursuit of self-interest in the 'looting model' analysis, since armed fighters and their leaders who identify easy rewards should seize them, in case others do so ahead of them. The 'looting model' does not explain how cooperation develops within some armed groups – but not in others in similar circumstances – to provide public goods where material short-term incentives should promote more predatory behaviour at the expense of any long-term collective action.

This framework to explain these differences focuses on three factors that weigh heavily in different ways in the cases below. First, it matters how close local authorities – state officials along with people who exercise local authority without the trappings of formal state office – have been to the centre of the pre-conflict regime's political networks. There is a strong correlation between the degree of closeness in relations between local elites and pre-conflict rulers and predatory behaviour among armed groups as conflict breaks out in collapsed states. Elites who were most excluded from centres of regime power during the immediate pre-war period tend to produce less predatory, if not less violent armed groups once conflict starts. Second, the extent to which local authorities in collapsed states, who eventually play a role in armed groups, adapt old arrangements to generate and distribute resources weighs heavily in determining the degree to which armed groups become predatory or protect local communities. This is because older ways of managing resources, even in clandestine trades in arms and illicit mineral exports, helped shield local communities from the predations of political networks attached to pre-war regimes. These strategies later gave these 'marginal' elites leverage over resources to equip and sustain armed young men, which they could use to exercise social control over them. Finally, the arrival of non-indigenous fighters, foreign military intervention, charitable aid, or new commercial networks enables violent entrepreneurs to ignore community demands or discard social constraints that other means of accessing resources might impose on otherwise predatory armed men.

This explanation for the behaviour of insurgents points to some shortcomings of broad studies that link increased vulnerability to violent conflict to a range of factors such as mineral resources or overseas sources of funding, at least to the extent that current African conflicts arise out of distinct circumstances. These relationships do exist and such studies are useful for detecting probabilities of risk (for example, Marshall and Gurr, 2003). What matters more is the social context in which resources are used. Broad collections of variables can miss how actors, rules and logics shaping violence are organised and how their interaction varies at different phases of conflicts. Nor do they necessarily explain outcomes of conflict. They cannot account for why conflict begins in one place, yet fails to appear, or appears in different forms in other places sharing similar risk factors. They do not explain variance in the behaviour of armed groups; why some sustain substantial inter-group stability and control members in the face of incentives for predations, while others fragment and become predatory.

Nigeria offers an ideal situation to investigate why armed groups develop different organisations and goals, even when confronted with similar incentives and resources. It is thus a good place to test the thesis that specific organisational interests and the political networks of state collapse survive collapsing state institutions and shape the character and aims of armed groups. These groups mobilise urban youth who suffer social consequences of corruption and economic mismanagement by the country's elite, even if this opposition does not take the liberal form that many students of democratisation prefer. Unlike some formal NGOs and donor-driven democratisation policies, youth gangs, some heavily armed, serve as repositories and organisers of knowledge and experiences of popular struggles by mass movements (Jega, 1998; Momoh, 2002). But as the cases below highlight, some end up fighting for personnel and networks of the political system that they say they hate, while others quite close by pose serious threats to it. The explanation for this variance and for the distinctive armed group behaviour that arises out of contemporary collapsing states, is the subject of the cases that follow. But first, to explain this context the specific nature of collapsed states is examined below.

The Distinctive Context for Violence in Collapsed States

What leads rulers to undermine their own state agencies intentionally? Most postcolonial rulers faced a dilemma in how to govern, especially in Africa, and arguably now in some parts of the periphery of the former Soviet Union. Many leaders simply articulated vague nationalist agendas. During the Cold War these usually found expression in domestic policies of economic self-sufficiency and the diplomacy of non-alignment. Ideally, economic prosperity would lift citizens out of poverty, generate more revenues for new state tasks and bolster the legitimacy of ruling cliques. This vision received support from foreign backers in the form of foreign aid, strategic alliances and tolerance of statist economic policies, at least up to the 1980s. This changed in the 1980s, as outsiders withdrew support for generic nationalist strategies. New ideologies of democracy and free markets did not address the political problems facing many of these rulers in maintaining stability, providing services to constituents and protecting their regimes. Indeed, new ideas such as reducing the powers of state administrators and empowering disgruntled sections of the population seemed to undermine the fundamental pursuit of holding weakly institutionalised states together.

Well before the 1980s many of these regimes faced considerable internal threats from their own ranks. Sudan suffered its first military coup in 1958, two years after independence. Through the period from 1970 to 1990, rulers in Africa faced a 72 per cent risk of violent removal from office. This risk declined to 45 per cent from 1990 to 2004 with the advent of regularly scheduled multi-party elections in many states (author's calculations). Even managing successions through elections poses considerable threats to the personal security of rulers. In 2002–04, for example, Burundi, the Democratic Republic of Congo, Côte d'Ivoire, Guinea-Bissau, Liberia, Nigeria, Somalia, Sudan and Uganda – nine of Africa's fifty-two states – hosted conflicts at the hands of a diverse range of non-state armed groups (Eriksson and Wallensteen, 2004: 532-46). Five conflicts included armed group leaders who were previously colleagues of the rulers who they now opposed. Elections have played important roles in sparking widespread violence in Republic of Congo, Nigeria, Tanzania, Guinea-Bissau, Central African Republic and Côte d'Ivoire. The 2000 elections in Zimbabwe demonstrated how multiparty elections were compatible with serious internal conflict; what Juan Linz calls 'chaosocracy' (2000: 253). Election violence is well known in Nigeria and is a major focus of the study of political behaviour in that country (Abdullahi Smith Centre for Historical Research, 2003).

Consequently, incumbent rulers tend to avoid centralising military command structures. Instead, they manipulate factional conflicts within security forces. To do so, they create multiple anti-crime units, violent 'tax enforcement' units, informal paramilitaries and palace guards to keep each other in check while still strong enough to suppress rulers' opponents. This explains preferences among Nigeria's rulers for overlapping state paramilitaries in a context of no significant external threats to the country's security. Prior to the establishment of the elected civilian government in 1999, personalised factional struggles took place within the country's military establishment, including in the army, the State Security Service, the National Guard, the Presidential Guard, and numerous special military-police units such as the Rivers State Internal Security Task Force, organised to suppress local protests. This strategy of fracturing the state's domination over the exercise of coercion provides greater short-term security for rulers who fear their own associates. The long-term impact, however, is seen in the wider spread of weapons and military expertise in societies, often into the hands of local strongmen and youth groups that were not initially associated with militaries or police.

Given this threat that institutionalised armed force poses to insecure leaders, the most efficient strategy in the short term is to distribute state assets as patronage at personal discretion. Though useful for building personal power bases, this practice undermines state capacities to provide services to the wider population. Once patronage politics dominates the political landscape, however, reform becomes extremely difficult. This is because any regime effort to carve out institutional space for efficient bureaucracies poses the risk of empowering people who could tap into citizen anger over favouritism and insider politics within the same political centre that sponsors reforms. In Ghana, for example, Lt. Jerry Rawlings benefited from popular disgust with corruption. But once his Revolutionary Councils began to organise this anger, Rawlings recognised that council members' calls for further political cleansing clashed with his need to manage Ghana's existing political establishment through patronage. In this regard, corrupt rulers may recognise the superior qualities of effective bureaucracies, but they manage political systems in which they would likely become easy victims of real reform as their old power-base used their control of violence to turn on their leader.

Potential reformers and revolutionaries face their own organisational problems, especially as external models for revolution and reform have grown scarce. The decline of external diplomatic and economic support for state-led development reduces material and intellectual support for insurgents who otherwise would have stressed modernisation. Marxists find no foreign backers. Libyan President Qadaffi's Pan-African 'Third Universal Principle' lost its sub-Saharan appeal as stories of race riots and expulsion of workers from Libya gained wide circulation and the mercurial colonel traded his radical credentials for an end to western sanctions. North Korean and Cuban models find few adherents. The decline in the prestige and prominence of outside models of rebellion and reform undermines the organisational prominence of educated intellectuals who sacrifice careers in exile to guide successful insurgencies. There is no clear replacement for the Marxist inspirations within the Eritrean People's Liberation Front. No strong Marxist or social democratic movements arise to fight inequality as they did in the African National Congress. The importance of these intellectuals and their models lay in their abilities to attract resources that they could use to discipline and reward people who supported a specific political project. Once empowered with resources and foreign supporters, such leaders could marginalise people who were more interested in looting and predation and provide a predictable pathway to power and prestige for the enterprising who would abide by the rules.

Strategies of Authority in Collapsing States

Alongside the recession of foreign models, many rulers in weakly institutionalised states further undermined their own state agencies. This profoundly changed how they exercised authority in these places and the shape that armed opposition would take. Since rulers often feared that their associates in state agencies could use their bureaucratic power-bases to oppose their patrons, personal security and patronage became higher priorities than spending on state services. Ultimately, spending on services like education and health care (reaching zero in 1992 in Zaire) would be wasted, according to this perspective. Such spending would divert resources from the more urgent task of managing powerful strongmen. Liberia's government, for example, reported a budget of $82 million for all of its official operations in 2000. Half of this was spent to protect the president, his private business associates, and a few other officials (IMF, 2002: 8). Meanwhile, President Charles Taylor personally controlled much greater resources to field informal militias, mostly from business transactions in violation of United Nations sanctions against his regime for his support of armed groups in neighbouring states.

As this defensive strategy strips rulers of state institutions and bureaucratic hierarchies used elsewhere to control associates and subordinates, these rulers manipulate markets to manage clients and punish and deny resources to others who otherwise might oppose them. Loyal associates are permitted access to economic opportunities such as smuggling or transactions in illicit goods. Thus rulers implant their personal political networks in place of the collapsing institutions of their own states. The sovereign façade of their political network remains valuable, however. Such rulers use their sovereign prerogatives to make laws to manipulate regulations to declare certain activities illegal. This permits them to sell exemption from enforcement to favoured individuals or groups, including those who wield their own private coercive power and who use it in the service of their economic positions, so long as this also helps maintain their patron's political dominance. These activities fuse the exercise of political power to violent predation in informal and clandestine markets. Thus these arenas of life that elsewhere are beyond the purview of state authority, become the mainspring of political domination in collapsing states well before these places come to international attention as conflict zones.

Such networks of authority force people who are struggling to survive the recession of state services to deal with corrupt officials even to gain access to informal 'unregulated' markets. It is not these people who pose threats to regimes. Instead, the main danger to authorities lies in the difficulty of dominating enough transactions to ensure that political clients do not exploit their local knowledge of markets and control over armed groups to enrich themselves without due obedience to their patrons. Thus many presidents build their own violent networks in this commercial world. Even as these rulers present themselves as beneficent patrons in this world of informal exchange, most people recognise that senior officials have little interest in governing, even in the sense of engaging in the social reciprocities that many expect of a good patron.

Old patrons have faced considerable challenge from subordinates since the end of the Cold War, however, even as threats from capable public agencies remain. As the 'looting model' predicts, the availability of small arms and increased regime reliance on rent-seeking sources of income play an important role. But at least as important is the pre-conflict organisation of coercion in the hands of presidential associates, including individuals such as key business partners and political advisors who may not have held formal state office. Nearly all 'warlords' in Africa, for example, occupied central positions in the authority structures of regimes that they later attacked. Most used their control of informal militias and armed gangs and wealth garnered from the commercial connections that they built up as part of old patronage networks to threaten their former benefactors. The Republic of Congo's Ninja militia, for example, backed Bernard Kolélas, Mayor of Brazzaville. The rival Zoulou militia fought for Professor Pascal Lissouba, a former Prime Minister, and victorious candidate for president in 1992

(Bazenguissa-Ganga, 1999: 37-54). Thus it is not the presence of resources, *per se*, that causes violence to take on such a predatory character. Instead, it is the nature of the patronage-based political system, particularly its tendency to fragment the control of coercion in its strategies of rule to avoid the threat of army coups. The decisive change, however, occurs as the former patron begins to lose the capacity to centralise and regulate his clients' exploitation of economic opportunities.

Highly educated people appear among war leaders (Professor Wamba-dia-Wamba and Dr Emile Ilunga of competing factions of the *Rassemblement Congolaise pour la Démocratie*, and Dr George Boley of the Liberian Peace Council), along with various generals and former ministers of government. These elite origins and close ties to the politics of incumbent rulers in many of Africa's internal wars highlight the ties between rebellion and the strategies of incumbent authorities in collapsing states. In earlier years, these individuals would have been in socially autonomous positions from which they would devise their critiques, recruit supporters, and receive aid and attention from abroad. Now the commercial networks that had been sinews of the ruler's authority provide challengers with the political raw materials to topple weakened patrons and fight off other claimants, including those who cling to more elaborate ideological critiques at the expense of exploiting these material opportunities. Liberia's warlord Charles Taylor, for example, procured supplies from abroad for President Samuel Doe (1980–89) before he turned against his boss. Mohammed Farah Aideed was a former Defence Minister and managed clandestine acquisitions of arms from abroad prior to Somalia's 1991 collapse. The son and business manager of former Zaire's President Mobutu (1965–97) leads insurgents who fight the son of a former smuggler who battled his way to State House. Insurgent commanders in Chechnya have professional resumés that include Soviet-era procurement directors and Red Army officers, job categories that give them access to networks to exploit clandestine economies and to procure sophisticated weapons.

The key to untangling the riddle of who becomes predatory and who maintains order lies in determining where these people were situated in pre-conflict political networks of collapsing states. For example, in places where local strongmen have controlled clandestine markets in defiance of presidential wishes, such as in northern Somalia in the 1980s, these politicians had to find safe niches and rely upon local customary authorities to help protect them and their transactions against presidential wrath. The earlier 'mistake' of northern Somalia's local elders and politicians lay in having supported a faction that was overthrown in 1969. The new ruler then excluded many of them from rackets that circumvented the government's own exchange and import controls out of suspicion that they still supported exiled separatists. Lacking the president's capabilities or influence, they had to use kinship networks and local elders to protect and guarantee their own 'unofficial' clandestine business operations. This alternative network included new ways to use customary guarantees of transactions to manage the transfer of overseas remittances outside of the reach of predatory officials. This limited what local authorities could do with these resources, as respected community leaders controlled their partners to a large enough extent that they could withhold resources and sanction politicians who preyed upon their own communities.

The nature of violence in Nigeria also shows that if local strongmen operate clandestine networks *in spite of* presidential wishes and can protect them from interference as state institutions collapse, armed groups in these areas tend to articulate a distinctive community-based programme, discipline predation among members, and resist co-optation into outside patronage networks. They remain relatively more immune to enticements or blandishments of other strongmen, especially outsiders. It is not clandestine markets and violent rackets *per se* that determine insurgent autonomy and behaviour. The degree of separation of these informal institutions from legitimate local authorities is most important. Alternatively, where control over rackets historically favoured longer-established and more localised patronage networks over the interests of new local elites with close ties to the capital, armed groups usually develop greater links to the interests of local communities and a greater capacity for collective action. This in turn reduces the risks of local violence and predation in those communities.

Predation and Authority in Nigeria

Nigeria seems to be brimming with youth groups that criticise corrupt and inept politicians and address fundamental ideological issues such as gross inequality. The OPC agitates for the autonomy of ethnic Yoruba parts of Nigeria and demands accountable, democratic governance in what they envision at the very least as a radically decentralised Nigerian federal system (Fasehun, 2003). They sponsor numerous youth groups and collaborate with other organisations to articulate a radically reformed alternative to existing Nigerian politics and even pose the creation of an alternative ethnic national homeland (Albert, 2002: 283-6). OPC also organises members as vigilantes to fight violent crime that Nigerian security forces cannot manage. Members also direct traffic, regulate markets and trades, and punish officials who take bribes, apparently as part of an effort to demonstrate to citizens the gross incapacity of the Nigerian state to serve public interests and to show potential supporters a different vision of their futures (Ajulo, 2000: 12; Olabisi, 2000: 5).

Nigeria's politicians and bureaucrats take seriously the threat that the OPC and groups like them pose to the country's political hierarchy. Gani Adams, head of a more radical faction of the OPC, compared this organisation to the African National Congress in South Africa in the 1980s and to Mau Mau nationalists in Kenya in the 1950s. He cited the African Charter on Human and Peoples Rights to justify his cause, stating that 'Colonised or oppressed peoples shall have the right to free themselves from the bonds of domination by resorting to any means recognised by the international community,' including autonomy (Adams, 2003: 3). One youth wing proposed creating an Oodu'a Republic (Oodu'a Youth Movement, 1994) and later pledged to 'raise and defend the full expression of their right to self-determination' (Oodu'a Youth Movement, 2001). The street-level activities of OPC's anti-crime campaign include attacking and killing policemen alleged to shield and collude with armed robbers. A Lagos State Senate investigation of OPC–police clashes in 1999 and 2000 determined that OPC fighters and police engaged in battles rooted in the suspicion among OPC members and citizens that local politicians and police sponsor armed robbers. Fighting took a toll of about 500 civilians, police and OPC members in 2002 (Mojeed, 2003b: 23).

The Bakassi Boys in eastern Nigeria also fight armed criminals. 'Bakassi Boys have a good name because they protect the people from daily humiliations and severe losses from armed bandits that operated freely in the markets and streets in general posing a threat to lives and property,' wrote one observer (Ukiwo, 2002: 2). The Niger Delta harbours armed youth groups such as the Ijaw Youth Congress (IYC), Movement for the Survival of Ogoni People (MOSOP), and Egbesu Boys where armed young men contest the failure of oil companies to compensate communities for environmental damages and the unwillingness of the Nigerian Federal Government to share oil revenues with oil producing communities. The Movement for the Actualization of the Sovereign State of Biafra (MASSOB) advertises its aims in its name. These groups confront state security forces such as the Rivers State Internal Security Task Force, which they claim has been responsible for transferring weapons to local allies and targeting local activists and popular local leaders in political violence (Human Rights Watch, 2003: 21-3). Their critics claim that these groups also include 'criminals who parade themselves as youth activists' and who are really interested in loot and extortion, rather than political programmes (Abugu, 2000: 2). Economic motivations for violence also appear. Youths have attacked installations of foreign oil producers and have extorted payments and stolen property that they have sold or converted to their own uses, activities that are difficult to isolate from general grievances over inequity (Ukeje, 2001: 346-7).

As in all conflicts, motives of personal gain and political grievance are inter-mingled. Most of these groups, however, are cohesive enough and articulate political programmes that should help them to follow the paths of revolutionary insurgencies instead of predatory bandits. Eric Wolf observed (of rural revolutionaries) that 'ultimately, the decisive factor in making a peasant rebellion possible lies in the relation of the peasantry to the field of power surrounding it;' what he calls 'fields of leverage'. That is, marginalisation from centres of power translates into organisational autonomy, while clandestine activities offer avenues for gathering resources to promote struggle and build followings (Wolf, 1999: 290). This kind of solidarity, born of the autonomy that exclusion affords at first appears to be widely present throughout Nigeria, as in many African states where abusive regimes place low priorities on administrative capabilities outside of coercive agencies. Nigeria's universities produce radical and reform-minded intellectuals in abundance. Many intellectuals and government critics support themselves as non-government organisations, seeking money and intellectual ties with exiled Nigerians and support groups from abroad, just as insurgents of earlier days relied upon solidarity networks for resources and political support.

Bakassi Boys vigilantes seem to offer this revolutionary potential too. They appeared in Ariaria Market in Aba in eastern Nigeria in 1998 to respond to widespread popular grievances about corrupt and irresponsible government, especially its inability to handle a terrible plague of armed robbery. Many even suspected that local police and some politicians were in collusion with these armed robbers. Colourful posters appeared in markets with titles such as 'The face up between the Bakassi Boys and Federal Government troops at Onitsha.' They depict machete-wielding fighters defying federal authorities. Popular videos such as *Down the River* show members humiliating corrupt judges and criminal courts. Action scenes feature the rapid summary justice of 'African Science' to discern a captive's guilt by holding up a special machete. A red machete means that heads will roll. Their popularity grew, and they spread to the market town of Onitsha. As a commander of Bakassi Boys explained: 'We deal with matters as fast as possible, unlike the courts.' He contrasts this with government courts: 'in 1959, when I was in primary school, there was a case in my village. It is still in court till today. Nobody knows when it will end!' (Umahi, 2001: 2)

Nigeria's actual 'fields of leverage', however, are minimal, at least in the sense of providing the organisational autonomy that Wolf and other scholars of resistance such as Scott (1987) describe. In particular, the evolution of informal political and clandestine economy networks amidst collapsing state institutions created numerous informal linkages between individuals within armed opposition groups and elite political networks. These linkages are centred in the junction between economic and political realms of the patronage-based political authority and are part of the violent appropriation of commerce that politicians used to control people and disrupt organisational alternatives. The social origins of Bakassi members highlight this linkage. A journalist observes: 'a good number of these [Bakassi] boys were also used for some of the dirty jobs carried out during the Abacha reign of terror, and they are all moving about freely, ready for the highest bidder to engage their services' (Agekameh, 2000b: 25). Some vigilantes allegedly include demobilised Nigerian soldiers that served in the ECOWAS Monitoring Group (ECOMOG) in Liberia and Sierra Leone and their behaviour reflects some of the techniques of fighting in those countries. A journalist observed that Bakassi Boys' 'judgment takes the form first of cutting off the hand from the elbow known as "short sleeve" or from the shoulders known as "long sleeve",' echoing techniques of Revolutionary United Front (RUF) rebels that ECOMOG fought in Sierra Leone (Agekameh, 2000a: 24-5; Ubani, 2000: 10). The demobilisation of paramilitaries and security agencies formed during General Sani Abacha's regime (1993-8) added to the weaponry and military expertise available to these groups (interview, Freetown, 9 May 2002). After Abacha died in 1998, it is unclear what happened to these weapons, although army officers repeatedly report that private individuals appear on bases to buy arms (Agekameh, 2001: 32).

More concrete connections appeared between Bakassi Boys and the former Anambra state governor, Chimaroke Mbadinuju, who elevated Bakassi Boys to the status of Anambra State Vigilante Service. The governor's political ties are especially important in this context. In 1967-70, the region that later became Anambra state was a centre of rebellion as separatist politicians fought to create an independent Biafra. Although the public policy of the victorious federal government stressed reconciliation, the reality was that few from this region were allowed access to high-level military careers. This exclusion was especially significant in light of the longevity of military rule, lasting until 1999, with the exception of a four-year interlude, 1979-83. Since local politicians could not become powerful at the federal level in their own right, they were forced to seek patronage from the country's military rulers if they hoped to be allowed to participate in the closely managed, phased transitions to civilian rule (in the 1970s and fairly continuously between 1985 and 1999). In practice this meant that local politicians who hoped to build their own local and regional patronage networks through access to state assets had to have strong ties to higher-level patrons in the capital. The military's victory in the civil war had limited the option of building a local opposition movement on the basis of autonomous local control over resources, especially as military government officials began to monopolise the distribution of 'private' and clandestine market opportunities, either through manipulating state regulations or simply crowding out truly autonomous clandestine market operators and replacing them with their own rackets. It is partly for this reason that many local citizens suspect that their political leaders and security forces are behind criminal activities.

This centralised control of resources, official and clandestine alike, provided military rulers with a lever to install dependent local supplicants in lucrative positions in return for obedience (Albert, 2002: 309-25). Such control over resources gave military rulers the capability to manipulate local politicians who owed their positions and resources to their distant positions. In relative terms the geographical and social gap between layers in this patronage system was greater in eastern and southern Nigeria in comparison to other regions of the country. In one sense, easterners who complain about their 'marginalisation' from centres of power in the patronage-based political networks and the formal institutions of the state are correct. But in another sense that is more important for how armed groups there behave, this form of dependence and oversight gives most enterprising local politicians greater incentives to cosy up to distant patrons at the expense of truly indigenous authorities. This relationship also gave military rulers more leeway to instigate local factional disputes. Constant disputes forced politicians to cultivate good relations in the capital, lest a shift in the interest of one's patron would spell the end of access to the portals of state-supplied benefits, clandestine and formal alike (Oyediran, 1997:193-211). It is in this context that a 'looting model' of rebellion develops. It is not because young rebels and other regime critics are inherently predatory. Instead, a key social space where rebels often build their own vision of their alternative political world – Wolf's 'field of leverage' – is the same social terrain in which the collapsing state and its officials dominate. As a consequence of its defeat in the civil war and the sidetracking of its own political networks, this characterised Nigeria's east even more than other parts of the country.

It was in this context that the Anambra State governor invited the Bakassi Boys to rid the commercial centre of Onitsha of armed robbers. The Abia State governor also extended an invitation to group members in his state. Since local factional battles in this part had been relatively closely integrated into national patronage networks, these men were well situated to exploit the junction of armed force and economic power. This remained the case even with the return to civilian rule in 1999 and elections in 2003 as 'some state governors were rumoured to have been deeply involved in arming thugs in the name of vigilante groups – all in preparation for this year's general elections' (Oshunkeye, 2003: 35).

Meanwhile, armed robbery did decline in Onitsha as Bakassi Boys killed suspects at the rate of five per day. This was compatible, however, with acting as a tool of the governor to extend his personal control over local commerce and capacity to fend off rivals. The Anambra State legislature legalised their activities, deputising them as the State Vigilante Service Committee answerable to the governor, while the Abia State government provided equipment to Bakassi Boys for its own Abia State Vigilante Services (Agekameh, 2000a: 23-7). This action gave Mbadinuju a double advantage – he could deputise a non-state armed group to seek out rival political and economic networks that posed a threat to his political power while at the same time benefiting from popular acclaim for appearing to do something about the plague of armed robbery.

It was not a positive development for the new civilian federal government that took power in 1999. The governor appeared to have begun to control his own armed force that was capable of settling political scores and seizing economic opportunities without assent from the political centre. The process mirrored similar developments in places like Liberia and Sierra Leone, where wars grew out of the fragmentation of political networks as local politicians began to exercise coercion against the interests of their old patrons.

Emeka Offor, head of the Anambra Patriotic Forum campaigning against the governor in the 2003 elections and perceived to be an agent of president Olusegun Obasanjo, accused the governor of using Bakassi Boys to murder two of his political opponents (Offor, 2001: 18). Governor Mbadinuju justified the Bakassi Boys' actions, saying:

> They came to me and said that they have been looking for this man [legislator]... and that they had gone to his house to catch him because he [legislator] committed criminal offences and I said no matter how highly placed a person is, anyone who is suspected of being an armed robber, we will bring him out and test him, so they [Bakassi Boys] tested him [legislator] as they normally test everybody and he didn't meet up with the test (Onwubiko, 2000: 11).

The incumbent governor showed an adept capacity to appropriate the language of anti-corruption to justify the Bakassi Boys' actions, stating that his opponent 'showed undue loyalty to some "money bags" who had sworn to destabilise state government' (Eke, 2000: 8). Likewise, the murdered Abia politician 'made confessional statements acknowledging his misdeeds before he was killed' (Akparanta, 2000: 17). The interventions of Bakassi Boys in bye-elections and in budget deliberations in the Anambra state legislature bolstered the governor's position in the guise of attacking 'corrupt politicians' in advance of the 2003 elections and strengthened his hand in his feud with Offor (Anayouchukwu, 2002: 36-7). At the level of rhetoric, reformist and radical inclinations of individual Bakassi Boys members remained compatible with engagement with politicians who were implicated in these vices. It is true that Bakassi Boys and other groups will kill members of other ethnic groups and defend particular communities from untrustworthy state institutions (Harnischfeger, 2003), but their manner of doing so also reinforces local aspects of the political economy that are responsible for these threats.

Developments in Anambra highlighted a related commercial dispute. During the 1993-8 Abacha dictatorship, the governor served as a legal advisor to the Anambra branch of a party that supported Abacha's continuation in office. Mbadinuju used that position to show local market associations that they had to deal with him to remain on good terms with authorities in the capital and with security forces in Anambra state. The kidnapped Anambra legislator championed a rival commercial organisation that backed what turned out to be the weaker local political faction during the Abacha years, and found that their fortunes took a turn for the worse when their patron's rival became governor after the 1999 election (Okebalama, 2000: 11). This remained the case, even after their patron could assert his client's interests in the state legislature where he won a seat in 1999. But his political clout dwindled when Mbadinuju removed the legislator and installed his personal assistant (known for ties to violent 'area boys') in the vacant seat. Subsequent clashes between Bakassi Boys and other armed groups from outside the state seemed to indicate that Mbadinuju's opponents were willing to use similar strategies. While political violence generally is disruptive of order, the important feature of this variety lay in the capacity of politicians to use it without reference to the interests of local communities, even if some people benefited from their actions. Mbadinuju used his vigilante force to control political assets and fight opponents directly. His opponents countered with political violence that appeared to enjoy support from the distant capital.

The political use of the group undermined ideological discipline among local Bakassi Boys. As powerful patrons came to determine how and when the group would get resources, 'the leadership of the group was soon embroiled in a bitter tussle over who would take ownership of the sleek silver colour Mercedes Benz car belonging to [the slain] Nwosu-Igbo' (Akparanta, 2000: 17). Matters got worse as a political rival of the Abia governor arrived in the state capital with members of MASSOB, the Niger Delta region separatist group noted above. Bakassi Boys responded by burning the rival's family home. The head of the Abia State Vigilante Services complained of the effect this had on Bakassi Boys goals and unity. 'We want the government to relocate us to a camp,' he urged, 'so that we can use regimental system to maintain discipline... Politicians are interfering with everything, lobbying this group against that group' (Agbo, 2001: 63). This action was especially striking, as MASSOB fighters were supporting clients of the federal government's president, their sworn foes in rhetoric.

Vigilantes in eastern Nigeria show how the shift of collapsed state politics into informal control of the local political economy destroys alternative avenues for organizational autonomy in which to build social movements and articulate ideologies of liberation. But as the case of the OPC below shows, it is not the clandestine economies or the violent nature of the groups that causes this outcome. Instead, behaviour is rooted in the nature of the patronage political networks' control over these resources and groups.

Circumstances Limiting Predation in Nigeria

In contrast to tight connections between Bakassi Boys and local elites who vied with each other for the benefit of powerful backers in a distant capital, the OPC has played a more autonomous role in regional politics. OPC was organised in the mid-1990s during the Abacha regime around the political agenda of protecting the interests of the Yoruba ethnic community. Like Bakassi Boys, OPC members responded to local insecurity, but elite members of this community never suffered the degree of subordination to central authorities that Anambra and Abia state political establishments did. After all, their political mentors participated in the civil war on the winning side. This left many Yoruba elites with more direct social control over local resources, although how these would be used depended on the nature of their political ties to the capital. These ties became strained in the extreme in the mid-1990s after Abacha's rejection of the results of the 12 June 1993 presidential election, in which M.K.O. Abiola, a Yoruba politician and businessman was widely considered to have won the popular vote.

Members of this wealthy business and political elite of western Nigeria incorporated the stolen election into a broader social vision that included a stronger Yoruba identity within Nigeria. This programme became synonymous with resistance to Abacha's continuation in office. The 'area boys' – urban toughs – that later became OPC leaders played significant roles in the mass civil disobedience and preparations for the Campaign for Democracy's armed struggle against military rule before Abacha's death in 1998 (interview with organiser, 12 Dec 2002). 'Area boys' also played a major role in leading the boycott of the May 1994 elections, the first significant popular challenge to the military regime. After 1998, the OPC split into a moderate and a radical wing. Moderate leaders have been more willing to tolerate the elected civilian government of Obasanjo. A radical wing opposes collaboration with Obasanjo's government, and argues for a wholesale renegotiation of southwestern Nigeria's relationship with the Nigerian federation with the option of complete independence.

This division among OPC members reflects a similar division within the Alliance for Democracy (AD), a party that draws support from Yoruba voters in the country's southwest. The split grows out of differences among elites in that region over how to deal with the political survival of politicians who had collaborated with the Abacha regime, some of whom face increasing pressures from legislatures to submit to investigations of misdeeds and corruption. Ultimately, this involves defining a vision for how ethnic Yoruba communities will participate in Nigerian politics, especially in light of widespread popular beliefs that a government dominated by Northerners has short-changed their communities. This split echoes political divisions in the 1960s among politicians who argued for closer collaboration with elites from other regions of Nigeria, versus those who favoured greater autonomy for the southwest. Thus OPC factional alignments trace other intra-Yoruba political splits, such as contention over appointment of a traditional leader in Ilorin. It is not surprising that OPC is tied to Yoruba elite politics. What is more significant for its organisational interests and behaviour, however, is the relative autonomy of southwestern elites in the political economy of the collapsing state. This is not necessarily intentional. It owes more to the failure of regional elites to exercise decisive control over the federal government and the formal and informal resources that this brings. Especially after Abacha's rise to power, they were forced to rely upon their own political and economic networks to survive, a feature that marks the character of the OPC. It helps to account for its relatively greater political autonomy, despite engagement in the region's factional politics.

Under the duress of the military regime, OPC patrons resorted to social capital and resources that have been relatively insulated from the predations of the collapsing state model of politics from which they now found themselves barred. In practical terms, this encouraged elite organisers of the OPC to link to a nineteenth-century tradition that provided a legitimate role for 'war chiefs' to defend local communities from marauders and kidnappers after the collapse of the Old Oyo Empire and the advent of widespread insecurity. In exchange, 'war chiefs' claimed a role in politics (Ajayi, 1965: 72-85), much as OPC styles itself as a vigilante organisation and contemporary defender of Yoruba interests. This gave OPC social sanction to use violence to defend local communities while giving new opportunities to youths who wanted to escape the strictures of parent and other social circumstances to struggle for power and wealth. At an individual level this is compatible with self-interested motivations prominent in the 'looting model' of rebellion, yet organises them in a way that disciplines their uses of violence.

Predation does occur among some OPC members. As among Bakassi Boys, OPC groups associate with local market organisations on the basis of shared linkages to key politicians. But the nature of the linkages to elites highlights the different configuration of social control of violence. The elderly Madam Tinubu, the boss of a powerful Lagos market association, mother of the current Lagos state governor, and backer of OPC illustrates this difference. Like *Iyalodes* of the nineteenth century, powerful women in this part of Nigeria play a prominent role in organising and regulating urban markets. In those days, *Iyalodes* also patronised 'war chiefs', providing them with ammunition and money to buy guns (Hinderer, 1872). The internal structure of the OPC also reflects earlier practice. *Eso* units within OPC are responsible for enforcing discipline within armed vigilante groups, at least in principle. These *Eso* units are the guarantors that the group will not prey upon its benefactors or side with political opponents as armed muscle, and report to suppliers of resources if members harm the greater interest. Other indigenous social structures such as *egbe* and *ogba* cultural groups play an important role in this context, as they carry out their customary roles of supporters of Yoruba culture and of rulers who respect community mores. This also incorporates community *elegbejegbe* groups that have become sources of recruits and provide a basis for organising local OPC branches (field observation, Ibadan, May 2003; Harunah, 2003).

OPC violence hardly offers an idealised version of 'civil society' as it perpetrates human rights abuses (Human Rights Watch, 2003a). Both factions of OPC have invaded market areas that are controlled by members of 'outsider' ethnic groups (Olukunle, 2000: 1-2; Alli, 2000: 6). Like Bakassi Boys, OPC members target corrupt politicians and police who intervene in factional conflicts. Justifications echo Bakassi Boys statements too. Reflecting widespread opinion in Lagos, 'Kayoade Williams, a repentant armed robber now an evangelist, told *Tell* that behind armed robbers are influential people in the society, including police officers who themselves are beneficiaries of robbers' exploits' (Agekameh, 2000b: 25). These attacks promote conflict between police and OPC members, while police have been accused of staging reprisal attacks and extra-judicial killings.

OPC members also appear to collaborate with at least some state agents. 'There are policemen, SS men who are OPC members. There are highly placed members of the society, even government officials, who cannot openly identify with us' says an OPC leader (Anon., 2000: 15). Furthermore, the Lagos State House of Assembly endorsed OPC as a 'legitimate anti-crime organisation' during one of the announced crackdowns. But OPC ties to politicians as an 'official' vigilante service put the group in a different situation, compared to the Bakassi Boys' role in politics. Local authorities are forced to at least consider localised forces of social control in their strategies, as these have the capacity to influence the recruitment, behaviour and resources available to OPC members. This stands in stark contrast to the dependence that Bakassi Boys members, even those with well developed personal ideological critiques, had on their political patrons and their bosses in the distant capital. While both engage in what the international community and many in Nigeria recognise as serious human rights violations, theirs is not the same thing as violence on the part of an armed group that emerges as an agent of manipulations from the centre of a patronage-based collapsed state administration. Members of each group engage in individual predation – as occurs in all conflicts – but the constraints that OPC members and their politician backers face in the form of autonomous social relationships that have bearing on the control of resources and violence produces a considerable difference in long-term outcomes. Frederick Fasehun's faction of OPC, for example, claimed the autonomy to patrol Lagos communities, 'as a vote of no confidence in the Nigeria police' in a manner that 'will force other [politicians] to remove themselves from the fence on important issues in this country' (Ebosele, 2000: 18), and not as an agent of a prominent politician or faction.

This autonomy can be traced to the decision of opposition forces in the south-west to launch a guerrilla struggle against Abacha's plan to transform himself into a civilian ruler. Ultimately Abacha's mysterious nocturnal demise in June 1998 – potent Viagra, acrobatic Indian prostitutes, and a massive heart attack according to local rumour – ended his self-succession plan. Yoruba politicians such as Lagos State governor, Ahmed Bola Tinubu, were left with armed youths, some who had travelled abroad for military training in conjunction with the planned armed insurgency. The advent of the elected civilian regime greatly improved prospects for these youths' benefactors as they entered state houses and assemblies. OPC members became burdens for Governor Tinubu, complicating his efforts to find a place in the new civilian administration. He and other politicians retained obligations to OPC members who supported them during Abacha's rule, reversing the social relation between Bakassi Boys and their local governors. Tinubu's strategy focused on efforts to set up a state-controlled police force as a counter to OPC, in contrast to the Anambra governor's 'State Vigilante Service Committee' that was to absorb Bakassi Boys. Public and federal opposition complicated Tinubu's plans, along with his own close attachment to politicians now in the Federal Government. The governor refrained from harsh criticism of OPC activities, causing some to suspect that his ability to control violence in Lagos was contingent on not antagonising the group (Adeyeye, 2004: 32). Some OPC support for Tinubu remained, as when members attacked Chief Gani Fawehinmi at the Lagos High Court, where he had appeared for a hearing to compel the Inspector-General of Police to investigate activities of the governor.

Some OPC activists became involved in intra-Yoruba splits prior to the 2003 elections. In December 2001, for example, the assassination of Nigeria's Attorney General Bola Ige followed his defection from the pan-Yoruba group *Afenifere* and his decision to side with the president's People's Democratic Party (PDP) to pursue his ambitions in the 2003 elections. Backers of the Attorney General and his rivals previously fought each other at PDP headquarters. Later, a gunfight took place in the Osun State House of Assembly. Each incident allegedly involved OPC factions (Mojeed, 2003a: 24).

Politicians associated with these factions appear to try to entangle OPC members in their political strategies in return for granting them a share of the material rewards of patronage. Likewise, some OPC members pursue personal interests. For example, some OPC members have been accused of intervening in landlord–tenant disputes and made their services available to dispose of unwanted renters. Such violence has extended to include protection for workers' guilds and attacks on their commercial rivals (Ozekhome, 2003: 193). OPC's Lagos area market invasions and attacks on ethnic Hausa long-distance truckers, with their added ethnic dimensions, puts looting opportunities at OPC members' disposal. These activities show the difficulty of disentangling personal economic motivations, elite factional politics and mass protest in the context of the collapse of state bureaucracies, as politicians use informal paramilitaries and control of economic opportunities to bolster their authority. But predation also is compatible with a rigid ethnic nationalist political vision that provides public goods to a defined group, even as it leaves outsiders as fair game for predation. At a minimum, the violence appears to follow a pattern of discipline that protects defined communities, even if it does so at the expense of pacific relations with their neighbours. If this occurs more widely, violence of this sort would be a form of 'community-building' (and state-building for those who dream of an Oodua Republic) even if it leaves some observers uncomfortable with the spectre of an ethnic homeland state and systematic human rights abuses.

Variations in the behaviours and political ties of the Bakassi Boys and the OPC show how resources and violence can have different characteristics, depending upon the natures of the social structures in which they are embedded. If Nigeria collapsed as a single political entity, it is likely that Bakassi Boys and similar groups would fit the 'looting model' of warfare. Their 'warlord' leaders would emerge from the local strongmen who previously depended upon the centralised distribution of patronage from a distant ruler, much as Governor Mbadinuju tried to fashion his political future. They and their collaborators would appropriate militarised commercial networks of the collapsing state. Disconnected from the informal institutions of control from the centre, yet not subservient to local interest groups in return for resources, they would further undermine remaining autonomous structures that provide order and security to communities. Perhaps the federal structure of Nigeria, both in formal and informal dimensions, has helped prevent this outcome. If it were a sovereign state, Anambra might resemble a collapsed state like Liberia or Sierra Leone, given its similarities of social organisation of violence and predation in local dimensions.

OPC may represent an 'indigenous solution' to disorder (especially if Nigeria were to collapse), though it would violate contemporary international norms in terms of its radical ethnic political vision, questioning of existing boundaries and violent methods. This manner of state-building follows many precedents in European history, but would alienate international backers today. Nevertheless, groups like OPC are likely sources of order in post-collapsed state conflicts. Like Sierra Leone's Kamajor ethnic militia, they reshape social solidarities and resources that were not included in the centre of collapsed state political economies, usually the results of historic accidents such as backing the wrong party at independence or ending up on the losing end of a past struggle to control state power. These different experiences also show the capacity of patronage-based political systems to destroy social autonomy and impose compromising collaboration upon people who may harbour quite sophisticated critiques and understandings of the mainsprings of local politics. It leaves radicalised social solidarities as the best refuge for people with different ideas about how to defend communities and pursue political change, at least in states where democratic political institutions have not restrained these internal strategies of elite authority (Bratton, Mattes and Gymah-Boadi, 2005: 130-59).

Other armed groups that emerge in collapsed states exhibit similar patterns of social relationships. In the cases discussed in this chapter, one again finds the crucial roles that relations of local elites to central patrons play in the behaviour of armed groups. The significance of outsiders, especially in realms of clandestine market control, also weighs heavily. These factors shape the interests of armed groups and tilt the 'fields of leverage' in various directions, sometimes favouring predatory individuals, and at other times favouring community defenders and political ideologues.

Broader Patterns of Collapsed State Violence

Armed groups in Sierra Leone's 1991-2002 war also reflected the nature of patronage politics amidst collapsing states as it shaped authority in local communities there. The majority – but not all – armed group violence was geared toward integration into existing patronage networks on better terms than seizing segments of them outright, along with their associated economic opportunities. Kandeh explains how politicians in Sierra Leone long had appropriated what he calls 'lumpen' violence; the protests and social deviance of unemployed and marginalised young men who found little or no opportunity in the economy that Sierra Leone's elite had monopolised. Once their centralised political network fragmented, 'armed marginals' pursued their own interests, especially among those in security forces in collusion with agents of the collapsed state much like Mbadinuju and Bakassi Boys in Nigeria (Kandeh 2004). A former minister of government at the time underlined the extent to which this violence was carried out in collaboration with state security forces: 'Government soldiers could use rebel tactics... or reach an accommodation with the RUF to exchange arms and uniforms for cash or diamonds' (Abraham, 2004: 107).

In Sierra Leone, however, 'armed marginals' pushed aside incumbent patrons, even more effectively than Mbadinuju's struggle to appropriate violence and negotiate better terms. But Sierra Leone's process of institutional state collapse also was more advanced than Nigeria's. Johnny Paul Koroma, a former army officer and head of the Armed Forces Ruling Council (AFRC), joined RUF rebels to seize the capital in May 1997. He repeated the pattern of politicians' appropriation of the country's main sources of wealth since at least the 1960s. By the late 1970s, the country's former president had destroyed most formal state institutions and ruled instead via an 'official' clandestine economy, subordinate to his personal discretion. Koroma and his associates seized these economic resources and established their own violent system of control. While the outbreak of war was a decisive event in the lives of people in Sierra Leone, the politics that the war brought were little different from what had prevailed in the decades before the war. What changed was the capacity of fragments of the old patronage system to appropriate resources directly and to integrate armed young men into their completing organisations.

A Sierra Leone journalist highlighted this continuity when he wrote of 'bush rebels' as 'young and old people (including children), all under the influence of hard drugs and always shabbily dressed.' He identified their links to 'town rebels' who 'work for the established government. They work in offices close to the seat of the President. They are present in all spheres of work... This class of rebels are responsible for the ugly state (and pleasant state) you are today... With just a signature they robbed your country of billions...' (Nasralla, 1999: 2). This continuity of patronage politics appeared in the statements of former RUF leader Foday Sankoh. He justified RUF violence as part of an effort to rectify wrongs in the method of distribution in the old patronage system, not as a revolutionary or reformist struggle: 'Why didn't they ask Jamil [a businessman] or Shaki [former president] that when the APC was in power? Yeah, we mine! We in RUF believe in wealth, arms and power in the hands of the people... We're not going to give up diamonds or our guns. And this is how we will get POWER now!' (Sankoh, 2000: 3) Diamonds were Sankoh's focus, even when he was included in a coalition government in 1999–2000. Not surprisingly, his behaviour generated considerable friction within the RUF as junior commanders strove to appropriate these resources for themselves (United Nations 2000a, paras. 72-81, 91-9).

The influence of patronage structures in the shaping of armed groups appears in other instances. For example, armed groups in Liberia's 1989-2003 war initially included commanders who articulated ideological programmes, much in the mould of Marxist and nationalist insurgencies in Africa in the 1960s and 1970s. An able commander associated with Charles Taylor, Elmer Johnson, articulated a popular critique of Liberia's dictatorship, which he used to mobilise a multi-ethnic group of followers in the early stages of the war. Local rumour held that Taylor found Johnson's popularity threatening to his leadership. Johnson was later shot under mysterious circumstances. Likewise, several Sierra Leone student radicals left for exile in Libya and trained with future commanders of the RUF. They produced articulate analyses of government corruption and identified the socially destructive effects of the politics of state collapse (Cumale, 1982), yet they were sidelined early in the conflict (Abdullah and Muana, 1998: 179).

In places where economic opportunities are fused to the exercise of political authority, ideologues find little time and resources to organise supporters. In a crowded field of combat with well-armed gangs, most tainted due to their previous associations with violent gangs and unpopular politicians with deep roots in clandestine economies or control over resources, these combatants possess a considerable short-term military advantage over their ideological cousins. Former Yugoslavia shows a similar dynamic: paramilitaries recruited from among economically marginalised youth. One leader, Zeljko Raznajatovic ('Arkan'), led the official fan club of Belgrade's soccer team after a career as a bank robber in Western Europe and assassin that Tito's regime used in the 1970s to target nationalist agitators. His paramilitary group found new patrons in Serb nationalist politicians, who were able to use their informal connections to violent groups in the old regime to fashion their new political strategies, adapted to the collapse of central authority. The Yugoslav army found that Arkan's and other groups' 'primary motive was not fighting against the enemy but robbery of private property and inhuman treatment of Croatian civilians' (United Nations 1994, para. 100). This was a classic case of predation, to be sure, but it also grew out of a distinctive political economy and operated in the service of a particular type of political authority.

However, like Nigeria, Sierra Leone's armed groups did not all behave in the same way. Community defence forces, known as Kamajors, appeared in the early 1990s in diamond mining towns close to the mining areas that RUF and army soldiers exploited. Kamajor groups were responsible for considerable human rights violations, but like OPC, they operated in a distinct community that they claimed to protect and were able to discipline members to limit predations. Once again, the presence or absence of lootable resources did not appear to be the primary factor governing armed group behaviour.

Discipline in these home guard forces was based on the adaptation of customary initiation rites that historically prepared young men to defend their communities. These practices survived in a context in which local political leaders had supported the 'wrong' party at independence. After their patrons were displaced in 1968, local chiefs and politicians lacked the trust of the new soon-to-be president for life. Thus they had to find new ways to protect their clandestine economic operations from his political network and to guarantee their own transactions. Chiefs also found that in the midst of political violence levelled against them in the 1970s, they could rally young men to protect their positions, provided they convinced the initiation rite authorities to support their cause (Lavalie, 1983).

Part of the cost of this support came in the demand among young men and local customary authorities that chiefs respect their duties as patrons (Dorjahn and Fyfe, 1962). In Sierra Leone, this meant acceptance of an elaborate set of customs governing landlord and tenant rights. In practice, that chiefs were obligated to protect outsiders and local people who they agreed could clandestinely mine diamonds on their land. In return, these people were supposed to become political muscle for chiefs and local politicians who supported them in their clandestine mining. Conflict took the form of political violence as armed gangs of politicians clashed. But the difference was found in the underlying social relations that shaped these uses of violence. Armed young men who fought to protect patrons in this instance could deny resources to those who became bad patrons, provided that existing social structures and respected intermediaries also reinforced this relationship. Therefore, once war became widespread in the 1990s, the self-interest of local strongmen intersected with the interests of local communities, at least to the extent that more predatory options were foreclosed.

Individual fighters harbour all sorts of grievances and interests that could become instrumental, depending upon the overall context of the conflict. They may hate the politics of their new patron. They may recognise that their predatory behaviour will not bring economic development and peace. Nonetheless, many will find that their pressing short-term need simply to survive means that it makes sense to join those with guns rather than to be a victim. In this event, indigenous efforts to create order out of collapsed states should always fail. Those who devote resources and time to cultivating political followings or who try to implement programmes in 'liberated zones' will find themselves at a permanent disadvantage to fighters who put all of their resources into attacking their rivals and seizing more wealth. Violent predators will destabilise what order exists, forcing their victims to seek protection from other violent entrepreneurs simply to survive.

But in spite of these short-term incentives and threats, not all join predatory gangs. Conflicts in the cases above include locally organised and armed home guard units and religious organisations that defend their own communities and provide what their communities regard as public goods. Such behaviour occurs in other places too. Taleban, its human rights violations and destruction of cultural monuments notwithstanding, exhibited a defined ideology and political programme. As noted above, its rulers in 2000 banned poppy cultivation despite the central role this crop played in foreign trade and in financing its acquisition of weapons. It also attracted supporters from religious schools inside Afghanistan and in neighbouring countries (United Nations, 2000b: paras. 71, 82). In this sense, Afghanistan's Taleban pursued interests greater than personal wealth or power, despite its diplomatic isolation, violent methods, poor international image, and exceptionally poor strategic choices. It built its politics on reshaping existing social solidarities that still regulated its access to resources. (This also became its weakness as US strategists succeeded in peeling these groups away from the Taleban coalition in the war that began in October 2001. The arrival of Taleban's 'Arab guests' and their money also demonstrated how outsiders both provided Taleban with short-term resources to advance their programmes at the expense of long-term reciprocities with social groups that turned out to hold the keys to the exercise of power in that country.)

This is not to excuse the behaviour of Taleban rulers, nor do global norms look kindly upon the sorts of political visions that OPC leaders occasionally articulate concerning an ethnically based Yoruba national homeland. Sierra Leone's Kamajor militia leaders currently stand charged of crimes against humanity before the UN-sanctioned Special Court for Sierra Leone (Special Court for Sierra Leone, 2004). But all point to important developments in the processes of armed conflicts in collapsing states. That is, in the absence of old Marxist and other reformist or revolutionary models, indigenous social solidarities and extreme ethnic chauvinism appears to many people to provide a model for reconstructing order and organising collective action amidst chaos. Ultimately, the key variable inhibiting the appearance of reformist and revolutionary groups is the nature of fragmentation of incumbent patronage networks in the context of prior institutional state collapse and the recruitment of violent groups among newly freelancing strongmen. This process destroys the social space that would otherwise harbour an alternative to their domination and poses a serious challenge for the international community that most often recognises occupants of State Houses as sovereign rulers, even if other groups actually govern these places much more effectively.

References

Abdullah, Ibrahim and Patrick Muana (1998) 'The Revolutionary United Front of Sierra Leone', in C. Clapham (ed.) *African Guerrillas*, London: James Currey, pp. 179-93.

Abdullahi Smith Centre for Historical Research (2003) *Election Violence in Nigeria: The Terrible Experience 1952-2002*, Kaduna: Abdullahi Smith Centre.

Abraham, Arthur (2004) 'State Complicity as a Factor in Perpetuating the Sierra Leone Civil War', in I. Abdullah (ed.) *Between Democracy and Terror: The Sierra Leone Civil War*, Dakar: CODESRIA, pp. 104-20.

Abugu, Uwakwe (2000) 'Armed Delta Youths to Face Robbery Charges', *Vanguard*, 3 July.

Adams, Gani (2003) 'The Rejection of Internal Colonialism', text in *Guardian*, 20 July.

Adeyeye, Joseph (2004) 'Tinubu's OPC Option against Laws of the Land-Police', *ThisDay*, 16 November.

Agbo, Anayochukwu (2001) 'Bakassi v MASSOB in Abia State', *Tell*, 26 Nov.

Agekameh, Dele (2000a) 'Blood Law of the Bakassi Boys', *Tell*, 28 Aug.

Agekameh, Dele (2000b) 'War of the Killer Gangs', *Tell*, 12 June.

Agekameh, Dele (2001) 'A Business Like Any Other', *Tell*, 6 Aug 2001.

Ajayi, Jacob (1965) 'Professional Warriors in Nineteenth Century Yoruba Politics', *Tarikh*, 1: 1, 72-81.

Ajulo, Steve (2000) 'Relief for Commuters as OPC Takes Over Traffic Control', *Guardian*, 11 Aug.

Akparanta, Ben (2000) 'We Assist Society – Bakassi Boys', *Guardian*, 22 July.

Albert, Isaac (2002) 'The Myth, Reality and Challenges of Nigeria's Reconciliation with *Ndigbo*', in E. Osaghae, E. Onwudiwe and R. Suberu (eds) *The Nigerian Civil War and Its Aftermath*, Ibadan: Programme on Ethnic and Federal Studies, pp. 309-25.

Alli, Yusuf (2000) 'Adesina Moves to Avert Fresh OPC, Traders Clash', *Punch*, 21 Aug.

Anayouchukwu, Arthur (2002) 'Wartime in Anambra', *Tell*, 4 Feb.

Anon. (2000) 'How OPC, Bakassi Boys Operate', *Saturday Punch*, 22 July.

Bazenguissa-Ganga, Rémy (1999) 'The Spread of Political Violence in Congo-Brazzaville', *African Affairs* 98(1): 37-54.

Bratton, Michael, Robert Mattes and Emmanuel Gymah-Boadi (2005) *Public Opinion, Democracy, and Market Reform in Africa*, New York: Cambridge University Press.

Collier, Paul (2000) 'Rebellion as a Quasi-Criminal Activity', *Journal of Conflict Resolution*, 44(6): 839-53.

Collier, Paul (2003) *Breaking the Conflict Trap: Civil Wars and Development Policy*, New York: Oxford University Press.

Cumale, Kwame (1982) 'The Oppressed Consciousness', *Awareness*, Freetown: Fourah Bay College, Feb.

Diouf, Mamadou (2003) 'Engaging Postcolonial Cultures: African Youth and Public Space', *African Studies Review*, 46(2): 1-12.

Dorjahn, Vernon and Christopher Fyfe (1962) 'Landlord and Strange: Change in Tenancy Relations in Sierra Leone', *Journal of African History*, 3(3): 391-7.

Ebosele, Moses (2000) 'Afenifere, Ohaneze for Security Body', *Guardian*, 26 July.

Eke, Emma (2000) 'Crisis is Part of Anambra State', *Guardian on Sunday*, 29 Oct.

Eriksson, Mikael and Peter Wallensteen (2004) 'Patterns of Major Armed Conflicts 1990-2003', in *SIPRI Yearbook 2004: Armaments, Disarmament and International Security*, New York: Oxford University Press, pp. 532-46.

Fasehun, Frederick (2003) 'The Failure of the Nigerian State and the Necessity for Identity Politics', in T. Babawale (ed.), *Urban Violence, Ethnic Militias and the Challenge of Democratic Consolidation in Nigeria*, Lagos: Malthouse Press Ltd, pp. 102-8.

Harnischfeger, Johannes (2003) 'The Bakassi Boys: Fighting Crime in Nigeria', *Journal of Modern African Studies*, 41:1 (March), 23-49.

Harunah, Hakeem (2003) *The Heritage of Our Pre-Colonial Culture of Peace*, Lagos: ERAF Foundation.

Hinderer, Anne (1872) *Seventeen Years in the Yoruba Country*, London: Seeley, Jackson and Halliday.

Hobsbawm, Eric (2000) *Bandits*. New York: New Press.

Human Rights Watch (2003) *The O'odua People's Congress: Fighting Violence with Violence*, New York: Human Rights Watch.

IMF (2002) *Liberia: Staff Report for the 2001 Article IV Consultation and Overdue Financial Obligations to the Fund*, Washington, DC: IMF African Department, 11 Feb.

Jega, Ataharu (1998) 'Youth Identity and Changing Roles in Urban Nigeria: Case Studies from Kano and Lagos', paper from Nordic Africa Institute, *Conference on Youth and Urban Popular Identities in Africa*.

Kandeh, Jimmy (2004) *Coups from Below: Armed Subalterns and State Power in West Africa*, New York: Palgrave.

Lavalie, Alpha (1983) 'SLPP: A Study of Political History of the Sierra Leone People's Party with Particular Reference to the Period, 1968-1978', MA Thesis. University of Sierra Leone.

Linz, Juan (2000) *Totalitarian and Authoritarian Regimes*, Boulder: Lynne Rienner Publishers.

Marshall, Monty F. and Ted Robert Gurr (2003) *Peace and Conflict 2003: A Global Survey of Armed Conflicts, Self-Determination Movements and Democracy*, College Park, MD: Center for International Development and Conflict Management.

Mojeed, Musikilu (2003a) 'In his Character', *Tell*, 24 Feb.

Mojeed, Musikilu (2003b) 'The Robbers in Uniform', *Tell*, 13 Jan.

Momoh, Albert (2002) 'Human Rights and the National Question on Nigeria', E. Osaghae & E. Onwudiwe (eds) *The Management of the National Question in Nigeria*, Ibadan: University of Ibadan, pp. 175-88.

Nasralla, A. [pseudonym] (1999) 'Types of Rebels', *For Di People*, 5 Feb.

Offor, Emeka (2001) 'Interview with Chief Offor', *The News*, 23 April.

Okebalama, Dozie (2000) 'Bakassi Boys and Anambra Politics', *Sunday Punch*, 17 Sept.

Oodu'a Youth Movement (1994) *Yoruba People's Charter of Self-Determination*, [pamphlet photocopy].

Oodu'a Youth Movement (2001) *The Yoruba Charter of Self-Determination*, [pamphlet].

Olabisi, Kolawole (2000) 'Teenager Kills Seven-Year-Old Boy for Ritual, Held by OPC', *Punch*, 27 Sept.

Olukunle, Akin (2000) '30 Killed in OPC, Police Clash', *Punch*, 17 July.

Oshunkeye, Shola (2003) 'The Reign of Guns', *Tell*, 24 March.

Oyediran, Oyeleye (1997) 'The Reorganization of Local Government'. L. Diamond, A. Kirk-Greene, O. Oyediran (eds) *Transition Without End: Nigerian Politics and Civil Society under Babangida*, Boulder,

CO.: Lynne Rienner Publishers, pp. 193-211.

Ozekhome, Mike (2003) 'Ethnic Militias and the Nigerian State: the challenges before civil society', in T. Babawale (ed.) *Urban Violence, Ethnic Militias and the Challenge of Democratic Consolidation in Nigeria*, Lagos: Malthouse Press Ltd, pp. 188-200.

Sankoh, Foday (2000) 'What Foday Sankoh Really Said in Makeni', *For Di People*, 1 February 2000.

Scott, James (1987) *Weapons of the Weak: Everyday Forms of Peasant Resistance*, New Haven: Yale University Press.

Special Court for Sierra Leone (2004) *The Prosecutor Against Samuel Hinga Norman, et al.* (Freetown: The Special Court for Sierra Leone.

Transparency International (2004) *Corruption Perceptions Index 2004*, www.transparency.org/cpi/cpi/2004.en.html#cpi2004, accessed 9 Jan 2005.

Ubani, Mike (2000) 'Bakassi Boys', *Tempo*, 3 Aug.

Ukeje, Charles (2001) 'Youths, Violence and the Collapse of Public Order in the Niger Delta of Nigeria', *Africa Development*, 26:1: 337-66.

Ukiwo, Ukowa (2002) 'Ethno-Religious Conflicts and the Crises of Democracy in Nigeria', paper presented at "An Assessment of Nigeria's Democratic Journey So Far', Centre for Advanced Social Science, Abuja, 18-21 February.

Umahi, Henry (2001) 'Interview with Henry Umahi', *Post Express*, 23 April.

United Nations (1994) *Final Report of the United Nations Commission of Experts Established Pursuant to Security Council Resolution 780 (1992), Annex III.A, Special Forces*, New York: United Nations.

United Nations (2000a) *Report of the Panel of Experts Appointed Pursuant to US Security Council Resolution 1306 (2000), Paragraph 19 in Relation to Sierra Leone*, New York: United Nations.

United Nations (2000b) *Report of the Secretary-General on the Situation in Afghanistan and Its' Implications for the International Suppression of Poppies*, New York: United Nations.

United Nations Drug Control Monitoring Programme (UNDCP) (2001) *Afghanistan Annual Opium Poppy Survey 2001*, Islamabad: UNDCP.

Wolf, Eric (1999) *Peasant Wars of the Twentieth Century*, Norman: University of Oklahoma Press.

World Bank (2004) *World Development Report 2005*, New York: Oxford University Press.

3

A Societal View on Violence and War
Conflict & Militia Formation in Eastern Congo[1]

KOEN VLASSENROOT

Beyond the Greed or Grievance Debate

The general inability of most observers to come to terms with the driving forces behind the conflict in eastern Congo finds expression in the numerous reports of present events in the DRC by foreign journalists and international aid organisations. For most outsiders, the dynamics behind this conflict are very hard to understand even without mentioning the difficulties in dealing with its origins. Although since early 1996 some human rights organisations had been reporting the growing abuses against the Tutsi populations in the eastern parts of the country, the first major military conflict in October 1996 took most Western observers by surprise. They only became aware of it when local Banyamulenge[2] and Rwandan forces were already in control of Uvira and were progressing towards Bukavu, yet they did not really comprehend what this crisis was about. An astonishingly simplistic explanation was the evident consequence. Two issues dominated their accounts. The war was seen as the next phase in the troubled and regional Hutu-Tutsi relationship and was linked to the position of the Banyarwanda and Banyamulenge communities in eastern Zaire.

When dealing with the AFDL rebellion, as was the case with the well-planned Rwandan genocide in 1994, 'it took time to detect the mix of skilful opportunism and local security concerns that caused an isolated rebellion' (Evans, 1997: 13). The final compromise was that a local reaction to ethnic purging in the eastern parts of Zaire ultimately led to the conjunction of local and foreign interests and the implementation of a rebel movement that removed the Mobutu regime from power with great ease. Thus, the end of Mobutism was not the result of state collapse but was caused by local and regional dynamics that fell completely outside the zone of control of the central government. Even though it can only be speculated whether the Zairian state would have survived much longer if the Rwandan regime had not started its campaign against the threat from the refugee camps and if it were not pushed to its knees by the AFDL coalition, a

[1] See also: Vlassenroot, Koen, 'The Making of a New Order? Dynamics of Conflict and Dialectics of War in South Kivu (DR Congo)', unpublished PhD dissertation, University of Ghent, June 2002.
[2] Ethnic Tutsi living in South Kivu.

closer look at the pre-war situation turns this question into a rhetorical one. The national army was in complete disintegration, the Kivu provinces were increasingly characterised by ethnic polarisation and conflict, and the democratisation process was in complete tatters, not even to mention the state of the health and education infrastructure or the escape strategies devised by the remains of Mobutu's regime.

Most observers would have come to a better understanding of the Kivu crisis if they had tried to unravel the recent history of the Zairian state. Strangely enough, it was a leading American political scientist who offered most observers the perfect excuse not to read the signals of impending state collapse and conflict. 'What is notable in these scenarios is the absence of clear turning points, warning signals, thresholds or pressure spots. The slippery slope, the descending spiral, and the downward trend are the mark of state collapse rather than deadlines and triggers,' William Zartman wrote (Zartman, 1995: 9).[3] It is sufficient to refer to Reno's, Reyntjens' or Lemarchand's alternative readings of the 1996 crisis to understand that their historical reconstructions clearly define the different turning points and the early warnings of an impeding collapse.

Most observers were even more troubled after the start of a new military campaign in August 1998 in eastern Congo, even if this conflict was also of no great surprise to careful observers. This time, no explanation could be offered by Zartman's theory of state collapse. Nevertheless, in 1998 it was much easier to identify when and where the conflict occurred than to explain its underlying logic. Once again, most observers limited their reasoning at the outset to regional dynamics and ethnic antagonisms. The newly created rebel movement was presented as a Banyamulenge-dominated force supported by the Rwandan army. This line of explanation, however, soon was replaced by the very popular 'greed' account,[4] which has come to dominate the present debate on internal conflicts.

On the surface, it seems that the present conflict in the eastern parts of the Democratic Republic of Congo is indeed all about gold, coltan, diamonds, petrol and timber rather than about security concerns, national power or political representation. For many reasons, the conflict in the Kivu has been presented in recent accounts as an illustration of the shift to a new type of conflict, in which national armies, liberation movements and political ideologies are replaced by warlords, informal economic networks, ethnic hatred and greed. The view of most observers is that the mineral trade is the driving force of the current conflict in the eastern Congo. When dealing with this war, most international attention is focused on the illegal extraction of natural resources by the different belligerents, particularly after a UN panel of experts in April and November 2001 came up with some remarkable research results. Based on the conclusions of this panel, most observers agree that the different actors direct their struggle mainly at the benefits to be gained from the vast Congolese mineral resources rather than at the achievement of long-term political aims.

[3] What can I say about his answer to the ultimate question of why states collapse? Because 'they can no longer perform the functions required for them to pass as states,' Zartman concludes (1995: 5). In other words, why do cars stop driving? Because, as Zartman would say, the engine no longer offers the energy needed for the car to drive.

[4] The least one can say about Collier and others' focus on war economies is that it highlights some thought-provoking issues. The thesis that 'it is the feasibility of predation which determines the risk of war' (Collier 2000: 3) forces observers to look at present conflicts from a new angle and to integrate the economic dimensions of civil war into their framework of analysis.

It is undoubtedly the case that the nature of conflict has changed, as is the fact that the present conflict in eastern Congo is a good illustration of many aspects of the new types of conflict. Yet the focus of discussion should be how to interpret these changes rather than to limit comprehension of these 'new wars' to ethnic hatreds, state collapse or to criminalised economic networks. Instead of focusing on wars as a breakdown of a particular system, one should try to understand how elites and societies are familiarising themselves with global changes and a context of war. What is easily interpreted as a return to African barbarism or greed-driven behaviour could also be understood as an outcome of political processes whereby large parts of the population are increasingly excluded and violence becomes institutionalised both as a strategy and as control and resistance.

The aim of this chapter is to present an alternative reading of the present conflict in the Kivu provinces and to make room for a sociological perspective on this civil war, because we believe that the purpose and reasons for conflict are located in those long term processes that define the conditions of everyday life (Duffield, 1998: 65-102). As Crummey noted, 'the real challenge is to see violence within its social setting, to appreciate its roots in social conflict, and to understand why and how people turn to it' (Crummey, 1996: 2). The strategy that looks into local society to understand conflict has some important advantages. First, it gives meaning to the global re-emergence of the concept of ethnicity. Embedded in popular political discourse, reference to ethnic belonging in most conflicts has encouraged a conflation between ethnicity, tribalism and the use of violence. Yet, as the conflict in the Kivus reveals, ethnicity should never be presented as the real cause of violence. Our research confirms what Martin says about the meaning of ethnic narratives in social and political processes:

> the identity narrative channels political emotions so that they can fuel efforts to modify a balance of power; it transforms the perceptions of the past and the present; it changes the organisation of human groups and creates new ones; it alters cultures by emphasising certain traits and skewing their meaning and logic. The identity narrative brings forth a new interpretation of the world in order to modify it (Martin, 1995: 13).

Second, a focus on the local society puts the analysis of militias into its social setting. As with ethnicity, local militias attempt to give meaning to the local and global social order and to modify the local social setting. As we will argue further in this chapter, in the case of the DRC one should not label these militias as just another new social or nationalistic movement, but analyse their nature in the concrete context. For marginalised youngsters, joining these militias offers them an alternative to exclusion and a way to benefit from modernisation. For those in charge of these militias, control over disorder produces the means to acquire access to economic resources and political objectives. In both cases, these strategies are to be seen as endeavours to become integrated into the global order. Third, a local perspective gives meaning to the widespread use of violence. In present day conflicts, violence is an opportunity rather than a problem; it covers functions ranging from military to psychological, while the objectives of violence are often very local and immediate rather than part of a liberation struggle.

In the following sections of this chapter, a general and multidimensional analysis of the conflict that has plagued the Kivu provinces since 1996 will be presented. First, the different origins and dynamics of the current conflict in eastern Congo will be identified. Second, the local dynamics of militia formation will be outlined, a development that Kaplan has explained as a revolt of 'loose molecules in a very unstable fluid, a fluid that was clearly on the verge of igniting' (Kaplan, 1994: 46). Thus in many accounts the rebellion of Mayi-Mayi fighters has been explained as a backlash or reprimitivisation of local society, even though on closer scrutiny one discerns the existence of a certain rationale behind these youngsters' acts of violence. To what extent the marginalised position of the younger generations offers a valid explanation for the development of these armed groupings is further explored.

Reading the Congolese Crisis:
The Local Dynamics of Exclusion

The Kivu region is located on the eastern side of the Congo and shares borders with Uganda, Rwanda and Burundi. As a highly populated and very fertile region, the highlands of Kivu reflect the realities of both the densely populated highlands of Rwanda in the east and the under-populated Congolese hinterland in the west. Originally, this region was one administrative unit but now consists of three provinces: Maniema, North Kivu and South Kivu. The two Kivus have always been a hotbed of conflict and turmoil. While the nature of the Congolese political system has undeniable impact, the local potential for social conflict rests on its geographical position and local history. Political events in both provinces have always been linked to the social and political dynamics of neighbouring Rwanda and Burundi, illustrated by the history of the Banyarwanda and Barundi migration to Congo. Long before the arrival of the colonists, there were important settlements of Kirundi and Kinyarwanda speakers living in what would later become the Belgian Congo. Between 1937 and 1955, the colonial authorities were responsible for the 'transplantation' of a large number of mainly Hutu-Rwandan as part of the 'Mission d'Immigration des Banyarwanda' (MIB). These new immigrants supplied the necessary labour for the large colonial coffee, tea or cotton estates and cattle ranches in the Kivu highlands, where they settled on land controlled by 'autochthonous' ethnic groups such as the Bahunde and Banyanga. Finally, as a result of the so-called Rwandan 'Social Revolution' of 1959 and its aftermath, a number of Rwandan Tutsi refugees settled in North and South Kivu. Clearly, the conflict in the Kivus was based mainly on issues of land access and citizenship.

When reading local explanations, however, another dimension prevails. Mamdani writes, 'Conventional wisdom in Goma and Bukavu has it that Kivu Province in eastern Congo is where losers in Rwanda traditionally end up, and it is from Kivu that they prepare to return to Rwanda' (Mamdani, 2001: 234). Indeed, when travelling through eastern Congo, the present war is often explained as a spill-over effect of the Rwandan ethnically explained conflict. As one local observer who Mamdani interviewed stated:

> These ethnic conflicts are cyclic, with each ethnic group (Tutsi versus Hutu) taking in turn power and misfortune. The fate of one today is the fate of the other tomorrow. The consequence of cyclical fortunes is that when they return, not everyone returns, some remain. Those who remain become Congolese' (Mamdani, 2001: 234).

This particular view leads many in eastern Congo to conclude that the Congolese would live in peace and harmony if they were just left to themselves. As inhabitants of the city of Goma explained after the eruption of the Nyiragongo volcano in January 2002: 'We are suffering now from two flows of lava. One is the lava stream of the volcano. The other is the armed presence of foreign troops on Congolese territory.'

It is quite evident that the current situation is strongly influenced by the political evolution in Burundi and Rwanda as are large parts of the local history. Closer scrutiny suggests the existence of a number of internal dynamics undermining stability in North and South Kivu. Shortly after its independence, Congo fell open to conflict for the first time. The immediate reaction to independence was an internal split between Congolese political forces and the development of several armed rebellions. Perhaps the most serious was the rebel movement led by Pierre Mulele. Although Mulele started his rebel career in Kwilu, his uprising soon spread to the eastern parts of the country, from where large parts of the country came under his control. The ease with which the uprising found fertile soil there can be explained by the fact that it offered several local communities the perfect pretext to raid other communities for cattle or to deny their owners access to land.

When analysing local history, it is easy to conclude that most conflicts in eastern Congo are centred around land disputes and cattle. In most cases, 'autochthonous' communities reject the land rights of 'exogenous' communities on the premise that, historically, the former are the sole owners of the land. Through a process of 'ethnic scapegoating', land rights of part of the population are rejected. In most cases local traditional authorities become actively involved in defending the customary land order, which secures their position of economic and political control. This was the case with the 'Guerre des Kinyarwanda' in 1963, which came down to a struggle for control over land access between the autochthonous populations that were holding the customary power, and the Banyarwanda community that was reacting against abuse by the traditional authorities.

At first sight, the different local conflicts that have erupted since the early nineties are but a continuation of history. The exclusionary campaign against the Banyarwanda in North Kivu as a result of the combination of continuous clashes over land use; the political tensions as a consequence of the promise of democratic elections; the conflict between Bafulero and Barundi in the Ruzizi Plain (South Kivu); the conflict between the Babembe and the Babuyu (South Kivu) and the tragic example of revived conflict between the Hema and the Lendu in Ituri, can all be explained as motivated mainly by land issues and opposing communities. An important factor contributing to the current crisis in Congo is the malfunctioning of the Congolese state.

However these conflicts cannot be analysed without considering the broader political environment. At the root of the political crisis in Congo is the crisis of the Congolese state that by its nature not only offered many opportunities to local strongmen but has been the key element in the historical dimensions of the social, political and economic alienation of large parts of society. Under Mobutu, political control was founded on the possibilities of extracting wealth through informal networks. Mobutu's political strategy had been straightforward from the start: divide the opposition, then gather up the 'tepid' and cash-strapped amongst opposing politicians and flood them with funds. As the politics of Zairianisation and the land law of 1973 have shown, Mobutu continuously converted economic assets into a stock of political resources for (re-)distribution to those who had shown political loyalty, while denying them the opportunity to become powerful enough to mount a leadership challenge. This required that they be regularly stripped of their privileges and 'recycled' as opposition politicians, possibly to be recalled. Even though individual members of the ruling class were never sure of their privileged position, this system created the necessary opportunities for the new ruling class as a whole. This strategy was not unique to Mobutu's practice of rule; it is a very old political ploy to offer stability to a ruling class and at the same time to deny stability to its individual members. Besides members of his own ethnic community, Mobutu sought support from those individuals (the Banyarwanda in the 1970s, then Kengo wa Dondo during the last years of his rule) who had no true popular basis and would never pose any serious political threat to his position. In doing so, he achieved hegemony and bureaucratic stability, as long as the required funds for distribution were available. The nature of the system made any serious opposition difficult because the exercise of political power through networks of patronage had an integrating effect. In the event that patronage failed and opposition appeared, Mobutu could always resort to techniques of terror and rely on coercive institutions such as the DSP (Division Spéciale Presidentielle). Thus, Mobutu's personalised system of power was based on two crucial elements: first, his capacity to create hegemony through the distribution of rewards to a ruling class via individual favouritism and second, his monopoly on violence, based on the loyalty of several bureaucratic institutions and factions in the army. As the father of the nation, he had the right to punish when needed.

For the rest of the population, the politics of patronage produced increasing political, social and economic marginalisation and exclusion, as they were denied political participation and their economic success was dependent mainly on their integration into the networks of patronage. As these were based on ethnic solidarity, the politics of patronage institutionalised ethnic communities as the organising principle of politics and economics, thereby creating structures of exclusion. Where this happened, in the eastern provinces, the Zairian regime failed to deal with two important local issues. First, it never seriously regulated the local political economy of land access. Second, political competition became inseparable from the nationality issue because the state never successfully determined the political and social position of the population with a Rwandan background (the Banyarwanda in North Kivu and the Banyamulenge in South Kivu). The source of conflict was ready made.

The first element of exclusion was related to the local political economy of land control. In the Kivu provinces, both internal (traditional use of space and the introduction of individual land property rights) and external elements (impact of colonisation) combined to produce a qualitatively different use of the available economic space and the mobility of labour within it. Traditionally, the economic use of space reflected social organisation and gave a material basis to ethnic belonging, a process that has been described more generally by John Lonsdale (1995) as 'moral ethnicity'. The reorganisation of that space by the arrival of new participants via politics and the market, however, eroded this customary social organisation. Agriculture was turned into a source of wealth accumulation and original customary powers were integrated into new networks of patronage after the introduction of the land law of 1973, seriously affecting local social cohesion. Lonsdale considers the overall effect of the market's entry to customary systems of economic and social organisation as depending on how far pre-capitalist hierarchies are friendly to the guest ('le visiteur du soir', as Bayart states [1981]) and in how far the capitalist caller turns into a loutish wrecker of the local moral economy (Lonsdale, 1995). In the case of the Kivu provinces, the impact was disastrous. The local politics of land access generated three effects: in the most populated regions, the shift in the economic use of space led to land dispossession and alienation and produced an agricultural labour surplus. In a reaction to growing marginalisation, most young men opted for temporary migration which had an impact on local mobility patterns. Finally, intensified competition for land led to a hardening of social and economic boundaries on an ethnic basis and disadvantaged the Banyarwanda and Banyamulenge communities. Considered to be non-indigenous citizens, they could not claim access to land under the customary laws.

The second element of exclusion was the nature of political identity. Since the Banyarwanda and Banyamulenge had no proper native authority, most of them were excluded from ethnic citizenship. This left them no option but to become subjects of the Congolese traditional authorities. For these two groups, it became clear that only national, civic citizenship could secure their economic and political rights. As neither the colonial administration nor the Zairian state was able to determine the legal status of the Banyarwanda communities living in eastern Congo, this part of the population was faced with permanent insecurity as to its political rights. During the 1970s, citizenship legislation permitted them to gain access to local economic resources, which provoked resentment from the local autochthonous elites. To limit the Banyarwanda's political influence and newly granted economic prosperity, a nationality law was passed in 1981 severely limiting their nationality rights. In the Kivus, this issue had the effect of hardening ethnic boundaries, yet at the same time gave direction to local political debate. Political exclusion turned out to be the key to the formation of conflicting identity. In the case of the Banyamulenge in South Kivu, their claims to political participation not only had the effect of hardening the boundaries between different identity groups but also facilitated the shift to massive violence as an enticing strategy of control and resistance.

Thresholds and Triggers to Conflict

The end of the eighties was a turning point in many ways. The politics of patronage had proved self-destructive. It ruined not only Zaire's formal economic fabric but also the very basis of the political elite. Patrimonial control over state resources conflicted with economic efficiency and the damage of this consumerism on the economy's productivity was enormous. The central problem that confronted Mobutu during his long hold on power, therefore, was how to continue to assert authority (and guarantee his hegemony) amidst declining resources. In addition, the breakdown of Cold War politics of containment ruptured international commitment to local clients and forced Mobutu to reposition himself.

At the end of the 1980s, growing economic decline and the weakening of state administration as a result of patronage, also led to an increase of the space that escaped state control. Contrary to the views of many observers, the development of this autonomous space was not only the result of a search for protection from state predation, or an expression of resistance by society against it, but also of the search for alternative means of wealth accumulation by members of the dominant class. This informal economy comprised two activities: a popular economy of survival and methods controlled by members of the local ruling class. Both sorts of activities escaped all legal control. Through their privileged access to the dominant class, local businessmen in the Kivus were able to develop unofficial trade patterns based on ethnic and personal ties and on the creation of a bridge between the two sorts of informal economic activities.

The end of external financial support and a deepening economic crisis in the late 1980s forced Mobutu to develop innovative strategies of survival. One of the ways in which he was able to continue to assert his authority was through control over markets rather than bureaucracies. Since the formal markets were in total collapse or had disappeared, Mobutu needed to search for alternative resources. He found these through an intensified participation in the informalised trade activities of high-value goods. Nevertheless, the destruction of the economic fabric had already created conditions for the development of decentralised networks of patronage, which became hard to control from the political centre. More successful was Mobutu's strategy of weakening the position of his political opponents. The best way to provoke intensified political competition between them was to introduce a process of democratisation. While this democratisation process brought renewed and multiple claims on the state, Mobutu prevented the formation of a strong opposition force by encouraging exit-strategies based on ethnic criteria, through the notion of 'géo-politique'. In reaction, local political leaders pushed forward the proposed expulsion of a particular group by mobilising others not belonging to that group. The effect of democratisation was to create new social and political boundaries on processes of inclusion, while campaigns of exclusion were the best strategies for local leaders to bind the grassroots population to their cause. A last element of Mobutu's survival strategy was to give the army freedom to act as a private militia.

Disorder in the Zairian context had nothing to do with anarchy but with deliberate strategies designed to preoccupy, destroy or disorganise rivals. Ethnicity proved to be the main guiding principle while the local youth militias were the best instruments. In Shaba, pushing the Baluba out towards their native Kasai by whatever means was a strategy to weaken the opposition and to undercut the power base of Mobutu's arch-rival Tshisekedi in this rich and strategic province. In North Kivu, Mobutu also actively encouraged the resurgence of ethnic resentment, which led to a violent campaign of exclusion against the Banyarwanda communities. The appearance of youth militias acting in defence of local strongmen only demonstrated how a situation of impunity created conditions for a skilful manipulation of disorder. The appearance of local militias from the beginning of the 1990s onwards, however, proved that the use of violence was not only to become part of a strategy of economic and political control but that it also advantaged local youth in their search for new forms of integration.

In the Kivu provinces, such dynamics initially led to an intensified competition between local political elites. Mobutu's divide-and-rule policy based on ethnic criteria was effective in preventing the local civil society from becoming a strong political force. Although it pretended to be a platform for dialogue and a guiding movement within the democratisation process, it never became a societal movement opposing central power, because networks of resistance and networks of dominance remained closely connected to each other and never transcended local ethnic tensions. In the Kivus, Mobutu's strategy produced four additional effects. First, the prospects of elections convinced Banyarwanda and Banyamulenge communities to organise in defence of citizenship rights, which only intensified the campaigns for their exclusion by local politicians. Second, local ethnically embedded associations shifted from protective organisations against the predatory state to forms of primordial solidarity and created the spaces in which local politicians, entrepreneurs and the urban population from the same ethnic background were reconnected. Third, the prospect of democratic elections introduced violence based on ethnic identity as a legitimate instrument to bring about change. Finally, the formation of the first local rural militias upgraded the status of young men who were marginalised in customary networks of dependency.

At this stage of the political crisis, Rwandan refugees entered the scene. Aside from a dollarisation of the local economy, the Rwandan refugee crisis had the effect of reinforcing the view that violence based on ethnicity and carried out by groups of mobile youth had become the dominant means of creating structural change. It is very likely that the refugee crisis would not have resulted in wide-scale violence if the Zairian regime had not been in near collapse and had not tried to rehabilitate itself through exploiting the tragedy. Given the situation in the Zairian state, the influx of more than one million refugees that were armed and resourced from the outside affected the local population in many ways and created the logic for future conflict, putting the Rwandan Hutu-Tutsi antagonism at the heart of local struggle. Local antagonism between autochthonous and Banyarwanda communities in North Kivu was altered by a new coalition of local Hutu-Banyarwanda, the refugee-leadership and militias. The new concept of 'Hutu-land' led to the tracking down of the local Tutsi population:

> The massive arrival of anti-Tutsi refugees, combined with the local anti-Tutsi sentiment fermented by local authorities and the Zairean government, largely contributed to the escalation of the conflict. The ex-FAR and the Interahamwe established de facto mini-republics over more than one million Hutu refugees and the local people with the full understanding of the Zairian government and the Forces Armées Zairoises (Gnamo, 1999: 327).

Local and Rwandan Hutu militias dreamed of a victorious campaign against the Tutsi population. From the refugee camps, extremist elements started undertaking small-scale incursions into Rwanda, without being prevented by the host regime. The position of the Mobutu regime towards the former Rwandan army and the Interahamwe militias provoked the formation of a regional coalition aimed at making Zaire safe for its eastern neighbours.

Both local and regional actors were forced to develop alternative strategies for their own survival, which explains the dynamics behind the formation of the 'Alliance des Forces Démocratiques pour la Libération du Congo/Zaïre' (AFDL). This alliance of local and regional forces easily defeated the remnants of the Mobutu regime. Yet, the key element for its military success became one of the most significant obstacles for the consolidation of its internal political power. While the regional allies were expecting some remuneration for their war efforts, the AFDL leadership felt a growing need to distance itself from them if it was to build its own domestic political power base. The dilemma of the new Congolese authorities turned out to be the 'raison d'être' of a second rebel movement, the 'Rassemblement Congolais pour la Démocratie' (RCD). Once again, the Kivu provinces were the territorial base for the military campaign against Kinshasa. The conflict produced a formidable coalition of regional and local forces. Yet, what was expected to be a simple imitation of the 1996 rebellion soon proved to be the beginning of a long-lasting conflict still without resolution. On the contrary, the second war has set in motion new strategies of political and economic control based on violence and leading to a reorganisation of the existing social and economic space. The DRC war could be explained as the next phase in a much larger and more deeply rooted conflict consisting of at least three different, yet closely related sets of dynamics. The most analysed of these is the regional dimension or the Great Lakes conflict, strongly linked to a larger regional struggle (involving at least six countries) for zones of political influence and economic control. The second level of conflict is the armed struggle among the Congolese themselves for the control of national political power. Finally, in both North and South Kivu, there is a historic but continuing conflict between different communities unrelated to, but highly influenced by events in neighbouring countries. All three levels have exhibited a certain logic of their own but have simultaneously influenced one another. In eastern Congo, however, the situation has become very particular since local, national and regional dynamics are closely intertwined. When analysing the current situation in the Kivus, the ten-year-old political crisis has resulted in a situation characterised by profound social disintegration, a shift from patrimonial to military control over resources, the growing importance of armed militia as an escape from further alienation (with violence becoming the main mode of discourse) and a total 're-tribalisation' of politics and society. These are the consequences of the search for strategies of control and resistance, where ethnic identity offers the perfect instrument.

Warlord Politics and Militia Formation

From this short overview, it can be concluded that the Congolese war should not be understood as an irrational, abnormal event or as a breakdown in a particular system, but as a complex of dynamics expressing the inner logic of the existing local social and political order. The war in eastern Congo represents the emergence of new, alternative systems of profit and power, introduced by those in power but replicated by numerous independent actors. In other words, the conflict in eastern Congo is not the final stage of the imported Rwandan political struggle but the end result of a weakening Zairian state and the latter's strategy to instrumentalise disorder. In the Kivu provinces today, violence is used as a means to reorganise the local social and economic space and to control mobility within and between spaces. Violence offers opportunities as strategies of survival for state actors and as strategies of resistance for a new class of local or regional strongmen. After two military campaigns and Mobutu's subsequent removal from office, three main consequences can be distinguished. First, ethnicity continues to be the main instrument to organise disorder: no other theme or issue has remotely similar mobilising power. Second, in the absence of any political space to express contention, the discourse of violence remains the sole legitimate expression of desire to bring about structural change. Third, the control of limited resources that allow the extraction of rent in terms of a reward for their mere possession remains central, even though these war economies should be understood as by-products of the local crisis. War economies help to explain how war is fought but not why. Rather than merely disrupting or destroying local social and economic fabric, this war creates new opportunities for some individuals even as it takes them away from many others.

One of the most notable aspects of the current conflict is the proliferation of localised (indigenous) rural militias. Marginalised socially and economically, scores of young people are increasingly attracted to the mobilising aims of new local figures. To reduce the explanation of the current crisis to an ethnic issue is generally sufficient to convince youngsters to join or form a militia, which is then presented – under franchise – as a local branch of the Mayi-Mayi movement. For young men banned from all political participation, such affiliation produces a semblance of social integration and a new social identity.

The term Mayi-Mayi covers a variety of groups including well-defined and structured groups with a clear political agenda and looser gangs of 'social bandits', using the title as a cover for predation upon the local rural population. Three different but related dynamics are apparent in the formation of these militias, accounting for much of the variation. The first relates to historical context, the second and third to the social and political. Most of the militias have a particular ethnic background and are struggling to improve the position of their own community. At the same time, the formation of various militias is in reaction to the effects of the existing patrimonial public order. Composed mainly of socially excluded youngsters, including educational dropouts (often because schools closed as a result of the wider conflict), the militias present an opportunity to escape further alienation. They constitute bottom-up violence against social and economic marginalisation. Because the formation of these militias is part of a social process that – in rejecting the current institutional order – is creating a rationality of its own, it is a very flexible phenomenon with shifting goals and objectives.

Their origins lie in hostilities at the end of the 1980s (de Villers and Willame, 1998) and these first generation militias were a result of a growing willingness of marginalised youngsters and school dropouts to form groups of under-aged combatants acting against every representative of modern political authority, and against their desperate feelings of exclusion. Most of these youngsters felt betrayed by their own governments, abandoned by international organisations and forgotten by the world. As they had nothing more to lose than their marginalisation, rebellion became an option both as a survival strategy and in self-defence against a predatory political and social order. The speed with which they changed ideologies and allies further proves what they wanted – alternatives to a situation of acute deprivation. Their proliferation in the most marginalised segments of Congolese society is additional evidence of this guiding logic.

At the end of the 1980s, local youth in Congo-Manday and Kasindi (North Kivu) formed rural and cross-border gangs known as the Kasindiens. They targeted the existing institutional political order, including the power of the traditional chiefs, who were considered to be 'prostitutes' of Mobutu. The phenomenon of militia-formation spread from the Kasindiens to other regions of eastern Congo. They soon started to cooperate with other militias: the Ngilima, based in Lubero and Beni (North Kivu) drawing its members mainly from the Nande (as the Kasindiens did), the Katuku, operating in the southern parts of Walikale (North Kivu), and the Batiri, operating in Masisi (North Kivu).

These militias only turned into important players in the local power-game after they had been mobilised by autochthonous traditional authorities and politicians, who were in competition with allotocthonous Banyarwanda communities. After 1990, a coalition of Nande and Hunde politicians who feared that they would lose political power if the Banyarwanda were registered as Zairian nationals and participated in elections, started a campaign to exclude the Banyarwanda from political life. In reaction, the local Banyarwanda association, Magrivi (Mutuelle des Agriculteurs de Virunga) in the Rutshuru region, encouraged its members to refuse to pay tribute to the autochthonous chiefs, or to recognise their authority. Tension mounted when poor Hutu farmers from Masisi who had lost their land because local chiefs sold it to rural capitalists of Banyarwanda origin, settled in Walikale, where they hoped to get access to land controlled by Nyanga chiefs. Fearing the growing influence of these newly arrived Hutu-Banyarwanda, both the local population and their chiefs protested against their presence and supported the formation of local militias. The Rwandan presidency fomented local tensions in order to cut support lines linking the local Tutsi population with the Rwandan Patriotic Front. Finally, the indigenous customary authorities in Masisi saw their position threatened by Banyarwanda communities and in a context of intense political animosity, decided they had no choice but to campaign against the 'foreigners'. The best way was to mobilise local youngsters who had already shown their readiness to take up bush knives for the defence of the community.

The first wave of inter-ethnic violence erupted in March 1993, when militia members killed several people at a local market in Ntoto. Although these attacks did not spread further into Walikale, Hunde militias started attacking Banyarwanda in Masisi district, receiving some support from Nande militias from Ruwenzori and local FAZ (Forces Armées Zairoises) elements. At the time, 'Mayi-Mayi/Bangilima' came into currency as a vague term to describe any local armed youth group, suggesting, somewhat prematurely the unification of all these local groupings. Since this first outbreak of massive violence in North Kivu, however, semantics and reality have grown closer together, as local militias began to play a crucial role in the elaboration of informal militarised social networks. Fighting became the safest way to escape marginalisation, because it offered militia members easy access to a livelihood.

The fragile settlement between the different communities in North Kivu, eventually forged at the end of 1993, lasted until the arrival of more than one million Hutu refugees from Rwanda and the settling of the ex-FAR (Forces Armées Rwandaises) and Interahamwe in different camps in Masisi and the Ruzizi Plain. The presence of the refugees had major effects on the local security situation, while creating new opportunities for local grassroots militias. The position of the Mayi-Mayi during this refugee crisis was confused since their ideology proved to be very flexible, directed at short-term and parochial goals. Two different dynamics interacted. Interahamwe violence was directed against local Tutsi populations or others unwilling to offer support. For many young men, membership in a rural militia was the only protection against harassment. On the other hand, a generation split – apparent in a widening gap between 'haves' and 'have-nots' – pushed an increasing number of marginalised and jobless young men towards the armed groups.

The start of the AFDL rebellion in October 1996 was the next turning point in the history of the Mayi-Mayi. In communities previously untouched by militia formation, rural armed groups started to mushroom. Particularly in South Kivu, newly formed militias became important components of the local political and military balance of power. In September 1996, after the first infiltration of Banyamulenge soldiers, a group of youngsters fleeing to Bukavu from the Ruzizi Plain was armed by FAZ factions and integrated into the defence forces as 'volunteers'. Others moved southwards to Fizi and Baraka, where they joined a local militia mainly drawing its members from the Bembe community. Here, retreating FAZ factions were ordered to hand over their arms, which permitted the Bembe militias to protect themselves against AFDL troops and to settle some of their old grievances with the Banyamulenge. After some Banyamulenge leaders were appointed to key positions within the new AFDL administration, more Bembe youngsters rallied to the Mayi-Mayi. Even more important were local developments in and around Bunyakiri, populated by the Batembo community. Local militias (known as Katuku) had been present in this region since the Masisi conflict of 1993. Only after the AFDL had taken Bukavu did these groups become significant players in the local power game. Initially, they formed a new alliance with Interahamwe and ex-FAR elements against the AFDL, understood to be a Tutsi-led movement. After a few meetings with Laurent Kabila, some Mayi-Mayi fighters joined AFDL forces. Others were kept in the forest to protect local populations.

From December 1996, some AFDL leaders intensified attempts to integrate local militia fighters into their forces, to continue their advance towards Kisangani. After Batembo leaders became convinced that the AFDL was a Congolese resistance movement aimed at liberating the country, an agreement was signed covering military cooperation. The AFDL was offered free passage to Kisangani (under the condition that only non-Tutsi fighters would pass through Bunyakiri) and several thousand Mayi-Mayi fighters joined the ranks of the AFDL. Yet not all Mayi-Mayi fighters reinforced the AFDL. Batembo leaders found it prudent to keep a large number behind for the protection of their own community. Local Interahamwe elements viewed this rapprochement as an act of betrayal of their Mayi-Mayi allies and retreated into the forest. Those who had stayed behind moved their headquarters to Kambale, where they came under the command of a certain Padiri. He disputed the recruitment of thousands of Mayi-Mayi fighters by the AFDL forces and invited the local traditional authorities and other local leaders to a meeting where he argued that the agreement with the AFDL would only bring more trouble. From his headquarters, Padiri started to reorganise the remaining parts of the Mayi-Mayi to continue his battle against the Kabila-led coalition.

After the start of the RCD (Rassemblement Congolais pour la Démocratie) rebellion, the local political and military landscape once again underwent a transformation. The changing political environment had a strong impact on the Mayi-Mayi militias, because the new context of war and state implosion linked grassroots realities directly to regional political dynamics, via informal militarised networks. The nature of this conflict gave the Mayi-Mayi movement fresh legitimacy in its struggle against Rwandan dominance. In this light, the promotion of some Mayi-Mayi commanders by Kabila has to be explained as a tactical ploy in pursuit of internal legitimacy, via an ultra-nationalist discourse. On the other hand, the state of disorder created the necessary conditions for the formation of new militias and, more importantly, for the spread of informal militarised social and economic networks. But as distinct from the recent history of militia formation in the Kivus, the proliferation of militias post-August 1998 was mainly limited to South Kivu. With the exception of a number of smaller Mayi-Mayi groupings between Beni and Butembo and in Walikale, the most important militias were subsequently to be found in South Kivu.

As the local balance of power and existing alliances drastically changed, Mayi-Mayi leaderships were forced to assume new political and military positions. Due to the efforts of a former FAC (Forces Armées Congolaises) general, Lwecha, who had become one of Kabila's closest allies, some Mayi-Mayi leaders were ready to reassess their relationship with Kinshasa. In return, the Kabila government supplied them with arms, ammunition and instructors, then awarded some of the militia leaders top positions within the FAC. From September 1998, Lwecha also tried to coordinate his efforts with the Padiri-led Mayi-Mayi groups along the road between Kisangani and Bukavu, the 'Forces d'Autodéfense Populaire' (FAP) in Fizi-Baraka, and with Burundian and Rwandan Hutu militias. In so doing, Kinshasa tried to regain some legitimacy in the east and, at the same time, extend its military capacities. Although most Mayi-Mayi representatives stressed that this material support was hardly sufficient to continue their activities, it was proof for most observers that the different militias in the east were an integral part of the official Congolese army. At least, material support from Kinshasa allowed Mayi-Mayi militias to intensify military activities and to switch tactics from hit-and-run methods to the longer-term occupation of large tracts of land. Their resistance against what was locally perceived as a 'foreign occupation' resulted in growing popular support and gave them new symbolic backing.

However, the RCD rebellion produced an additional effect. A context of growing impunity and a crisis of authority gave a new significance to the formation of local militias. Originally, formation could be considered bottom-up violence in response to social and economic marginalisation. Most militias adopted the appearance of rural-based movements for civil defence. Since August 1998, the distinction between some Mayi-Mayi chiefs and local warlords has become less clear. In the context of state implosion and conflict, the Mayi-Mayi have taken on a new role, due to attempts by a new class of local strongman to unify different ethnically embedded armed groups in defence of vested interests. Militarised informal networks have enabled the continuation of profit-seeking activities through violence. Local economic interests have become linked to a much larger political context leading to further militarisation of local society. Violence has become an opportunity in itself, while the control of disorder is the main strategy for the pursuit of local and short-term interests. Neo-liberal 'greed, not grievance' is not the cause of the violence but seems to be its ultimate outcome.

Violence and the Social Setting

From this short historical narrative of the Mayi-Mayi militias, a number of arguments help to explain their proliferation and the attraction of the rebel as social model. A first argument is about the attractiveness of the Mayi-Mayi. For many members, the militias are an alternative to desolation. Violence in most militia groups has to be seen as a reaction to the effects of a long process of social deterioration and political destruction. As Jourdan has pointed out, 'young combatants use violence to their own profit, in order to renegotiate and improve their social status. In this sense, violent practices have a political value because they manifest a will to undermine the social order, promoting at the same time new forms of organisation' (Jourdan, 2004: 162). It is important to note the strong reference to ethnic belonging, which is part of a deliberate strategy to strengthen the internal cohesion and mobilising power of the armed groups. As a consequence, the activities of the Mayi-Mayi have the effect of strengthening social boundaries. Second, in the chaotic and disorderly context of eastern Congo, the choice of enrolment has not only further divided local society, but has also produced greater violence and disorder.

A further argument is that these militias have created new, basic values and beliefs and provided members with renewed identities, in their position as Mayi-Mayi fighters. These elements served two important functions: to protect the fighters in battle and to increase the internal cohesion of the militia grouping. After being initiated, fighters live in a separate environment, characterised by a different order and authority structure from the society in which they originate. Even when the rural population supports the activities of the militias, its members become alienated from their own families. This is how their recourse to magic and the introduction of new codes of social conduct should be understood. These are sources of reassurance for the militia fighters, while producing internal cohesion within the armed band. In the end, the rituals symbolise that the militia fighter's social environment no longer corresponds to his former social background, that his enrolment into the militia provides him with a new social identity and that he is able to cope with the effects of the use of violence. The impact of these new social identities should not be underestimated. For most young Kivutiens, the identity of young combatant has become a strong model in youth imagination. In their search for access to modernity, young people have developed a number of strategies, ranging from gold mining to armed predation. In essence, these strategies all express the desire to reverse the existing social structures and to:

> impose their own rules and, at the same time, to be able to accede to modernity that is shown off through the metaphors of their body ... The daily experience of young combatants is embodied: tattoos made by Mayi-Mayi, amulets around ankles and wrists, extravagant uniforms, hats from cowboy style to bandana, sun glasses and body postures that recall Hollywood action movies. A list that could be very long and that cannot leave out the Kalashnikov – the rebels 'gun par excellence' which, because of its continual presence and ostentation, seems almost to represent a prosthesis of the combatants' bodies (Jourdan, 2004: 163).

Finally, it may be argued that these new social identities (which have become a strong model in local youth imaginary) and the use of violence, have had a great impact on the wider social environment. In eastern Congo today, violence has a clear function. While it gives access to modernity and its symbols, it should be recognised that violence in Kivu has become the only means to attain economic and social success. Given the harsh living conditions of a farmer or a miner, being a combatant is the only model of modernity that is accessible. Violence has become the only tool to give meaning to the social environment.

However, the use of violence has created a reality that can no longer be understood, one that violence has turned into 'non-sense'. The real danger is that in the absence of a social contract, such violent behaviour may become the unconditional rule of individual behaviour. This is summarised in the comment of Ryszard Kapuscinski that in a situation of enduring poverty and exploitation, everyone ultimately becomes an opportunist (Kapucinski, 1997). In the context of general despair, opportunism nonetheless forms an easy excuse for generalised violence. Individuals who in normal circumstances would not be attracted to violent behaviour are suddenly seen to be colluding with armed agents, thieves or social bandits who are themselves engaged in predatory activities. In addition, the 'streetlords' and other incontrollable recruits have set up their own private protection mechanisms between themselves and the suffering population as a result of rebel factionalism. This 'trafic d'influence', or passive corruption is generally accepted to have replaced the social pact that existed between the Mobutist state and its citizens. Today, people do not address their personal problems to weakened administrations but go to their local 'streetlord' who – for a small reward – will take care of the person that is causing trouble. The sad result of this process is a criminalised society in which everyone might become one's enemy. The factional behaviour of rebels and bandits is affecting entire communities, all pitched against each other in a fierce battle over exhausted resources.

Conclusion

Contrary to most observers, I have tried to understand the Mayi-Mayi militias as an autonomous dynamic instead of a local reaction against the presence of foreign troops. Categorising these militias in terms of their own self-description would be as misleading as condemning the militia fighters as social deviants, encouraged by their Rwandan or Tutsi enemies. Rather than defining the Mayi-Mayi fighters as a resistance movement driven by nationalistic ideals, I have tried to present their rebellion as a reaction to marginalisation, exclusion and as an alternative to despair. Even though many youngsters have felt attracted to the anti-Rwandan discourse of their leaders, this hostility was not a cause of their existence but facilitated the proliferation of militias by offering a new, attractive ideological underpinning.

The question remains what will be the next step in the history of the Mayi-Mayi. Their existence and behaviour has produced a considerable impact on the social context. The Congolese conflict and the proliferation of armed militias has realised a shift in authority to the advantage of those in charge of armed groupings and has provoked a fierce competition between a new generation of militia leaders and local traditional authorities. This is not a new phenomenon. The guiding aims of some militia members back in the 1960s were to replace the traditional chiefs and become the new leaders of their own ethnic community. Today some Mayi-Mayi leaders have been more successful in those aims and have replaced the traditional authorities to become the true leaders of the regions they control. In addition, the militias have provided fighters with a renewed identity, defined by their position as Mayi-Mayi and have alienated them from their original social environments. Initiation rituals have transformed these fighters into guardians of their community, but at the same time have clearly cut the existing links with their former social environment. Even where the rural population has supported the activities of the militias, its members have become alienated from their own families. Yet, these militia fighters are role models for the younger generations. While marginalisation and exclusion are the main causes for the existence of and enrolment into militias, the bitter result is that militias have helped to reinforce the view that violence is a legitimate strategy of defence or for creating change, as well as a strategy for identity making and of improving an individual's social position. Thus, militia fighters have further alienated themselves from existing local societies. Demobilisation and reintegration may well be arduous enterprises, as their success depends on the ability to break down the mechanisms that reproduce violence and that have become part of everyday life.

References

Bayart, Jean-François (1981) 'La Politique par le bas en Afrique-noire', *Politique Africaine* no. 1: 53-83.

Collier, Paul (2000) *Economic Causes of Civil Conflict and their Implications for Policy. World Policy Research Paper*, Washington: World Bank.

Crummey, Donald (1996) 'Introduction', in D. Crummey (ed.) *Banditry, Rebellion and Social Protest in Africa*, London: James Currey and Portsmouth: Heinemann.

Duffield, Mark (1998) 'Post-Modern Conflict: Warlords, Post-Adjustment States and Private Protection', *Civil Wars*, vol. 1, no. 1, Spring 1998: 65-102.

Evans, Glynne (1997) 'Responding to Crises in the African Great Lakes', *Adelphi Papers*, No. 311, Oxford: Oxford University Press.

Gnamo, Abbas H. (1999) 'The Rwandan Genocide and the Collapse of Mobutu's Kleptocracy', in Howard Adelman and Astri Suhrke (eds) *The Path of Genocide. The Rwanda Crisis from Uganda to Zaire*. Uppsala: Nordiska Afrikainstitutet, pp. 321-50.

Jourdan, Luca (2004) 'Being at War, Being Young: Violence and Youth in North Kivu', in K. Vlassenroot. and T. Raeymaekers (eds) *Conflict and Social Transformation in Eastern DR Congo*, Ghent: Academia Press, pp. 157-76.

Kaplan, Robert (1994) 'The Coming Anarchy. How Scarcity, Crime, Overpopulation, Tribalism, and Disease are Rapidly Destroying the Social Fabric of our Planet', *The Atlantic Monthly*, February 1994, pp. 44-76.

Kapucinski, Ryszard (1997) *Lapidaria*, Warsaw: Czytelnik.

Lonsdale, John (1995) 'Moral Ethnicity, Ethnic Nationalism and Political Tribalism: the Case of the Kikuyu', in *Staat und Gesellschaft in Afrika, Jahrestagung Vereinigung von Afrikanisten in Deutschland*, 28-30 April 1995, pp. 93-106.

Mamdani, Mahmood (2001) *When Victims Become Killers. Colonialism, Nativism, and the Genocide in Rwanda*, Princeton: Princeton University Press and Oxford: James Currey.

Martin, Dennis-Constant (1995) 'The Choices of Identity', *Social Identities*, Vol. 1, no. 1: 5-20.

de Villers, Gauthier and Jean-Claude Willame (1998), 'Republique Démocratique d'un entre-deux-guerres', *Cahiers Africains*, CEDAF, No. 35-36.

Vlassenroot, Koen (2002) 'The Making of a New Order? Dynamics of Conflict and dialectics in South Kivu (DR Congo)'. Unpublished PhD Thesis, University of Ghent, June 2002.

Zartman, William (ed.) (1995) *Collapsed States: The Disintegration and Restoration of Legitimate Authority*. Boulder, CO.: Lynne Rienner.

4

Debating
the Rwandan Genocide

NIGEL ELTRINGHAM

*Convention on the Prevention and Punishment of the Crime of Genocide
(UNCG), Adopted by Resolution 260 (III) A of the U.N. General Assembly
on 9 December 1948. Entry into force: 12 January 1951.*

Article II

In the present Convention, genocide means any of the following acts committed
with intent to destroy, in whole or in part, a national, ethnical, racial or religious
group, as such:

(a) Killing members of the group;
(b) Causing serious bodily or mental harm to members of the group;
(c) Deliberately inflicting on the group conditions of life calculated to bring about
     its physical destruction in whole or in part;
(d) Imposing measures intended to prevent births within the group;
(e) Forcibly transferring children of the group to another group.

Article III

The following acts shall be punishable:

(a) Genocide;
(b) Conspiracy to commit genocide;
(c) Direct and public incitement to commit genocide;
(d) Attempt to commit genocide;
(e) Complicity in genocide.

Article IV

Persons committing genocide or any of the other acts enumerated in article III
shall be punished, whether they are constitutionally responsible rulers, public
officials or private individuals.

Introduction

From 6 April to mid-July 1994, between 507,000 (HRW and FIDH, 1999:15) and 937,000 (IRIN, 2004) ethnic Tutsi were murdered in massacres committed by militias (principally the *interahamwe*) and elements of the army, often with the participation of the local population.[1] Not until 29 April 1994 did the UN Secretary-General, Boutrus Boutrus Ghali, acknowledge that the civil war was distinct from the massacre of civilians. Despite this, in its resolution of 8 June, the UN Security Council (henceforth UNSC) spoke only of 'acts of genocide' rather than 'genocide'. Only on 28 June, did the UN Commission on Human Rights' Special Rapporteur on Rwanda, René Degni-Ségui, present his first report in which Article II of the UNGC was quoted verbatim. Degni-Ségui concluded 'The conditions laid down by the 1948 Convention are thus met' (UN, 1994a: para 48). Subsequently, both the mandate of the International Criminal Tribunal for Rwanda (ICTR)[2] and Rwanda's domestic law regarding genocide[3] define the crime according to the UNGC.

From its inception, the UNGC has been the subject of much criticism (see Gellately and Kiernan, 2003: 14-20),[4] described as 'a purely political ploy' (Bauer, 1998: 33) and 'a rhetorical rather than a juridical device' (Novick, 2001: 101). In the aftermath of the 1994 Rwandan genocide, however, it has been demonstrated that with political will (albeit delayed), the UNGC could be deployed juridically, although this has been neither a straightforward process, nor one whose purpose is without controversy (see Akhavan, 1997; Eltringham, 2004: 27-33; ICG, 1999; 2001; Maogoto, 2003). Whatever the faults of the UNGC, it is 'finally being enforced and developed in several international courts [and] remains the best starting point for discussions of genocide' (Gellately and Kiernan, 2003: 19).

As regards the logocentrism of defining events as crimes, Mertus (2000: 148) notes that for the 'international community' the *naming* of crimes is an opportunity to establish/refine/enforce the boundaries of international law and serves that community's interest in explaining its own failure to stop crimes it has itself

---

[1] The preliminary report of the Rwandan Government's census of August 2001 stated that the names of 951,018 victims had been established and that 1,074,017 people had been killed in massacres and genocide between 1 October 1991 and 31 December 1994 and that of those killed, 97.3 per cent were Tutsi (IRIN 2001). The final report of the 2001 census put the death toll for April–July 1994 at 937,000 which includes the deaths of ethnic Hutu (see IRIN, 2004).

[2] Security Council Resolution 955 (8 November 1994) in which Article II of the *Statute of the International Tribunal for Rwanda* contains Articles II and III of the UNGC (UN 1994c). The ICTR was the first international tribunal to convict for the crime of genocide based on a trial (rather than a guilty plea): Jean-Paul Akayesu 2 September 1998.

[3] Mirroring the ICTR, Rwanda's domestic law regarding genocide, 'Organic Law No. 08/96 of August 30, 1996 on the *Organisation of Prosecutions for Offences constituting the Crime of Genocide or Crimes against Humanity* committed since October 1, 1990 (Article Ia) states 'genocide ... as defined in the Convention on the Prevention and Punishment of the Crime of Genocide of 9 December 1948'.

[4] According to genocide scholars, the Convention has three key weaknesses. First, although commonly perceived as referring to 'mass killing', the Convention co-mingles lethal and non-lethal acts. Second, the ambiguity of 'destruction in whole or in part' (Fein, 1993: 10). This lack of quantitative criteria means that the threshold between one or two massacres and an episode of genocide 'remains inherently indeterminate' (Harff and Gurr, 1988: 366) and demonstrating intent becomes paramount. Third, the Convention excludes the annihilation of political groups (see Chalk, 1989: 151; du Preez, 1994: 8; Whitaker, 1985).

proscribed (Mertus, 2000: 149; see Melvern, 2000; Power, 2003). However, while trials (domestic or international) may be 'meaningful to lawyers drafting pleonastic documents', Mertus notes that 'little satisfaction will come to survivors [whose] voices will remain largely unheard and unaddressed' or traumatically constrained by courtroom performance (Mertus, 2000:142; see Mertus, 2003; Ross, 2003a; 2003b).[5]

In the wake of massive violence there is, at an individual and collective level, a desire to establish a coherent, causal narrative (see Sanford, 2003). This need is emulated by law, where trials 'aspire to produce a coherent narrative: one that explains and interprets as well as records' (Maier, 2000: 271). Trials seek to provide a 'temporal causal sequencing' that 'makes sense of action' so that 'violence that shatters lives and bodies can be comprehended' (ibid.) through an 'authoritative version' extracted from a 'confusing welter of oral reports' (ibid.: 272).

And yet, to synthesise or 'fabricate' an authoritative narrative from diverse sources and voices, trials necessarily, 'privilege certain voices while suppressing others' (Gready, 2003: 1). As they constrain/repackage testimony to create a new master narrative, trials only admit 'enough information to prove the issue at hand' (Mertus, 2000: 144; see Conley and O'Barr, 1990). Trials must 'vastly simplify' in order to render justice (Maier, 2000: 267). And, what matters, are 'hard facts', in which 'subjectivity and information not immediately relevant to the prosecution of the individual case is dismissed' (Wilson, 1997: 146, 153; see Maier, 2000: 272; Osiel, 1997: 103-4).

Informing this process is the (preordained) spatial-temporal gaze of any criminal trial, the delineation of 'the crime' and its methodologically individual reductionism. In the context of the trial of Adolf Eichmann in 1961, Hannah Arendt noted that trials may not satisfy those who wish to locate events within a broader historical landscape:

> Justice demands that the accused be prosecuted, defended and judged, and that all the other questions of seemingly greater import – of 'How could it happen?' and 'Why did it happen?', of 'Why the Jews?' and 'Why the Germans?' ... be left in abeyance. Justice insists on the importance of Adolf Eichmann. ... On trial are his deeds, not the sufferings of the Jews, not the German people or mankind (Arendt, 1994 [1963]: 5).

There is a tension between putting the individual and/or 'history' at the centre of the trial.[6]

Mertus (2000: 149) suggests that authoritative, legal nomenclature is of instrumental use to elites as a resource that demonises former power-holders and creates a new image of a 'liberated' nation that legitimises their rule (see Wilson, 2001). In the context considered here, both the current elite in power and its exile 'shadow' agree on the key assertion that the Tutsi were victims of a genocide between April and July 1994. And yet, despite purported fixity, this key assertion sets in motion the search for causal narratives. Irrespective of whether elites are knowledgeable of the actual content of trials, or agree with their stated purposes, juridical recognition furnishes this key assertion. Just as the teleological illusion of history appears to answer the question 'How-did-the-past-create-the-present?'

---

[5] Likewise, and despite claims to the contrary, 'truth acknowledgement' exercises are similarly unable to satisfy desires (often competing) to locate events comparatively or within the local past (see Minow, 1998: 128-9; Wilson, 2001).
[6] For a detailed discussion of whether trials can or should 'write history' see Osiel (1997: 79-141) and Maier (2000: 261-78).

(Chapman, Tonkin and McDonald, 1989: 5) when the content of historical narratives is determined by contemporary social and political needs (see Friedlander, 1992: 1; Eltringham, 2004: 158-60), so a key juridical assertion *awaits* its causal narrative, to be placed at the apex of a 'causal-temporal-logical line' (see Errington, 1979: 239). To construct this narrative(s), elites engage in 'selecting and adapting thoughts, mutating and creating them, in the continued struggle for argumentative victory against rival thinkers' (Hajer, 1995: 53; see Billig, 1987: 82). In so doing, translocal interlocutors use certain discursive practices as they struggle for 'argumentative victory' over opponents. These practices include drawing on 'analogies, historical references, clichés, appeals to collective fears, or senses of guilt' (Hajer, 1995: 63). Such practices, although set in motion by a fixed legal designation, inevitably deploy notions of the inveterate and appeal to analogy beyond the restricted individual, temporal-spatial gaze implied by the legal designation.

Rwanda is a context in which 'History is incessantly invoked' (Chrétien, 2003: 39), referred to 'at every political level, from a president speaking to an international audience ... to the piercing return of history in political party programs' (ibid.: 37-8). In such a context, 'history' will, inevitably, remain 'contrapuntal, not harmonic' (Maier, 2000: 275; see Eltringham, 2004: 147-79) and will evade the singular delineated master narrative that, it is hoped, will result from naming crimes.

The promise of the panacea of 'record making', oriented around central propositions (the immovable fixity that legal categories appear to furnish) undoubtedly informs debate, but it remains in tension with the desire to call upon notions of the inveterate and analogy that breaches the constrained gaze of law, its deracinated mapping and *singular* narration of reality oriented around the individual defendant. The selective accenting *within* atomistic trials exists simultaneously with a process by which gravity is articulated through the inveterate and analogy beyond the immediacy that is the imperative of legal naming and process (see Arendt, 1994 [1963]: 285).

Debating the Rwandan Genocide

The material considered here is drawn from interviews conducted between 1996 and 1999 in Rwanda among Government officials, pro-government journalists and civil society leaders (henceforth 'Rwandan Government'),[7] and in Europe among exiled Rwandan academics, former Government officials and civil society leaders (henceforth 'exiles').[8] As regards the focus on elite discourse, Robert Gellately and Ben Kiernan (2003: 10-12) note that a 'top-down' ('intentionalist') approach to genocide (that concentrates on elites) and a 'bottom-up' ('interactive') approach (that concentrates on those who do the killing and the experiences of victims and survivors) should not be considered exclusive, but form the basis of

[7] 'Returnee' indicates that the respondent had returned to Rwanda after the genocide. 'RPF' indicates membership of the Rwandan Patriotic Front.
[8] Although all exiles referred to here were opposed to the Rwandan Government, not all were ethnic Hutu (according to the ascribed ethno-racial identity found on her or his pre-1997 ID card). The use of the categories 'Rwandan Government' and 'exiles' is not meant to imply that *all* members of either group would make (or agree with) the statements considered here.

complementary research. The multifarious research agenda proposed by Timothy Longman (2004) reflects this position and examples of the latter can be seen in recent work (see Mironko, 2004). The elite-oriented position taken here, proceeds from both the recognition that the 1994 genocide 'stemmed from a deliberate choice by a modern élite' (Chrétien, 2003: 331; see Eltringham, 2004: xii) and the broader concern within anthropology that one should give as much attention to elites as to studies of what are described as 'ordinary people' (see Nader, 1972; Sluka, 1999).

As noted above, the discourse of the Rwandan exiles did not subvert the key juridical assertion that a genocide of ethnic Tutsi took place in 1994. None of the exiles I interviewed[9] denied the use of the term genocide in relation to the events of April–July 1994. For example:

> I think that the killing of Rwandan Tutsis was a genocide. Because that was the slogan. Kill the Tutsis, kill the women, kill the children, kill them all. That is genocide. The slogan was clear: 'Kill the Tutsi.' Therefore, without a doubt it should be classed as genocide (Rwandan Academic, exile, France, July 1999).

Rather, debate concerns two lenses through which those interviewed attempt to interpret the 1994 genocide: its relation to the Holocaust and where, within Rwanda's past, should one locate precursors?

Comparison with the Holocaust: Rwandan Government

Members of the then Rwandan Government and press appeared acquainted with *aspects* of the UNGC. Genocide is described as 'an attempt to make one single group extinct' (Rwandan Government Spokesperson, (RPF), returnee, Kigali, June 1998); that 'the genocide was prepared, organised systematically and methodically executed' (Karasira, 1996: 12); and that it was a 'state sanctioned genocide' (Victor, 1998: 1). And yet, while such statements correspond to aspects of the UNGC, none of the members of the Rwandan Government interviewed referred to the Convention by name. Rather, the principal referent was the Holocaust and its associated lexicon. For example, the association of the Habyarimana regime with 'fascism' (Member of the Rwandan Parliament, (RPF), returnee, Kigali, April 1998; see also Visathan, 1996; Mikekemo, 1996; Munyaneza, 1996); describing the genocide as 'a final solution' (Rwandan Government Official, Kigali, returnee, June 1998; see Gachinya, 1996b) and as a 'Holocaust' (Mikekemo, 1998; Victor, 1998; New Times Editorial, 1996: 2). Likewise:

> Two and a half years ago the word 'genocide' was just lying in the history books of the Tsiganes [Roma, 'gypsies'], the Armenians and the Jews – and some dictionaries. Then came the end of April 1994 when genocide was already half way in Rwanda and a hot debate erupted in the [UN]. Was it genocide? The UN Security Council finally found no other description of what was happening in Rwanda. The word 'genocide' invaded the world media (Ruhumuriza, 1996: 8).

The word 'genocide' was not 'lying in the history books', but was the subject of an international convention, ratified by 113 states as of 24 March 1994. Circumventing the UNGC, members (and supporters) of the Rwandan Government used

[9] None of those interviewed are accused of participation in the genocide.

analogy with the Holocaust in a number of ways: for example, that the Rwandan genocide was more proximate to the Holocaust than the Armenian genocide of 1915 (and 1918 to 1923):[10]

> Great numbers of deaths, organisation, systematic elimination, this is a genocide. In this way, the Holocaust resembles events in Rwanda, as does the genocide of Armenians. But, the Armenians were killed because they had a different language and culture.[11] In contrast, the Jews had the same language and culture as the Germans which was also the case in Rwanda (RPF Supporter, non-exile, Europe, July 1999).

While actors drew attention to certain differences between the Holocaust and the 1994 genocide, the thrust of their statements was to draw parallels:

> There are similarities in its execution. To exterminate a people because of who they are, not because of what they have done. There was no Auschwitz in Rwanda, therefore, it was different. But, people were still killed because of what they were, not what they had done. It is similar [to the Holocaust], because the victims killed in 1994 had never heard about politics (RPF Representative, non-exile, Europe, February 1999).

Similar analogies were made with the Holocaust regarding the ideological foundations of the genocide in Rwanda:

> Habyarimana's reign gave birth to a crop of Hutu intellectuals who were very similar to those that emerged during the reign of Hitler in Germany .... The Hutu were given to believe that they were a race of supermen, that the world and everything in it was, and will be, for the Bahutu. Hitler used such methods to arouse Germans soon after the First World War (Gachinya, 1996a).

When clear distinctions were drawn with the Holocaust, it was not to insist on difference *per se*, but to imply that the Rwandan genocide was 'worse' than the Holocaust, in terms of both the speed of killing and the participation of the population. For example:

> There is a difference in time between Nazi Germany and the long time it took to exterminate six million Jews and over one million killed in such a short time in Rwanda (Rwandan NGO Worker, returnee, Kigali, May 1998).

> The Nazi holocaust was different to the genocide here in Rwanda because the state machinery planned and carried out the killing. Here, the state machinery planned the killing, but it was carried out by the population (Rwandan Presidential Advisor, (RPF) returnee, Kigali, May 1998).

> If you talk with Germans about their war, they will say – it was not us, only the Gestapo who killed. But in Rwanda the population itself killed. ... Fifty-six methods of killing were counted before the researchers stopped counting. If you talk to Jews they speak of gas being used or deportation – very mechanical methods of torture – but in Rwanda there were so many methods (Member of the Rwandan Parliament, (RPF), returnee, Kigali, October 1998).

> [The Rwandan Genocide was] the worst genocide ever because members of communities both caused and were victims of the genocide (Member of the Rwandan Parliament, (RPF), returnee, Kigali, October 1998).

---

[10] More than 1.5 million Armenians were murdered between 1915 and 1923 (see Melson, 1992; Hovannisian, 1999; Dadrian, 1995).

[11] For a discussion of how perpetrators constructed the Tutsi as a target, see Eltringham (2004: 19-33).

Comparisons with the Holocaust: Rwandan Exiles

The exiles accepted the fundamental similarity between the Holocaust and the 1994 genocide

> The Holocaust was the same because they killed innocent people according to their race or because of their convictions, religion etc, and that's terrible. Genocide is unacceptable. We cannot accept what has happened in Rwanda (Former Rwandan Government Official, exile, Belgium, March 1999).

> It's the same thing, it was the innocents who were killed and there was an ideology of extermination. But, for me, the similarities stop there (Rwandan NGO Worker, exile, Belgium, March 1999).

> The only comparison is that there are innocent, unresisting victims, whether they were killed fast or slowly. What is important is exterminating a group and the personal suffering each person undergoes. What is common is the innocence of the victims (Former Rwandan Minister, exile, Switzerland, May 1999).

And yet, they also argued that the two events should not be considered identical:

> They [the Rwandan Government] compare the situation in 1994 with the Holocaust; the situations are not the same. That is to say it is not necessary to compare. It is necessary to take a situation in its own context, where there is an intention to destroy an ethnic group. That is genocide. But, I don't think that it is necessary to compare. It is necessary to consider such things in their own context (Rwandan NGO Worker, exile, Belgium, March 1999).

Some exiles insisted that the preceding civil war[12] prevented direct comparison:

> The similarities stop there ... From Hitler's rise to power it was clear. The exclusion of the Jews was a policy. In contrast, in Rwanda one can say that there was exclusion and ethnic discrimination, but one also saw strong ethnic integration and there was regional discrimination among the Hutu. But Hutu and Tutsi always found space for economic and social activities without a problem. That is the great difference (Rwandan NGO Worker, exile, Belgium, March 1999).

The exiles argued that, while the civil war (1990-93) and the genocide were distinct, the genocide emerged from the context of a conflict between two definable and armed parties. In contrast, there was no objective dynamic in which the Jews as a group threatened the Nazi monopoly of state power (see Newbury and Newbury 2003: 140).[13] For example:

> The RPF compares the genocide in Rwanda with the genocide committed against the Jews by the Germans, but the Jews did not attack the Germans (Former Rwandan Government Official, exile, Belgium, March 1999).

---

[12] The RPF entered Rwanda from Uganda on 1 October 1990. Despite initial success, the Front was then forced to conduct a guerrilla war. In May 1992 an RPF offensive resulted in 350,000 people being internally displaced, with a further 800,000 being displaced following the RPF offensive of February 1993. In August 1993, with the signing of the Arusha Peace Accords, the fighting ended (see HRW and FIDH, 1999: 48ff, for details).

[13] It should be noted, however, that the RPF was to be part of a new transitional government under the 1993 Arusha Peace Accords (see Eltringham 2004: 84-5) and was considered (with the internal opposition) as a threat to the monopoly of the state held by President Habyarimana and his party. Furthermore, in genocidal propaganda Tutsi civilians within Rwanda were explicitly designated as 'accomplices' of the RPF (see ibid.: 91-4).

It is not true that the Rwandan genocide is the same as the Holocaust. The Jews did not enter a war for Germany against the Germans. In Rwanda there was a war. Tutsi were an invading army. It is not the same relationship. There was a war, an attack from outside (Rwandan Academic, exile, Belgium, February 1999).

For the exiles, the objective of the Rwandan Government in drawing parallels between the 1994 genocide and the Holocaust was to misrepresent those events by obscuring contextual differences. As one exile argued:

[Paul] Kagame is exploiting the Holocaust. Both Tutsi and Jews have suffered, but in a different manner and for different reasons. Rwanda is different. I myself am a *rescapé* [a survivor of the genocide]. The *interahamwe* killed Hutus, but they are completely forgotten for official reasons.[14] I have no right to say my brothers have been killed. Rwanda is a whole different case to the Holocaust (Former Rwandan Minister, exile, Belgium, February 1999).

Likewise, according to the exiles, drawing such parallels misrepresents pre-genocide Rwandan society (at least before 1990) and the lack of a sophisticated, articulated ideology as found in Nazi Germany:

In the Jewish case you had the Nazis, you know how their ideology was constructed. We never had such a thing in Rwanda. Some say in Rwanda there was a Nazi system. This is completely wrong. In Rwanda the genocide was caused by the selfishness of a certain elite group wanting to cling to power. There was no theory to that power struggle, one group used fear to cause harm. As such, there was no Hutu hatred for Tutsi or *vice versa*. Yes, there were extremists, but a system constructed on ethnic hatred did not exist. This is a major difference between the two situations (Former Rwandan Minister, exile, Switzerland, May 1999).

Finally, the exiles consider there to have been an element of 'politicide'[15] in the events of Rwanda in 1994 (although they do not use this term nor the relevant aspect of 'crimes against humanity') and that this also sets the Rwandan case apart from the Holocaust:

1994 was genocide, but not exactly the same as the Nazi genocide. Genocide has a philosophical basis, a superior race that wants to eliminate an inferior race absolutely, without exception. In 1994 there was a genocide, but a political type in order to maintain political power. Hutu massacred Tutsi because they were seen as political opponents. One cannot compare the genocide of Rwanda with the Nazi genocide (Rwandan Journalist, exile, France, July 1999).

In 1994 there were the moderate Hutu and the Tutsi, it was not only a question of ethnicity. It's more correct to say, there were people killed in 1994 and that they were killed by a Hutu group (Rwandan NGO Worker, exile, Belgium, March 1999).

Comparisons with the Holocaust: Comment

Interpreting events in the Great Lakes region through the prism of the Holocaust is neither unique to Rwanda nor the events of 1994. Bertrand Russell described the 1963 massacre of Tutsi in Rwanda (see below) as 'the most horrible

---

[14] For a discussion of the anomalous status of Hutu victims, see Eltringham (2004: 97-9).

[15] 'In genocides the victimised groups are defined primarily in terms of their communal characteristics, i.e. ethnicity, religion or nationality. In politicides the victim groups are defined primarily in terms of their hierarchical position or political opposition to the regime and dominant groups' (Harff and Gurr, 1988: 362).

systematic human massacre we have had occasion to witness since the extermination of the Jews by the Nazis'. Similarly, the killing of between 100,000 and 200,000 Hutu in Burundi in 1972 by the Tutsi-dominated army is described by Stephen Weissman as 'the first clear genocide since the Holocaust' (1997: 55) and is the subject of an article by Stanley Meisler entitled 'Holocaust in Burundi' (1976; see Lemarchand and Martin, 1974; Bowen, Freeman and Miller, 1973).

From a detached analytical perspective one can draw numerous parallels with the Holocaust (see Levene, 1999; Miles, 2000). First, in both cases 'a modern bureaucratic state organised the forces of violence, mobilised its citizens, and directed them to kill people of a particular category' (Newbury and Newbury, 2003: 135; see HRW and FIDH, 1999: 1). Both Tutsi and Jews were dehumanised/demonised (see Prunier, 1995: 143n. 27; Destexhe, 1994 :50). Just as it was widely believed that Jews killed children at Passover and drank their blood (Staub, 1989: 102) so Tutsi/RPF were portrayed as 'cannibals' (Chrétien, Dupaquier, Kabanda and Ngarambe, 1995: 162,189; Article XIX, 1996: 112). Both the Rwandan genocide and the Holocaust involved an imagined transnational plot. Like the 'Jewish-Bolshevik conspiracy', genocidal propaganda in Rwanda claimed there was a 'Hima-Tutsi' plan to colonise Central Africa with the support of Uganda and Burundi (Chrétien, Dupaquier, Kabanda and Ngarambe, 1995: 167-75; HRW and FIDH, 1999: 111). Just as the forged *Protocole des Sages de Sion* (see du Preez, 1994: 36; Cohn, 1980) claimed there was a global Jewish conspiracy, so the extremist newspaper *Kangura* referred to a 'letter' (undoubtedly forged) which it claimed had been found in 1962 and contained 19 points detailing how 'the Tutsi' should surreptitiously take over the Great Lakes Region (Chrétien, Dupaquier, Kabanda and Ngarambe, 1995: 163ff; see Hintjens, 1999: 263). There is a clear resemblance between the concept of *Volksgemeinschaft* (a folk or racial community) and the ubiquitous references in genocidal propaganda to *Rubanda Nyamwinshi* or rule by *le peuple majoritaire* – rule by the demographic majority: the Hutu. In both cases, the perpetrators insisted it was necessary to kill women and children to prevent future 'revenge'.[16] One could argue that there is a parallel between the international silence regarding the massacre of Hutu in Burundi in 1972 and 1993 and Hitler's question 'Who, after all, speaks today of the annihilation of the Armenians?' (quoted in Bardakjian, 1985: 43; see Newbury and Newbury, 2003: 138).[17] In both cases, non-killing demagogues played a critical role; in Nazi Germany Julius Streicher (editor of *Der Stürmer*) and in Rwanda, Ferdinand Nahimana (editor of *Kangura*). In both cases, perpetrators were obsessed with 'racial hybridity'. In Nazi Germany, *Rasenschänder* ('desecrators of the race') and *Mischlinge* ('half breeds') and in Rwanda *abaguze ubwoko* ('ethnic cheaters') and *ibiymanyi*

---

[16] In a speech on 5 May 1944 Himmler stated that 'In my view, we as Germans, however deeply we may feel in our hearts, are not entitled to allow a generation of avengers filled with hatred to grow up with whom our children and grandchildren will have to deal because we, too weak and cowardly, left it to them' (quoted in Bartov, 1998: 785 n.22). In a leaflet distributed in Ruhengeri *préfecture* in early 1991, it was stated 'Go do a special *umuganda*. Destroy all the bushes and the *Inkotanyi* who are hiding there. And don't forget that those who are destroying the weeds must also get rid of the roots [i.e. women and children]' (quoted in Article XIX, 1996: 34).

[17] As Alison des Forges notes 'In October 1993 there were 500,000 people killed in Burundi and no one [internationally] did anything and this encouraged extremists [in Rwanda] to argue to other people "Look we can get away with it. Why not do it?"' (quoted in Fein, 1998: 16; see Eltringham, 2004: 90).

('hybrids'). The most chilling similarity: seventy per cent of European Jewry and seventy-seven per cent of the Tutsi population of Rwanda were murdered.

And yet, making the Holocaust the 'paradigmatic genocide' has its dangers.[18] First, the utility of the Holocaust as comparator has been weakened as it has been transformed into an 'emblematic horror' (Novick, 2001: 255). For example, Peter Novick quotes Al Gore (a senator at the time) talking of 'An Ecological Kristallnacht' with an 'environmental Holocaust' to follow (Gore, 1989, cited in Novick, 2001: 231). Likewise, anti-Castro activists in Miami erected a monument to the 'Cuban Holocaust' (Swarns, 1994; cited in Novik, 2001: 231). While such analogies are insensitive, we must recognise that 'Individuals from every point of the political compass can find the lessons they wish in the Holocaust; it has become a moral and ideological Rorshach test' (Novick, 2001: 12, 241ff.). In this way, comparison between the Rwandan genocide and the Holocaust takes place in a environment in which the term 'Holocaust' suffers from 'semantic stretch' (Fein, 1994a: 95).

Use of the Holocaust as the 'paradigmatic genocide' may also lead to the axiom that only a western, industrialised power (armed with a sophisticated, pseudo-scientific ideology) can achieve mass murder (Harff and Gurr, 1988: 361).[19] Helen Fein (1993: 6) notes that between 1960 and 1979 there were at least a dozen genocides and genocidal massacres, but that these events went 'virtually unnoted in the western press and not remarked on in world forums'. In her opinion, this was due, in part, to the Holocaust having become the paradigmatic genocide which 'diminished observation of less planned, less total, and less rationalised cases of extermination' (ibid.; see du Preez, 1994: ii; Power, 2003: 358). As a consequence of 'making the Holocaust the emblematic atrocity, have we made resemblance to it the criterion by which we decide what horrors command our attention?' (Novick, 2001: 257).

Genocide cannot be reduced to a singular, recurring script, as Roger Smith's five-part typology demonstrates:

> (1) *retributive genocide*, which is based on the desire for revenge; (2) *institutional genocide*, frequently incidental to military conquest and prevalent in the ancient and medieval worlds; (3) *utilitarian genocide*, motivated by the desire for material gain; (4) *monopolistic genocide*, originating from the desire to monopolise power, particularly in plural societies; and (5) *ideological genocide*, motivated by the desire to impose a particular notion of salvation or purification on an entire society and most commonly found in the 20th-century (1987: 24-7; see Freeman, 1991: 189-90).

Smith's five archetypes are not designed to be mutually exclusive, but represent only the predominant (or at least verbalised) motive of genocide perpetrators. In any actual case more than one of these motives will be present (Chalk and Jonassohn, 1990: 35). Smith considers the Holocaust to have been over-whelmingly 'ideological'. In contrast, the most frequent source of genocide in the

---

[18] By presenting the Holocaust as the archetypal genocide the Turkish government has sought to deny the genocide of the Armenians (Fein, 1993: 56; see Smith, 1992).

[19] As Fein points out 'Although most contemporary genocides take place in the Third World, much of the theory about genocide is derived from a dominant or exclusive focus on the Holocaust, which occurred in a modern, Western, Christian and post-Christian society' (1993: xv; see du Preez, 1994: ii).

[20] 'One major difference between the Holocaust and other forms of genocide is that pragmatic considerations were central with all other genocides, abstract ideological motivations less so' (Bauer 2001: 47).

twentieth century was the struggle to monopolise state power (Smith, 1987: 26).[20] In the case of Rwanda, one could argue that the 1994 genocide had 'retributive',[21] 'monopolistic',[22] 'utilitarian'[23] and 'ideological' (see Eltringham, 2004: 19-27) components. It is necessary, however, to recognise that the particular fusion of motives is unique to each episode. An over-emphasis on the ideological component of the Rwandan genocide (in comparison with the Holocaust) may detract from its monopolistic features and contemporary issues regarding the control of state institutions (see ICG, 2002; HRW, 2003).

Genocide scholars have suggested a further distinction between 'pragmatic' and 'transcendental' genocide (du Preez, 1994: 11; see Freeman, 1991: 189). If genocide has a clear economic or political 'pragmatic' purpose it will continue until that purpose is achieved. Pragmatic genocide is devoid of vision.[24] In contrast, 'transcendental' genocide will continue until all members of a target group have been eliminated.[25] Clearly, the Nazi genocide was predominantly transcendental.[26] While in the case of Rwanda there was a transcendental element ('racial purity') there is also a clear sense of its pragmatic nature in the desire of the Habyarimana regime to hold on to power in the context of the Arusha Accords (1993) which would have forced him (and his associates) to share power with the RPF and the internal opposition (see Eltringham, 2004: 76-91).[27] While the Nazis saw extermination of 'lesser races' as a natural expression of Aryan power, 'the Hutu extremists saw elimination of the Tutsi as a practical solution to the political problem of retaining control of the state' (Linden, 1997: 48). By overplaying comparison with the Holocaust this pragmatic component in Rwanda may be obscured. Again, the archetypes of 'pragmatic' and 'transcendental' are not mutually exclusive (see du Preez, 1994: 67). In order to mobilise killers, genocidal propaganda may contain both transcendental and pragmatic elements. As with Smith's typology, the relative importance of any element will be unique in each specific case. Each genocide is a unique constellation of these components.

Comparison based on the Holocaust as archetype, which assumes there is one mechanically recurring script, are 'bound to be misleading' (Fein, 1993: 56). Each occurrence of genocide is distinct, involving specific victims, perpetrators,

---

[21] Fein refers to the 1994 genocide as 'retributive'. Her meaning is slightly different to that found in Smith's typology, but corresponds with 'monopolistic': 'the perpetrators represent an élite or segment of the dominant ethnic group that felt threatened by the imposition of a new structure in which their ethnic group's interests could be subordinated' (Fein, 1998: 160).

[22] As Degni-Ségui observed in June 1994 'The reason for what is taking place in Rwanda is not ethnic as such, but rather political, the aim being the seizure of political power, or rather the retention of power, by the representatives of one ethnic group ... who are using every means, principally the elimination of the opposing ethnic group, but also the elimination of political opponents within their own group' (UN 1994a para 56).

[23] '[The genocide] was, among other things, largely a fight for good jobs, administrative control and economic advantage' (Prunier, 1995: 227).

[24] Du Preez (1994: 68) gives the German genocide of Herero (see Bridgman, 1981; Drechsler, 1980; Hull, and the postcolonial genocide of Ibo as examples of pragmatic genocides.

[25] Du Preez (1994: 68) gives the Nazi genocide of Jews and Roma/'gypsies'; the Stalinist genocide of Kulaks, the Khmer Rouge genocide of bourgeoisie and the Turkish genocide of Armenians as examples of transcendent genocide.

[26] '[T]he assault on the Jews was purely ideological; that is, it had no *a priori* pragmatic elements, as in the case of literally all genocidal attempts we know of' (Bauer, 1998: 39).

[27] 'The wanton killing of Tutsi civilians ... became the quickest and most "rational" way of eliminating all basis of agreement with the RPF' (Lemarchand 1995: 9-10; see Fein, 1994b: 5).

motives, methods and consequences (Smith, 1998:4; see Hirsch, 1995: 34). We require, therefore, 'discernment within comparison' (Fein, 1993: 54) the recognition that every historical event, including the Holocaust, resembles in some ways other events to which it might be compared and differs from them in others (Novick, 2001: 9; see Freeman, 1991: 188; Maier, 1988:69; Harff, 1992: 30).[28] The point of comparison is not comparison for its own sake, to satisfy 'some abstract intellectual urge' (Bauer, 1998:32; see Bartov, 2003). Rather, it is critical in designing pre-emptive, generic models of genocide aimed at early warning and detection (Stanton, 1998; Hinton, 2002: 29-30; Kuper, 1985: 218-28; Little, 1991; Whitaker, 1985: 41-5).

In seeking to demonstrate how the Rwandan genocide emulates the Holocaust, actors inadvertently perpetuate the Holocaust's superlative status, rather than demonstrate the parity of the two events. Given this drawback, what is the function of drawing analogies with the Holocaust?

Numerous authors have demonstrated how the international media represented the Rwandan genocide as 'tribalistic savagery' drawing on fundamentally racist perceptions of Africa (see JEEAR, 1996: Study II, para 4.3; Power, 2003: 355-6; Hawk, 1992). As early as February 1994 headlines such as 'Tribal Feuds Throw Rwanda in Crisis' (Watson, 1994) began to appear. During the genocide *Time Magazine* described events as 'Pure tribal enmity' (Michaels, 1994a), a 'tribal bloodlust' and 'tribal carnage' (Michaels, 1994b) and *The Times* wrote about 'tribal slaughter' (Kiley, 1994a) and 'tribal pogrom' (Kiley, 1994b). The genocide was presented as spontaneous, primordial bloodlust – rather than a premeditated, well-organised attempt to annihilate the Tutsi. Reference to 'tribalism' implicitly refers to a concept of social evolution, especially Elman Service's 'band → tribe → chiefdom → state' typology (1962; 1975). 'Tribes', therefore, are well down the 'evolutionary chain', implying that Rwanda in 1994 had not yet reached the level of state formation, that it was merely a 'shell state', one of many 'artificial political entities' (Kaplan, 1994b) with 'fictitious' sovereignty (Kaplan, 1994a) in which the 'paraphernalia of the state' was merely hollow window-dressing for the real motivating force: *tribalism*.

As a consequence, the use of the term 'tribal(ism)' does two things. First, it obliterates the critical role played in the genocide by state-sanctioned actors (see HRW and FIDH, 1999: 234). Second, it replaces this role with the image of an 'ancient', superorganic, all-consuming compulsion, which denies individual agency and obscures the concerted, *desperate* effort required by extremist newspapers such as *Kangura* and the extremist radio station *Radio Télévision Libre des Mille Collines* (*RTLM*) – both *modern* technologies – to construct an image of irreconcilable difference between Hutu and Tutsi (see Vidal, 1998: 659). Furthermore, 'tribal(ism)' generates the image of a conflict between two homogeneous, distinct sides or 'two quasi-nations' (Kagabo and Vidal, 1994: 545) rather than one-sided mass murder. Thus, media representations which referred to 'tribalism' paralleled genocidal propaganda which evoked the image of a 'final battle' (the *Simusiga*) between Hutu and Tutsi and in so doing obfuscated genocide as 'warfare' (see Chrétien, Dupaquier, Kabanda and Ngarambe, 1995: 192). This tribal motif naturalises the distinctly constructed character of racial distinction in

---

28 For a discussion of debates regarding the 'uniqueness' of the Holocaust and the Rwandan genocide see Eltringham (2004: 8-9). For the relation of this debate to criminal trials for genocide see Osiel (1997: 121-41).

Rwanda (see Eltringham, 2004: 12-27), detracting culpability from the instigators of the genocide and dispersing responsibility among a multitude of automatons driven by a semi-mystical, primeval imperative. As Omer Bartov (1998: 799) notes:

> Having created a reality beyond its wildest fantasies, humanity cannot imagine what it created ... human agency becomes tenuous, the disaster being ascribed either to insane genius or to anonymous forces.

'Tribal(ism)' obscures the fact that the genocide was 'a political phenomenon – thought about, spoken about, organised and planned by political actors' who were part of the state and its institutions (Kagabo and Vidal, 1994: 545; see Newbury and Newbury, 2003: 136).

Thus, a function of drawing analogies with the Holocaust is as a response to these forms of misrepresentation. When faced with such distortion, the Rwandan government has been both pushed and pulled to draw such analogies. Pushed, because of the 'tribalism' projected on to Rwanda by international coverage and pulled by the privileged place given to the Holocaust in *western* public consciousness. For, although the Holocaust may be a global paradigm, it is also 'the best known genocide *in the Western world*' (Fein, 1993: 55; emphasis added) in contrast to other genocidal episodes such as the killing of Armenians 1915-23 (see Dadrian, 1995); Indonesian 'communists' in 1965-6 (see Dwyer and Santikarma, 2003), Biafra in 1966 (see Saro-Wiwa, 1989), Bangladesh in 1971 (see Jahan, 2004), Burundi 1972 (see Lemarchand and Martin, 1974), Cambodia 1975-8 (see Kiernan, 1996), or East Timor 1975-2000 (see Taylor, 2003).

In this sense, the analogies drawn by the Rwandan Government with the Holocaust appear to be a legitimate response to the representation of the Rwandan genocide as tribalistic savagery in the 'Dark Heart of Africa'. No-one would seriously contend that the Holocaust – however brutal – was the outcome of primordial tribalism. It was clearly a premeditated, thoroughly modern, organised campaign in which irrational 'savagery' gave way to its polar opposite; clinical state bureaucracy (see Steiner, 1977: 99). It is racist misrepresentation coupled with ethnocentrism that forces the Rwandan Government to draw parallels with the Holocaust in order that the Rwandan genocide be given parity in public consciousness – they are forced to demonstrate that this was a 'black Holocaust'. For example, prior to President Clinton's visit to Rwanda in March 1998, a Rwandan journalist hoped that the President would 'acknowledge how the genocide in Rwanda is similar to the genocide in Europe and elsewhere' (Mucyo, 1998; see Xinhua, 1998).

Precursors to 1994: Rwandan Government

In 1959 the Tutsi monarchy was overthrown by a Hutu intelligentsia supported by the Belgian colonial authorities and elements within the Roman Catholic Church. Tutsi were killed and tens of thousands fled to neighbouring countries (see Eltringham, 2004: 34-5). These events were formerly described as the 'Hutu' or 'Social Revolution'. For the Rwandan Government, however, these events are the '1959 Genocide' that marked the beginning of the intermittent genocide of Tutsi:

The first genocidal massacres were in 1959, propagated by the Belgians in close collaboration with the Catholic Church (Rwandan Presidential Advisor, (RPF), returnee, Kigali, May 1998).

The first acts of genocide were committed in 1959, 1960, 1961 (RPF Party Official, returnee, Kigali, June 1998).

First attempt at genocide in 1959 (Official Rwandan Government Spokesperson, (RPF), returnee, Kigali, June 1998).

The 1994 genocide had been planned since 1959. A philosophy for thirty-five years which accepted that Hutu should kill Tutsi (Official Rwandan Government Spokesperson, (RPF), returnee, Kigali, June 1998).

Genocide started in 1959, then 1963, 1966, 1967, 1973, 1993, 1994 (Paul Kagame, quoted in Jere-Malanda, 2000).

Precursors to 1994: Rwandan Exiles

Although the statements above refer to a number of genocidal episodes (1963, 1972 etc.), as a consequence of the emphasis being placed on 1959 (as the 'inaugural' year) the debate focuses on those events. While the exiles do not deny that both massacres and serious human rights abuses were committed in 1959, they dispute the designation of those events as an episode of genocide:

I know that there were some terrible events. People were killed. But, to call it genocide is inappropriate. There were deaths. That must be regretted. But it was not a genocide. For me, it was a revolution (Former Rwandan Minister, Exile, Belgium, March, 1999).

Yes, a revolution in 1959, of course. Yes, Tutsi were killed in a genocide in 1994, but not in 1959 (Rwandan Academic, Exile, France, July, 1999)

The main argument proffered by exiles to object to 1959 being considered a genocide is that, in their opinion, the 'social revolution' was only directed against a Tutsi political elite in a context of democratisation rather than an intention to eliminate all Tutsi:

One cannot speak of genocide because there was no intention to kill all Tutsi (Rwandan Journalist, exile, Switzerland, June 1999).

It was really those in power who were targeted. The violence was not generalised to all Tutsi (Rwandan NGO Worker, exile, Switzerland, May 1999).

During the years after 1959 the exiled Tutsi launched attacks [*Inyenzi* attacks, March 1961 to November 1966]. In certain parts of Rwanda – Gitarama and Gikongoro – the Tutsi who stayed were massacred. I don't understand those massacres and I condemn them. But, that was not the case with the 1959 revolution – it was aimed at those who were in power (Rwandan NGO Worker, exile, Belgium, March 1999).

Likewise, other exiles point out that those Tutsi who were not members of the elite, and were therefore neither killed nor fled to surrounding countries, were 'integrated' in to post-independence Rwanda (Rwandan Academic, exile, France, July 1999). Another argument advanced by exiles (premised on the widely held – although erroneous – assumption that only a 'state' can commit genocide) is that as the Rwandan state was not under 'Hutu control' in 1959, the killings of 1959 cannot be considered as a genocide committed by a Hutu Government (as in 1994). Thus, 'Among the population, the Hutu were the majority, but they had no power. How can a dominated people plan and execute a genocide if they have no power?' (Rwandan Journalist, Exile, Switzerland, June, 1999). A third argument made by the exiles is that the first killings in 1959 were of Hutu leaders:

> The killings began after the Tutsi had killed Hutu leaders. For example, Kayibanda[29] was saved by the Belgians (Rwandan Academic, Exile, France, July, 1999).

> It is true that in 1959 there were massacres, but they were started by the assassination of Hutu leaders (Rwandan Journalist, Exile, Switzerland, June, 1999).

The exile's fourth argument that 1959 was not a genocide is the small number of victims killed in 1959 in comparison with 1994:

> There were not many killed in 1959, they were only chased away (Rwandan Academic, Exile, France, July, 1999).

> Only 1,000 people were killed (Rwandan NGO Worker, Exile, Belgium, March, 1999).

> I thought a lot were killed, but in fact there were very few (Rwandan Academic, Exile, France, July, 1999).

In the opinion of the exiles, their assertion that 1959 was not an episode of genocide in no way diminishes the reality of genocide in 1994. For example, 'Yes, a revolution in 1959, of course. Two groups, slaves and leaders. Some Tutsi were innocent while others started planning to kill the Hutu leaders. Yes, Tutsi were killed in 1994, in a genocide, but not in 1959' (Rwandan Academic, Exile, France, July, 1999).

On four counts the exiles argue that 1959 was *not* an episode of genocide. They do not accept that 1959 was a generalised attack on Tutsi – rather it was an attack on a ruling elite who subjugated both Hutu and lower status Tutsi (see Eltringham, 2004: 15, 78-9). While the exiles are prepared to admit that there were moments of violence in 1959, they insist that this was a revolution based upon a genuine demand for democracy, social justice which took place in the context of de-colonisation and the end of indirect Belgian rule.

Precursors to 1994: Comment

Members of the Rwandan Government may be right to consider 1959 an episode of genocide. The failure to legally recognise episodes of genocide has been commonplace since the inception of the UNGC in 1948 and its 'Entry into Force' on 12 January 1951. As already mentioned, Fein notes that between 1960 and 1979 there were at least a dozen genocides and genocidal massacres that went virtually unnoted (1993: 6).

Two important issues arise from the debate reviewed above. First, in their arguments against 1959 as genocide (in comparison with 1994) the exiles demonstrate a limited grasp of the UNGC, the very convention by which 1994 was classed as genocide, a designation with which they agree. Second, while the debate concentrates on the events of 1959, there are far more compelling

---

[29] Between 1956 and 1958 Grégoire Kayibanda was editor of *Kinyamateka* (the official newspaper of the Roman Catholic Church in Rwanda). He became leader of *Parmehutu* (*Parti du mouvement d'émancipation Hutu* – Party of the Movement for Hutu Emancipation) and was elected President on Rwandan independence (1962).

arguments that the events of 1963 were genocide – according to the UNGC – and thus constitute a pre-cursor to 1994. This raises the question of *why* the Rwandan Government chooses to place the emphasis on 1959?

In many respects, the exiles are right in their assertions regarding 1959. Communal elections were held in 1960,[30] in January 1961 a 'coup' removed the monarchy and Rwanda declared a republic[31] (confirmed in a referendum in September 1961 in which eighty per cent of votes supported the abolition of the monarchy). Independence followed on 1 July 1962. Thus, as the exiles argue, the 'revolution' and independence were not simultaneous. Furthermore, Belgian colonial authorities were tacitly and actively involved in the 'revolution'.[32] Similarly, the violence of 1959 was indeed sparked by an attack on the *Parmehutu* activist Dominique Mbonyumutwa on 1 November 1959 by members of the monarchist UNAR[33] party (although contrary to popular opinion/ *Parmehutu* propaganda he was not killed). Inter-ethnic violence followed in which a UN commission (visiting in 1960) estimated at least 200 people had been killed, although it added that 'the number may even be higher since the people preferred to bury their dead silently' (UN, 1960: 31; quoted in Lemarchand, 1970b: 906). As regards the targets of the violence 'much of the violence was aimed against those who held administrative posts (such as chiefs and subchiefs) and members of the Tutsi aristocracy, rather than directed indiscriminately at all Tutsi' (Newbury, 1998: 13). By the start of November 1959, twenty-one Tutsi chiefs (of forty-three) had been killed, made destitute, or gone into exile, while 314 Tutsi sub-chiefs (of 549) had been killed or fled (Reyntjens, 1994: 27).

Despite the specific targeting of Tutsi chiefs, the UN also reported actions which would now be interpreted as a form of 'ethnic cleansing' (see Bell-Fialkoff, 1996):

> incendiaries set off in bands of ten. Armed with matches and paraffin ... they pillaged the Tutsi houses they passed on their way and set fire to them. ... day after day fires spread from hill to hill. Generally speaking the incendiaries, who were often unarmed, did not attack the inhabitants of the huts, and were content with pillaging and setting fire to them (UN, 1960: paras 202-3).

On the whole, violence appears to have been 'primarily focused against property rather than against persons or institutions' (Lemarchand, 1970b: 806). There was, however, regional differentiation: 'where violence did carry some political implications, as in the Gitarama and Ruhengeri districts, it was aimed against individual chiefs, not against the monarchy' (ibid.). There is, however, little

---

[30] Pro-Hutu parties (*Parmehutu* and *Aprosoma*) won 84 per cent of the seats while the two 'Tutsi' parties (UNAR and RADER) won less than 9 per cent. (Lemarchand, 1970b: 911). As a consequence, *Parmerhutu* won 160 *burgomestres* (out of 229 (Chrétien, 1985a: 158).

[31] The 'Coup of Gitarama' – 28 January 1961. Recently elected communal councillors and *burgomestres* (who administered the 299 *communes*) formed themselves into a Legislative Assembly; Grégoire Kayibanda was appointed Prime Minister; the monarchy was abolished and Rwanda declared a republic.

[32] In January 1960, Colonel Guy Logiest (Belgian Special Resident) had declared '[W]e must take action in favour of the Hutu. By virtue of the situation we are led to take sides. We cannot stay neutral and sit' (quoted in Lemarchand, 1970b: 909). The last Belgian vice-governor general, Jean-Paul Harroy described 1959 as an 'assisted revolution' (1984: 292).

[33] *Union Nationale Rwandaise*, formed 3 September 1959; dedicated to a constitutional monarchy; and maintained that the Hutu-Tutsi problem was a creation of colonialism. Although under the nominal presidency of a Hutu, the party was mainly a Tutsi party, its leadership dominated by Tutsi chiefs.

evidence of central planning or co-ordination (Lemarchand, 1970a: 163-4). Conversely, UNAR organised a campaign against opponents, killing the Secretary-General of APROSOMA[34] and when UNAR reported that a Tutsi crowd had been machine-gunned, the accusation was made against the *Belgian* authorities, not against Hutu militants (ibid.: 166, 167 n. 35). There was, however, significant population displacement with 20,000 Tutsi from the north resettling to Bugesera in the south. By the start of 1960, more than 10,000 Tutsi refugees had fled to Uganda, Tanzania, Burundi and the Belgian Congo (Reyntjens, 1994: 27 n. 33). It could be argued that this forced displacement of Tutsi corresponds to Article II(b) and (c) of the UNGC. Similarly, acts of 'deportation' and 'persecution on political ... grounds' committed 'against a civilian population' could, at the time, have been considered as 'crimes against humanity' as defined in the 1950 'Principles of International Law Recognised in the Charter of the Nuremberg Tribunal and in the Judgement of the Tribunal' as adopted by the International Law Commission of the UN.

What emerges from statements by exiles is the limited grasp they have of what constitutes genocide under the UNGC, despite being adamant elsewhere that 1994 was a case of genocide (determined by the same Convention). On four counts, they argue that 1959 was not genocide: not all Tutsi were targeted; the killings were not committed by a 'Hutu state'; the killing of Tutsi was in response to the killing of Hutu leaders; and, there were only a small number of victims. None of these assertions categorically impedes 1959 from being considered genocide under the UNGC. Given that the Convention talks of 'intent to destroy in whole *or in part*, a national, ethnical, racial or religious group' (emphasis added) then targeting only the Tutsi elite does not disqualify the events as genocide. Likewise, the Convention does not indicate that genocide must be committed by a state, it can equally be committed by private individuals (Article IV). Similarly, nowhere in the Convention are retaliatory killings disqualified from being acts of genocide. Finally, the Convention gives no quantitative criteria on the number of victims. Although the exiles are adamant that 1994 was a case of genocide, they appear to possess a limited understanding of the very Convention by which those events were categorised as such.

More regrettable is that by placing the emphasis on the events of 1959 attention is detracted from more pertinent comparisons to be drawn between the genocide of 1994 and the events of 1963. Although the question of refugee figures is contentious (see Reyntjens, 1994: 139-41) when independence was declared on 1 July 1962, it was estimated that 300,000 Tutsi had been displaced, of which 120,000 were outside the country (Guichaoua, 1992: 17ff.). By 1964, a census taken by the UNHCR and the ICRC (in camps under their control) estimated 336,000 refugees *outside* the country (of whom 200,000 were in Burundi; 78,000 in Uganda; 36,000 in Tanzania; and 22,000 in the Belgian Congo [ibid.]). As a whole, the figures amounted to between forty and seventy per cent of the Tutsi population. Between July 1962 and the UNHCR/ICRC report of 1964, the Tutsi refugee population outside Rwanda appears to have grown by 216,000. In other words, sixty-four per cent of Tutsi who found themselves outside Rwanda by 1964 had left between the second half of 1962 and early 1964.

[34] *Association pour la Promotion Sociale de la Masse*, formed 15 February 1959. Although primarily a Hutu party, its progressive 'populist' stance was directed at the 'poor' both Hutu and Tutsi.

What, therefore, had occurred in the intervening period and can parallels be drawn with 1994? In 1963, as in 1990, an armed incursion by Tutsi refugees who had been prevented from returning to Rwanda (the *Inyenzi* in 1963, the RPF in 1990) was manipulated by state officials to incite the massacre of Tutsi civilians. Although in the 1990s four years passed between the invasion by the RPF (October 1990) and the 1994 genocide, the massacre of Tutsi began immediately, with 348 Tutsi killed in Kibilira commune in October 1990. In January 1991 300-1,000 Bagogwe (considered as Tutsi) were murdered (see Chrétien, Dupaquier, Kabanda and Ngarambe, 1995: 175–9; Prunier, 1995: 136). In January and February 1991 further massacres took place in the communes of Mukingo, Kinigi, Gaseke, Giciye, Karago and Mutura. In March 1992 at least 300 Tutsi were killed in Bugesera. Further massacres took place in Kibuye in August 1992 and again in the north-west in December 1992 and January 1993 (see HRW and FIDH, 1999: 87ff.) and between February and August 1993 a further 300 Tutsi and political opponents were killed in the north-west (UN, 1993:10). Thus, although the genocide did not immediately follow the RPF attack, anti-Tutsi pogroms (on the basis that all Tutsi were 'accomplices' of the RPF) began immediately. Similarly, the killing of Tutsi in 1963 was not solely a response to the attack by the *Inyenzi* in that year. *Inyenzi* raids had taken place from 1961 onwards and had resulted in the massacre of Tutsi. After a raid in Byumba in March 1962 'Between 1,000 and 2,000 Tutsi men, women and children were massacred and buried on the spot, their huts burned and pillaged and their property divided among the Hutu population' (Lemarchand, 1970a: 217-19). Thus, the widespread massacre of Tutsi in 1963 was (like the 1994 genocide) the culmination of intermittent violence.

On 21 December 1963, 200 to 300 armed Tutsi refugees crossed into Rwanda from Burundi. With their numbers swollen to 1,000 they got within twelve miles of Kigali before being stopped by the *Garde Nationale* under Belgian command (see Reyntjens, 1985: 461 n. 27). As in 1990 (following the RPF invasion) hundreds of influential Tutsi and certain Hutu were arrested (ibid.: 463). As was to occur in 1994, killing began with the elimination of political opponents (the leadership of the UNAR and RADER).[35] Then, as in 1994, the killing took on an indiscriminate character. While the Rwandan government was to admit to 870 dead, it was estimated that in the period 24–28 December 1963 between 5,000 and 8,000 Tutsi were killed in the single *préfecture* of Gikongoro (ten to twenty per cent of the Tutsi population of that *préfecture* [Reyntjens 1985: 465]). According to figures cited by the World Council of Churches, between 10,000 and 14,000 Tutsi were murdered between December 1963 and January 1964 (see Lemarchand, 1970a: 225; Chrétien, 1985: 158). As Filip Reyntjens notes, however, these 'cold figures hide the extreme violence of which innocent Tutsi were the victims' (1985: 468). According to André Guichaoua, a 'veritable "Tutsi-hunt" took place throughout the country' (1992: 9).[36] An article in *Le Monde* on 4 February 1964, written by Denis Vuillemin (a UNESCO schoolteacher in Butare) stated 'the repression carried out in the *préfecture* of Gikongoro is indeed a true

---

[35] RADER, the *Rassemblement Démocratique Rwandais*, created in 1959 and composed of 'progressive' Tutsi monarchists. Between 15 and 20 of the most important Tutsi politicians (including members of the government) were summarily executed (Lemarchand, 1970a: 223).

[36] This echoes Degni-Ségui's statement in June 1994 that 'Veritable manhunts [for Tutsi] have been carried out' (UN 1994a, para 23).

genocide' (quoted in de Heusch 1995: 7) while a story in *The World Today* was entitled 'Attempted Genocide in Ruanda [*sic*]' (Reyntjens, 1985: 466 n. 48).

An investigation was launched at the request of the Swiss Government. Under the *Procureur de la République* the investigation found 89 individuals guilty, including two ministers and a number of local officials (*préfets* and *burgomestres*). The Rwandan President, Grégoire Kayibanda, refused to accept these findings and ordered a new investigation. The new investigation incriminated only a handful of individuals all of whom received light sentences (Lemarchand, 1970a: 226). One can only speculate whether an international tribunal would have found individuals guilty of crimes of genocide in 1963 in addition to clear crimes against humanity. There remains, however, a striking similarity in the way the massacres of 1963 and 1994 were perpetrated, even if the time-scale in 1963 was considerably shorter than in 1994. From March 1992 onwards, various elements close to Habyarimana initiated the organisation of 'self-defence groups' (see HRW and FIDH, 1999: 102-3, 110–11, 139-40). Likewise, in 1963 the organisation of 'self-defence groups' was put in the hands of *burgomestres* and *préfets*. Just as in 1994 Théodore Sindikubwabo (the interim President during the genocide) travelled to Butare to initiate the genocide, so in 1963 ministers were sent to each *préfecture* to 'clean' the country of a potential fifth column (see Lemarchand, 1970a: 223). In 1963 (as in 1994) radio broadcasts asked the population to be 'constantly' on the 'alert' for Tutsi terrorists and were used to facilitate massacres. In 1963 (as in 1994) references were made in official statements to 'accomplices' of the *Inyenzi* and to 'popular anger' as a justification for killing (see Chrétien, Dupaquier, Kabanda and Ngarambe, 1995: 124, 196, 301; Article XIX, 1996: 138; Prunier, 1995: 139). Echoing the initial failure of the UN to recognise genocide in 1994 (see Barnett, 2003), the UN's Special Representative to Rwanda, Max Dorsinville, absolved the Rwandan Government by emphasising that it did not deny there had been 'excesses' and that 'despite the violent reprisals at the end of December, one cannot speak of elimination or systematic extermination of Tutsi, nor as genocide, as some sources quickly described the events' (UN 1964, quoted in Reyntjens, 1985: 467). A letter from to the Rwandan President from Dorsinville merely stated that he hoped the government 'would do its utmost to calm and pacify ethnic rivalries' (quoted in Lemarchand, 1970a: 227). As an American journalist observed at the time, 'not a finger was raised by the UN, under whose official tutelage the trusteeship region of Rwanda was given its independence' (ibid.). Given these significant similarities, the massacres of 1963 must be seen as a 'preamble to the planned genocide that was to take place thirty years later' (de Heusch, 1995: 5). Even if many features of 1963–4 distinguish it from 1994 (for example, the fact that thousands of Tutsi refugees were *allowed* to leave Rwanda) it remains the case that if Rwandese wish to compare 1994 with massacres in the period around independence, then 1963–4 proposes itself as a more relevant candidate for comparison than 1959.

In contrast to 1963, the events of 1959 had features not present in 1994: the context of independence; participation of a colonial authority; retaliatory killings; and apparently more discriminate targeting. One can envisage, therefore, a more productive and persuasive debate concerning the recurring features of genocidal violence in Rwanda, if actors concentrated on comparing the events of 1963 with those of 1994.

One can only speculate why the members of the Rwandan Government chose to place the emphasis on 1959. The most obvious reason is that 1959 constituted the first episode of inter-ethnic violence and therefore must be accorded pre-eminence. Alternatively, RPF members of the current Rwandan government may want to avoid unfavourable comparison between themselves and the *Inyenzi*, to avoid simplistic accusations that they had not learned the lesson of 1963: if Tutsi outside attack, then Tutsi inside the country will be killed. Catharine Newbury (1998: 16) observes that the victims in 1963–4 had done nothing wrong, but were 'punished as scapegoats because their "ethnic" brothers ... had attacked the country. A similar dynamic was evident in 1990, in the wake of the RPF attack on Rwanda.' As mentioned above, earlier incursions by the *Inyenzi* had led to the massacre of Tutsi. As a consequence, the UNAR (Tutsi) leadership *within* Rwanda and many Tutsi refugees were categorically opposed to the December 1963 attack (Lemarchand, 1970a: 216, 220). Fearing the consequences, even the exiled *mwami* (king) had forbidden the 1963 attack (Reyntjens, 1985: 469).[37]

Another reason why the RPF may wish to detract attention from 1963 is that between 1990 and 1994 genocidal propaganda strongly associated the *Inyenzi* with the RPF. The full name used in the 1960s by Tutsi insurgents based in Burundi was *ingangurarugo ziyemeje kuba ingenzi,* the name of one of the armies of *mwami* Rwabugiri (1860–95) meaning 'the brave ones in the service of the king's army.' Thus, *Ingenzi* ('brave') was deliberately transformed into *Inyenzi* the *Kinyarwandan* word for 'cockroach' (Lemarchand, 2001: n. 18) perhaps because the insurgents 'came out at night' (Reyntjens, 1985: 460). From 1990 onwards, members of the RPF called themselves *Inkotanyi* ('the warriors who fight valiantly'). As with *Ingenzi*, *Inkotanyi* refers to one of *mwami* Rwabugiri's warrior groups, although it is not clear whether the RPF leadership were aware of this historical reference and its monarchist association (Reyntjens, 1994: 91 n. 7).

Despite this, the character of the RPF was very different to that of the *Inyenzi*: twenty to thirty per cent of RPF soldiers were Hutu (Alison des Forges, cited in Taylor, 1999: 85); with the emergence of the democratic opposition in Rwanda (see Eltringham, 2004: 76-8), the RPF could not claim (as the *Inyenzi* had done) that they were the only opposition to a dictatorial regime; and while the *Inyenzi* had been committed *only* to the return of Tutsi refugees, the RPF 'eight point plan' spoke of 'national unity' and the elimination of corruption, placing the return of refugees as only a fifth objective and omitting any reference to the monarchy (see Prunier, 1995: 156). In fact, the RPF ideology was decidedly anti-monarchy. When, the Rwandan Alliance for National Unity (RANU) was formed in Kampala in 1980, it called for the abolition of the monarchy (Cyrus-Reed, 1996: 484). In December 1987, RANU was renamed the Rwandan Patriotic Front. The rift between monarchists and the RPF was clear in October 1990, when Claude Rukeba (son of François Rukeba who had led the *Inyenzi* in Burundi) appeared to denounce the RPF invasion, referring to himself as 'leader of the UNAR' (Reyntjens, 1994: 149). This rift has continued (see HRW, 2000).

Despite these differences, from 1990 onwards, genocidal propaganda associated the *Inkotanyi* with the *Inyenzi*. For example, 'first they were Tutsi, then they came

---

[37] The UNAR newspaper printed in Rwanda – *L'Unité* – declared (in July 1962) that 'UNAR assures the government of its total support in the fight against terrorism'. The party expelled the *Inyenzi* leaders and called on surrounding countries not to allow 'terrorist' bases (Reyntjens, 1985: 462).

as *Inyenzi* ... and finally they have come as *Inkotanyi'* (*RTLM*, 5 June 1994; quoted in Chrétien, Dupaquier, Kabanda and Ngarambe, 1995: 130) and 'There is no difference between the RPF and the *Inyenzi* ... they are the same [people] that attacked us up to 1967 [they] have regrouped and called themselves the RPF' (*RTLM*, 6 April 1994; quoted in Chrétien, Dupaquier, Kabanda and Ngarambe, 1995: 131). One can speculate, therefore, that members of the RPF would not wish to draw attention to the events of 1963–4 to avoid this distortion and distance their pan-Rwandan political project from being portrayed as latter-day *Inyenzi*, 'nostalgic for [monarchical] power, who have never and will never recognise the realities of the 1959 social revolution' (*communiqué* from Col. Déogratias Nsabimana, FAR Chief-of-Staff, 21 September 1992; quoted in HRW and FIDH 1999: 62). By placing the emphasis on 1959, however, members of the Rwandan Government detracted attention from the blatant genocidal character of 1963, which, as a pre-cursor of 1994 would reveal recurring features of genocidal violence in Rwanda.

Conclusion

Both the international and domestic trials of those responsible for the 1994 genocide are premised on a notion of deterrence by ending a 'culture of impunity' (see Schabas, 2000: 447).[38] While the importance of retributive justice and the acknowledgement of individual criminal acts should not be underestimated, the statements considered here interpret the genocide through prisms of analogy and by tracing inveterate continuity which generate fluidity, debate and competing narratives that can, in turn, be interrogated. Such interrogation reveals partiality and suggests we should remain wary of final accounts 'that purport to set the record straight', for after all, 'There is no whole picture that can be "filled in", since the perception and filling of a gap lead to the awareness of other gaps' (Clifford, 1986: 18). This is in contrast to the purported fixity that the designation of crimes and subsequent trials seek to establish. Whatever the success in the rarefied atmosphere of the courtroom of establishing/refining/enforcing the boundaries of international criminal law (Mertus, 2000: 149), key juridical assertions will always generate such 'adversarial stories' (Maier, 2000: 275).

[38] This is a stated aim of the current Rwandan government. Although the Rwandan representative at the UNSC voted against the November 1994 UN Security Council resolution that established the ICTR (UN, 1994b), he endorsed the merits of establishing individual criminal responsibility 'The Tribunal will help national reconciliation and the construction of a new society based on social justice and respect for the fundamental rights of the human person, all of which will be possible only if those responsible for the Rwandese tragedy are brought to justice' (UN, 1994b; see Eltringham, 2004: 145-6). For a critique of the 'deterrence function' of trials see Maogoto (2003: 11-13).

References

Akhavan, Payam (1997) 'Justice and reconciliation in the Great Lakes Region of Africa: The contribution of the International Criminal Tribunal for Rwanda', *Duke Journal of Comparative and International Law* 7(2). <www.law.duke.edu/journals/djcil/articles/djcil7p325.htm>. Accessed 27 February 2005.

Arendt, Hannah (1994 [1963]) *Eichmann in Jerusalem: A Report on the Banality of Evil*, Revised edn, Harmondworth: Penguin.

Article XIX (1996) *Broadcasting Genocide: Censorship, Propaganda and State-Sponsored Violence in Rwanda 1990–1994*, London: Article XIX.

Bardakjian, Kevork (1985) *Hitler and the Armenian Genocide*, Cambridge MA: Zoryan Institute.

Barnett, Michael (2003) *Eyewitness to a Genocide: The United Nations and Rwanda*, Ithaca, NY: Cornell University Press.

Bartov, Omer (1998) 'Defining Enemies, Making Victims: Germans, Jews, and the Holocaust', *The American Historical Review* 103(3): 771-816.

Bartov, Omer (2003) 'Seeking the Roots of Modern Genocide: On the Macro- and Microhistory of Mass Murder', in Robert Gellately and Ben Kiernan (eds) (2003) *The Specter of Genocide: Mass Murder in Historical Perspective*, Cambridge: Cambridge University Press.

Bauer, Yehuda (1998) 'Comparison of Genocides', in Levon Chorbajian and George Shirinian (eds) *Studies in Comparative Genocide*, Basingstoke: Macmillan Press.

Bell-Fialkoff, Andrew (1996) *Ethnic Cleansing*, Basingstoke: Macmillan.

Billig, Michael (1987) *Arguing and Thinking: A Rhetorical Approach to Social Psychology*, Cambridge: Cambridge University Press.

Bowen, Michael, Gary Freeman and Kay Miller (1973) *Passing By: The United States and Genocide in Burundi, 1972*, New York: Carnegie Endowment for International Peace.

Bridgman, Jon M. (1981) *The Revolt of the Hereros*, Berkeley, CA: University of California Press.

Chalk, Frank (1989) 'Genocide in the 20ᵗʰ Century: Definitions of Genocide and their Implications for Predication and Prevention', *Holocaust and Genocide Studies* 4 (2): 149-60.

Chalk, Frank and Kurt Jonassohn (1990) 'The Conceptual Framework', in Frank Chalk and Kurt Jonassohn (eds) *The History and Sociology of Genocide: Analyses and Case Studies*. New Haven CT. and London: Yale University Press.

Chapman, Malcolm, Elizabeth Tonkin and Maryon McDonald (1989) 'Introduction', in Elizabeth Tonkin, Maryon McDonald and Malcolm Chapman (eds) *History and Ethnicity*, London: Routledge.

Chrétien, Jean-Pierre (1985) 'Hutu et Tutsi au Rwanda et au Burundi', in Jean-Loup Amselle and Elikia M'Bokolo (eds) *Au Coeur de l'Ethnie: ethnies, tribalisme et état en Afrique*, Paris: Éditions la Découverte.

Chrétien, Jean-Pierre (2003) *The Great Lakes of Africa: Two Thousand Years of History*, trans. Scott Strauss, New York: Zone Books.

Chrétien, Jean-Pierre, Jean-François Dupaquier, Marcel Kabanda and Joseph Ngarambe (1995) *Rwanda: Les Médias du génocide*, Paris: Éditions Karthala.

Clifford, James (1986) 'Introduction: Partial Truths', in Clifford, James and George E. Marcus (eds) *Writing Culture: The Poetics and Politics of Ethnography*, Berkeley, CA: University of California Press.

Cohn, Norman (1980) *Warrant for Genocide: The Myth of the Jewish World Conspiracy and the Protocols of the Elders of Zion*, New York: Scholars Press.

Conley, John M. and William M. O'Barr (1990) *Rules versus Relationships: The Ethnography of Legal Discourse*, Chicago: University of Chicago Press.

Cyrus-Reed, William (1996) 'Exile, Reform, and the Rise of the Rwandan Patriotic Front', *The Journal of Modern African Studies* 34(3): 479-501.

Dadrian, Vohakn (1995) *The History of the Armenian Genocide: Ethnic Conflict from the Balkans to Anatolia to the Caucasus*, Oxford: Berghahn Books.

de Heusch, Luc (1995) 'Rwanda: responsibilities for genocide', *Anthropology Today* 11(4): 3-7.

Destexhe, Alain (1995) *Rwanda and Genocide in the Twentieth Century*, London: Pluto.

Drechsler. Horst (1980) *Let us Die Fighting: The Struggle of the Herero and the Nama against German Imperialism (1884–1915)*, London: Zed Books.

du Preez, Peter (1994) *Genocide: The Psychology of Mass Murder*, London: Bowerdean.

Dwyer, Leslie and Dequng Santikarma (2003) '"When the World Turned to Chaos": 1965 and Its Aftermath in Bali, Indonesia', in Robert Gellately and Ben Kiernan (eds) *The Specter of Genocide: Mass Murder in Historical Perspective*, Cambridge: Cambridge University Press.

Eltringham, Nigel P. (2004) *Accounting for Horror: Post-Genocide Debates in Rwanda*, London: Pluto Press.

Errington, Shelly (1979) 'Some Comments on Style in the Meaning of the Past', *Journal of Asian Studies*, 38(2): 231–44.

Fein, Helen (1993) *Genocide: A Sociological Perspective*, London: Sage.

Fein, Helen (1994a) 'Genocide, Terror, Life Integrity, and War Crimes', in George J. Andreopoulos (ed.) *Genocide, Conceptual and Historical Dimensions*, Philadelphia, PA: University of Pennsylvania Press.

Fein, Helen (1994b) 'Patrons, Prevention and Punishment of Genocide: Observations on Bosnia and Rwanda', in Helen Fein (ed.) *The Prevention of Genocide: Rwanda and Yugoslavia Reconsidered*, New York: Institute for the Study of Genocide.

Fein, Helen (1998) 'Testing Theories Brutally: Armenia (1915), Bosnia (1992) and Rwanda (1994)', in L. Chorbajian and G. Shirinian (eds) *Studies in Comparative Genocide*, Basingstoke: Macmillan Press.

Freeman, Michael (1991) 'The Theory and Prevention of Genocide', *Holocaust and Genocide Studies* 6(2): 185–99.

Friedlander, Saul (1992) 'Introduction', in Saul Friedlander (ed.) *Probing the Limits of Representation: Nazism and the 'Final Solution'*, Cambridge MA: Harvard University Press.

Gachinya, Faustin (1996a) 'The Tutsi Republic: Will it do Better?' *New Times*, Kigali, July 1996: 7.

Gachinya, Faustin (1996b) 'Let Our People Go!' *New Times*, October 1996.

Gellately, Robert and Ben Kiernan (2003) 'The Study of Mass Murder and Genocide', in Robert Gellately and Ben Kiernan (eds) *The Specter of Genocide: Mass Murder in Historical Perspective*, Cambridge: Cambridge University Press.

Gore, Al (1989) 'An Ecological Kristallnacht: Listen', *New York Times*, 19 March 1989: 27.

Gready, Paul (2003) 'Introduction', in Paul Gready (ed.) *Political Transition: Politics and Culture*, London: Pluto.

Guichaoua, André (1992) *The Problem of the Rwandese Refugees and the Banyarwanda Populations in the Great Lakes Region*, Geneva: UNHCR.

Hajer, Maarten (1995) *The Politics of Environmental Discourse: Ecological Modernisation and the Policy Process*, Oxford: Clarendon Press.

Harff, Barbara (1991) 'Recognising Genocides and Politicides', in Helen Fein (ed.), *Genocide Watch*, New Haven, CT: Yale University Press.

Harff, Barbara and Ted Gurr (1988) 'Research Note: Toward Empirical Theory of Genocides and Politicides: Identification and Measurement of Cases since 1945', *International Studies Quarterly* 32(1988): 359–71.

Harroy, Jean-Paul (1984) *Rwanda: De la féodalité à la démocratie*, Brussels: Hayez.

Hawk, Beverly (1992) *Africa's Media Image*, New York: Praeger.

Hintjens, Helen (1999) 'Explaining the 1994 Genocide in Rwanda', *Journal of Modern African Studies* 37(2): 241-86.

Hinton, Alexander L. (2002) 'Introduction: Genocide and Anthropology', in Alexander L. Hinton (ed.) *Genocide: An Anthropological Reader*, Oxford: Blackwell.

Hirsch, Herbert (1995) *Genocide and the Politics of Memory: Studying Death to Preserve Life*, Chapel Hill, NC and London: The University of North Carolina Press.

Hovannisian, Richard G. (ed.) (1999) *Remembrance and Denial: The Case of the Armenian Genocide*, Detroit, MI: Wayne State University Press.

Hull, Isabel (2003) 'Military Culture and the Production of "Final Solutions" in the Colonies: The Example of Wilhelminian Germany', in Robert Gellately and Ben Kiernan (eds), *The Specter of Genocide: Mass Murder in Historical Perspective*, Cambridge: Cambridge University Press.

Human Rights Watch (HRW) (2000) *Rwanda: The Search for Security and Human Rights Abuses*, April 2000, New York: Human Rights Watch.

Human Rights Watch (HRW) (2003) *Preparing for Elections: Tightening Control in the Name of Unity*, New York: Human Rights Watch.

Human Rights Watch (HRW) and Fédération Internationale des Ligues des Droits de l'Homme (FIDH) (1999) *'Leave None to Tell the story': Genocide in Rwanda*, New York: Human Rights Watch.

International Crisis Group (ICG) (1999) *Five Years After the Genocide in Rwanda: Justice in Question*, Brussels: International Crisis Group.

International Crisis Group (ICG) (2001) *The International Criminal Tribunal for Rwanda: Justice Delayed*, Brussels: International Crisis Group.

International Crisis Group (ICG) (2002) *Tribunal Pénal International Pour le Rwanda: Le Compte à Rebours*, Brussels: International Crisis Group.

IRIN, (2001) RWANDA: *Government puts genocide victims at 1.07 million*, United Nations: Office for the Co-ordination of Humanitarian Affairs Integrated Regional Information Network for Central and Eastern Africa, 19 December 2001.

IRIN, (2004) RWANDA: *Census finds 937,000 died in genocide*. United Nations: Office for the Co-ordination of Humanitarian Affairs Integrated Regional Information Network for Central and Eastern Africa, 2 April 2004.

Jahan, Rounaq (2004 [1997]) 'Genocide in Bangladesh', in Samuel Totten, William S. Parsons and Israel W. Charny (eds) *Century of Genocide: Critical Essays and Eyewitness Accounts*, 2nd edn, Abingdon: Routledge.

JEEAR (1996) 'The media. In The International Response to Conflict and Genocide: Lessons from the Rwanda Experience. Study II Early Warning and Conflict Management', Copenhagen: Steering Committee of the Joint Evaluation of Emergency Assistance to Rwanda. <www.reliefweb.int/library/nordic/book2/pb021h.html>. Accessed 27 February 2005.

Jere-Malanda, Regina (2000) 'Interview with Paul Kagame', *New African Magazine*, July 2000. <www.rwanda1.com/government/interviews_newafricanmag.htm>. Accessed 22 January 2003.

Kagabo, José and Claudine Vidal (1994) 'L'extermination des Rwandais tutsi', *Cahiers d'Études africaines* 34(4): 537–47.

Kaplan, Robert D. (1994a) 'The Coming Anarchy: How Scarcity, Crime, Overpopulation and Disease are Rapidly Destroying the Social Fabric of our Planet', *Atlantic Monthly*, February 1994.

Kaplan, Robert D. (1994b) 'Into the Bloody New World: A Moral Pragmatism for America in an Age of Mini-holocausts', *Washington Post*, 17 April 1994.

Karasira, Peter (1996) 'ICTR Kigali Office in Disarray'. *New Times*, Kigali, October 1996: 12.

Kiernan, Ben (1996) *The Pol Pot Regime: Race, Power and Genocide in Cambodia Under the Khmer Rouge, 1975–79*, Cambridge, MA: Yale University Press.

Kiley, Sam (1994a) 'I Saw Hills Covered with Bodies Resembling Lawns of Flesh', *The Times*, 14 May 1994.

Kiley, Sam (1994b) 'Tutsi Refugees Face Choice of Starvation or Being Murdered', *The Times*, 14 May 1994.

Kuper, Leo (1985) *The Prevention of Genocide*, New Haven: Yale University Press.

Lemarchand, Réné (1970a) *Rwanda and Burundi*, London: Pall Mall Press.

Lemarchand, Réné (1970b) 'The Coup in Rwanda', in Robert I. Rothberg and Ali A. Mazrui (eds) *Protest and Power in Black Africa*, New York: Oxford University Press.

Lemarchand, René (1995) 'Rwanda: The Rationality of Genocide', *Issue: Journal of Opinion* 23(2):8-11.

Lemarchand, René (2001) 'Disconnecting the Threads: Rwanda and the Holocaust Reconsidered', *Idea: A Journal of Social Issues*. <www.ideajournal.com/genocide-2001-lemarchand.html>. Accessed 27 January 2005.

Lemarchand, Réné and David Martin (1974) *Selective Genocide in Burundi*, Report no. 20, London: Minority Rights Group.

Levene, Mark (1999) 'Connecting Threads: Rwanda, the Holocaust and the Pattern of Contemporary Genocide', in R. Smith (ed.) *Genocide: Essays Toward Understanding, Early-Warning and Prevention*, Williamsburg, VA: Association of Genocide Scholars.

Linden, Ian (1997) 'The Church and Genocide: Lessons from the Rwandan Tragedy', in Gregory Baum and Harold Wells (eds) *The Reconciliation of Peoples: Challenge to the Churches*, Geneva: WCC Publications.

Little, Franklin H. (1991) 'Early Warning: Detecting Potentially Genocidal Movements', in Peter Hayes (ed.) *Lessons and Legacies: The Meaning of the Holocaust in a Changing World*, Evanston, ILL: Northwestern University Press.

Longman, Timothy (2004) 'Placing Genocide in Context: Research Priorities for the Rwandan Genocide', *Journal of Genocide Research* 6(1): 29-46.

Maier, Charles S. (1988) *The Unmasterable Past: History, Holocaust and German National Identity*, Cambridge, MA: Harvard University Press.

Maier, Charles S. (2000) 'Doing History, Doing Justice: The Narrative of the Historian and the Truth Commission', in Robert I. Rotberg and Dennis Thompson (eds) *Truth v. Justice: The Morality of Truth Commissions*, Princeton, NJ: Princeton University Press.

Maogoto, Jackson N. (2003) 'The International Criminal Tribunal for Rwanda: A Distorting Mirror; Casting Doubt on its Actor-Oriented Approach in Addressing the Rwandan Genocide', *Africa Journal on Conflict Resolution* 3(1): 55-97.

Meisler, Stanley (1976) 'Holocaust in Burundi, 1972', in Willem A. Veenhoven (ed.) *Case Studies on Human Rights and Fundamental Freedoms: A World Survey*, The Hague: Nijhoff.

Melson, Robert (1992) *Revolution and Genocide: On the Origins of the Armenian Genocide and the Holocaust*, Cambridge: Cambridge University Press.

Melvern, Linda R. (2000) *A People Betrayed: The Role of the West in Rwanda's Genocide*, London: Zed Books.

Mertus, Julie (2000) 'Truth in a Box: The Limits of Justice through Judicial Mechanisms', in Amadiume, Ilfi and Abdullahi An-Na'im (eds) *The Politics of Memory: Truth, Healing and Social Justice*, London: Zed Books.

Mertus, Julie (2003) 'The Politics of Memory and International Trials for Wartime Rape', in Gready, P. (ed.) *Political Transition: Politics and Cultures*, London: Pluto.

Michaels, Marguerite (1994a) 'Descent into Mayhem', *Time Magazine*, 18 April 1994.

Michaels, Marguerite (1994b) 'Streets of Slaughter', *Time Magazine*, 25 April 1994.

Mikekemo, Kamyamanza (1996) 'The Conspiracy of Silence', *New Times*, Kigali, October 1996: 7.

Mikekemo, Kamyamanza (1998) 'Capital Punishment Deserving for Rwandan Genocide Perpetrators', *New Times*, Kigali, 27 April-3 May 1998: 3.

Miles, William (2000) 'Hamites and Hebrews: Problems in "Judaizing" the Rwandan Genocide', *Journal of Genocide Research* 2(1): 107-15.

Minow, Martha (1998) *Between Vengeance and Forgiveness: Facing History after Genocide and Mass Violence*, Boston MA: Beacon.

Mironko, Charles (2004) '*Igetero*: Means and Motive in the Rwandan Genocide', *Journal of Genocide Research* 6(1): 47-60.

Mucyo, J. (1998) 'Clinton's Historic Visit to Rwanda', *New Times*, Kigali, 14–21 March 1998: 1-2.

Munyaneza, Charles (1996) 'Could Genocide Have Been Avoided?' *New Times*, Kigali, January–February 1996: 8.

Nader, Laura (1972) 'Up the Anthropologist: Perspectives Gained from Studying Up', in Dell Hymes (ed.) *Reinventing Anthropology*, New York, Pantheon Books.

New Times Editorial (1996) 'When the Guilty Have no Conscience', *New Times*, Kigali, July 1996: 2.

Newbury, Catharine (1998) 'Ethnicity and the Politics of History in Rwanda', *Africa Today* 45(1): 7-24

Newbury, Catharine and David Newbury (2003) 'The Genocide in Rwanda and the Holocaust in Germany: Parallels and Pitfalls', *Journal of Genocide Research* 5(1): 135-45.

Novick, Peter (2001) *The Holocaust and Collective Memory: The American Experience*, London: Bloomsbury (paperback edition).

Osiel, Mark (1997) *Mass Atrocity, Collective Memory, and the Law*, London: Transaction Publishers.

Power, Samantha (2003) '*A Problem from Hell*': America and the Age of Genocide, London: Flamingo.

Prunier, Gérard (1995) *The Rwanda Crisis: History of a Genocide (1959-1994)*, Expanded edn, London: C. Hurst and Co.

Reyntjens, Filip (1994) *L'Afrique des Grands Lacs en Crise Rwanda-Burundi 1988-1994*, Paris: Karthala.

Reyntjens, Filip (1985) *Pouvoir et Droit au Rwanda. Droit public et évolution politique 1916-1973*, Brussels: Musée Royal de l'Afrique Centrale, Tervuren.

Ross, Fiona C. (2003a) 'The Construction of Voice and Identity in the South African Truth and Reconciliation Commission', in Paul Gready (ed.) (2003) *Political Transition: Politics and Cultures*, London: Pluto.

Ross, Fiona C. (2003b) *Bearing Witness: Women and the Truth and Reconciliation Commission in South Africa*, London: Pluto Press.

Ruhumuriza, Ellis (1996) 'How France Covered up Genocide in Rwanda', *New Times*, Kigali, 16–25 December 1996: 8.

Sanford, Victoria (2003) 'What is Written in Our Hearts': Memory, Justice and the Healing of Fragmented Communities', in Paul Gready (ed.) *Political Transition: Politics and Culture*, London: Pluto.

Saro-Wiwa, Ken (1989) *On a Darkling Plain: An Account of the Nigerian Civil War*, London: Saros International Publishers.

Schabas, William (2000) *Genocide in International Law*, Cambridge: Cambridge University Press.

Service, Elman R. (1962) *Primitive Social Organization: An Evolutionary Perspective*, New York: Random House.

Service, Elman R. (1975) *Origins of the State and Civilization: The Process of Cultural Evolution*, New York: W. W. Norton and Company.

Sluka, Jeffrey A. (1999) 'State Terror and Anthropology', in Jeffrey A. Sluka (ed.) *Death Squad: The Anthropology of State Terror*, Philadelphia, PA: University of Pennsylvania Press.

Smith, Roger W. (1987) 'Human Destructiveness and Politics: The Twentieth Century as an Age of Genocide', in I. Wallimann and N. Dobkowski (eds) *Genocide and the Modern Age: Etiology and Case*

Studies of Mass Death, New York: Greenwood.

Smith, Roger W. (1992) 'The Armenian Genocide: Memory, Politics, and the Future', in Richard G. Hovannisian (ed.) *The Armenian Genocide: History, Politics, Ethics*, New York: St Martin's Press.

Smith, Roger W. (1998) 'State Power and Genocide Intent: On the Uses of Genocide in the Twentieth Century', in Levon Chorbajian and George Shirinian (eds) *Studies in Comparative Genocide*, Basingstoke: Macmillan Press.

Stanton, George (1998) *Eight Stages of Genocide*, Washington DC: Genocide Watch. <www.genocidewatch.org/8stages.htm>. Accessed 27 February 2005.

Staub, Ervin (1989) *The Roots of Evil: The Origins of Genocide and Other Group Violence*, Cambridge: Cambridge University Press.

Steiner, George (1977) *Language and Silence*, New York: Atheneum.

Swarns, Rachel L. (1994) 'A Debate Over Definitions: "Cuban Holocaust" Memorial Dismays Many Jews', *Miami Herald*, 6 November 1994: 1A.

Taylor, Christopher (1999) *Sacrifice as Terror: The Rwandan Genocide of 1994*, Oxford and New York: Berg.

Taylor, John G. (2003) '"Encirclement and Annihilation": The Indonesian Occupation of East Timor', in Robert Gellately and Ben Kiernan (eds) *The Specter of Genocide: Mass Murder in Historial Perspective*, Cambridge, Cambridge University Press.

United Nations (UN) (1960) UN Visiting Mission to Trust Territories in East Africa: Report on Ruanda-Urundi, UN Doc. T/551.

United Nations (UN) (1993) Report by B. W. Ndiaye, Special Rapporteur, on his Mission to Rwanda from 8 to 17 April 1993, 11 August 1993, UN Doc. E/CN.4/1994/7/Add.1. <www.preventgenocide.org/prevent/UNdocs/ndiaye1993.htm>. Accessed 27 February 2005.

United Nations (UN) (1994a) Report on the situation of human rights in Rwanda submitted by Mr. R. Degni-Ségui, Special Rapporteur of the Commission on Human Rights, under paragraph 20 of Commission resolution E/CN.4/S-3/1 of 25 May 1994, 28 June 1994, UN Doc. E/CN.4/1995/7. <http://193.194.138.190/Huridocda/Huridoca.nsf/TestFrame/d32234b56f1324558025671600 3356b6?Opendocument>. Accessed 27 February 2005.

United Nations (UN) (1994b) Verbatim record of the 3453rd meeting of the Security Council, 8 November 1994, UN Doc. S/PV.3453.

United Nations (UN) (1994c) Security Council Resolution Establishing the ICTR. 8 November 1994, UN Doc. S/RES/955 (1994). <www.ictr.org/ENGLISH/Resolutions/955e.htm> Accessed 27 February 2005.

Victor, K. (1998) 'Bisesero: a symbol of resistance', *New Times*, Kigali, 17-24 April 1998: 1.

Vidal, Claudine (1998) 'Le genocide des Rwandais tutsi et l'usage public de l'histoire', *Cahiers d'Etudes africaines*, 38(2-4): 653-64.

Visathan, Victor (1996) 'Hutuland Tutsiland?' *New Times*, Kigali, January-February 1996: 12.

Watson, Paul (1994) 'Tribal Feuds Throw Rwanda in Crisis', *Toronto Star*, 23 February 1994.

Weissman, Stephen (1997) 'Living with Genocide: The U.S. Could Play a Significant Role in Stopping African Genocide-but It Doesn't', *Tikkun* 12(4): 53-68.

Whitaker, Benjamin (1985) *Revised and Updated Report on the Question of the Prevention and Punishment of the Crime of Genocide*, 2 July 1985, UN Doc. E/CN.4/Sub.2/1985/6. <www.preventgenocide.org/ prevent/UNdocs/whitaker>. Accessed 27 February 2005.

Wilson, Richard (1997) 'Representing Human Rights Violations: Social Contexts and Subjectivities', in Richard Wilson (ed.) *Human Rights, Culture and Context, Anthropological Perspectives*, London: Pluto Press.

Wilson, Richard (2001) *The Politics of Truth and Reconciliation in South Africa: Legitimizing the Post-Apartheid State*, Cambridge: Cambridge University Press.

Xinhua, (1998) 'Extradite Criminals says the Government', *New Times*, Kigali, 11-18 May 1998: 2.

5

Darfur
Peace, Genocide & Crimes Against Humanity in Sudan

DOUGLAS H. JOHNSON

The war in Darfur has become an analytical problem for the international community. Coinciding as it did with the commemoration of two historic genocides – ten years after Rwanda and sixty years after the Nazi holocaust – it stirred the world's conscience in a way that no other report of slavery, mass civilian deaths or other atrocities in the Sudan did during the previous twenty-one years of civil war in the South. The recognition of 'genocide', however, became entangled in the arguments for and against intervention; for the United Nations Convention on Genocide (1948) requires the international community to act once genocide is recognised. 'Genocide' thus became less an objective description of events, and more an indicator of political priorities. A purely racial definition of genocide sometimes has been applied on both sides of the argument. 'Race – not religion – is the fundamental fault line in Sudan...' an African commentator declared, urging the African Union to put an end to the racist hypocrisy of Afro-Arab states and the genocidal policies of the government of Sudan (Mutua, 2004). A more conservative approach was equally certain in invoking the immutable categories of race and tribe as arguments *against* such international action. William Lind, the Director of the Center for Cultural Conservatism, for instance, propounded the 'realist' attitude that the conflict was the outcome of peoples fighting for 'their primary loyalty' of tribe and race, something they had done since 'history's dawn' (Lind, 2004). Some on the left, particularly those opposed to Western aggression in the Third World, adapted this tribal argument to the older idea of the desert and the sown, to explain Darfur as an ecological problem that cannot be fixed by external intervention (Steele, 2004).[1] It is not surprising, therefore, that there is no consensus about the events in Darfur, and descriptions have run the gamut from genocide (Crawford, 2004) to the lesser categories of ethnic cleansing (Human Rights Watch, 2004b) and 'crimes against humanity' (United Nations, 2005).

Genocide or no genocide, one argument against intervention that Western

---

[1] In this case Steele cited my earlier description of droughts and the struggle for new home territories in the 1980s (Johnson 2003: 139-41) in support for this ecological interpretation of the current war in Darfur. He chose to ignore my linking that period of environmental stress to the structural marginalisation of Darfur within the Sudanese state, and the increasing use of a racial ideology by external actors in Darfur's internal conflicts.

diplomats and journalists frequently put forward was that intervention over Darfur threatened to derail the peace negotiations between Khartoum and the Sudan People's Liberation Movement (SPLM), then winding their tortuous way to a resolution in Kenya. The conflicts in the South and Darfur, it was almost universally agreed, were unrelated and required separate solutions. Peace in the South was seen as something that could be achieved even as war in Darfur escalated.

So, is there a connection between Darfur and the longer-running southern civil war? Or is Darfur merely the outbreak of ethnic violence, further evidence of the fragmentation of the Sudan into its component tribal parts?

I start from four premises. First, despite what diplomats and journalists insist, the war in Darfur *is* related to the longer civil wars in the South, the Nuba Mountains and Blue Nile, and its timing is connected to the peace process that culminated in a formal peace agreement in January 2005. Second, as Paul Richards has recently pointed out, the 'new wars' of the post-Cold War era happen on the margins of weak and retreating states (Richards, 2005b: 13). Third, again to cite Richards, 'war does not break out because conditions happen to be "right", but because it has to be organised... The venture has to be planned... This is the work of specific groups in society; understanding the character, organization and beliefs of these groups, and their impact on other groups supporting, resisting or victimised by their activities is an essential task for the analyst' (Richards, 2005b: 4). Fourth, as Jan Ovesen has written about Cambodia, to understand 'genocide' one must analyse not just the violent events themselves, but the violence that preceded, and even followed, them (Ovesen, 2005). Weaving 'these events back into their social context may help us see important connections with "low intensity" violent conflict' (Richards, 2005b: 14).

The Antecedents to Darfur's War

The Sudan as a nation is a constellation of underdeveloped regions and the violence and civil strife that has spread throughout many parts of the country since the early 1980s can be seen as a sequence of interlocking civil wars (Johnson, 2003). The grievances of the regions began to be articulated soon after the Sudan's independence and gave birth to a fledgling federalist movement in the 1950s which began to attract support from the ethnically and religiously dissimilar regions of the South, the Nuba Mountains, the East and Darfur before the Sudan's first military government put an end to parliamentary democracy in 1958. From then on the central government viewed federalism as tantamount to secessionism and suppressed it vigorously.

With the negotiated end to the first civil war in the South in 1972 and the creation of the semi-autonomous Southern region, federalism was revived in its more muted form of decentralisation and applied to the whole country. But the decentralisation that created regional governments throughout the northern Sudan was a sham. Democratic choice was limited and regional governors were still appointed by the president and military ruler, Jaafar Nimeiri. The central government delegated responsibility for basic services to the regions, but not the revenues or revenue raising capacity. Resources were retained and redistributed by the central government.

Darfur was to suffer particularly from this arrangement during the famine of 1984–5. It had been a single province until 1976, when it was divided into two during an earlier decentralisation programme, and then reconstituted as single region in 1981. This coincided with a sharp decline in rainfall throughout the 1970s, affecting Northern Darfur at first, but moving progressively southwards. The drought precipitated a movement of peoples out of the north into the southern farming belt, and this was further complicated by refugee movements from Chad in the west, as many armed nomadic peoples resettled in Darfur during the Chadian civil war. During this time the central government failed to provide Darfur with the necessary financial and material resources with which to deal with displacement and famine relief. It had also previously abolished the structures of tribal administration, whose authorities had routinely negotiated and regulated seasonal and temporary movements of persons and livestock (Prunier, 1991; Harir, 1993: 20-2).

It should be emphasised that at first the pastoralists displaced by drought included Arabs as well as the non-Arab Zaghawa, and the land they began to encroach on in the central farming belt belonged to farming people (e.g. Fur; Birgid; Tunjur) as well as pastoralists (e.g. Rizeigat), Arabs (e.g. Rizeigat; Bani Helba) as well as non-Arabs (e.g. Fur, etc.) (Harir, 1993: 21). The conflicts that developed over nomad occupation of abandoned farmland at this time could be described as 'tribal', in that they involved disputes over territory belonging to one group or another, but they were not 'racial': there was not a general mobilisation of 'Arabs' against 'Africans'. If anything, the conflict was at first identified as being primarily between the pastoral Zaghawa and the agricultural Fur (Harir, 1993: 23-4), two groups that are now identified as 'African' and are allied in the current struggle against the Khartoum government.

It was then that the politics of the Chadian civil war began to have an impact on Darfur. Chad's civil war, ostensibly between an Arab minority in the north and an African majority in the south, had been internationalised in the 1980s as a battleground for the indirect confrontation between Libya and the United States. The US and its ally, Nimeiri, bolstered Hissen Habré's non-Arab government against Libya's expansionist policies. While US military assistance flowed into southern Chad through Darfur, Qadaffi formed an Islamic Legion first to take control of, and then push south from, northern Chad. The recruits to this Islamic Legion came from many Arabic-speaking groups of the Sahel and the Sudan, including exile Umma party opponents to Nimeiri, and pastoralists who straddled the Chad-Darfur border. The ideology they were inculcated with was not just pan-Islamic, but pan-Arab, stemming from Qadaffi's political vision of creating an 'Arab belt' across the Sahel. With the dismantling of the Islamic Legion following Libya's defeat in 1988, many of its former members – armed, trained, and imbued with a new ideology – crossed into Darfur (de Waal, 2004: 26).

The state retreated further after the fall of Nimeiri in 1985. It increasingly abdicated its responsibilities, especially in the preservation of public order, during the government led by the Umma party of Sadiq al-Mahdi (1986–9). With easy access to arms from the Chadian civil war, many groups, including the Fur, Zaghawa and Arab pastoralists, armed themselves and formed their own militias. In this many received external support, either from the Libyan government (who still saw them as allies in Chad), or from political parties such as the Umma and

National Islamic Front (NIF), based in Khartoum (Harir, 1993: 23-4; Verney, 1995: 29). The Arab Alliance, formed in 1987, was founded by former members of the Islamic Legion (de Waal, 2004: 26). It was during this time that land grabs by Arab militias (*janjawid*)[2] became more frequent, and an explicit racist ideology transplanted Qadaffi's idea of a Sahelian 'Arab belt' into Darfur, now seeing itself as confronting the 'Black (*zuruq*) belt' of non-Arab farmers (Harir, 1994; Verney, 1995: 30). The first targets of the *janjawid* were the Fur, and a description of *janjawid* tactics published in 1994 now has a familiar ring:

> The *modus operandi* of the Arab *janjawid* and knights [*fursan*] was not only characterized by brutality towards fellow human beings as long as they were Fur, it also opted for a complete destruction of orchards, farms, vegetable fields and villages. It was deliberately designed to end up in the migration of most of the Fur from their home territory which could have become a *de facto* Arab home-territory as a result. In fact, the extension of the Arab Belt as an ideology was reinforced by the naming of the territories temporarily occupied during this war as 'liberated territories'. Whole Fur *omodiyas* (districts) were occupied after their populations were forced to migrate under the threat of extinction by horse-mounted and gun-blazing Arab *janjawid*. (Harir, 1994: 181-2)

Throughout this time, of course, the escalating conflict in Darfur was being played out against the background of civil war in the South, which had broken out in 1983. The war in the South soon expanded into the 'northern' areas of the Nuba Mountains and Blue Nile, and established patterns and precedents that were ultimately transferred to Darfur.

National Objectives and Tribal Militias in the Civil War

The Sudan is an Arab county, according to John Ryle's apt analogy, in the same way that the United States is an Anglo-Saxon country (Ryle, 2004). The founding mythologies of each country give a streamlined genealogy that masks the varied origins of their inhabitants. In the Sudan the history of Arab migration is represented in the myth of the 'wise stranger', a wandering Muslim holy man who is granted land by a local sultan, marries the sultan's daughter or sister, introduces Islam, and superimposes an Arab patriline on the ruling family (James, 1977: 120-4). In the process of Islamisation of the northern Sudan political legitimacy was bolstered by establishing a genealogical link to a Muslim – which ultimately meant Arab – ancestor, and genealogies establishing such links have been manufactured for generations, including in the 'Baggara' belt[3] of the western Sudan (Cunnison, 1971).

The reality of the genealogies founded by 'wise strangers' was somewhat

[2] There is some confusion over the origin and meaning of the term *janjawid*. It is applied to the militias by their victims, not by themselves, and has been widely used to describe any group of marauding bandits. As such the government has been able to deny any connection with the militias, on the grounds that *janjawid* are bandits, and 'bandits' is how the government regularly characterises rebel forces, whether in the South or Darfur. An historical equivalent to the *janjawid* would be the Confederate 'bushwhackers' who operated in the absence of regular Confederate troops during the American Civil War in Missouri and Kansas, but in support of Confederate strategic aims and the Confederate state government in exile (Fellman 1989). Reciting the phrase 'Jesse James was a *janjawid*,' will remind the reader of the character of the *janjawid* in all their manifestations.

[3] Baggara (*baqqara*) is Arabic for cattle keeper, and refers to the cattle- (as opposed to camel-) keeping semi-nomadic peoples of Kordofan and Darfur.

different. Many of the names of the late medieval founding 'Arab' ancestors of the peoples of the central and northern Nile valley in fact date from the eighteenth century, and can be found on land grants issued by the sultans of Sennar, at a time when the kingdom of Sennar was itself in retreat. The sultans conferred a grant of land to local leaders, who by this means gained recognition of a territory, or *dar* (homeland), of their own. This in effect created new tribes around the state's newly recognised sheikhs (Spaulding, 1985). This system of incorporating new tribes through the granting of new territory was later to be revived by the current regime in Khartoum.

Political legitimacy has been harder to establish in post-independence Sudan, where many peoples are not Muslim, and among those who are, many do not claim to be Arab. Post-independence governments have tended to try to forge a national identity based on Islam and Arabism,[4] and in this they have frequently been assisted by more powerful and richer regional neighbours, such as Nasser's Egypt, Qaddafi's Libya, Saddam Hussein's Iraq, and Saudi Arabia. Resistance to the forced spread of Islam and Arabism have been strong factors in the outbreaks of both civil wars in the South.

The national project of linking Islam with Arabism was one element in the development of the use of militias during the second civil war in the South and it took advantage of environmental and economic pressures along the North's borderlands with the South. This was the recruitment and organisation of militias from among the Baggara Arab tribes of Kordofan and Darfur (the Missiriya and Rizeigat in particular) who shared seasonal pastures with the Dinka of Bahr al-Ghazal and Abyei. The Baggara had suffered the contraction of their own grazing areas throughout the 1970s and 1980s from two sides: from drought caused by reduced rainfall and from the alienation of land by the government for use in mechanised farming schemes. In organising militias to fight against the SPLA and their civilian base further South, the government took advantage of the Baggara distress (caused as much by government policies as by drought) and offered them a means whereby they could pass on their own losses to the government's enemies. The militias were rarely used in military confrontations with organised forces of the SPLA. Most often they attacked the livelihood of the civilian populations of the South, in what became a war of targeting resources (Johnson, 2003: 151-9).

The tactics of the militias in Abyei, northern Bahr al-Ghazal and the Nuba Mountains were to strike at civilian settlements, seizing livestock and people, burning crops and houses. The aim was not only to deprive the SPLA of a civilian support-base, but to drive civilians permanently out of whole territories, making these areas available either for government occupation or militia settlement, or both. The work of government militias was the principal cause of the 1998 Bahr al-Ghazal famine (Human Rights Watch, 1999). In a revival of the old *dar* land grants of the kingdom of Sennar, a number of militias have been encouraged to participate by offers of land seized in war. Groups of West African Muslim 'Fellata' (Fulani) migrants, who have never before been accepted in the Northern Sudan, have been offered their own *dars* carved out of land occupied in the Nuba Mountains and Abyei. Other land-hungry groups, such as the Missiriya of Kordofan, also have been offered land taken from the Dinka in Abyei.

---

[4] See Abd al-Rahim (1969) for the classic statement of the essential link between Arabism and Sudanese nationalism.

Initially militias were surrogate forces, but they became part of a more systematic political project in the 1990s with the creation of the Popular Defence Forces (PDF). The PDF often use the tribal idiom in their organisation, but they are more often subversive of older tribal social structures. After seizing power in 1989 the NIF attempted to recruit former Umma Party supporters among the Baggara into their militias as a way of undermining Umma support in their traditional heartland. They also armed jobless youth and encouraged them to ignore the customary sheikhly power structure within their tribe. In fact, many of the militia leaders have no 'tribal' base at all, but are from the merchant class and have gone into the raising of militias – much as European entrepreneurs of the Renaissance and the Thirty Years War did – as an extension of business. As we have noted above, the government has often used the militias as a colonising force, seizing control of areas of potential or actual wealth (the rain-fed lands of the Nuba Mountains, the pastures of the Kordofan-Bahr al-Ghazal border, the oil fields in Kordofan and Upper Nile) through the deployment of militias. It is a method by which the regime retains control over an increasingly restless and marginalised Sudanese population (Lavergne, 2004).

The PDF were under the direct control of the security forces, not the military, and recruits were not only given military instruction, but religious indoctrination (de Waal, 1991). They thus became the front line manifestation of the Islamist/ Arabist national project. As such their role was redefined, not as plundering, but as *jihad*, and militiamen were elevated to the status of *mujahidin* in government propaganda, as well as in their own eyes (Ryle, 2004).

This was to lead to two further developments in the war against civilians. The first was the extension of *jihad* to the government's Muslim opponents. Muslims who opposed the government, especially in the war in the Nuba Mountains, were declared unbelievers, whom it was legal to kill (African Rights, 1995: 289).[5] The second was the legitimation of rape as a weapon of war. Militia forces commonly raped Dinka and Nuba women, whether in their own villages or in the 'Peace Camps' established in government controlled areas. Rape was primarily an assault on family and social cohesion of the communities under attack (African Rights, 1995: 221-42). But in so far as rape was forced on non-Arab peoples (whether or not they were Muslim), it was also a re-enactment of the myth of Arab expansion into Sudan and the insertion of Arab patrilines among non-Arab peoples (cf. James, 1977).

The Southern Peace Process

The official SPLM position has been that they were fighting for a 'New Sudan', which was specifically non-sectarian, and where power was not concentrated in the hands of a particular group within the North. Secession for the South was presented as a secondary option, should the 'New Sudan' be unobtainable. In effect the SPLM has demanded that the Northern parties choose between a unity, which would include the South, or an Islamic state, which would exclude it. Negotiations on this basis were about to start between the SPLM and the

---

[5] It should be noted that the SPLA included Muslim soldiers from the outset of the civil war, and the *fatwa* declaring insurgent Muslims apostates applied to all war fronts.

government of Sadiq al-Mahdi when the NIF of Hassan al-Turabi and a faction of the army under Omar Bashir seized power in a coup in 1989.

When face-to-face negotiations finally did take place at Abuja in 1992, secession had moved up higher in the SPLA agenda. A proposal for self-determination for the South, the Nuba Mountains and Blue Nile was flatly rejected by the government delegation, who announced that separation could only come through 'the mouth of the gun', not through negotiation (Wöndu and Lesch, 2000: 51). This was widely reported at the time, and the government's refusal to accept the prospect of self-determination as one avenue for ending the war was a major factor in stalling peace negotiations for the next ten years. It was largely because of international pressure, coinciding with the fall-out of the war against terrorism, that led to peace talks resuming under IGAD chairmanship at Machakos in Kenya in 2002.[6] The compromise that was brokered at Machakos in July 2002 finally recognised that the retention of an Islamic state in the Sudan would require the reciprocal acceptance of the right of self-determination for the South.

This framework did not apply to the 'Three Areas' outside 'the South' where the SPLA was active: Abyei (a Dinka district in Western Kordofan), the Nuba Mountains (Southern Kordofan) and Blue Nile. The SPLA leadership in both the Nuba Mountains and Blue Nile were Muslim, as were many of their soldiers. They articulated their grievances with Khartoum as a rejection of both the Islamist interpretation of Islam – the position of the current government – and the racist ideology of 'Arabism' aligned with Islam that a succession of governments in Khartoum had adopted in fighting the wars in the South.

The SPLM/A could not ignore the demands of their constituents in the Three Areas and therefore insisted that they be included on the agenda for a comprehensive peace. Khartoum resisted, but finally had to accede, not only because of the SPLA presence in each area, but because of international pressure. Despite this, they continued to try to evade the issue throughout the next two years, first by refusing to send a negotiating delegation to the first session at which the Three Areas were to be discussed in January 2003, and then by raising procedural questions at subsequent sessions. That the last protocol to be agreed and signed in May 2004 (again, due to international pressure) was about the Three Areas is proof of the political sensitivity of the issue.

That agreement set up the basis of semi-autonomous regional governments in the Nuba Mountains and Blue Nile. While neither region will have the right to vote to secede (and neither has asked for that right), the local autonomy provisions do mean that there is the possibility that either region – or both – will set themselves as non-Islamist enclaves within the Islamic state of the North. It is precisely this precedent that Khartoum has tried to avoid, because it undermines the project of an unitary Islamic state for the North. If Blue Nile and the Nuba Mountains were to opt out of the Islamic state as it is currently constructed, how could that right not be extended to other regions as well, including the mixed population of the nation's capital, Khartoum?

In February 2003, just as negotiations over the Three Areas began, Darfur blew up over many of the same issues that the SPLM representatives of the Nuba Mountains and Blue Nile had just presented to the international observers at the

[6] The Inter-Governmental Authority for Development, representing the governments of Kenya, Uganda, Ethiopia and Eritrea, had initiated a forum for peace talks in 1993.

Kenya peace talks. The timing was not lost on politically active Darfuris, who soon petitioned to be included in the IGAD talks (Darfur Human Rights Forum 2003). Khartoum responded to Darfur and the peace talks in two ways. It tried to crush the resurgence of fighting in Darfur as quickly and completely as possible so that there would be no question of extending the Nuba/Blue Nile option to Darfur. It also dragged out the peace talks (especially when it came to the Three Areas) to allow the government time to deal with Darfur and avoid it being complicated by international interventions, whether diplomatic, humanitarian or military.

The War in Darfur

The war in Darfur, as we have already seen, did not start in February 2003 when the Darfur Liberation Front launched a new offensive and renamed itself the Sudan Liberation Movement/Army (SLM/A). Government interventions in Darfur after 1989 had failed to deal with the land issue, which lay at the heart of many local conflicts. There was a further retreat of government from the processes of mediation in favour of direct intervention in disputes through support for specific militias. The government at first did not take a consistent line in siding with one or other group, but did so more out of a concern to display its power than to resolve issues on the ground. This led to a further erosion of government legitimacy among many of the peoples of Darfur (Harir, 1993: 25), especially as increasingly the government sided with and supplied the militias of Arab groups (Ryle, 2004). By 2002, other communities not involved in the original clashes of the 1980s, such as the Masalit, were reporting not only increased depopulation of their territory through raids by Arab militias, but increased arrest and detention of community leaders by the government (Baum, 2002). There was more to the Darfur crisis than events in Darfur. The government's response was influenced by events at the heart of government as well

One of Turabi's political strategies had been to recruit Darfuris into NIF, urging them to reject the older sectarian parties (especially the Umma Party) that had alternated governing the Sudan since independence. Many Darfuris thus participated in the central government through party affiliation as a way of overcoming Darfur's regional marginalisation. However, the perception grew among Darfuris that Khartoum was not, in fact, including them in the centre of government, nor was the new highly centralised federal system truly devolving power. The fragmentation of the Islamist movement with the split between Turabi and Bashir in 1999 only deepened the disillusionment of Darfur Islamists, who felt, once again, marginalised, with their own interests subordinated to the interests of the commercial and political elite of the central Nile Valley.

This was the allegation of 'The Black Book', surreptitiously circulated by the new Justice and Equality Movement (JEM) in Khartoum in 2000. It was a critique, not of the 'Arabs' in Darfur, but of the dominance of a specific alliance of three tribes from the Northern region (the Shaigiya, Ja'aliyin and Danagla), who between them have dominated the upper levels of commerce, government and the army since independence. It was not just this general complaint that motivated the writers of the Black Book, but the decline of western Sudanese (e.g.

Darfuri) representation in the government in the first ten years since the NIF coup, in which they participated, and the progressive impoverishment of the western regions as a result of specific policies of the government which, so they claimed, had further concentrated economic power in the hands of the elite of the Northern region ('Seekers of Truth and Justice', 2004 [2000]: 1-2, 7-9).

The Darfur opposition may have shared common grievances, and had a common perception of the cause of their marginalisation, but they had more difficulty in creating a common front. This is in part because of the difficulty of communication between the internal and external opposition groups. The Sudan Federal Democratic Alliance, led by Darfur's former governor Ahmad Ibrahim Diraige, had established training camps in Eritrea along with other groups of the opposition National Democratic Alliance as early as 1997. The Darfur Liberation Front (aka SLM/A) was able to establish a military presence inside Darfur, close to the Chad border, in part through its links with the SPLA. The JEM included many former NIF members among its founders. The political divisions of the previous twenty years, which saw people from Darfur ranged against each other along the political spectrum, were difficult to overcome. But another factor was the clandestine nature of recruitment imposed on the internal opposition because of the pervasiveness of the state security apparatus. Both the SLM/A and JEM tended to recruit through family and personal ties, rather than through mass organisation. Given this personal network of initial recruitment both groups are also highly mixed, with Fur, Zaghawa and others being found in both organisations.

Many of the people who sided with Turabi against his erstwhile lieutenant, Ali Uthman Muhammad Taha, and President Bashir in the internal NIF split were Muslims from Darfur. The government therefore was doubly paranoid about the escalation of the fighting, because they feared Turabi's hand stirring up trouble in Darfur. The government was also aware that because of the high proportion of soldiers from Darfur in the national army, the army itself would become even more unreliable the longer the Darfur conflict went on. This was certainly one incentive to rely on the militia network rather than the conscript army.

The militias of the PDF were placed in the front line, with active support from units of the army and air force. Their main targets were civilian villages, not armed units of the main guerrilla forces. The tactics were the same as those used earlier in Bahr al-Ghazal and the Nuba mountains, and those used by independent militias in Darfur in the 1980s. As in these earlier theatres of conflict, there are reports of rewards of territory being granted to the militias, including some drawn from immigrant groups from Chad; thus tying them to the personal leadership of the state in much the same way the land grants of the old sultanates did.

For those familiar with the war in the South, Darfur followed a familiar pattern. Clashes between a local resistance army and government forces were first dismissed by the government as banditry, then as tribal fighting. International attention focused on those groups identified as Arab tribal militias, the colloquially-named *janjawid*, who were accused of terrorising various groups of Muslim African farmers. As in the South, the fighting was given a racial inter-pretation, of Arab against African (Amnesty International, 2003a&b, 2004a&b; Human Rights Watch, 2004a&b; International Crisis Group, 2004).

It was counter insurgency on the cheap, with an introduction of the racist element already seen in the use of militias in Bahr al-Ghazal and the Nuba Mountains, even against Muslim peoples (de Waal, 2004: 26). The expression of this racism is particularly evident in the widespread rape of Muslim women from non-Arab groups (Amnesty International, 2004d), whether in the act of rape, when victims are also verbally insulted as black slaves, or in denying allegations of rape. Musa Hilal, the leader of one of the largest militias repudiated such claims, asking, '"Why would we rape them? They disgust us." He adds that black women have such wanton sexual habits, as can be seen from the way they dance, that there would be no need for anyone to use force with them' (Anon, 2004: 47).

But despite this recourse to a combination of racist ideology and cupidity to gain the active complicity of militiamen, not all of the Arab pastoralists of Darfur have been so easily turned against their neighbours. The Rizeigat Baggara of Southern Kordofan have been ready and willing participants in military activity against the Dinka pastoralists to the south, but many have refused to use their militia organisations against their farming neighbours to the north.

Conclusion

If we 'weave' the most recent events in Darfur back into their social and political context we can see in the Sudan, as Ovesen sees in Cambodia (Ovesen, 2005: 37), that what is now called genocide is part of a long continuum of political violence. What has happened in Darfur is part of an established – and ongoing – pattern of state-directed violence, first adopted in the South, but also in the other areas where the SPLA has been active, which has increased the circle of the state's enemies by defining them through exclusion. As Paul Richards has stated above, this war was organised, it did not just happen. The environmental distress of Darfur was not the cause of the conflict, but merely a contributing factor that successive governments in Khartoum have used to their advantage in offering incentives to locally raised militias – now in Darfur, but earlier in Kordofan and Bahr al-Ghazal. The racial antagonism between 'Arab' and 'African' does not lie at the heart of the local war. The 'Arabs' that black Darfuris feel have marginalised them are not their neighbours, but the elite of the central Nile valley who have formed the majority of the leadership of the parliamentary and military governments since independence. The racial difference between black 'Africans' and black 'Arabs' in Darfur has been part of the manipulation of the national project emanating from the centre that has equated Islam with Arabism, reinforced by the specific manifestation of pan-Arabism promoted by Libya during the Chadian civil war. The *janjawid* militias obtain both their inspiration and their military strength not from their ideology and sense of racial superiority, but from government supplies and training, and the coordinated support from the government air force and army.

A manipulated sense of difference is not enough to explain recent events. There needs to be a motive or a reward for complicity. In this case the state has provided tangible rewards – in land, in loot, in local political patronage – to the militia leaders and their recruits. Just as the current regime once played on the Darfuris' sense of political exclusion from the state to recruit them into the movement that seized power in Khartoum, so they have now played on the Arab pastoralists' sense of local marginalisation to help keep the regime in power against this most recent insurrection.[7]

If genocide, in the broad construction of the term, has taken place in Darfur (Crawford, 2004), then it has certainly also taken place in parts of the South and the Nuba Mountains before now, and is likely to continue. There is a threat that the pattern will continue even in those areas of the Sudan now declared at peace. During the final year of negotiations in the South there was a formal agreement between the government and the SPLA to control the use of militias and refrain from attacking civilian settlements. This agreement was monitored by an international team, but it was never enforced. Khartoum's many violations went reported but unpunished. The most violent and systematic case was the use of local militias, supported by the army and air force, in clearing out the civilian settlements of southern Shillukland along the White Nile (Ajawin, 2004; CPMT, 2004), at the same time that fighting in Darfur was escalating. This went largely unreported in the Western media. The failure of the international community supporting the IGAD talks to take action against Khartoum's violations was certainly a factor in convincing Khartoum it could act the same way with impunity in Darfur. There is evidence now emerging that the government is organising other militia groups in areas along the border of the South, as well as inside areas such as Upper Nile where the active oil fields are located, as a way of positioning themselves to prevent the full implementation of the Southern peace agreement.

The United States, having taken the lead in pronouncing genocide in Darfur, did not follow the logic of its pronouncement with action. In the UN, China and Russia's growing interest in the Sudan's oil has prevented the Security Council from taking more robust action, preferring to refer 'crimes against humanity' in Darfur to the International Court of Human Rights (United Nations, 2005), a court the US does not recognise. Yet if the US is restrained, it is not only because its overstretched military capacity no longer enables it to act on its own in the face of a new coalition of the unwilling, but because it continues to harbour the belief that too forceful action in Darfur could still derail the Southern peace process. The foregoing examination of events would suggest otherwise. The world should not have been surprised by events in Darfur, as they were a continuation of events that had unfolded over twenty-one years elsewhere in the Sudan. Having failed to take action in Darfur, they should not be later surprised if these same events ultimately undermine the longed-for Southern peace.

---

[7] Darfuris have been used in the army in the South and the Nuba Mountains, as well as in the security branches in Khartoum. As one Khartoum resident told me, when he was arrested in 1997, the jailors who tortured him were from Darfur. In many of the asylum appeals in the United Kingdom that I have been asked to comment on, Nuba detainees have reported that their jailors heaped the same terms of racial abuse on them that the *janjawid* are now reported to be using in Darfur. It would be interesting to know just how many of the jailors who routinely abused Nuba prisoners in Khartoum as blacks fit only to be slaves were themselves Darfuris. The old sultanate of Darfur, after all, was originally built as a slave-raiding state.

References

Abd al-Rahim, Muddathir (1969) *Imperialism and Nationalism in the Sudan: A Study in Constitutional and Political Development 1899-1956*, Oxford: The Clarendon Press.

African Rights (1995) *Facing Genocide: The Nuba of Sudan*, London: African Rights.

Ajawin, Yoanes (2004) 'Terror on the Nile', *Parliamentary Brief*, August, pp. 19-20.

Amnesty International (2003a) 'Urgent Call for Commission of Inquiry in Darfur as Situation Deteriorates', *AI Index: AFR* 54/004/2003, February.

Amnesty International (2003b) 'Sudan: Empty Promises? Human Rights Violations in Government-controlled Areas', *AI Index: AFR* 54/036/2003, July.

Amnesty International (2004a) 'Darfur: Too Many People Killed Over No Reason', 3 February.

Amnesty International (2004b) 'Sudan: Darfur – attacks against civilians ongoing', *AI Index: AFR* 54/000/2004, March.

Amnesty International (2004c) 'Sudan. At the Mercy of Killers – Destruction of Villages in Darfur', *AI Index: AFR* 54/072/2004, July.

Amnesty International (2004d) 'Sudan, Darfur: Rape as a Weapon of War. Sexual Violence and its Consequences', *AI Index: AFR* 54/076/2004, July.

Anon (2004) 'The world notices Darfur', *The Economist*, 31 July: 47-8.

Baum, Gerhart (2002) 'Situation of Human Rights in the Sudan. Report of the Special Rapporteur', New York: United Nations, Fifty-Seventh Session, August.

CPMT (Civilian Protection Monitoring Team) (2004) 'Final Report of Investigation No. 36: Fighting in The Shilluk Kingdom and Killing of Civilians', www.cpmtsudan.org

Crawford, Roderick (2004) 'This *is* Genocide', *Parliamentary Brief*, August 4.

Cunnison, Ian (1971) 'Classification by Genealogy: A Problem of the Baqqara Belt', in Yusuf Fadl Hassan (ed.) *Sudan in Africa*, Khartoum: Khartoum University Press, pp. 186-96.

Darfur Human Rights Forum (2003) Letter to General Sumbeiywo, 2 July.

de Waal, Alex (1991) 'Some Comments on Militias in Contemporary Sudan', in H. Bleuchot, C. Delmet and D. Hopwood (eds) *Sudan: History, Identity, Ideology/Histoire, identités, idéologies*, Reading: Ithaca Press, pp. 71-83.

de Waal, Alex (2004) 'Counter-Insurgency on the Cheap', *London Review of Books*, 5 August: 25-7.

Fellman, Michael (1989) *Inside War. The Guerrilla Conflict in Missouri during the American Civil War*, New York and Oxford: Oxford University Press.

International Crisis Group (2004), 'Darfur Rising: Sudan's New Crisis', 25 March.

Harir, Sharif (1993) 'Militarization of Conflict, Displacement and the Legitimacy of the State: A Case from Dar Fur, Western Sudan', in Terje Tvedt (ed.) *Conflicts in the Horn of Africa: Human and Ecological Consequences of Warfare*, Uppsala, EPOS, pp. 14-26.

Harir, Sharif (1994) '"Arab belt" versus "African belt": Ethno-political Conflict in Dar Fur and the Regional Cultural Factors', in Sharif Harir and Terje Tvedt (eds) *Short-Cut to Decay: The Case of the Sudan*, Uppsala: Nordiska Afrikainistitutet, pp. 144-85.

Human Rights Watch (1999) *Famine in Sudan, 1998: The Human Rights Causes*, NY/Washington DC/London/Brussels: Human Rights Watch.

Human Rights Watch (2004a) 'Darfur in Flames: Atrocities in Western Sudan', 16/5A, April.

Human Rights Watch (2004b) 'Darfur Destroyed: Ethnic Cleansing by Government and Militia Forces in Western Sudan', 16/6A, May.

James, Wendy (1977) 'The Funj Mystique: Approaches to a Problem of Sudan History', in R. K. Jain (ed.) *Text and Context: The Social Anthropology of Tradition*, Philadelphia: ISHI, pp. 95-133.

Johnson, Douglas H. (2003) *The Root Causes of Sudan's Civil Wars*, Oxford/Bloomington, IN: James Currey/Indiana University Press.

Lavergne, Marc (2004) 'Ethnicity as a Weapon: the Divide and Rule Motto Revisited', paper presented at the annual meeting of the Sudan Studies Society of the United Kingdom, 25 September.

Lind, William S. (2004) 'Fourth Generation War in the Sudan', 16 July, www.antiwar.com

Mutua, Makau (2004) 'Racism at Root of Sudan's Darfur Crisis', *The Christian Science Monitor*, 14 July: 10.

Ovesen, Jan (2005) 'Political Violence in Cambodia & the Khmer Rouge "Genocide"', in Richards (2005a), pp. 22-39.

Prunier, Gérard (1991) 'Ecologie, structures ethniques et conflits politiques au Dar Fur', in Hervé Bleuchot, Christian Delmet and Derek Hopwood (eds) *Sudan: History, Identity, Ideology/Histoire, identités, idéologies,* Reading: Ithaca Press, pp. 85-103.

Richards, Paul (ed.) (2005a) *No Peace, No War: An Anthropology of Contemporary Armed Conflicts,* Oxford/Athens OH, James Currey/Ohio University Press.

Richards, Paul (2005b) 'New War: An Ethnographic Approach', in Richards (2005a), pp. 1-21.

Ryle, John (2004) 'Disaster in Darfur', *New York Review of Books* 51(13), 12 August.

'Seekers of Truth and Justice' (2004 [2000]), *The Black Book: Imbalance of Power and Wealth in Sudan,* English translation: anonymous, March.

Spaulding, Jay (1985) *The Heroic Age in Sinnar,* East Lansing MI: African Studies Centre, Michigan State University.

Steele, Jonathan (2004) 'Diplomacy is Forgotten in the Mania for Intervention', *The Guardian,* 6 August, p. 26.

United Nations (2005) International Commission of Inquiry on Darfur, Report to the Secretary-General, Geneva, 25 January.

Verney, Peter (ed.) (1995) *Sudan: Conflict and Minorities,* Minority Rights Group Report 95/3, London: Minority Rights Group International.

Wöndu, Steven and Ann Lesch (2000), *Battle for Peace in Sudan: An Analysis of the Abuja Conferences 1992-1993,* Lanham MD: University Press of America.

6

Legacies of Violence
in Matabeleland, Zimbabwe

JOCELYN ALEXANDER

The processes by which people seek to confront the legacies of state violence and war offer a unique window on their relationships with the state and with their political, community and religious leaders. Efforts to invoke and deal with past violence in public create arenas of interaction in which historical narratives and political relationships are made and unmade. They also shape and in turn are shaped by wider political struggles. In the Matabeleland region of Zimbabwe, people have sought to confront their violent pasts in a range of ways, from locally initiated ceremonies and burials to carefully stage-managed commemorative events organised by national political leaders. The two ends of the spectrum interacted with one another: the power of elite-generated narratives to prevent other pasts from articulating themselves often came at the price of failing to convince and so placing silenced communities outside the nation, while local processes of memorialisation, commemoration and history-making acted to undermine the political purposes of the nation-state (see Fritzsche, 2001; Cole, 2002; Klein, 2000). The implications for political legitimacy and for citizenship of these interactions are important: as Richard Werbner writes, silencing 'popular commemoration' comes at a 'very real, lingering cost' to ruling elites (Werbner, 1998a: 9; see also Hutchinson, 1998; Cole, 1998). Battles over 'counter-memories' and 'buried memories' (Werbner, 1998b) are closely linked to debates over the moral and political obligations of leaders, local and national, and they have important consequences for people's political understandings and aspirations. In moments of political contestation, memories of past violence can play a pivotal role, as they have in the last decade in Zimbabwe.

In exploring these themes, I draw on research carried out by myself, JoAnn McGregor and Terence Ranger in the former Shangani Reserve, now divided into the rural districts of Nkayi and Lupane (Alexander, McGregor and Ranger, 2000; Alexander and McGregor, 2001). This is a work of synthesis, reliant on our collective research and that of the Zimbabweans with whom we collaborated in the field. It revisits this work in the context of newly heated debates over the past provoked by the political crisis that engulfed Zimbabwe in 2000.

Researching the Shangani

Located north of Matabeleland's provincial capital of Bulawayo, the Shangani region was in the nineteenth century a forested backwater located on the margins of the pre-colonial Ndebele state. Over the twentieth century it was settled by diverse groups of people with a range of ethnic identities and religious beliefs. In the 1940s and 1950s, a significant group of people, notable for their political activism and modern, Ndebele identity, were forcibly evicted into the Shangani (Alexander and McGregor, 1997). They were central to the rapid transformation of the region into a political hotbed, fiercely loyal to the nationalist party ZAPU. During the liberation war, this area was one of the key fronts of ZAPU's liberation army, ZIPRA. It was not, however, ZAPU which triumphed in the 1980 elections, but Robert Mugabe's ZANU-PF. This region and others that supported ZAPU were subsequently subjected to extreme state repression, a devastating period known as the *gukurahundi*. It was intended to destroy the only significant political alternative to ZANU-PF, but was also cast by government forces – and popularly understood – in ethnic terms as a war against the 'Ndebele'. The war came to a close with the Unity Accord of 1987 under which ZAPU was absorbed into ZANU-PF. Former ZAPU leaders took up posts in the ZANU-PF government, and peace prevailed in Matabeleland.

An intense period of reckoning with the past and political contestation followed, during which we undertook our research. The claims and counter-claims launched in the mid- to late-1990s provided in some ways an ideal context for exploring the violent past. The Unity Accord had brought high expectations of state investment after so many years of devastation, as well as of recognition of ZAPU's contribution to the nation. People in Matabeleland wanted to speak out about past state violence; they were actively engaged in making claims on the state which were developmental in intent as well as about asserting the claims of citizenship. History was centrally deployed in making these claims, just as it was in confronting the multifarious consequences of past violence. The individuals we interviewed were actively engaged in constructing narratives about the past. They were keen to have their stories heard and told.

Our interviews were loosely chronologically structured, taking each individual's life story as the starting point, and ranging over a variety of social and political questions. The ways in which people spoke about the violent past differed markedly. We found that political leaders – whether at village, district, provincial or national level – had a clearer story to tell, shaped by a political narrative that laid blame and offered explication. Others operated in different idioms. Religion was at times invoked as a prophetic or explanatory force. For those who bore arms, stories of war were centrally about an individual's move-ment over time and space from one identity to another, from the lowly status of herd or school boy to professional soldier, with trials, ordeals and epiphanies marking the way (Alexander and McGregor, 2004). For those to whom the languages of politics and religion and soldiering did not offer an overarching narrative able to integrate experience in an orderly and understandable fashion, stories of past violence were the most difficult to articulate (compare to Merridale, 1999).

Within all these categories, there were still of course profound disagreements. And within each account, there were events and episodes which could not be explained and which did not make sense to those who had experienced them. Memories of war and state violence were not easily placed into seamless, useful narratives even by seasoned politicians. Group discussions inevitably provoked debates over the past and what it meant. The words of guerrillas, as with some former nationalist leaders, were in addition constrained by the legacy of war-time restrictions on revealing secrets. In such cases, close collaboration with the Mafela Trust, established by former ZIPRA guerrillas to identify and commemorate the war dead, was essential (see Brickhill, 1995).

Research of this kind also required following the networks which shaped the worlds to which people referred. It was necessary to go to other regions in order to trace the routes people travelled in making political and spiritual connections. Religious affiliations were divided among the Nevana medium to the north, the Matopos shrines of the High God Mwali in southern Matabeleland, and a host of Christian denominations; the provincial capital of Bulawayo was home to many of the region's political leaders; guerrillas who operated in this region often lived far afield. Retracing these routes was an essential part of understanding the movement of symbols, metaphors and ideas back and forth over space and through political and religious hierarchies. It was important to understanding the shifting nature of institutions and social relationships.

Our research has not relied on oral history alone: it has woven together archival, written and oral material. We have been interested in both memory and history. Oral history has served the purpose of exploring how the past was remembered and refashioned in the present by different individuals, as well as – to put it simply – what happened. We have sought both to reconstruct events and processes and to understand how they were evaluated, interpreted and perceived. There were clearly political narratives of the past; there were clearly mythologised events; there were topics around which there was silence; the state's archives told a very different story from those it administered. By building on a wide range of oral interviews as well as rich archival and written sources it has been possible to identify and evaluate the nature of the remembered past, and to question the myths and the lacunae in archives and individual accounts. Exploring the memories and legacies of violence did not produce a monolithic account, save perhaps in the sense that ZAPU's nationalist history was so firmly stamped upon it, but rather a fractured and painful set of stories that were contested both within communities and across a wider social and political field. Moreover, these stories could shift over time: amidst the political crisis since 2000 narratives were recrafted, memories revalued, and the obligations of leaders reassessed, though always around a central and indelible sequence of violence.

The Shangani in the 1990s

Prior to the renewed political violence of 2000 and after, the sequence of violence in the Shangani had encompassed the armed conquest of the region in the 1890s, the colonial state's forced evictions and coercive agricultural interventions, the nationalist struggle, the liberation war of the 1970s, and the post-independence *gukurahundi*. Efforts to confront this history in the 1990s were shaped by this whole range of events as well as by the contemporary political context. The mid-1990s was a time of devastating drought and economic hardship in which disaffection spread through the country as a whole. The ruling elite's developmental programme, which was an important source of its legitimacy, came under angry criticism, as did its claims to the nationalist mantle. History was a heated focus of debate and challenging official narratives was a powerful means of making claims on the state and politicians. In Matabeleland, the failure of the Unity Accord to bring either development or an acknowledgement of ZAPU's history made for a particularly insistent challenge to ZANU-PF leaders.

In the following sections I explore some of our findings regarding the ways in which people sought to confront the legacies of violence. It is a story of the struggle of individuals, communities and soldiers to become part of the nation's narrative, and citizens of its polity, on terms that did justice to their understanding of the past and their aspirations for the present. It demonstrates the labyrinthine inter-linkages among political, religious and other institutions, across national, regional and local arenas, and between the political and cultural. Let me start with the national debates which set the scene for regional and local initiatives.

National Debates

The 1990s were rife with challenges to the ruling party's use of the narratives and symbols of nationalist history. Debates over the legacies of war focused on both the liberation war of the 1970s and the post-independence war of the 1980s, but in very different ways. The former guerrillas who had made up Zimbabwe's two liberation armies used a variety of public fora to make strident demands for material compensation, while public revelations about the 1980s war led to demands for what Werbner has called 'recountability', that is the right 'to make a citizen's memory known, and acknowledged in the public sphere' (1998a: 1).

Former guerrillas played on the official role in which they had been cast in the commemoration of the war for independence, and the constitution of the historical narrative of the new nation. Norma Kriger has explored the process by which ZANU-PF sought to ground a unified national identity in the liberation war through establishing a hierarchy of 'Heroes' Acres' – burial grounds for guerrillas and nationalists, at national, provincial and district levels (Kriger, 1995; Werbner, 1998b). The symbolism of these sites was not, however, always convincing to the fighters or their nationalist leaders. ZAPU and ZIPRA leaders had long charged that the identification of heroes was partisan, and had launched their own efforts to commemorate the war dead. With the unification of veterans from both liberation war armies in one War Veterans' Association, many more criticisms were voiced. Former guerrillas demanded a say in deciding who was a hero and they criticised the hierarchal nature of heroes' acres. They and their political allies pointedly noted the poverty in which many living 'heroes' lived while the carefully selected dead were feted. In 1997, they responded to the 'looting' of official war compensation funds by the political elite with protest and riot.

Guerrillas' demands for recognition and material compensation came to a head in late 1997 when President Mugabe promised lump sum payments and pensions to all veterans: their contestation of official historical narratives and patronage politics was about to produce a major shift in their relationship with the ruling party and in the stories they told about themselves (see Alexander and McGregor, 2003). This act did not, however, silence a broader debate about historical obligation and sacrifice. Ex-detainees and youth who had aided guerrillas but had not received the now re-valued title of 'veteran' also demanded compensation – and threatened to reveal alternative, divisive narratives of war if they were ignored. The economic crisis triggered by the payouts and the taxes imposed to pay for them also sparked massive demonstrations and claims from trade unionists and others that the war had affected all: alternative views of the debts of war and of the ideals for which it had been fought were loudly voiced on the streets and in the media. All this marked a wide-ranging reassessment of the nationalist leaders' relationship to their divided constituencies and called into question their capacity to root their claims to political legitimacy in a particular narrative of the past.

It was in this volatile period that the violence of the 1980s began to be publicly explored. Reports of mass graves and massacres appeared in the press in piecemeal fashion in the aftermath of the Unity Accord and a horrifyingly detailed human rights report was released in 1997 (CCJP/LRF, 1997). The evidence of state atrocity had been firmly placed in the public sphere and sparked a difficult to control debate. President Mugabe's response was cannily ambiguous. 'History' was dangerous, he said: it threatened to 'tear our people apart'. But it was at the same time necessary to preserve the historical 'record' in order to 'remind us what never to do'. The state's use of violence against its own citizens had to be both remembered and forgotten if the nation was to be peaceful and united. In the letters pages of the media the debate regularly invoked the metaphor of 'opening old wounds'. These 'wounds' stood as markers of a history of violence – they were 'intractable traces of the past', 'felt on people's bodies, known in their landscapes, landmarks and souvenirs'. They begged difficult questions regarding the proper commemoration of the dead and the appropriate ways in which history might be invoked in the present (Werbner, 1998a: 2-3).

Parallel to and in constant tension with the shifting processes of official memory-making and debates over commemoration ran a tremendously varied struggle at local and regional levels over the legacies of the violent past.

Commemoration in the Shangani

The national debate over the narratives of the nation and the violence of the 1980s created the context in which local initiatives were taken to reinstate in the public memory those who had been excluded from ZANU-PF leaders' version of history. In the Shangani there was a particularly powerful demand for commemoration, for public acknowledgement and for ritual resolution of the history of violence. It revealed – and required the renegotiation of – political relationships and historical narratives.

Two events illustrate these processes: one was a high profile effort to anoint the site known as Pupu as both a shrine and provincial heroes' acre; the other involved a modest attempt to commemorate a handful of the victims of post-independence violence. The Pupu site was steeped in the history of the last hundred years of violence: it was the location of a great battle between the warriors of the Ndebele state and settler forces; it contained a Rhodesian obelisk to their war dead as well as a ritually important tree at which ceremonies were held for the Ndebele dead and it had been regularly visited by guerrillas in the liberation war. It was thus important to the making of Rhodesian, Ndebele and nationalist identity.

When peace returned in 1987, local leaders nominated this site as a heroes' acre. Leading ZIPRA figures took the initiative, and liaised with chiefs, spiritual leaders and nationalist politicians of the former ZAPU. A commemorative event was held in 1992 which was far more multi-voiced, popular and historically sweeping than anything that normally occurred at official heroes' acre celebrations. But silences remained: it had been intended that ZANU-PF politicians would attend but they did not; ex-guerrillas were refused a platform in favour of (formerly ZAPU) politicians who emphasised the need for unity. No mention was made of the 1980s violence, and efforts to establish a shrine for the several generations of war dead came to nothing. Instead, a full five years later, an official monument to the unknown soldier was unveiled at another site in the district. This met with a distinct lack of enthusiasm. Few attended the ceremony, and those who did – veterans and others bussed in for the purpose – were unmoved by the monument's symbolism. Former guerrillas wondered how a soldier could be 'unknown': they wanted to know who he was, where he was from and they wondered what purpose a single soldier could possibly serve. The substitution of the unknown soldier for the many hoped-for historical figures indicated the silencing of still controversial aspects of the nation's memory: acknowledgement of the pre-colonial Ndebele state's war dead, ZIPRA's contribution to the liberation struggle and the victims of the 1980s violence. Both of these events revealed the limits of popular and official commemoration and the extent to which history could be publicly shaped by either the ruling elite or its errant constituencies.

In 1997 a different commemoration of the dead was planned in the region, this time with the explicit goal of memorialising those killed after independence. The community of Daluka planned a public ceremony at one of the district's mass graves, located in a school yard and containing the bodies of five people killed by government forces. They intended to erect a gravestone with the names of the dead inscribed upon it. Local leaders raised the necessary funds, the MP and Provincial Governor were invited, and the event was publicised in the newspaper. This was to be a first step in resolving the spiritual and social problems caused by the unacknowledged dead. But the ceremony was not to be. Politicians said it would hinder development while the intelligence organisation, responsible for so much terror in this region, returned to disrupt the event. In the end, the families of the dead built a makeshift grave, inscribing only the date on the headstone. A narrative of unity was thus enforced: it could not tolerate the inscription on the landscape of the names of those who had died in a moment of national division. This remained an 'unsettled struggle against state-buried memory' (Werbner, 1998b: 98).

Independent Zimbabwe's leaders expended tremendous energy in seeking to craft and to discipline public memory. They did so because acts of commemoration and the telling of political narratives were crucial to their legitimacy and to the creation of a national identity. The control they exercised over the nation's memory was never, however, complete, and in the 1990s it suffered unprece-dented challenge. The events at Pupu, at the unknown soldiers' monument and at Daluka underlined the political dangers of silenced memory, and the failures to convince of a bowdlerised official memory. Such cases represented one set of arenas in which people struggled to confront the legacies of violence. There were others: debates over the meaning and consequences of past violence shaped a much wider set of institutions and ideas, interacting with drought, the ritual demands of post-war cleansing and the many ways in which people sought to make their leaders accountable to them.

Drought, Cleansing and Accountability

Drought was a central focus of political debate in 1990s Zimbabwe, providing the impetus for a far-reaching moral and religious reappraisal of the state and nation (see Mawere and Wilson, 1995; Mafu, 1995). In Matabeleland, understandings of drought were linked to the desire for a cleansing of the metaphysical and physical traces of violence. Attempts to locate the causes of drought and to carry out acts of cleansing laid bare the political and spiritual relationships between leaders and their constituencies, highlighting diverse notions of accountability. At one level, popular debates focused on the legitimacy of the national leaders, drawing on concepts of leaders' responsibilities to God, the ancestors and through them their followers. At another level, criticism focused on more accessible local spiritual and secular leaders, and was about both their consumptive excesses and ongoing social struggles within communities. The two levels of debate intersected in the initiatives taken to confront drought and the legacies of war, illustrating the complex interplay of the local and national, the political and the cultural.

The widespread belief that Zimbabwe's liberation war had been supported by the ancestors and the powers of both the Matopos rain shrines in Matabeleland South and the Nevana medium to the north, formed the basis for a critique of national leaders and a common thread in debates over post-war cleansing and drought. People in Matabeleland charged national leaders with neglecting the rain shrines after they had come to power. They had failed to 'report' properly to the shrines, to thank the spirits and the High God Mwali for their support, to offer an apology for the violence and to lead the way in cleansing the nation of the effects of war.

In the Shangani, ZAPU's nationalism had invoked the goals of freedom, equality and 'one man, one vote', but had also cast ZAPU leader Joshua Nkomo as the 'father of the nation', sanctioned by the Matopos shrines and the ancestors. He was responsible for maintaining relationships with the ancestors and had particular duties with regard to rainmaking. For many ZAPU leaders in the Shangani, this meant only he could legitimately rule the nation. Because he did not, the ancestors and God had turned against them. Nkomo had in fact held ceremonies at the Matopos shrines after independence but these were criticised as incomplete: he had focused on his own glory. He had not properly reported the dead or cleansed the effects of guns, gases and bombs. But if Nkomo had acted improperly, Mugabe had done much worse. He was said to have desecrated the central Matopos shrine of Njelele, to have angered God through his illegitimate and violent rule and so brought drought. Christians invoked biblical comparisons, likening Mugabe to King Nebuchadnezzar.

The crucial role attributed to nationalist leaders in these accounts highlighted the continued potency of the political and spiritual relationships defined through decades of building rural nationalism and war. They comprised a compelling means by which the nationalist 'fathers' could be taken to task, adding an additional layer of relationships to those constituted through electoral politics, one in which the violent past was central. Nationalist leaders were, however, rarely directly accessible to the people of the Shangani. In contrast, local religious leaders could be confronted in debates over the causes of drought and the nature of misrule. The Njelele shrine keepers in the Matopos, the many shrine messengers and mediums, the Nevana medium and chiefs all came in for a share of the blame. The relationship with these figures was understood differently from that with nationalist leaders and it was expressed in a different idiom.

People from the Shangani regularly travelled to the Nevana medium and the Njelele shrine and both were also the subject of much rumour. There were tales of corruption, of excessive fees being charged, the misuse of sacred sites, and in the case of the Nevana medium a propensity to love all things flashy and modern. Criticism was also directed at individuals and groups within the Shangani. Here there was no agreement as to the causes of drought. Religious specialists and chiefs came under attack for their ignorance, youth or corruption. Disputes divided communities along longstanding lines between different generations of settlers, chiefs and their followers, religion and generation. Christians came under severe criticism for their failure to respect the shrines but stuck by an alternative, apocalyptic explanation for drought that linked biblical prophecies of famine, disease, war and false prophets to the end of the world.

Despite the strength of division and the failures of nationalist leaders, people in the Shangani did seek to find ways to confront the legacies of war and drought. They made efforts to 'clean' the forests and to hold ceremonies at local rain shrines. While far from uncontroversial, these efforts underlined the link between drought and the history of war. The years of violence had left human bones in the forests which caused grave offence; cleansing ceremonies had often not been held for years due to a fear of entering the forests, leaving the disturbing residue of violence to fester among the trees.

Other initiatives involved a much wider set of actors, bringing local concerns into a regional context and into interaction with national leaders. The most ambitious of these was instigated by a Shangani man named Nkanyezi. He was an ex-combatant and *inyanga* or traditional healer, with senior posts in the provincial war veterans' association and traditional healers' association. He had been called upon by his spirits to make an offering at Njelele and to install the 'proper' keeper. To do so, he invoked the nineteenth-century practices of the Ndebele state as his model. Chiefs in the Shangani organised donations to purchase beasts to send to the shrine as pre-colonial Ndebele leaders had done. Nkanyezi subsequently set about organising a series of cleansing ceremonies for guerrillas to be held at the shrine, taking up a problem widely seen as sorely neglected by the nationalist leaders. Guerrillas held that they had not been properly cleansed after the liberation war because their return from war had not been reported to the spiritual authorities and so they were not at peace. This sort of cleansing was not about individual acts of violence but about the violence of the war as a whole, of an army. Nkanyezi was able to draw on his links in the veteran and healer associations and to gain the approval of senior politicians and military commanders for his actions. The cleansing ceremonies, like Nkanyezi's previous initiative, drew their form and legitimacy through reference to the nineteenth-century Ndebele state. This made sense to guerrillas in this region who cast the liberation war as a direct continuation of the Ndebele state's struggle against conquest. Those who attended the ceremonies believed the dual goals of cleansing and 'reporting' to have been accomplished. The ceremonies did not, however, successfully incorporate the nationalist leaders: they kept away and were again harshly criticised for neglecting their obligations.

Like the efforts at memorialisation and commemoration, cleansing and drought-related initiatives invoked a lengthy history. They delved into the nineteenth-century past and drew on the political and spiritual links built between leaders and led, through nationalism and guerrilla war. They occupied a different and in some ways less threatening political space, however. The nation's leaders actively sought to shape public memory and to silence alternative narratives about the violent past but their response to demands for accountability to their fighters and for the land's fertility, expressed through involvement in ritual and ceremony, was simply omission. This means of silencing, or more accurately refusing to hear, did not prevent local debates and initiatives from surviving or even thriving and it tolerated the building of new linkages across institutions and space. These political and cultural idioms retained a central place in people's understandings of themselves as political actors and of the obligations, met and unmet, of their leaders as Zimbabwe entered a new era of violent change.

Politics and the Legacies of Violence in 2000 and After

We concluded our book *Violence and Memory* by arguing that the *longue durée* of violence in the Shangani was central to people's understanding of their role as citizens. I want now to look at how the political crisis since 2000 has played out on this terrain.

In the late 1990s, Zimbabwe entered a period of upheaval in which violence, past and present, played a crucial role. Mugabe's decision to accede to the demands of former guerrillas for compensation in 1997 marked a key step in building a new constituency for an embattled ruling party and in remaking nationalist history. In the run up to the constitutional referendum of early 2000, ZANU-PF struggled with internal divisions, a crumbling economy and an ever more confident and outspoken opposition movement. The ruling party's defeat in the referendum led ZANU-PF to further elaboration, in interaction with its veteran allies, of a nationalist history that excluded those who now constituted a potent opposition in the form of the Movement for Democratic Change (MDC). Mugabe donned combat fatigues, made frequent reference to the liberation war and frequent use of its language of 'enemies' and 'sell outs'. His rhetoric targeted the MDC's urban, trade union and intellectual roots, seeking to exclude these groups from the nation's history, which was now narrowed to the heroic successes of fighting men and the struggle for the land rather than the far broader constituency and ideals that nationalism had once encompassed (Raftopoulos and Phimister, 2004; Ranger, 2003).

In the parliamentary elections of 2000 and presidential elections of 2002, these ideas were elaborated at great length in the media. As Terence Ranger has suggested, at core lay an argument about history. ZANU-PF's slogans in 2000 were all about reclaiming the land and were accompanied by widespread occupations of white-owned land, led by war veterans; in 2002 it was 'Zimbabwe will never be a colony again.' State-run television and the government press were filled with stories about slavery, Africa's imperial partition, the guerrilla war, colonial brutalities and 'heritage'. ZANU-PF was cast as the sole representative of the liberation movement and African authenticity, while the MDC 'had abolished history', proclaiming its irrelevance in an 'age of globalisation'. They merely promised prosperity and were prepared to 'reverse' Zimbabwe's history in order to achieve it, even if this meant 'turning Zimbabwe into a British and American overseas territory'.[1] The MDC's leader Morgan Tsvangirai was attacked for not having contributed anything to Zimbabwe's history, and indeed not understanding what it was. In Ranger's view, ZANU-PF politics opposed history to 'the end of history' (Ranger, 2004: 220; also see Ranger 2002; Raftopoulos 2002).

ZANU-PF in Matabeleland

How did all this shape Matabeleland's perceptions of the past and politics of the present? For ten years following the Unity Accord of 1987, Matabeleland's voters had remained loyal to ZANU-PF. But by the late 1990s, this support had started to fray, as JoAnn McGregor and I have explored.[2] Many issues echoed nationwide complaints – unemployment, inflation, corruption – but others related to the memories of the region's past, specifically of violence and the political obligations it was understood to have created. The enforced silences regarding the 1980s violence, the failure to grant ZAPU and ZIPRA their due and the lack of developmental investment following the Unity Accord were all widely voiced complaints. Mugabe was not unaware of the dangers. He belatedly and unconvincingly apologised for the state violence of the 1980s and promised, but did not deliver, compensation for its victims. Only ZIPRA veterans were to receive compensation of any kind and that was not for their suffering at the hands of the ZANU-PF government in the 1980s but for their sacrifices on behalf of the nation in the 1970s.

Mugabe found his efforts to impose his narrowed interpretation of liberation war history difficult in this region, even with the help of the newly co-opted war veterans. The veteran association had spearheaded land occupations across the country. It was important not only because it offered an effective national organisation, reaching down to district levels that could be used in political mobilisation but also because of the symbolic importance of veterans as exemplars of the liberation war credentials Mugabe stressed. Veterans are, however, a diverse group and not all shared Mugabe's vision of the past or of the role allotted them in the present. In May 2000, a group of veterans formed the Zimbabwe Liberators' Platform. They spoke out angrily against what they saw as

---

[1] Ranger (2004: 219), quoting a newspaper article by Godfrey Chikowore in *The Herald*, 16 June 2002.

[2] In this and the next sub-section, I draw primarily on Alexander and McGregor, 2001.

the exploitation of veterans by a weak and unpopular party and they overtly challenged Mugabe's version of liberation war history (see Raftopoulos, 2003: 217-18). Everywhere there were veterans who supported the MDC. In Matabeleland, ZIPRA guerrillas had been singled out for attack in the 1980s, and they remembered a much longer history of tension between the two nationalist parties and their armies during the liberation war. Some ZIPRA veterans publicly distanced themselves from ZANU-PF's strategies and from its increasing use of violence. Their anti-violence stance was reinforced by significant numbers of local ZANU-PF leaders (themselves formerly ZAPU and hence once also subjected to ZANU-PF violence) in the region.

The use of violence in the run up to the 2000 elections was heavily laden with historical reference. Some ZANU-PF candidates went so far as to say that the *gukurahundi* would be repeated, that the notorious Fifth Brigade, responsible for the murder of thousands of civilians, would return, if Matabeleland voted for the MDC. They stressed notions of loyalty cast in the liberation war language of the 'sell-out', and bearing the same mortal threat. The levels of violence in this period were, however, far less severe than that of the 1980s. It was largely the work of ZANU-PF, the intelligence organisation and veterans, rather than the security forces. These people lived locally and their use of violence was limited by networks of kin, church, schools, drinking fraternities and the like. Intimidation nonetheless forced many MDC candidates and supporters to flee or go under-ground. For ZANU-PF it looked like an easy victory was to hand; from the point of view of the MDC, however, a very different dynamic was being played out in the long history of ZANU-PF violence.

The MDC in Matabeleland

The MDC had been established only nine months prior to the 2000 election. It was largely urban based, had little access to the media and was consistently portrayed as a front for white farmers and 'Rhodesian' and British imperialism. It was said to want to reverse the gains of independence. Many people found these ideas at least in part plausible. So how did the MDC overcome these disabilities in Matabeleland?

In organisational terms, the MDC made significant headway in recruiting a constituency of rural service centre workers, unemployed youth, educated war veterans, teachers, school kids and business people as well as members of church and NGO networks, all of whom worked to spread the message through the rural areas (see Alexander and McGregor, 2001). The MDC's message appealed for its economic critique and attacks on corruption but also centrally due to its recrafting of the nation's history. The MDC worked to relate the party's national slogans and symbols to local contexts and histories. Far from trumpeting the 'end of history', the MDC engaged directly with it. The national slogan 'time for change' had a countrywide appeal, but the symbol of the open hand had a unique significance here: people associated it with former ZAPU leader Joshua Nkomo's rallies both before and after independence. Local MDC campaign leaders opened their rallies by praising and remembering Nkomo as the father of nationalism. They cast the MDC as the successor to this nationalist tradition. The period when ZAPU had been subsumed into ZANU-PF was repressed. Instead, a new narrative was constructed in which Matabeleland had always been ZAPU, the thirteen years of 'unity' had meant nothing, and the MDC now offered the opportunity for ZAPU's true spirit to re-emerge: if ZANU-PF enforced silences of one kind, the MDC's counter-narratives created silences of another.

What the MDC so effectively offered was a persuasive, historically rooted, moral argument about the region's history of violence. MDC candidates opened meetings with a minute's silence for the victims of the 1980s. Some had particular success in mobilising ZIPRA veterans by reminding them of the time when they were 'hunted down' by the very same ZANU-PF their colleagues now supported. The violence employed by ZANU-PF and war veterans in the course of campaigning in 2000 helped the MDC make its case. Threats to redeploy the hated Fifth Brigade of the *gukurahundi* era were certainly greeted with fear but also with tremendous outrage. People recalled how they had resisted violence in the past, how violence had strengthened their resolve to vote against ZANU-PF the last time there had been a credible opposition in the form of ZAPU, in 1985. They felt they knew about ZANU-PF's violence and they could draw on their memories in order to resist it again. In fact, the MDC did draw effectively on the region's long experience of clandestine organisation, skillfully circumventing existing power structures and making much use of dissimulation and disciplined secrecy.

The MDC's strategy was extraordinarily successful throughout Matabeleland. In the rural seats of Matabeleland North, it won by margins of fifty-nine to eighty-six per cent, much to the shock and dismay of local ZANU-PF leaders and veterans. The MDC's youthful leaders cast the result as an overwhelming rejection of ZANU-PF's version of unity and the exclusive and intolerant national-ism that characterised it. For them it was ZANU-PF that had been left behind by history: it was 'the party of the old people, especially the uneducated – people who can be used, people who you can tell "come beat these ones", and then just buy them [a beer].' They saw their politics as introducing a long delayed citizen's revolution; they spoke of 'voting the torturers out'. The violence of the 1980s weighed heavily in this. One elder convert to the MDC stressed, 'we cannot forget the *gukurahundi*'. In their own post-mortems, district ZANU-PF committees also stressed the history of violence in explaining their defeat: 'The President has not said "Sorry to those victims about what the Fifth Brigade did [in the 1980s] in this region." They are hungry for that word "SORRY".' In 2000, the chasm between official narratives of the past, and the nature of citizenship they implied, and the political aspirations and popular memory of violence in Matabeleland proved too wide to bridge.

The period immediately after the 2000 parliamentary elections was a time of reflection and relatively open debate. It did not, however, last long. Uncertainty was rapidly replaced by mounting instability and renewed violence. The politics of land entered a new phase as ZANU-PF implemented its Fast Track resettle-ment programme, involving the movement of hundreds of thousands of people onto largely white-owned commercial farms. War veterans and increasingly youth militia played a key role in ZANU-PF's evolving and increasingly violent strategy. This led to not only on-going violence on the farms but also to the closure of local councils, arrests, beatings and killings of MDC activists, the suspension of many local government personnel and other civil servants and to threats to and attacks on teachers and NGO staff accused of supporting the opposition.[3] Those identified as MDC were told to go to their own leaders for land, for drought relief, for medical services. They were no longer deemed to be a part of the Zimbabwean nation and no longer deemed to enjoy rights as its citizens. ZANU-PF did not pull back from its narrowed version of the nation's narrative. Instead it increased the levels of violence necessary to enforce it, through systematically destroying the independence of state institutions, creating new avenues of patronage and discipline, and expending far more energy both in silencing those proclaiming an alternative vision of the past and for the future and in aggressively promoting its own vision.

Texts, Memory and the Dead in 2002

Two documents to be found circulating in Matabeleland in 2002 illustrated the ongoing battle over histories silenced and distorted by violence. In this highly literate society, texts provided a crucial means of communication and medium for debate, alongside the practices of religious ritual, memorialisation, commemoration and daily conversation.

The first text is a collection of speeches given by Robert Mugabe, entitled *Inside the Third Chimurenga*, and used to 'educate' the youth militia who became such a central part of ZANU-PF's persecution of the opposition in the aftermath of the 2000 elections (Mugabe, 2001: 38; cf. Solidarity Peace Trust, 2003; Reeler, 2003). It is of the same stable as the 'patriotic history' projected in the state-controlled media (see Ranger, 2004). Much of it is crude and repetitive in its appeals. The liberation war and the heroic dead are constantly invoked, while Britain is repeatedly blamed for its betrayals and never ending imperial ambitions, and land issues stand centre stage:

> We are a Government born out of the liberation struggle. The poor send their children to war to recover their heritage ... What message do we give them today as they wallow in their pre-independence poverty? That those you fought against have refused [you] the land and you may no[t] have it? How will they respond to us when they cannot see their children who perished in slaughter? Do we go back to war? ... The colonial power has reneged on its promise (Mugabe, 2001: 38).

White Zimbabweans come in for repeated attack as the 'local agents' of imperialism. Urban people and intellectuals are cast as untrustworthy, as people who recite 'borrowed and stereotype[d]' positions and who are the 'worst collaborators' with the 'embittered racist Rhodesians and their foreign supporters' (ibid.: 40). How different are the 'fresh and original thoughts' of the 'firm and steadfast' peasant (ibid.: 50-1). The MDC's successes are put down to its access to 'foreign money', the 'filthy lucre' that lured it into working against the national interest. Defectors from ZANU-PF are 'Judas Iscariots who left because of pieces of silver dangled before their faint, materialistic and purchasable hearts' (ibid.: 76-7).

This is a history in which the enemies of the liberation struggle, live and breathe, constantly threatening to betray the heroic sacrifices of the dead and their memory among the living. The youth recruited to militia camps are cast as the offspring of this perpetually about-to-be-betrayed generation, now given the chance to redeem beyond question their forebears' sacrifices. The youth 'trainees'

[3] This was an extremely complex process. For the best exploration of its dynamcs, see McGregor 2002.

are thus inducted into an inter-generational dynamic wherein their own political role must be defined if they are to be morally valorised, according to the aims of the war dead of the 1970s. As human rights groups have documented, the narrative circulated by means of this text was constantly tied directly to past uses of violence (the good violence of the liberators and the bad violence of the white and British oppressors) and to the need for violence to be used again in the present (see Solidarity Peace Trust 2003). This was, of course, a wholly different dynamic from that which had characterised the debates of the Shangani. There, the ancestors' endorsement of the liberation war was used as a means by which people might hold leaders accountable for post-war failings. Here it was the leaders who invoked the ancestors to create obligations among the nation's youth in a kind of reverse accountability.

The second text is a photocopied document of uncertain origin titled 'Progress Review on the 1979 Grand Plan'. It is undated and signed cryptically 'From the Core'. This is an explicitly tribalist tract that lionises Mugabe as the 'ideal Shona person', and lauds his battles against the 'crimes' committed by both the Ndebele and the Europeans. As the title indicates, the text claims to be a progress report on a plan hatched within ZANU in 1979, at the end of the liberation war. It recounts Zimbabwean history from the point of view of a unified Shona 'race', first colonised by the Ndebele and then by whites. The Shona did not succeed in resisting until the emergence of a 'Shona led political party' – ZANU – which fought for 'Shona Majority Rule'. ZAPU was a confused Ndebele party that sought 'Black Majority Rule' not realising that any majority rule would be by definition Shona. After independence, Mugabe realised he had to deal with the Ndebele, and so he orchestrated a conflict, sending in the Fifth Brigade to 'smash' ZAPU. It was then possible to establish the dominance of Shona heritage and language, Shona control of state offices, media, schools, churches, businesses and banks, and now the land, through its occupation and distribution to Shonas.

The rewriting of the liberation struggle and post-independence repression as the execution of a straightforward plan designed to leave 'the Shona' in a position of total domination is the sort of conspiracy theory that one might hope would be easily dismissed. Instead, this document was avidly read and circulated in Matabeleland (despite its front page warning 'For the Eyes of the Shona Elite Only!') and widely believed, even or perhaps especially by those still working within ZANU-PF.[4] It has become yet another artefact in the ongoing debates over Matabeleland's place in the nation and over the political dangers of ZANU-PF for those who would claim the rights of citizens. The indelible nature of the long history of violence in Matabeleland and the ways in which people refuse to allow its removal from the political arena, were underlined once again in 2002 when ZANU-PF sought to proclaim the 22 December anniversary of the Unity Accord as a day of national celebration. The secretary of the Zimbabwe Liberators' Platform, a ZIPRA veteran, retorted that it should instead be a day of national mourning, of remembrance for those who 'lie in mass graves' (Ranger, 2004: 233). The betrayal of the dead of the 1980s did not enter into the education of the youth militia or the pantheon of patriotic history, but they too are ancestors whose shadowy presence continues to be felt in the political sphere.

---

[4] I say this on the basis of numerous discussions in Matabeleland of the 'Grand Plan', with members of the MDC as well as Zanu(PF) and war veterans.

In her fascinating exploration of the assassination of ZANU leader Herbert Chitepo in Zambia in 1975, Luise White has argued that texts compete by 'claiming (and proclaiming) their truth' (White, 2003: 1 and chapters 1 and 6). Narratives about the past are produced and reproduced, and power is produced and reproduced through them; some are more powerful and some more believable than others. Writing about the period from 2000 to 2002, when history was so heatedly contested, she shows how the serialisation in the embattled independent press of the Chitepo Commission report on the assassination was used to remind Zimbabweans of a time when ZANU-PF was fragmented and weak, its army divided against itself. This reminded Zimbabweans that the liberation war had been an international endeavour dependent on international support and that nationality was not tied to territoriality. The report made ZANU-PF's exclusionary language of race and citizenship, its invocation of unity and sovereignty, look like such a poor fit with its own history.[5] These three texts stand as part of an ongoing debate over history circulating in the towns and rural areas. They are tied to political interests, social institutions and the uses of violence, all struggling to proclaim their 'truth'.

Conclusion

A key aspect of Zimbabwe's recent politics has revolved around contesting and creating national narratives. Nowhere has this been more fraught than in Matabeleland where violence played such a profound role in shaping political understandings and memories. In the 1990s it was possible to track a complex politics that sought to confront the legacies of one hundred years of violence through a host of different strategies: it demarcated and challenged the relationships between leaders and led, between both and the spiritual world. The failures to address the silences of this period and the mismatch that remained between ZANU-PF's nation and that envisioned by its Matabeleland constituency produced a spectacular shift of allegiance in the 2000 elections. Matabeleland's past was aligned with that of ZAPU's never realised promise, while ZANU-PF was cast as the party of unrepentant violence, deaf to the claims of its citizenry. However, this was not the end of the story. A new chapter of violence has since been written and it has created a new round of 'buried memory' and 'counter-memories', grounded in the past and invoked in the present. The dead of Zimbabwe's violent past remain a potent presence in the politics of the living.

[5] See Worby's discussion of Zanu(PF)'s uses of the concept of sovereignty (2003).

References

Alexander, Jocelyn and JoAnn McGregor (1997) 'Modernity and Ethnicity in a Frontier Society: Understanding Difference in Northwestern Zimbabwe', *Journal of Southern African Studies* 23(2): 187-201.

Alexander, Jocelyn and JoAnn McGregor (2001) 'Elections, Land and the Politics of Opposition in Matabeland', *Journal of Agrarian Change* 1(4): 510-33.

Alexander, Jocelyn and JoAnn McGregor (2003) 'Veterans, Violence and Nationalism in Zimbabwe', paper delivered to the conference on 'Africa and Violence: Identities, Histories and Representations', Emory, Atlanta, 11-13 September.

Alexander, Jocelyn and JoAnn McGregor (2004) 'War Stories: Guerrilla Narratives of Zimbabwe's Liberation War', *History Workshop Journal* 57(1): 79-100.

Alexander, Jocelyn, JoAnn McGregor and Terence Ranger (2000) *Violence and Memory: One Hundred Years in the 'Dark Forests' of Matabeleland*, Oxford: James Currey.

Brickhill, Jeremy (1995) 'Making Peace with the Past: War Victims and the Work of the Mafela Trust', in Ngwabi Bhebe and Terence Ranger (eds) *Soldiers in Zimbabwe's Liberation War*, Oxford: James Currey.

Catholic Commission for Justice and Peace/Legal Resources Foundation [CCJP/LRF] (1997) *Breaking the Silence, Building True Peace: A Report on the Disturbances in Matabeleland and the Midlands, 1980 to 1988*, Harare: CCJP/LRF.

Cole, Jennifer (1998) 'The Uses of Defeat: Memory and Political Morality in East Madagascar', in Richard Werbner (ed.) *Memory and the Postcolony: African Anthropology and the Critique of Power*, London: Zed Books.

Cole, Tim (2002) 'Scales of Memory, Layers of Memory: Recent Works on Memories of the Second World War and the Holocaust', *Journal of Modern Contemporary History* 37(1): 129-38.

Fritzsche, P. (2001) 'The Case of Modern Memory', *Journal of Modern History* 73: 87-117.

Hutchinson, Sharon E. (1998) 'Death, Memory and the Politics of Legitimation: Nuer Experiences of the Continuing Second Sudanese Civil War', in Richard Werbner (ed.) *Memory and the Postcolony: African Anthropology and the Critique of Power*, London: Zed Books.

Klein, Kerwin Lee (2000) 'On the Emergence of Memory in Historical Discourse', *Representations* 69: 127-50.

Kriger, Norma (1995) 'The Politics of Creating National Heroes: The Search for Political Legitimacy and National Identity', in Ngwabi Bhebe and Terence Ranger (eds) *Soldiers in Zimbabwe's Liberation War*, Oxford: James Currey.

Mafu, Hezekiel (1995) 'The 1991-2 Zimbabwean Drought and Some Religious Reactions', *Journal of Religion in Africa* 25(3): 288-309.

Mawere, Abraham and Ken Wilson (1995) 'Socio-Religious Movements, the State and Community Change: Some Reflections on the Ambuya Juliana Cult of Southern Zimbabwe', *Journal of Religion in Africa* 25(3): 252-87.

McGregor, JoAnn (2002) 'The Politics of Disruption: War Veterans and the Local State in Zimbabwe', *African Affairs* 402: 9-37.

Merridale, Catherine (1999) 'War, Death and Remembrance in Soviet Russia', in Jay Winter and Emmanuel Sivans (eds) *War and Remembrance in the Twentieth Century*, Cambridge: Cambridge University Press.

Mugabe, Robert Gabriel (2001) *Inside the Third Chimurenga*, Harare: Department of Information and Publicity, Office of the President and Cabinet.

Raftopoulos, Brian (2000) 'Constitutionalism and Opposition in Zimbabwe', African Studies Seminar, Oxford, June.

Raftopoulos, Brian (2001) 'The Labour Movement and the Emergence of Opposition Politics in Zimbabwe', in Brian Raftopoulos and Lloyd Sachikonye (eds) *Striking Back: The Labour Movement and the Post-Colonial State in Zimbabwe, 1980-2000*, Harare: Weaver Press.

Raftopoulos, Brian (2002) 'Briefing: Zimbabwe's 2002 Presidential Election', *African Affairs*, 404: 413-26.

Raftopoulos, Brian (2003) 'The State in Crisis: Authoritarian Nationalism, Selective Citizenship and Distortions of Democracy in Zimbabwe', in Amanda Hammar, Brian Raftopoulos and Stig Jensen (eds) *Zimbabwe's Unfinished Business: Rethinking Land, State and Nation in the Context of Crisis*, Harare: Weaver Press.

Raftopoulos, Brian and Ian Phimister (2004) 'Zimbabwe Now: Challenging the Political Economy of Crisis and Coercion', *Historical Materialism* 12 (4): 355-82.

Ranger, Terence (2002) 'The Zimbabwe Presidential Elections: A Personal Experience', *Zimbabwe Review*, Britain-Zimbabwe Society, 02/2, May 2002.

Ranger, Terence (ed.) (2003) *The Historical Dimensions of Democracy and Human Rights in Zimbabwe: Nationalism, Democracy and Human Rights*, Volume 2, Harare: University of Zimbabwe Publications.

Ranger, Terence (2004) 'Nationalist Historiography, Patriotic History and the History of the Nation: The Struggle over the Past in Zimbabwe', *Journal of Southern African Studies* 30(2): 215-34.

Reeler, Tony (2003) 'The Role of Militia Groups in Maintaining ZANU-PF's Political Power', unpublished paper, March. Excerpts downloadable from http://www.kubatana.net/html/archive/hr/030331ar.asp?sector=hr.

Solidarity Peace Trust (2003) 'National Youth Training Service: "Shaping youths in a truly Zimbabwean manner". An overview of youth militia training activities in Zimbabwe, October 2000-August 2003', 5 September.

Werbner, Richard (1998a) 'Beyond Oblivion: Confronting Memory Crisis', in Richard Werbner (ed.) *Memory and the Postcolony: African Anthropology and the Critique of Power*, London: Zed Books.

Werbner, Richard (1998b) 'Smoke from the Barrel of a Gun: Postwars of the Dead, Memory and Reinscription in Zimbabwe', in Richard Werbner (ed.) *Memory and the Postcolony: African Anthropology and the Critique of Power*, London: Zed Books.

White, Luise (2003) *The Assassination of Herbert Chitepo: Texts and Politics in Zimbabwe*, Bloomington, IN: Indiana University Press.

Worby, Eric (2003) 'The End of Modernity in Zimbabwe? Passages from Development to Sovereignty', in Amanda Hammar, Brian Raftopoulos and Stig Jensen (eds) *Zimbabwe's Unfinished Business: Rethinking Land, State and Nation in the Context of Crisis*, Harare: Weaver Press.

7

The Past as Contested Terrain
Commemorating New Sites of Memory in War-Torn Ethiopia

ALESSANDRO TRIULZI

Since the early 1990s, Ethiopia's past has been challenged from various corners in renewed attempts to modify the hegemonic narrative of the country – the narration centred around Christian highland ('Abyssinian') rulers and their historical achievements – and to adapt it to changing political conditions and to new visions of the country's future. Most critics challenged the traditional state-centred and 'Whig interpretation' of Ethiopia's past (the progressive march of the Ethiopian state towards unity and modernity) which they substituted with competing mythologies based on group memories and newly imagined projections of the collective self.[1] Thus Ethiopia's past has become in recent years a particularly 'contested terrain. Selectively remembered, conveniently forgotten, or sometimes invented to the exclusion and silencing of certain voices and substitution of a hegemonic mythology' (Sorenson, 1993: 38).

The debate over the reading of the country's past has mainly focused on diverging views over the nature of the multi-ethnic state and the process of expansion and amalgamation of its different nationalities: to some, mainly belonging to the Christian highland groups, the 'unity of the nation was assumed and largely unquestioned'; they genuinely shared the long-held imperial view that 'Ethiopia was Abyssinia writ larger. The nation did not need to be built; it simply existed' (McClellan, 1996: 69, fn. 38). To others, mainly from the southwestern and eastern border regions which had been forcefully annexed by Emperor Menelik II at the end of the nineteenth century, the Empire was a mere product of 'internal colonialism' and a 'prison-house of nations if ever there was one' (Gellner, 1983: 85. See also Holcomb and Ibssa, 1990; Jalata, 1993).

The measure of individual and collective violence which accompanied the historical unfolding of the country has been differently evaluated by observers (Zewde, 1991; Hassen, 1994; Baxter, Hultin and Triulzi, 1996; James, Donham, Kurimoto and Triulzi, 2002; Clapham, 1999, 2000; Abbay, 2004) but has

---

[1] See Sorenson, 1991, 1993; Hassen, 1990; Jalata, 1993, 1998; de Waal, 1994; Tibebu, 1995; Adhana, 1994; Tadesse, 1999; Clapham, 2002, Triulzi, 2002a. Earlier drafts of this paper were presented at Conferences held in Cape Town (August 2000) and Lisbon (February 2002) , and during Seminars held at the universities of Paris (May 1999), Edinburgh (November 2003), and Basel (November 2004). An earlier version appeared in *Cadernos de Estudos Africanos* (Triulzi, 2002b).

become today a crucial bone of contention in public discourse over the country's destiny since 'a gradual rooting of violence as a pattern and ideology of behaviour' (Abbink 1995: 71) has become an institutional component of the Ethiopian experience in recent years. The growing culture of violence which accompanied the Eritrean war has also affected the debate over the growth and destiny of the Ethiopian state. According to Jon Abbink, this 'legacy of violence' goes back to the very foundation of the Ethiopian state, and must include both the forced incorporation of its neighbouring peoples and the brutal colonial repression of the Fascist period (1935-41), as well as the domestic violence of Haile Sellassie's modernisation policies. The boundless state violence which became a daily practice during the Revolutionary years of 1974-91 finally gave way to the gradual 'crumbling of the Ethiopian state and of the imagination of a common Ethiopian identity' – not just 'the alienation of people from the state, but also from each other' (Abbink, 1995: 71). The memory of this enduring structure of violence has lingered on more in private perceptions and individual and family remembrance than in public discourse. For the most part, the public acknowledgement of the country's past divisions has tended to remain till recently silent or muted.

The recent war with Eritrea reopened the debate over the country's past and its repressed layers of memories and resentments over the national question. In continuity with Ethiopian tradition, the state has been part of this process just as have opposition groups, nationalist movements and diaspora intellectuals, each of them proposing conflicting and often exclusive versions of their own past. The result, as in other parts of postcolonial Africa, has been that both historians and public practitioners have acted 'more like construction workers than researchers', linking glorious past to radiant futures in such a way that 'their quickly laid layer of asphalt covers the myriad ancient paths connecting the past to the present' (Mudimbe and Jewsiewicki, 1993: 4). The current debate over the politics of historical representations in Ethiopia begs the question of recovering new semantic codes for a shared collective memory in the country. Recent attempts to re-appropriate new 'sites of memory' in the country's past run the risk of gathering 'a meaningful configuration of selected, negotiated events' which may 'construct a community' but dictate at the same time 'the categorical exclusion of those who do not participate in the recollection' (ibid.: 10).

In this chapter I will attempt to show how, during the recent conflict (1998-2000) which opposed the old mother-country, Ethiopia, to her ex-northern province, now independent Eritrea, over the old (colonial) border along the Mareb River in the north, a heated debate over the country's past was openly raised to extol the new identity of the nation-at-war, and to strengthen the fragile political basis of the coalition government around the regained unity of its peoples. Paradoxically, it was the EPRDF coalition government which ruled the country since 1991 under the leadership of the Tigrayan People's Liberation Front (TPLF), which first ignited the process of historical redefinition of the country's identity by enforcing a highly contested policy of controlled decentralisation and 'ethnic federalism' (Zegeye and Pausewang, 1994: 209-79). As the traditional representation of Ethiopia's identity withered away amidst opposing claims, a revised set of historical representations was introduced in the national debate which aimed at a 'usable' reading of the country's past.[2] As new actors attempted to

---

[2] The term 'usable past' has been coined by Ranger (1976) to denote the use of the past for nationalistic reasons.

retrieve from the country's past the historical signs of their role in today's political arena, a conglomeration of assertive and exclusive claims denouncing other groups' historical wrongs and disclaiming their belonging to the national mould quickly won the day. The result was the denial of existing interethnic links and bridges and of the long 'history of interaction, overlay, penetration, ambivalence, and constant change' which characterised the troubled but dense historical heritage of the region (Clapham, 2002: 49).

The conflict with neighbouring Eritrea, which ended with a frail peace agreement signed in Algiers in December 2000 after two years of protracted trench warfare,[3] thus created new venues for historical assertions and denials in the region of the Horn. In the course of the war, which confronted for the first time on the ground two opposing visions of national identity, one of which was carved out of a previously shared one, the two sides resorted to a 'war of words' (Abbink, 1998: 554) which was fought in the field as well as in printed statements and on the web. The vocal conflict was aimed not only at defending the reciprocal rights of each country over the disputed border but also at projecting the newly found national identity and consolidating its collective perception internally. The fact that the Eritrean identity had to be carved out of a previously shared Ethiopian one made matters all the more painful. Acknowledging a tense past between the two 'brothers at war' (Negash and Tronvoll, 2000) became a way of distinguishing the 'nation' from its enemy. The bitter war of words which was fought throughout the conflict was carried out through debasing accusations and reciprocal insults which were voiced in the media and increasingly, on the air.[4] The respective diaspora joined in and loudly took part in the globalised realm of the internet which soon became a new frontline for confrontation.[5]

Commemorating War Events: The Struggle Over Adwa

Throughout the conflict, suppressed memories came to be articulated in a fierce battle of definitions and slogans concerning the 'we' and 'them', the 'nation' and its 'enemy'. New sites of memory came to be proposed, while old ones were revisited and rewritten in the battlefield. War events were thus lived as occasions of memory, 'history-repeating-itself' in such a way as to confirm the new identity of the nation-in-the-making, offended and denied by the other side's national destiny. Thus war itself became a living *lieu de mémoire* (Nora 1984), a realm

[3] The conflict started on 6 May 1998 and ended on 12 December 2000. The war caused close to 100,000 deaths, about 300,000 displaced from the border areas and a heavy toll of destruction. The Algiers settlement provided for the installation of a 4200-member UN peace-keeping force (UNMEE), and the creation of a jointly-appointed Eritrea-Ethiopia Border Commission (EEBC) working under the auspices of the Permanent Court of Arbitration in the Hague, whose decision on the border would be accepted as final by both Parties. As I happened to visit Ethiopia regularly before and during the conflict, I was able to witness the rituals of war and memory which are discussed in this chapter.
[4] For a detailed account of the cyberspace exchange during the war, see Guazzini (2001).
[5] For Ethiopia see in particular the *Ethiopia-Eritrea Conflict Webpage* run by an anonymous Ethiopian signing himself as Dagmawi (the Amharic title for Emperor); the formally independent but pro-TPLF *Walta Information Center (WIC)* whose collection of 'Despatches' have now been printed (see Walta Information Center, n.d.); or the web pages of the unofficial *Warka*, *Ethioforum*, or *Ras_Alula.net*. For Eritrea, see in particular *Dehai – Eritrea Online*, *The Eritrean–mail network*, or *Asmarino.com*. For a more complete list, see Guazzini, 2001: 535-47.

which visibly revealed old rivalries and unveiled long felt chains of collective resentment. The war at the border was soon to be accompanied and sustained by a parallel war of memories inside the country.[6]

Commemorating war events thus became a way to come to terms publicly with a troubled past, to disentangle oneself, so to speak, from the once shared collective memory of the country. As elsewhere, the open recognition of 'a right of recountability' (Werbner, 1998: 1) in the public sphere encouraged a revisionist vein in national memory while new forms of 'state memorialism' were encouraged to justify the historical predicament confronting the country. The appropriation of war events of the past, particularly of their symbolic significance, became an intricate bone of contention. It is no wonder, then, that a powerful site of memory such as the Battle of Adwa, with its highly symbolic charge and differentiated interpretations, soon became an easy prey to the war climate.

The debate surrounding the 1896 Victory over the Italians will be taken here as an example of how a long-shared memory may become a divided one in times of war, and how it can be used in the political arena to forge a divisive future. In many ways, the Adwa case represents a turning point in the politics of memory being carried out in the region. It shows how a national event of great symbolic significance in colonial Africa is in fact an intricate web of diverse and even opposing memories, and can be perceived in post-colonial times both as a momentous event in the nation's past and as a painful scar to be healed or concealed within the new body politic. Just as in other 'memories of empires' which are increasingly questioned today (Dakhlia, 2000), hybridity and polysemic values appear to connote present-day revisitations of the country's past, particularly when – as in the Ethiopian case – the hidden history they conceal shows the recurrence of both the glorious 'victories' and the painful 'agonies' of a unified past which is as yet not equally shared among the nation's subjects (Strecker, 1994). Hence the peculiar 'efflorescence of state memorialism and popular counter-memory' (Werbner, 1998) which has characterised the recent debate over the country's past.

This is why the *internal* significance of the Adwa event has been increasingly scrutinised in Ethiopia as part of the enquiry into the country's troubled past. Adwa has been traditionally described as Ethiopia's most important *external* accomplishment to defend its sovereignty against colonial encroachment: 'Adwa ... has been subjected to this drum-and-trumpet treatment since 1896. The Ethiopian ruling elites have always tried to make certain that Adwa is present in our collective memory uniquely and only as *an externally oriented event*, as an affair between two states, Ethiopia and Italy' (Mennasemay, 1997: 49). Yet, Adwa's internal aspect is far more important as it 'raises issues more fundamental than the external one – hence the struggle to appropriate it by the opposing visions of Ethiopia that have emerged since the conquest of power by the TPLF' (ibid.: 43). In fact:

> It is the very category of 'Ethiopian' that is currently contested. Who are we? Just a collection of ethnic groups, unwillingly squatting beside each other, preparing for the right time to implement what the 1994 Ethiopian constitution calls the right of

---

[6] For a useful parallel of a 'redefined' past to show that people who had been neighbours since childhood could live no longer in the same territory, see the case of Serbia as described by Turton (1997: 82).

secession? Or, does Adwa intimate a new way of being Ethiopian such that the present conflicts of interpretation are but contradictory expressions of the difficult unfolding of the aspirations for freedom and national unity conceived at Adwa? (ibid.: 45).

It is this sort of questioning that made the celebrations of the Adwa centenary in 1996 a tense affair. When I went to Ethiopia in February of that year to help coordinate a group of Italian scholars wishing to take part in the centenary celebrations – itself a no less tense affair in view of the contrary 'epic of defeat' which the Battle of Adwa generated in my country[7] – I was taken aback by the strong emotions the Adwa victory was still able to evoke within Ethiopian intellectual society. In spite of the centenary festive mood and the jubilant tone of the celebrations, one could feel an undercurrent of tensions, ambiguities and silences which spoke unequivocally of the mixed feelings which the 1996 centenary unveiled. Throughout the lengthy preparations, in the debates at the international conference which was held in Addis Ababa on the eve of the anniversary and particularly during the ground celebrations which were locally carried out in Adwa itself, the northern town in Tigray, it was clear that the battle meant different things to different people.

To many Ethiopians and particularly to the Shoan-Amhara – the old power-holder group which presided over much of Ethiopia's political history and who were ousted from power in 1991 after the fall of the Derg – Adwa was the culmination of the unification process carried out by Emperor Menelik, the battle itself being 'an eloquent demonstration of national unity' and the high point of its national independence (Zewde, 1991: 76). Further, by extending Ethiopia's national borders, Menelik

> pushed the frontier of the Ethiopian state to areas beyond the reach even of such a renowned medieval empire-builder as *Negusa Nagast* Amda-Tseyon (1314-44). In the process, the Ethiopia of today was born, its shape consecrated by the boundary agreements made after the Battle of Adwa in 1896 with the adjoining colonial powers (ibid.: 60).

Yet, in Adwa town itself, the battle was mainly portrayed as 'a Tigray-Italian conflict' which helped Menelik divide the northern country and limit the power of Tigrayan hegemony in the region.[8] In so doing the Ethiopian monarch, while successfully repelling the Italian attack, allowed historic Tigray to be to cut in two, thus allowing the Tigrayan territory (Kebessa) north of the Mareb River to be part of Italian Eritrea (Abbay, 1998). Unlike Emperor Yohannes, the Tigrayan ruler who is praised today for using 'his military strength to defend the state-nation against foreign invaders ... rather than for a brutal subjugation of what he considered component regions of the state-nation' (Adhana, 1994: 23), Menelik exploited his victory over the Italians by subjugating peoples and nationalities north and south. An oral testimony collected by Jenny Hammond near Adwa vividly recalls this feeling:

---

[7] I have argued elsewhere that the memory surrounding the Battle of Adwa in my own country needed revisiting as it carries no less ambiguous emotions in today's perceptions of our colonial past (Triulzi 2003: 95-108).

[8] According to Mennasemay (1997: 81, fn. 3), a nucleus of Tigrayan intellectuals, who were well represented at the Adwa Centenary Conference in 1996, made sure that Adwa was seen mainly 'as a Tigray-Italian conflict'. Sven Rubenson (1996: 35) quotes the statement by Iyassu Gayim to the effect that 'the Italian Army "was crushed by the the the Tigrayans, who were assisted by Emperor Menelik".' See the debate over the Adwa issue in *Ethiopian Register*, Los Angeles, April 1999: 2-36.

For six or seven months, Menelik's army in Adwa ate everything, looted everything, burned houses for firewood. Before he had come to Adwa, Menelik had declared to his soldiers, 'Don't bring food! Tigray is a very strong enemy. We will eat their food and take their resources' ... Through all the feudal battles, the *akeytai* [imperial army] always depended on the people to feed the army, for fodder – all this came from the people in the villages, but in Tigray at this time they also had the express and explicit motive to weaken the Tigrayan economy and reduce the political threat. 'Even if he [Tigray] doesn't have anything to eat, he can still pay in money. Press him, press him.' The army also burned huts for firewood. The force was approximately 70,000, although it included a significant number of Tigrayans (Jenny Hammond, Adwa field notes, personal communication).

Finally, to many Oromo, numerically the most important group in Ethiopia, Adwa signalled the epic struggle between two colonial powers, Italy and Ethiopia, in which the Oromo peoples and the other southern nationalities saw no benefit or advantage. Menilik is viewed by Oromo nationalist historians as an internal coloniser who, with the success achieved over the Italians, accomplished a long-term project of brutal expansion by forcefully extending 'Abyssinian colonialism' (that is, Amhara-Tigrayan power and control) well beyond its traditional borders. The Battle of Adwa was no signal for black emancipation:

> With this victory Menelik defended not only historic Abyssinia, but also the southern colony he had already acquired through brutal conquest; conquest initiated by Shoan predecessors, but largely carried out by himself, an act without which the triumph of Adwa would not have been possible (Haj, 1994: 17).[9]

Hence, at the centennial celebrations of the Battle in 1996, the untold but central event was 'the struggle to appropriate Adwa' by its various contenders. The EPRDF coalition government then ruling the country was in fact in a *cul-de-sac*. On one side, it could not give the national event the importance it deserved without acknowledging Menelik's role in carrying out the Ethiopian victory over colonialism; at the same time it was unwilling to concede the internal 'drum-and-trumpet' effect in favour of Menelik's accomplishment to the detriment of local memories and repressed feelings within the coalition partners. That the Oromo, however under-represented in the government coalition, would not accept any glorification of Emperor Menelik was clearly stated by President Nagaso Gidada at the official opening of the centenary celebrations on Masqal Square on 2 March:

> Emperor Menelik invaded the people in southern, eastern and western Ethiopia and imposed upon them a brutal national oppression ... The expansionist invasion that Menelik had carried out caused the massacre of numerous people, inflicted on the rest humiliation and national oppression (*Ethiopian Herald*, 3 March 1996).

The result was an intricate web of official statements and silences, and the adoption of an all-endorsing pan-African symbolism which became the official slogan of the celebration: Adwa, an African victory (*Adwa: ya-Afrika dil*). A pamphlet publicising the centenary extolled the Ethiopian victory as the beginning 'of the struggle toward freedom, self-determination and self-rule of the peoples of Africa; a struggle which finally ended a hundred years later with the successful defeat of apartheid in South Africa.' By so doing, the coalition government attempted to achieve several conflicting aims in the newly exclusive national

---

[9] The classic colonial stand has been argued by Holcomb and Ibssa (1990). For recent criticism of the internal colonial theory, see Strecker, 1994: 306-12; Mennasemay, 1997: 54-61; Clapham, 2002: 42-3.

memory: to bypass the Amhara myth of national unification without hurting the Oromo and southern feelings of collective subjugation; to vindicate the all-Ethiopian aspect of the battle as a form of anticipation of the coalition-led government which presided over the commemoration and, finally, to play the African card of anti-colonialism without hurting the western allies and particularly the donor countries among which Italy (the ex-enemy) was a prominent member. Hence the 'considerable ambivalence and confusion' which marked the commemoration of the Adwa victory denounced by Bahru Zewde, the Director of the Institute of Ethiopian Studies, in his opening address to the Adwa Victory centenary conference which opened on 26 February:

> It remains a curious historical irony that the commemoration of such an event as Adwa, which was notable above all for its demonstration of supreme national consensus and single-mindedness, could be attended by doubt and uncertainty (Abdussamed and Pankhurst, 1998: 8).[10]

Two years later, while a prolonged and bloody conflict raged over the northern border (Abbink, 1998; Trivelli, 1998; Battera, 1999; Tadesse, 1999; Milkias, 1999; Berhane, 1999; Negash and Tronvoll, 2000; Abbink, 2003), a further dimension came to surround the Adwa event and its historical interpretation. All along the two-year conflict, war events were locally commented on with a constant 'look backward' effect, the Eritrean enemy being portrayed as the new external threat to the country's integrity as colonial Italy had been in the past. Old and new sites of memory thus emerged during the conflict and Adwa's memory was summoned back, this time as a *memory-against* colonial Eritrea. Although the historical analogy with colonial Italy reflected in many ways a search for legitimacy by the Tigrayan leadership over a fractured country, there is no doubt that the traumatic war experience of the past, or rather the representations of such experiences which were shaped in the course of the recent conflict, helped sustain the war effort and were used to instil a national sense of belonging of which the Eritreans were no longer part.

Badme: The Second Adwa

This became particularly clear after Ethiopia's counter-offensive of February 1999 which disrupted the Eritrean line of defence around the town of Badme and repelled the enemy across the border.[11] The crushing victory at the Badme front followed nine months of desultory trench warfare and extensive military build-up during which the Government had been repeatedly called to task for inaction. The military victory over the Eritrean enemy was to be celebrated accordingly. Thus, although the official news of the successful counter-offensive against Eritrean troops at the Badme front was announced on 27 February,

---

[10] Bahru Zewde was himself removed from office a few months after the centenary celebrations ended.
[11] The victory of Badme, which left on the ground an estimated 20,000 casualties on both sides, saw a gruesome three-day Ethiopian assault on fortified Eritrean positions. The battle was fought between 23-6 February with mop up operations the following day. The military operation, which was titled *Operation Sunset*, derived its name from a quote by the Eritrean President, Isayas Afeworki, that Eritreans would not withdraw from the occupied territories 'not even if the sun doesn't rise' (Press Digest (English, private weekly, hence PD), 4 March 1999: 1-3). For an account of the battle, see Milkias 1999, particularly pp. 44-6.

the government did not encourage street celebrations on the subsequent days. The TPLF government wanted to score a propaganda victory as well by delaying it until the 103rd Anniversary of the famous Victory of the Battle of Adwa, thereby equating the Badme success with the glorious victory of Adwa. Thus on the eve of the 103rd anniversary, the *Lualawinet* and Security Committee of Addis Ababa City Council called on the people to come out into Mesqel Square to celebrate the double victory on March 2, 1999 (*Ethiopian Register*, April 1999: 10).

On that day, the traditional commemoration of the Battle of Adwa saw a 'mammoth crowd' variously estimated between 500,000 and one million people gather in the capital's main celebration area in Mesqel Square.[12] The unusual mass attendance – possibly the greatest gathering of city residents since the coming to power of the new government – was due to the official announcement on 27 February that Operation Sunset, the Ethiopian counter-offensive against Eritrean troops at the Badme front, had resulted in a major victory over the occupying forces. Richard Lee, BBC correspondent in Addis Ababa, reported the event in these terms:

> There were remarkable scenes this morning in Addis Ababa ... The Mesqel Square which used to be known as Revolution Square was overflowing with up to a million people. There were groups of people chanting and dancing, singing praise songs for the soldiers at the front and also denouncing the Eritrean government. Many people were carrying placards... At one point, there was an effigy of the Eritrean President which was paraded around the square. They tried to burn it but they were stopped by the police. So, instead, they just threw it on the ground and kicked and tore it to shreds (*The Monitor*, 4 March 1999: 10).

Clearly, the tension which had accumulated in Ethiopia in the long 'nine months of patience',[13] and during the heated propaganda war which was daily exchanged between the two countries throughout the conflict (Abbink, 1998: 554; Guazzini, 2001: 550-62; Muchie, 1999: 32-6), found in the anniversary of the 1896 major victory over the Italian army a long repressed relief. But there was more to it. Because of the calculated matching of the dates of the two war events, the Battle of Badme soon came to be equalled to its more famous predecessor, the Battle of Adwa. Thus Badme was conveniently labelled 'the second Adwa'. During the following week practically all electronic and print media equalled 'Ethiopia's resounding defeat over a numerically mammoth Eritrean army' to the 'historic feat' accomplished at Adwa in 1896 (*PD*, 4 March and 11 March 1999). The argument was best synthesised by *Abyiotawi Demokrasi*, a private Amharic weekly in these terms:

> Some 103 years ago a historic feat was accomplished: Ethiopian warriors, armed with primitive weapons but full of courage, trounced a well-armed, well organized aggressor army from Italy. Forty years later, Fascist Italy's army invaded Ethiopia once again. Its cowardly army used internationally prohibited poison gas. Its victory was short-lived, and was finally kicked out, humiliated. Nine months ago, Issaias Afeworki, a brainchild of his Italian colonial masters, invaded Ethiopia. True to their history, Ethiopians once again punished and will continue to punish this latest aggressor (*Abyiotawi Demokrasi* 2-8 March, as quoted in *PD*, 11 March 1999: 11).

[12] See a report in PD of 11 March 1999: 9. Ethiopian Police gave the lower figure the day after the event (*The Monitor*, Addis Ababa (English, private weekly), 4 March 1999).

[13] 'We endured foreign occupation and humiliation for nine months in the hope that the international community would convince Eritrea to accept a peaceful solution to the conflict', (Office of the Government Spokesperson, Official Statement, 6 March 1999, *Addis Zemen* (Amharic, Government daily) 7 March 1999 as quoted in *PD*, 11 March 1999: 11).

The *Ethiopian Register*, an Amhara-based diaspora journal normally quite critical of the Tigrayan-led Ethiopian Government at home, commented on the event in no less glowing terms:

> Whether there is coincidence or not, March 2 is the 103rd anniversary of the Italian defeat at Adwa under the leadership of *Atse* Menelik. Whether intended or not, or by coincidence or not, the symbolic metaphor is not lost that yet another arrogant enemy was humiliated on the same day as the Italian colonialists were routed. There was national unity then, as there was unprecedented national unity now, against aggression (Muchie, 1999: 332).

The new political climate favoured a further step in the display of public memory in the country. If the Ethiopian victory at Badme was to be seen as 'the second Adwa', the victory of 1896, which had been celebrated only three years earlier, had to be adjusted to the new conditions prevailing in the country. The war laid the ground for the needed revision. It was pointed out that the Adwa Victory Centenary Conference in 1996 had not been attended by Eritrean scholars from Asmara. Eritrean feelings towards Adwa were voiced by Irma Taddia and Uoldelul Chelati Dirar in the following terms:

> On the one hand, in the collective memory of the Eritreans, the battle of Adwa represents the definitive act separating the Mareb-Mellasc [the area north of Mareb, i.e., Eritrea] from the rest of Ethiopia... Adwa is an Ethiopian matter. Why should Eritreans celebrate an Ethiopian victory that was used as an ideological weapon of Pan-Ethiopianism? ... Adwa surely represents a challenge to colonialism for many African people[s], but as far as Eritrea is concerned, a paradox emerges. Adwa actually strengthened the colonial power, it legitimated the colonial borders, and at the same time it represented a significant landmark towards the definition of Eritrea as a separate colonial society (Abdussamed and Pankhurst, 1998: 555, 563).

Four years later, the victory of Badme came to be charged with new meanings, particularly after the victorious offensive of the Ethiopian army in May 2000 which swept away Eritrean resistance and routed its army. The new victory made it clear that the Adwa-Badme association was meant to remain, as Badme was now called upon to symbolise the 'new' war-united Ethiopia under Tigrayan leadership, once again rejecting the old Eritrean aggressor. In so doing, the war appeared to redeem the silenced years of the post-liberation period up to the 1993 referendum when the Eritreans, said to have 'grown arrogant' because of their ex-colonial imprint and of their alliance with TPLF, were accused of maintaining a continued attitude of superiority and disdain towards their cousins across the Mareb River while taking full benefit of their double identity and privileged position within Ethiopian society.[14]

Settling Accounts with the Past

The historical comparison between Adwa and Badme was not unexpected. The war of words which had preceded the Ethiopian victory on the Badme front engendered a massive propaganda effort on both sides which made frequent use

[14] Examples of this kind of argument abounded in the Ethiopian press during the conflict. See in particular Tolosa Bedane 1999; Ahmed 1999; Sotal 1999. The historical background for anti-Tigrayan prejudice during the colonial period are examined in Abbay 1998: 21-68, and Berhe 2004.

of insulting epithets and debasing accusations. On the Ethiopian side (the only one I can bear witness to here), war propaganda closely associated Eritrean aggression to Italian colonial ambitions in the region and to the legacy of racist arrogance their colonial masters had left behind. Reacting to Eritrean President Issayas' remarks made on 18 July 1998 that the 'elite of Tigray have this baggage of feeling inferior, marginalised and wanting to assert itself by expanding territory,' the Ethiopian *Dagmawi* ('Emperor') quickly responded on the web by indicting

> *Fascist ideology* humiliated Eritreans and relegated them to sub-human status. In the search for positive self-identity, those Eritrean elites who had adopted some superficial Italian cultural aspects began to look down upon their 'uncivilised' fellowmen. The self-hatred caused by Italian colonialism was turned around and reflected on the common people of Ethiopia and Eritrea who were still in tune with their culture. It is this attitude which has been perpetuated through the past several decades, sadly contaminating the Eritrean identity. It is this phenomenon which has created the paradox whereby the indigenous cultural heritage of Axum is disparaged and the current inhabitants of the town derided as 'Agames'. In its place the Eritreans substitute the foreign trappings left behind by the departing Italians and cherish these relics as if they created them themselves (*Dagmawi*, 30 September 1998, in Walta Information Centre, n.d.: 117).

Although the state media were more restrained in their formal statements and official declarations,[15] both electronic and printed media, particularly in the private press, made recurrent use of Italian war images of the Fascist period manipulating faces and slogans to indict the new Eritrean 'fascists' and their coarse parroting of their ex-colonial masters. Thus a *National Geographic* picture of 1935 showing young Eritrean boys swearing 'to become loyal balillas' was turned into 'Issayas and Eritrean boys take the oath and swear to become loyal balillas,' the Eritrean President's face being cleverly superimposed on those of the Eritrean boys' and of the Italian militia officer.[16] Terms such as '*banda*', 'fascist', '*ascari*', '*agame*', people affected by 'the mulatto disease' or by 'the abused wife syndrome' were often used to indicate the Eritrean enemy in the Ethiopian media and the private press, thus indicating the continuity between the old Eritrean 'collaborators' and their heirs in the new 'colonial' regime at Asmara. In the Ethiopian Press, the Eritrean government was always labelled with its derivative '*sha'biyya*' ('popular') from the old title of the warring enemy Front, while the term '*woyane*', after the Tigrayan W*eyane* (peasant) rebellion of 1943, was always used in Eritrea to denote the Ethiopian TPLF 'revolutionary' leadership.[17]

> With the sounds of gunfire – so writes Ruth Iyob – also arose a crescendo of pent-up feelings of resentment in the form of ethnic slurs and re-interpretations of past grievances between the peoples of Eritrea and Ethiopia. That discourse reached an unprecedented level of ugliness when Radio Woyane (TPLF Radio) broadcast a speech

[15] Not so the Ethiopian daily radio broadcasts in Tigrinya addressed to the Eritrean public, themselves an answer to the vitriolic propaganda daily broadcast in Amharic from Asmara.
[16] The war of words was very much a war of images as well. The *National Geographic* picture was shown repeatedly on Internet in the *Ethio-Eritrean Conflict Home Page*, a private pro-Ethiopian network. See http://www.geocities.com (consulted 13.05.1999). For other images, notably the one where Hitler is pictured talking to Mussolini who states, in the superimposed caption pointing to a smiling Issayas, 'He is MY student and I have taught him well,' see the 'forum' of ethio.com at http://www2.ethio.com (consulted 13.05.1999).
[17] Several examples are quoted in Guazzini, 2001: 565-7. For the conflict being mainly an 'ascari's war', see Yilma, 1999. For the Weyane revolt see Tareke, 1996: 87-124.

by a high official accusing Eritreans of arrogance and superiority complex and claiming that 'they had threatened to wipe out the peoples of Tigray as if they were *kunchi* [fleas] with a can of anti-vermin spray' – words reminiscent of the early Hutu renditions of Tutsi bands as *inyenzi*, or cockroaches (Radio Woyane, 28 May 1998). Eritrean authorities responded that the *Woyane* (TPLF) did not constitute the legitimate Ethiopian government (Iyob, 2000: 677).[18]

The crude labelling was not just a rhetorical device which graphically aired the growing resentment among the Tigray leadership vis-à-vis the old allies now turned into enemies. As the conflict built up, the deep contrasts between the two Fronts, which had accompanied all along the uneasy anti-Mengistu alliance,[19] were gradually divulged breaking a tradition of secrecy which had been typical of the two Fronts but which had not surfaced in the public debate till then. In fact, the internal contrasts between the old allies in the field – TPLF and EPLF – were soon submerged by a much broader and widespread anti-Eritrean resentment which openly surfaced within the Ethiopian public, promptly stimulated by the war climate. The resentment had many causes, of which the forced independence of Eritrea agreed by the two Fronts in the absence of a public debate, and the expulsion of over 100,000 Ethiopians from independent Eritrea, were by no means the only ones. Equally important factors were the privileged position Eritrean citizens maintained in Ethiopia particularly after the 1993 referendum, their enjoying a *de facto* dual citizenship which allowed them to keep positions of power and wealth in the two countries, and the protection accorded them by the EPRDF government. The ensuing deportation of some 60,000 Ethiopian citizens of Eritrean origin was the sad outcome and the late replica of the earlier expulsions from independent Eritrea of the Ethiopian military and administrative personnel and their families.[20]

Yet the war unleashed another tense but hidden memory: that of the Eritrean collaborators in the 1935 Italian occupation of the country. Until the recent conflict, on the whole, Eritreans had not been held accountable for their past participation in the Italian colonial venture and occupation of the country. Following the liberation in 1941, and particularly after the federation with Eritrea in 1952, the nationalistic mythology which developed around the anti-Fascist resistance required a certain 'degree of historical amnesia' which was to soothe the newly found unity between the resisters, exiles and collaborators:

> In this nationalistic environment, tacit encouragement was given to amplify one's contribution and tactfully to avoid discussion of the deficiencies of others. Individuals who had served the Italians as *askaris* (regular soldiers) or *bande* (irregulars) largely became mute, unwilling and unencouraged to say much about the wartime experiences. Certainly the history books did not record their involvement (or did so minimally) and there was little serious effort to understand why they made the choices that they did (McClellan, 1996: 66).

---

[18] Ruth Iyob appears to be unaware that the image of anti-vermin spraying over the Ethiopian population was used in Fascist cartoons dating back to the Italian occupation period with clear reference to the use of mustard gas.

[19] On the contrasts between TPLF and EPLF, see in particular Young, 1996; Abbink, 1998; Trivelli, 1998; Berhe, 2004.

[20] The trauma of the reciprocal deportations and dehumanising modalities which accompanied them will remain in the collective memory of both Ethiopians and Eritreans as yet another unacknowledged structure of violence in the region. On this point see Gilkes and Plaut, 1999: 11, 54-56; Legesse, 1999; Assefa, 1999; Kibreab, 1999.

Thus, throughout the post-liberation period, it was the Eritrean patriots' resistance to Italian rule which was celebrated and many Eritreans were called in to help in the post-war reconstruction effort.[21] Thus, the fact that Eritrean troops had accompanied the Italian colonial army in 1896, and had been massively used in the repression of the Ethiopian resistance during the short-lived Fascist occupation of the country, became part of a grieved yet silenced past. Ironically, the Eritrean 'colonial' factor was not allowed to surface in Ethiopian society till the Eritrean liberation movement decided to use it to define its strategy for independence and even then it was openly dismissed by Ethiopia in her consistent denial of Eritrea's request for independence as an ex-colonial country wanting to decolonise. Yet, in a few months, the war with Ethiopia changed all this and freely unleashed an anti-Eritrean 'colonial' memory that had been repressed or removed till then.

Thus the war at the border was charged with a new symbolic function: to settle accounts with the past and ensure that the final separation between the two 'brother' countries became a living reality as it transformed, although traumatically, a political event agreed upon by the two Fronts (the Eritrean independence) into a cultural one. In this sense, the conflict has been a fatal turning point for both countries and the lengthy war, possibly miscalculated at first, helped consolidate a separate identity for both: this is perhaps one of the main reasons why it lasted so long. The conflict helped forge, perhaps irrevocably, an Eritrean national alterity which was denied throughout thirty years of war but which was openly vented during the thirty months of hostilities between the two countries. If Ethiopia was to be separated from Eritrea, it needed an irrevocable caesura. The war events helped to provide it:

> Badme is a place of no particular consequence in the highlands between Ethiopia and its much smaller kin, Eritrea, two nations of great promise in the Horn of Africa. But lying on the battlefields near the town are the corpses of 10,000 soldiers – maybe less, maybe more – who died over the last month because each nation claims Badme and the surrounding area as its own (Fisher, 1999).

It is the corpses of those 10,000 soldiers, 'maybe less, maybe more', that are making the irrevocable difference deep inside the Ethiopian nation and its ethos of wounded outrage and irreparable moral offence:

> The cluster bombs dropped [over] elementary schools killing children, and the bombs dropped on innocent civilians who were in line to receive food assistance in Adigrat, and the exodus of the Eritreans from Ethiopia and Ethiopians from Eritrea have assured us that we will be two separate and distinct countries (Sotal, 1999: II: 8).

As the TPLF-led coalition gradually consolidated its leadership over a country-in-arms, the war appeared to achieve important political assets for the Ethiopian government. Although its policies were critically exposed in the private press before the war, the political returns of the victorious events were now clearly perceived:

> The Ethiopian Government, which had low support in the country because of the ever deteriorating economy, has now allied Ethiopians behind it and garnered a lot of support. Though Ethiopians may have their domestic grievances, they are ready to defend their country ... No doubt that the Government of Ethiopia has taken full advantage of this war, which is indeed a blessing to it. It has armed and fortified itself

---

[21] On the involvement of Eritreans in the Ethiopian resistance movement, see Berhe, 2003: 106.

and maybe for the first time has become untouchable both for domestic and outside threat (Ahmed, 1999).[22]

And again, soon after the end of hostilities, observers agreed that

> Ethiopia's latest offensive against Eritrea has undoubtedly strengthened the position of the ruling coalition government. The war has produced a new sense of national unity and removed much of the suspicion and distrust with which the EPRDF administration has been viewed by many Ethiopians previously concerned about Tigrayan dominance in national politics (Biles, 2000: 22).

At the historiographical level, the conflict further inspired a new Tigrayan-oriented historical revisionism which the field victory over Eritrea appeared to sanction and legitimate on the ground. According to Medhane Tadesse's historical reconstruction of the conflict (1999),[23] Tigray always acted in Ethiopian history as the 'senior partner' of the wider Tigrinya-speaking region. The Tigray lords are said to have had 'precedence and grandeur' over their northern rivals since Alvarez' time and always 'acted as protectors of their junior partners to the north of the Mereb' (ibid.: 5-7).[24] It was the Italian colonial presence that first instilled 'an incipient supremacist feeling among the Tigrinya-speaking Eritrean urban elite vis-à-vis the Tigray and other Ethiopian nationalities', while colonial Fascism inevitably bred 'the mutation in the character, behaviour as well as socio-cultural identity' particularly of the urbanised Eritrean elite. 'Fiat cars and Italian villas' thus gave the Eritreans a false sense of superiority which entrenched itself and affected Eritrean nationalism at a time when Tigray was impoverished and starved by a centralised feudal state (ibid.: 26-43).

But the Tigray political elite, the author tells us, did not fall into the easy trap of Eritrean-Tigrinya nationalism. From the beginning it opted for Ethiopia and maintained its pledge throughout. Thus the anti-Mengistu struggle which was fought together with the ex-Eritrean allies is explained today by Tigrayan intellectuals as being only tactical, beleaguered as it was by continuous superiority complexes and arrogant behaviour on behalf of the EPLF, and by deep strategic and political divergences (ibid.: 50-86; see also Adhana, 1994; Young, 1996; Berhe, 2004). Thus, while TPLF reorganised the country under a coalition government and, although traumatically, 'applied the principle of self-determination and ethnic federalism', EPLF went on building, as it had been doing from the start, 'a nation from above'. The two governments are said to have adopted 'diametrically opposite and even hostile political systems' (Tadesse, 1999: 102 – but see also Tadesse and Young, 2003).

A War-Created Unity

Seen in this perspective, the victory over the Eritrean aggressor is indeed a 'second Adwa', a major war of national identity and the beginning of a new cycle

---

[22] Not all private press subscribed to the newly-found unity. On June 3 *Tobyia* (Amharic private weekly) wrote: 'We had thought that we have avoided war once and for all and restored lasting peace in our country. Sad enough, we have once again slid into another morass of war – a war of destruction and misery... [while] another round of drought and famine is hovering over the country.' See *PD*, 10 June 1999:6.

[23] Though not an official publication, the volume has been massively diffused in Addis Ababa and debated in the media.

[24] Francisco Alvarez was a member of the Portuguese embassy who visited Ethiopia in 1520.

of state formation and consolidation of supremacy in the region of the Horn. The war has helped the government to redefine an enduring site of memory and charge it with new symbolic meanings which were sanctioned on an everyday basis by the conflict itself. It is through war that Ethiopian society was brought to internalise the political wound of Eritrean independence, while strengthening at the same time the feeling of unity in the country.[25]

How flimsy this war-created unity was, became clear by post-war events. Although political tension over the conduct of the war had been rampant within both fronts during the conflict, public dissent was only voiced in public in the aftermath of its settlement. Between spring and summer 2001, a series of political crises of unprecedented nature shook both the Ethiopian and the Eritrean governments, with serious splits among the two leading political fronts, mass arrest of opponents following student protests and a dramatic tightening of state security and repression.[26] In the meantime, while the internationally supervised demarcation of the border was delayed on the ground pending the decision of the agreed-upon Boundary Commission (the EEBC) to decide on the disputed border, tension grew again when the Commission released its decision in April 2002 and it soon became clear that neither party could claim victory, although both governments had done so at the beginning.[27] When the news was finally released that the village of Badme on the Western Sector of the Border had been assigned to Eritrea, the Ethiopian government repeatedly raised its voice in protest and in September 2003 formally rejected the Commission's decision as 'illegal, unjust and irresponsible' and appealed to the United Nations Security Council.[28] Faced by international hostility and the rejection by the UN of her appeal, the Ethiopian government has been confronted since by renewed public outcry and internal opposition over the loss of Badme to the Eritreans.

In November 2003 the Eritrean government withdrew its representative from Addis Ababa, and officially proposed that the seat of the African Union be moved away from the Ethiopian capital. In return, the Ethiopian government has advanced a new political platform, which has been rejected by Eritrea, of formal acceptance of the verdict together with parallel renegotiation of the territory within the Badme area. In December 2004, it was reported that a policy of 'voluntary resettlement' of Tigrayan families was being encouraged in the area of Badme, and voter registration for national elections was being carried out in Badme as late as January 2005.[29] The matter is not over yet, and the fate of Badme will continue to be a political test of defiance for both countries.[30]

[25] In this sense also Clapham 2000. Quoting Edward Luttwak's article 'Give War a Chance', Clapham critically analyses the use of war as a state-formation device in countries such as Ethiopia where the 'nation' has been imposed from above and there is no inclusive national feeling as yet.

[26] Two articles (Tadesse and Young, 2003, and Hedru, 2003) have argued that the war represented a watershed in the recent history of both countries and their leadership, weakening the position of the respective fronts and opening the way to renewed forms of coercion and personal rule.

[27] The Commission issued its decision on 13 April 2002. Although it mentioned the towns of Tserona and Fort Cadorna (assigned to Eritrea) and Zalambessa (assigned to Ethiopia) in the central sector, with an equal sharing of the area of Bure in the east, no mention was made of Badme, in the western sector, which continued to be under Ethiopian administration (see White, 2002).

[28] The UN upheld the Commission's decision. See United Nations Security Council, 'Progress Report of the Secretary-General on Ethiopia and Eritrea', 19 December 2003.

[29] *Sudan Tribune*, 8.12.2004; and *Addis Triubune*, 28.01.2005.

[30] In a recent article posted on the web, Jon Abbink, 2003, has defined Badme as 'the linchpin of national integrity … and whoever would be accorded it under the EEBC decision would carry the day and be perceived as the ultimate victor of the war.'

Clearly, the 'nature of the violence perpetrated in this two-year war has sunk deep into the public consciousness' and has been dangerously 'internalised'. If the rationale of the war was to '"create difference" and anchor it psychologically' in the country at large, the war has been an easy win, and its net result will inevitably be 'the impending creation of an iron-clad, physical border between Ethiopia and Eritrea, in an area of trans-border contacts and shared identities' (Abbink, 2001: 448-53; see also Tronvoll, 1999).

Whatever the decision will be, such a border has been and will remain of an artificial nature. It will definitively separate frontier peoples and local communities, such as the Irob, the Kunama and the Afar, who have always lived side by side at the periphery of equally exploiting colonial or internal governments, whether of 'hegemonic' or 'diasporic' nature (Iyob, 2000; Abbink, 2001), by forging cross-border contacts and alliances which are no longer possible:

> This war is easier for someone from Addis Ababa and Asmara than those living in Zalambessa, Irob, and Badme. People there on both sides of the border have more in common with the 'enemy' than with their countrymen. This is a conflict that splits family members into two military camps. It has brought Cousin against Cousin. Trying to draw a straight boundary line through the people above is in itself a crime. ... Hatred that has already been plowed will be harvested, and there will not be an end after the conclusion of the war. ... The most probable outcome of this war [is] that there will not be a winner and a loser, only two losers (Sotal, 1999, I: 9).

The tremendous social and human costs of the Ethio-Eritrean war, the toll of human and material destruction caused in the border region and the new unacknowledged 'legacy of violence' shovelled on the peoples of the Horn, may soon form a new intractable web of divisive memories which may be even more difficult to acknowledge, let alone commemorate, in the future. Writing history in war will not help reconcile divided memories in the region or the building of new bridges over a common if troubled past.

References

Abbay, Alemseged (1998) *Identity Jilted or Re-Imagining Identity? The Divergent Paths of the Eritrean and Tigrayan Nationalist Struggles*, Lawrenceville, NJ and Asmara: The Red Sea Press.

Abbay, Alemseged (2004) 'Diversity and State-Building in Ethiopia', *African Affairs* 103: 593-614.

Abbink, Jon (1995) 'Transformations of Violence in Twentieth-Century Ethiopia: Cultural Roots, Political Conjunctures', *Focaal* 25: 57-77.

Abbink, Jon (1998) 'Briefing: The Eritrean-Ethiopian Border Dispute', *African Affairs* 97: 551-65.

Abbink, Jon (2001) 'Creating Borders: Exploring the Impact of the Ethio-Eritrean War on the Local Population', *Africa* (Roma) 56(4): 447-58.

Abbink, Jon (2003) 'Badme and the Ethiopia-Eritrea Conflict. Back to Square One?' *Perihelion Working Papers* (http://www.erpic.org/perihelion/wps/ethiopia.hlm)

Abdussamed, Ahmed and Richard Pankhurst (eds) (1998) *Adwa Victory Centenary Conference 26 February–2 March 1996*, Addis Ababa: Institute of Ethiopian Studies, Addis Ababa University.

Adhana, Adhana Haile (1994) 'Mutation of Statehood and Contemporary Politics in Ethiopia', in Abebe Zegeye and Siegfried Pausewang (eds) *Ethiopia in Change. Peasantry, Nationalism and Democracy*, London and New York: British Academy Press, pp. 12-44.

Ahmed, Hashim A. (1999) 'Eritrea's Problem is a Leadership Future', *Addis Tribune*, 12 March.

Assefa, Samuel (1999) 'On Deportations', *Addis Tribune*, Part I: 7 May, Part II: 14 May, Part III: 21 May (also printed in *The Ethiopian Herald*, 21, 22, 23 May).

Battera, Federico (1999) 'Il conflitto Etiopia-Eritrea e is uoi effetti sulla crisi permanente del Corno d'Africa', *Africa* (Rome) 56(4): 492-531.

Baxter, Paul, Jan Hultin and Alessandro Triulzi (eds) (1996) *Being and Becoming Oromo: Historical and Anthropological Approaches*. Uppsala: Nordic Africa Institute, pp. 7-25.

Bedane, Tolosa (1999) 'The Genesis of the Ethio-Eritrean Crisis', *The Ethiopian Herald*, February 10.

Berhane, Mekonnen (1999) 'Imagined Versus Actual Impacts of the Eritrean-Ethiopian Conflict', *Horn of Africa* 17: 72-87.

Berhe, Aregawi (2003) 'Revisiting Resistance in Italian-occupied Ethiopia: The Patriots' Movement and the Redefinition of Post-War Ethiopia (1936-1941)', in Jon Abbink, Mirjam de Bruijn, Klaas van Walraven (eds) *Rethinking Resistance. Revolt and Violence in African History*, Leiden: Brill, pp. 87-113.

Berhe, Aregawi (2004) 'Origins of the Tigray People's Liberation Front', *African Affairs* 103: 569-92.

Biles, Peter (2000) 'Bitter Foes', *Diplomatic Briefings* (Addis Ababa): 15(72).

Clapham, Christopher (1999) 'Menelik's People. The Difficulty of Defining Ethiopia', *Times Literary Supplement*, 7 May: 4-5.

Clapham, Christopher (2000) 'War and State Formation in Ethiopia and Eritrea', *Critique Internationale*, Fall; reprinted in Italian in *Afriche e Orienti*, 3/4: 110-18.

Clapham, Christopher (2002) 'Rewriting Ethiopian History', *Annales d'Ethiopie* 18: 37-54.

Dakhlia, Jocelyn (2000) 'Introduction' to the international conference on 'Mémoires d'empires', Paris: EHESS.

de Waal, Alex (1994) 'Rethinking Ethiopia', in Charles Gurdon (ed.) *The Horn of Africa*, SOAS-GRC Geopolitical Series, London: UCL Press.

Fisher, Ian (1999) 'Wherever That Town Is, Someone Will Die for It', *The Reporter*, Addis, 24 March.

Gellner, Ernest (1983) *Nations and Nationalism*, London: Blackwell.

Gilkes, Patrick and Martin Plaut (1999) *War in the Horn: The Conflict between Eritrea and Ethiopia*, London: The Royal Institute of International Affairs.

Guazzini, Federica (2001) 'Riflessioni sulle identità di guerra nel cyberspazio: il caso eritreo-etiopico', *Africa* (Rome) 56(4): 532-72.

Haj, Abbas (1994) 'Menelik's Conquest as the Genesis of Ethiopian Crises. A Case of the Arsi Oromo', *The Oromo Commentary*, 4(2): 17-23.

Hassen, Mohammed (1990) *The Oromo of Ethiopia: A History 1570-1860*, Cambridge: Cambridge University Press.

Hassen, Mohammed (1994) 'Some Aspects of Oromo History That Have Been Misunderstood', *The Journal of Oromo Studies* 1(2): 77-90.

Hedru, Debessay (2003) 'Eritrea: Transition to Dictatorship, 1991-2003', *Review of African Political Economy*, 97: 435-44.

Holcomb, Bonnie and Sisay Ibssa (1990) *The Invention of Ethiopia: The Making of a Dependent Colonial State in Northeast Africa*, Trenton, NJ: The Red Sea Press.

Iyob, Ruth (2000) 'The Ethiopian-Eritrean Conflict: Diasporic vs. Hegemonic States in the Horn of Africa, 1991-2000', *The Journal of Modern African Studies* 38(4): 659-82.

Jalata, Asafa (1993) *Oromia and Ethiopia: State Formation and Ethnonational Conflict, 1868-1992*. Boulder and London: Lynne Rienner Publications.

Jalata, Asafa (ed.) *Oromo Nationalism and the Ethiopian Discourse. The Search for Freedom and Democracy*, Lawrenceville NJ: The Red Sea Press.

James, Wendy, Donald L. Donham, Eisei Kurimoto and Alessandro Triulzi (eds) (2002) *Remapping Ethiopia: Socialism and After*, Oxford: James Currey.

Kibreab, Gaim (1999) 'Mass Expulsion of Eritreans and Ethiopians of Eritrean Origin from Ethiopia and Human Rights Violations', *Eritrean Studies Review* 3(2): 107-37.

Lata, Leenco (2003) 'The Ethiopia-Eritrea War', *Review of African Political Economy* 97: 369-88.

Legesse, Asmarom (1999) *The Uprooted*, Asmara: Citizens for Peace in Eritrea.

Luttwak, Edward (1999) 'Give War a Chance', *Foreign Affairs* 78: 4.

McClellan, Charles (1996) 'Observations on the Ethiopian Nation, Its Nationalism, and the Italo-Ethiopian War', *Journal of African Studies* 3(1): 57-86.

Mennasemay, Maimire (1997) 'Adwa: A Dialogue between the Past and the Present', *Northeast African Studies* 4(2) (new series): 43-89.

Milkias, Paulos (1999) 'Ethiopia and Eritrea at War: Saga of Triumph and Tragedy at the Dawn of the Millennium', *Horn of Africa* 17: 33-71.

Muchie, Mamo (1999) 'From Adwa to Badme: Lessons from History', *Ethiopian Register* 4: 32-6.

Mudimbe, Valentin-Yves and Bogumil Jewsiewicki (1993) 'Africans' Memories and Contemporary History of Africa', *History and Theory* 32(4): 1-11.

Negash, Tekeste and Kjetil Tronvoll (2000) *Brothers at War. Making Sense of the Eritrean-Ethiopian*

War, Oxford: James Currey.

Nora, Pierre (1984) *Les lieux de mémoire*, vol. I Paris: Gallimard.

Ranger, T. O. (1976) 'Towards a Usable African Past', in Christopher H. Fyfe (ed.) *African Studies since 1945: A Tribute to Basil Davidson*, London: Longman, pp. 28-39.

Rubenson, Sven (1996) 'The Falsification of History: When,Who and Why', *Ethiopian Register*, 3(3): 35.

Sorenson, John (1991) 'Discourse on Eritrean Nationalism and Identity', *Journal of Modern African Studies* 29(2): 301-17.

Sorenson, John (1993) *Imagining Ethiopia. Struggles for History and Identity in the Horn of Africa*, New Brunswick, NJ: Rutgers University Press.

Sotal [pseudonym] (1999) 'Eritrean and Ethiopian Bitter Divorce', *Addis Tribune* Part I: 5 March; Part II: 12 March.

Strecker, Ivo (1994) 'Glories and Agonies of the Ethiopian Past', *Social Anthropology* 2(3): 303-12.

Tadesse, Medhane (1999) *The Eritrean-Ethiopian War: Retrospect and Prospects. Reflections on the Making of Conflicts in the Horn of Africa, 1991-1998*, Addis Ababa: Mega Printing Enterprise.

Tadesse, Medhane and John Young (2003) 'TPLF: Reform or Decline?', *Review of African Political Economy* 97: 389-403.

Tareke, Gebru (1996) *Ethiopia: Power and Protest. Peasant Revolts in the Twentieth Century*, Lawrenceville, NJ and Asmara: The Red Sea Press.

Tibebu, Teshale (1995) *The Making of Modern Ethiopia 1896-1970*, Lawrenceville, NJ: Red Sea Press.

Triulzi, Alessandro (2002a) 'Battling with the Past: New Frameworks for Ethiopian Historiography', in Wendy James, Donald Donham, Eisei Kurimoto and Alessandro Triulzi (eds) *Remapping Ethiopia: Socialism and After*, Oxford: James Currey, pp. 276-88.

Triulzi, Alessandro (2002b) 'Violence and the Acknowledgement of Tense Past in the Horn: A Note on the Ethio-Eritrean War (1998-2000)', *Cadernos de Estudos Africanos* 2: 91-102.

Trivelli, Richard M. (1998) 'Divided Histories, Opportunistic Alliances: Background Notes on the Ethiopian-Eritrean War', *Afrika Spectrum* 33(3): 257-89.

Tronvoll, Kjetil (1999) 'Borders of Violence – Boundaries of Identity: Demarcating the Eritrean Nation State', *Ethnic and Racial Studies* 42(6): 1037-60.

Turton, David (1997) 'War and Ethnicity: Global Connections and Local Violence in North East Africa and Former Yugoslavia', *Journal of Oxford Development Studies* 25(2): 77-94.

Walta Information Center n.d. [2000] *Dispatches from the Electronic Front: Internet Responses to the Ethio-Eritrean Conflict*, Addis Ababa: Berhanena Selam.

Werbner, Richard (1998) 'Introduction', in R. Werbner (ed.) *Memory and the Postcolony: African Anthropology and the Critique of Power*, London and New York, Zed Books.

White, Philip (2002) 'The Eritrea-Ethiopia Border Arbitration', *Review of African Political Economy* 96: 345-56.

Yilma, Tilahun (1999) 'The Eritrean and Tigrean Askaris War in Defence of a Colonial Boundary', *Ethiopian Register* 6(7):18-23.

Young, John (1996) 'The Tigray and Eritrean Liberation Front: A History of Tensions and Pragmatism', *The Journal of Modern African Studies* 34(1): 105-20.

Zegeye, Abebe and Siegfried Pausewang (eds) (1994) *Ethiopia in Change: Peasantry, Nationalism and Democracy*, London: British Academic Press.

Zewde, Bahru (1991) *A History of Modern Ethiopia, 1855-1974*, London: James Currey.

8

Violence as Signifier
Politics & Generational Struggle in KwaZulu-Natal

PREBEN KAARSHOLM

Introduction: The Meaning of Violence

The last decade of apartheid rule in South Africa from the mid-1980s to the mid-1990s was characterised by high levels of political violence which were obviously 'meaningful' inasmuch as they related to the struggle for and against democratisation and majority rule. But the more specific 'meanings' of forms of violence, their intensity and their background in local micro-politics and understandings of antagonisms were perhaps less clear – not least in politically complex areas like KwaZulu-Natal where the battle was not only between supporters and opponents of the apartheid state, but also between the Inkatha Freedom Party (IFP) on the one hand and the United Democratic Front (UDF) and the African National Congress (ANC) on the other to control or 'liberate' individual communities internally.

Since the transition from apartheid in 1994, openly political violence of the above type has abated and resurfaced mainly when balances in the distribution of power bastions have been challenged, or when new political actors – like the United Democratic Movement (UDM) – have tried to get a foothold in new local contexts. Otherwise, forms of violence which have continued at high levels, again, not least in areas like KwaZulu-Natal, have tended to be seen as criminal or – as I have written myself – as 'acts of meaningless terror and depredation' marring everyday life (see Kaarsholm, 2000; Marks, 2004).

In this chapter, I shall discuss in some detail the ways in which violence has unfolded and been used within one particular urban slum settlement outside Durban in KwaZulu-Natal, but let me first relate the issue to a more overall discussion of backgrounds to violent conflict and violence escalation in Africa.

In *Fighting for the Rain Forest: War, Youth and Resources in Sierra Leone* (1996), Paul Richards questions formulations of 'random violence', 'the irrationality of violence', 'meaningless violence' and so on as used to describe the tactics of killings and mutilations employed by the RUF (Revolutionary United Front) rebel movement in Sierra Leone, often carried out by child or teenage soldiers of the forest (see also Richards, 2000).

Richards is targeting in particular writings such as Robert Kaplan's much discussed essay on 'The Coming Anarchy' (1994) and Kaplan's assertion that the form of recent conflicts in Liberia, Sierra Leone, Rwanda, Somalia signals the coming to life of a 'new barbarism' in Africa.

As to RUF action, Richards goes on to work out an explanation (or rather two explanations) for the 'rationality' underlying the violence of the youthful rebels. In his first explanation, the violence is related to the radical marginalisation and social exclusion of youth in the hinterland diamond and forest zones of Sierra Leone. Their world views and ambitions are basically modernist but their hopes of progress and livelihood vested in education and opportunities facilitated through the state have not been fulfilled. As traditional forms of patronage have also been undermined, a large class has emerged of 'excluded intellectuals', 'embittered pedagogues', 'internal exiles' with no access to employment or career except for the illegal digging of alluvial diamonds.

Such groups have formed a significant part of the RUF's forced or voluntary recruitment, and in Richards' view the forms of extreme violence committed against the civilians of the countryside – precisely the population that one would expect to support the rebel movement – may be explained through particularly intellectual and theoretical notions of rationality, rooted in this sociological background. The violence is a scream coming from those *in extremis*, directed more at listeners in the capital and in the outside world than at local people. It calls attention to the plight of those marginalised in the backwoods of globalisation. In this respect, Richards compares the rationality of thinking in the Qadaffi-inspired RUF cadres with that of the similarly 'didactic' Maoist Shining Path movement in Peru (Richards, 2000: 28).

In a postscript to the second edition of his book, Richards goes on to offer a second, more elaborate, explanation. The original scenario of the rebellion was one in which marginalised young 'intellectuals' faced a system of 'state patri-monialism' which had abandoned its obligations towards them. Thus they confronted it with an alternative model of radically egalitarian meritocracy. This two-pole model of understanding no longer sufficed with the entry onto the scene of the *kamajo* militias. Significantly, these 'hunter' militias, linked to chiefly authority and utilising traditional 'bush craft' as well as local forms of magic and medicine, were brought into the war by the Kabbah government from 1996. Alongside South African Executive Outcomes mercenaries, their task was to hunt down the elusive units of the RUF and penetrate the no-go-zones which protected the fortress-like purity of RUF-controlled 'enclaves'. The militias were very successful:

> [B]y origin at least, *kamajo* militia units represented a revival of an older local patrimonial power, untrammelled by state interference... Paramount chiefs, in local tradition, first asserted their title to the forest through prowess in hunting. [A] young *kamajo* informant stresses that *kamajo* fighters, as revitalised citizens of the 'dead' zone, had the magical power to move at will, and control all spaces,... appearing in places where you would not expect ... *Kamajo* magical powers of movement and bullet protection actually worked, he vehemently asserted... The RUF/SL seem, equally to have been in no doubt that that the *kamajo* threat was real. Prepared to battle corrupted state patrimonialism, the movement seems to have become badly disoriented by this unexpected resurgence of a more authentic local patrimonial power threatening to take away its protective 'wall' (Richards, 1996: 182).

So when eventually the hunter militias also broke away from the Government to represent an alternative social movement, rivalling that of the RUF, this led to an acceleration of the RUF's radical egalitarianism. It was at this stage that the violence of the movement also escalated: when peasants have their hands cut off to prevent them from harvesting, their fingers mutilated to keep them from voting and their feet amputated to prevent them from running back to their chiefs. RUF violence, in Richards' view, can thus be seen as an 'extreme form of "rationalist" response to the patrimonial magic of the *kamajo*' while the militias themselves have retaliated with further atrocities such as beheadings, which have clear connotations of magic (Richards, 1996: 182). In this way, the confrontation became one not just between rebels and the state, but also between 'modernist' and 'traditionalist' movements and ideologies of opposition, between ideas of radical egalitarian renewal and of moral and cultural rearmament as the alternative to the decay of state patrimonialism.

A similar analysis is presented by Koen Vlassenroot in an essay on confrontations in the Congo-Rwanda border region, where he attempts to explain the violence of *mayi-mayi* youth militias as occurring in the context of 'democratic' reforms imposed from the central state and undermining structures of local patrimony (see Vlassenroot, 2000, cf. Vlassenroot's chapter in this collection).

Interesting in Richards' analysis is his interpretation of the RUF youth soldiers' use of modern global visual media and in particular their reception and interpretation of the violent Sylvester Stallone movie *First Blood* (which initiated the *Rambo* series). Such media inspiration – also recognisable in the scary costumes, masks and performance styles of youthful Liberian rebels entering Monrovia in 1990 and transmitted through to TV screens all over the world – has been pointed out as another instance of the 'new barbarism' breaking forth in Africa. But in his interviews and analysis, Richards shows the reception and utilisation of *First Blood* and the Rambo imagery to be much more complex:

> Video has had a wide impact in the forested diamond districts of Sierra Leone, and this little drama of the social exclusion of the miseducated is often cited by young people as one of their favourite films, or the film they found most enlightening (significantly, the word they most often use in this context is 'educative'). *First Blood* has several times been compared, by informants, to the impact of studying Shakespeare's *Macbeth* at school. *Macbeth* strips the mask of public service from politics to reveal naked personal ambition beneath. The point that strikes home about Rambo is social exclusion. Ejected from town by the corrupt and comfortable forces of law and order, with only his wits for protection, Rambo is on his own in the forest. The *result* of social exclusion, the film seems to say, is unconstrained violence. That violence is cathartic, since it serves to wake up society at large to the neglected cleverness of youth. The film speaks eloquently to young people in Sierra Leone fearing a collapse of patrimonial support in an era of state recession (Richards, 1996: 57-8).

Rather than an instance of 'violence-as-entertainment' as seen perhaps by western audiences, *First Blood* in mobile forest video parlours as well as on urban murals in Sierra Leone became an 'epic of self-empowerment', with Rambo being identified with trickster figures of Mende narrative traditions and advocating either revolutionary egalitarianism, or possibly just a need 'not to clear away the old system entirely, but to establish a national debate about a new and fairer patrimonialism' (ibid.: 58-9).

Globalised media messages and symbolisms thus meet with locally differentiated receptions and responses. Besides Sierra Leone, Rambo, *ninjas* and *kung fu* master fighters enter the cultural stages and inner worlds of villages in the Indian highlands of Guatemala, the video parlours in the townships of Nairobi, and into the preferences, conversations, life styles and identifications of youth in urban shack settlements of post-apartheid South Africa.

South Africa is a long way from Sierra Leone; the political dynamics of violence and identity formation in KwaZulu-Natal in the 1990s is very different from that of the diamond fields in the rain forest. There is not anything essentially 'African' that unites them (as a 'new barbarist' might think). Still, it appears to me helpful to enter into dialogue with Paul Richards' interpretation of the possible meanings of violence in Sierra Leone and to confront this with the ways in which violence figures in the life of youth in Amaoti – a slum settlement in Inanda on the outskirts of Durban and an area intensely disputed and violently fought over in the process of apartheid's collapse and the emergence of the new South Africa.

Context: Place and History

The word Amaoti is said to mean 'more wood' and is the name of an area within Inanda, situated about 35 kilometres from the centre of Durban and allegedly named so because it used to be a forested and uninhabited place. In the late nineteenth century, workers on neighbouring sugar estates would be directed to fetch firewood there (interview J-13, 25 September 1999). The history of the area is linked to that of the Inanda mission reserve and of the Qadi chieftainship and until the 1960s, Amaoti remained a quiet rural place where land was divided among often quite prosperous Indian and African freehold farmers and smallholders who were allocated land by the Qadi chief or his *induna* (Hughes, 1985 and 1998).

That African freehold should be possible so close to centre of Durban and to the prime sugar lands of Natal has to do with the history of the extensive tracts of land which were given to the American Board of Commissioners for Foreign Missions at Inanda in the 1840s as a mission reserve, and from which the missionaries for a period from the 1850s sold off plots of freehold land to individual African converts. From the late nineteenth century, other freehold plots were acquired by Indian labourers who had completed their contracts for indenture on the sugar plantations and now established themselves as traders, maize growers and market gardeners on the outskirts of Durban (Hughes, 1985: 6).

Out of these African and Indian middle-class environments in Inanda emerged prominent intellectuals, educationalists and political leaders such as John Dube, Isaiah Shembe, A. W. G. Champion and Mohandas Gandhi. At the same time, possibilities for social and cultural development in Inanda were minimised through the reductions of mission reserve holdings, and of areas available for African freehold, proclaimed in the land acts of 1913 and 1936, and by segregation measures directed against Indians. Thus from 1936, large tracts of land in Inanda became designated a 'released area' which meant that they would be held in Government trust with a view to their eventually being made available for African communal use within a system of segregation, but without any specific plan or time schedule being worked out for this process.

Together with land which was being sub-let by freeholders for whom 'rent farming' had become more profitable than the growing of crops, from the 1960s these 'released' lands became an area of refuge for growing numbers of sub-letters and squatters who were alienated from more formal kinds of settlement through the policies of 'high' apartheid. Durban's two big formal townships of Umlazi (to the south) and KwaMashu (to the north-west) were established from the late 1950s with the clear intention that they would eventually be incorporated into a nationally independent Zulu 'homeland' – providing rurally based 'labour lungs' for the city of Durban – and that residence within them would be given preferentially to people of Zulu identity. With the development of the KwaZulu administration through the 1970s, these requirements became increasingly formalised, but already from the time that the famous informal settlement of Cato Manor was cleared around 1960, Inanda, with its fairly vague and unpoliced planning regulations, became a favourite site to seek residence for people who did not fit or did not want to fit in with the designs for settlement of the Group Areas Act.

Furthermore, Inanda was relatively close to the urban centre and was there-fore attractive for people looking for formal or informal employment in the dockyards, in Durban industries, as house servants, or generally seeking their fortune in town. In particular, it presented a stepping stone into urban life for people arriving from outside Natal and Zululand: for Xhosa speakers coming in from Pondoland and Transkei, for Chewa speakers with Malawian family histories and for Shangaans speakers seeking employment or escaping violence and destabilisation in Mozambique. Such settlers would mix with migrants arriving from poverty-stricken areas of rural Zululand and, as the 1980s progressed, with people fleeing from the upheavals and clashes accompanying the break-up of apartheid, or taking advantage of the fact that influx controls were no longer being enforced as vigorously as before. Thus, in the 1980s, Amaoti became home to groups of Xhosa speakers who had run away from conflicts and political violence in the coastal area south of Durban and who used networks of family and home association to find settlement at Inanda.

In the process, Amaoti and other Inanda areas like neighbouring Bhambayi ('Bombay') – home to Gandhi's famous Phoenix settlement – were transformed into overpopulated shack settlements without services of sanitation, water supply or electricity. At the same time, the communities became increasingly torn by the forms of instability and violence from which people had run away, such as by political conflict between the UDF and the IFP and by struggles over access to and control over local resources. These conflicts were intensified significantly through the interference of the apartheid state. Regarding settlements like Amaoti, apartheid policy remained undecided. In the late 1970s, the immediate threat appeared to be forced removals of squatters under the Group Areas Act to make space for an expansion of the neighbouring Indian area of Phoenix. Later plans moved in the direction of transforming this and other parts of Inanda into formalised African townships. Following periods of drought and outbreaks of typhoid and cholera, pressure was put on landlords to either supply water and sewage or evict their tenants. This led to tension between tenants and particularly Indian land owners, culminating in August 1985, when confronta-tions between UDF supporting youth and the police, backed by Inkatha supporting elders, led to attacks on Indians. Shops and houses were burnt, the Gandhi settlement destroyed, and the majority of Indians in 'mixed' areas like

Amaoti and Bhambayi were forced to leave their properties and seek refuge in Phoenix (Hughes, 1987).

In the late 1980s and early 1990s, violence and political confrontation was predominantly between the UDF and the IFP with the police openly or clandestinely backing the IFP or acting as a 'third force', setting off violence to destabilise communities and any capacity for opposition. An Amaoti-based 'Internal Stability Unit' was notorious in this respect and Indian members of the Unit were accused of seeking racist revenge (Ainslie and de Haas, 1995:11). From 1989-90 onwards, however, the war between the UDF and Inkatha in both Bhambayi and Amaoti appeared to have been won by the UDF, and IFP supporters either left these areas or kept their political sympathies quiet. In this process, young men, in particular those who had dropped out of school during the boycotts, came to the forefront as activists and marshals, and for a period stood out as the effective leaders and organisers of local society within a context of 'ungovernability' (Hemson, 1996).

In an interview, a woman from Amaoti (born 1956) tells her story of the two principal forms of violence which she saw as ravaging the community between 1986 and 1989:

> I lived first in Tintown and then in Odlameni – 'the place of violence'. It was given this name because initially it had been allocated to Indians, but during the violence between Indians and Africans, it was taken over by Africans ... What happened was that young men and boys used to go around in Indian areas throwing petrol bombs in the houses which belonged to Indians and taking whatever was in the houses. A lot of Indians were beaten up. The last Indian to leave was from Ritrivier. He had to climb on the roof and shoot at people who were advancing so as to prevent the loss of his possessions. However, that Indian was rescued by the arrival of the police and he lost all his possessions.
>
> This violence started in 1985-1986 after the killing of Mrs Mxenge, an activist and also the wife of a popular lawyer who was killed by the security police ... We did not like it. Just to give you an example, there was an Indian who was like a member of our family. He even used to have breakfast at our house in some instances. When that violence started we were separated and we became enemies, which was not good ... A lot of Indian people were greatly affected. They lost their goods, and the people who suffered most were Indians.
>
> In the long run, Africans were affected too ... When Africans went to look for work in Indian areas like Phoenix, they were denied work because they said we had chased them away from their places. At times they would give you work but refuse to pay you when you have finished the work. Some Indians even resorted to cruel ways like putting people in hot water in the bath, and taking them out when they are dead. Some of those were arrested. They did that, and that showed us that Indians were so much affected that they planned to revenge for the suffering caused to them ... There were Africans who worked as shoe-repairers in the Indian areas, and also those who did some work in there. What Indians used to do was to ask those Africans to repair shoes for them but once they are inside the yard they just killed them. We used to fetch a number of people, who had been killed there ...
>
> The second type of violence was that started by Mr Gcobhoza – an IFP member – and this was the most destructive violence because people were killed, and houses were destroyed. People died for absolutely nothing. I personally lost lots of possessions. There was a day when I had visited a friend of mine. When I came back I discovered that the war was on. My kids were saved miraculously. I came into the house and took them to the other side of the place. That day alone led to the death of nine people.

Some people died, others survived and some were crippled for life ... There was no education taking place. Pupils could not go to school. What Gcobhoza used to do was that he fetched school boys and drafted them into his army. Since transport came to a standstill people could not go to work. We were looking at each other like animals ...

This violence came to a halt after a battle in 1989 which led to the death of 32 people, and Mr Cele – who was also one of the perpetrators of violence – was killed. The community felt that in order to stop this violence they had to kill him. Mr Cele used to get traditional medicine for Gcobhoza so that he could be difficult to kill ... He was called to a meeting where he was told it was about peace. He agreed reluctantly but he did come because there was going to be another IFP leader present in the meeting. The coming of that IFP leader was just a lie to get that Mr Cele to arrive in the meeting. Whilst the meeting was on the assault on Gcobhoza and Mr Cele started. They both tried to escape but they caught Cele, killed him and Gcobhoza survived. Gcobhoza survived but they discovered his *inyanga* and the *inyanga* told the people that Gcobhoza had requested his medicine to strengthen him as security because he owned a night club. Gcobhoza killed a lot of people; more that one hundred. The one case which caused Gcobhoza to be caught and be charged for murder was the killing of the Ntombela twins. He was then jailed, and violence then ended in about September 1989. But 23 April 1989 was the last situation where the two factions met each other in a conventional warfare. Late in September it was just a few individuals. Things then came back to normal. People were affected badly. We could not even go to town because they attacked taxis and buses. So it was dangerous to go to town. Possessions were stolen and people could not work (Interview J-12, 1 October 1999).

Thus UDF/ANC control was victoriously established, and the forces of the IFP expelled. In this woman's narrative, the latter are linked to those of 'tradition' and *muti* (medicines). At the same time, police attempts at destabilisation continued and conflicts and violence emerged between different groups within the ANC. This had to do with patterns of fighting strategy; structures of alternative government; 'people's courts' which had been established within the context of 'ungovernability', but also with issues of control over economic activity. In Bhambayi, for example, a system of committees would deal with incoming settlers and claim a fee from them. Such committees would be linked to associations of 'home' – also in the sense of networks through which informal economic activity (like the extensive trade in *dagga*) would be channelled. Committees would regulate the moral and social life of the community, sit in judgement and impose fines or other kinds of punishment on designated offenders. In terms of defence or fighting, there would be systems of authority over the 'moving into camp' – the procedure when women and children were sent 'into the bush' and away from homes likely to be targets of attacks. The men got together in special 'camping grounds' to prepare themselves for battle, be armed, and take *muti* – medicines to fortify and make themselves invulnerable (Ainslie and de Haas, 1995: 8; see Blose and Hurst, 1998).

Such systems of authority and regulation necessarily involved interpretation of the meanings of custom, culture and morality, and this in Bhambayi brought about a more or less clear spatial division between an upper and a lower court area which were controlled by different groupings:

For example, there appear to have been significant differences in ethos between the courts of the Upper and Lower zones/areas. The Upper court was controlled by members of the ANC Youth League, who were described by certain long-standing residents as 'politically mature' in meting out appropriate punishment, including fines, for misdemeanours. Those administering the court were also described as 'progressive' as opposed to the more conservative, older men associated with the Lower court, who were accused of being resistant to change, and prone to abuse of power (Ainslie and de Haas, 1995: 8).

Ainslie and de Haas even depict the difference as one between 'political cultures' which would then move on to take different sides in battle, distinguished by, respectively, red (for the young progressives) and green head bands (for the older conservatives).[1]

This distinction between a modernisation-oriented progressiveness and a moral rearmament-directed upholding of tradition is not dissimilar to the one which had been seen by many people as a basic marker of difference between the UDF/ANC and the IFP. Ainslie and de Haas claim that in the period preceding the 1994 national election, support for the green bands did indeed provide an avenue through which the IFP, with the support of the police, could seek re-entry and effect destabilisation of the area. Both 'green' and 'red' factions were dominated by Xhosa speakers; and therefore Zulu nationalism was not on the agenda of even the conservative faction.

In Bhambayi, such differences between cultural camps and orientations within the UDF/ANC has represented a continuous potential for violence, both in the period leading up to the first democratic national elections in 1994 and, indeed, to the present day. The cracks of similarly uneasy alliances in Amaoti appear to have been less visible until the local elections of 1996. As in Bhambayi, after the violent confrontations of 1989–90, Amaoti came under the solid and exclusive control of the UDF/ANC. The dismissal of the IFP meant that the Qadi chiefly structures, which had been linked to Inkatha, lost their authority and that civic associations dominated by youth and activists came to the fore, 'modernity' thus seemingly overpowering 'tradition'. Civics, however, were still forced to base their power in the locality on alliances with informal structures like people's courts and networks of elders in control of *insizwas* (see below). On this basis, patterns of almost totally exclusive one-party rule were established: in the local elections of 1996, the ANC in Bhambayi pulled 4,141 votes against 497 for the IFP, while in Amaoti the ANC got a total of 9,637 and the IFP 380 (Project Vote, 1996: 15f.).[2]

In Amaoti, the local elections returned two ANC councillors (against only one in Bhambayi) with a significant number of votes cast for each of them – 5,365 for G. A. Phewa and 4,272 for S. B. Khumalo (ibid.). Gilbert Phewa's background was in the trade unions as a shop steward, with a history of activism with the civic associations of Amaoti and Inanda; Bethuel Khumalo (in spite of his Zulu name and first language) derived his support more in the networks of conservative and moral rearmament-oriented Xhosa-speaking patriarchs in Amaoti, whose stronghold is the section called Lusaka.[3] In quite complex ways,

[1] At least from 1998 onwards, this division seems to have been complemented by antagonisms within the Upper Court of 'progressives' over the accountability and styles of leadership of politicians which have involved violent confrontations. In 1999 this led to the arrest on a murder charge of the ANC councillor for Bhambayi and Ohlange: Lenford Mdibi, an old-standing SACP activist, trade unionist and ex-mine worker.

[2] This pattern was continued in the December 2000 municipal elections, where ward boundaries were changed, and the Democratic Alliance overtook the IFP as the second 'biggest' party (see www.elections.org.za).

[3] Lusaka, Cuba, Angola, Libya etc. are all UDF names for the different sections within Amaoti –

the oppositions between 'modernist' and 'traditionalist' outlooks and between generations were thus overlayed with registers of ethnic differentiation.

When the two councillors failed to agree on how to divide their powers and cooperate, violence broke out, members of the Civic Association were harassed and intimidated by supporters of Khumalo and some of them were forced to leave the community. In January 1997, in the Amaoti area of Cuba, next door to Lusaka the home of councillor Phewa was attacked and it was rumoured that the instigators were supporters of councillor Khumalo:

> As you can see while we are talking, I am just staying in an unfinished house, but I used to have a nice house up there. Last year – in 1997, January 7, I was attacked by a mob of Transkeians. They just burnt my house down, they shot us, but lucky enough, because of God... I think sometimes to be a Christian I used to be saved from some bad things like that. It's not that there was something wrong I had done, but they were used by a certain element to further their interest... My partner, he just organised these Transkeians to come and kill me by thinking that might gain my support if I'm dead. He thought very wrong – instead of trying to work hand in hand with me so that he can see how I move – swiftly with the people – he tried to attack me by using these people (interview with G. Phewa, Amaoti, 25 August 1998).

Following this, councillor Phewa had to seek refuge for eleven months across the Ohlange (Riet) River in Indian Phoenix while a new house was being built for him, next door to the Amaoti police station. Meanwhile, councillor Khumalo's house was also set ablaze and he was suspended from the Durban Metropolitan Council while his case was being investigated. During his suspension, however, he continued to act as a local authority, moving around Amaoti armed with a hand gun and campaigning against crime and the lack of respect in the youth. To back him up, he could draw on the support of *insizwas* (groups of young men) under the control of the Lusaka people's courts and allied with similar outfits based in neighbouring Bhambayi. On 2 February 1999, Bethuel Khumalo was shot dead at mid-day at a central tuck shop in Amaoti. His killer was recognised as man called Songqengqe and was himself killed a month later during an attempt to rob a police man of his pistol at a local hospital. The case of Khumalo's murder has not been solved. A few months' later there seems to have been something like a regular battle between different groups, in which seven supporters of the Lusaka courts were killed by young opponents. This happened in Angola section which has been a stronghold of opposition to the courts of elders based in Lusaka.[4]

Doing Research in Amaoti

Potential for conflict, dynamics of violence and oppositions of cultural styles at a more everyday level can be illustrated through a brief account of some of my field work experiences.

[3] (contd) replacing official denominations and referring to places where the ANC in exile had camps and where refugees had gone to, or else countries supporting the South African liberation struggle.
[4] The last section is based on an interview with a senior police officer in Amaoti on 1 December 1999 and with Hlengiwe Hlophe, the widow of councillor Khumalo, on 7 November 2000. In the local elections held in December 2000, Mrs Hlophe stood as a candidate against councillor Phewa and won (cf. Kaarsholm, 2005).

My first contact in Amaoti was with a group of youngsters who called themselves the 'Amaoti Save the Youth Project'. In early 1998, a University of Natal assistant had been conducting interviews for me in Bhambayi and had heard of this group in the neighbouring locality who had just organised a successful beauty contest – a popular pastime for both male and female youth – and who were now planning to organise a cultural festival centred on virginity testing.[5] When I returned to Durban in July 1998, we went to Amaoti and did group interviews with 'Save the Youth' and with two of their leaders, Mfanafuti and Mandla.

'Save the Youth' was set up with the aim of saving youth from crime, thus benefiting local society by reducing crime, but also of saving youth from discrimination and harassment by elders. The group's core members themselves had backgrounds in gangsterism, and particularly with a gang or a style referred to as 'trompies'. These young men now claimed to have been saved and reformed, and were attempting to raise funds for the new initiative from tuck shop owners and other Amaoti entrepreneurs, some of whom had been victims of gangsterism in the past. They said that youth in Amaoti were regularly and indiscriminately taken to task, disciplined and beaten by groups of elders and by *insizwas* supporting them. Such beatings would often take place after drinking parties of the elder men who would then go looking for youngsters to punish and would identify anyone with a hip-hop hat or baggy trousers as a gangster. The young men further alleged that these vigilante-like outfits were both supporting and supported by Mr Khumalo, one of the two ANC councillors, whereas Mr Phewa, the other councillor, according to them, was a friend of youth:

> Various bad things have been happening at Amaoti – for instance this crime which is caused by groups like the 'trompies' and others. There has also been corruption by the councillors, and they don't like to work together. These high structures meet and come to certain conclusions, and you always find that young people are not represented there. This disturbed us. People came to the conclusion that young people were criminals ... We have been trying to organise young people for four years, but the councillors would not allow us, since there were already these other party political youth structures ... Of course, all these other structures were under the ANC, the ANC is the only political organisation that exists here at Amaoti ...
>
> There has been a lot of conflict going on ... the most active youth is the youth of Angola. There have been people who have moved from here to other places to call these men who have then come with spears to clean the area. We realised that most of the people that they aimed at 'cleaning out' were youth who are already suffering in their environment – some of them have no parents and no place to stay... We wanted to confront these people who took the law into their own hands. So many young people have been killed here by those who said they were cleansing the area of criminals. In fact, we regarded those people who came to clean as the most dangerous criminals, because they have been killing people in the name of cleaning ...
>
> These are old people. One of the councillors organised these people when they went on a killing spree. We had to look at this, and after a lot of people had been killed, the people at the Civic Association helped us and got us this small office to meet in. We could not have our meetings at someone's home because – in the past – whenever we did this, people would say that we were making bombs ... We are still working on the constitution of 'Amaoti Save the Youth Project' ... The name Amaoti might change,

[5] Virginity tests are claimed by their supporters to be traditional performances through which young girls prove themselves to be passing into adulthood in purity, and acknowledging the values and authority of custom (cf. Kaarsholm,1999a: 108; Kaarsholm, 2005: 146-50).

because we want all the youth of Inanda to become part of this project, we want this to be the 'Inanda Save the Youth Project' ...

Usually, we send letters to both councillors, but we know that this other councillor does not want us because whenever we do fund-raising, he follows us and claims to be doing the same thing we had planned to do. He wants to create confusion. Mr Phewa is the one on our side – when we have organised something, he attends, and we also wish that one day the other councillor can come and be with us. Mr Phewa has been very helpful to us in terms of fund-raising and helped us talk to business people around here – some of them helped us a lot. The problem is we don't have money, and that makes our work very difficult ... You see now we don't even have money for a ribbon for this printing machine, now that we should be writing invitation letters for the [virginity testing] function on 1 August ... There are about 50 girls who have put their names down to be tested (interview with Mfanafuti, 13 July 1998).

We also talked about my research and got into discussion about what it was good for, and what people would get out of it. I explained that my research was academic and aimed at furthering a better general understanding of the problems I was looking at, but was not carried out in preparation for a development project that would try to alleviate these problems. I argued that perhaps an improved general understanding might help people to see the problems more clearly so that they would themselves be in a better position to design or present a demand for appropriate projects. I underlined that if I paid people to give me information, this would immediately render the information worthless, because informants would then just tell me anything to get paid. We thus ended in the kind of stalemate I had experienced before in townships and shanty towns, where people have experienced many visits from researchers, and where we could all see how the research would be useful to me, but not agree on how it would help or be of interest to them.

A similar discussion took place, when we went to visit councillor Phewa, the friend of the youth, who gave us a good briefing on the situation of young people in the locality, on the 60 per cent unemployed, the poverty, the break-up of families, the rapes, assaults and housebreaking, the drinking and the drugs.

He told us how he had tried in vain to find funds for projects to address the problems – for a community hall and sports venues, for an organiser who would take on youth work in the community, for youth to organise themselves and do self-help projects. So what he needed was money for projects and an organiser. Research was something that came and went and was always there without one seeing any benefits; researchers would come and do their thing, then they would go away, and you never heard from them again. Anyway, if I wanted to work with a group of youngsters in Amaoti, I would do much better to work with a group of his own: more organised youth contacts who were all ANC members and would be much more reliable to work with than 'Save the Youth'. The latter were suspected by many in the community not to be quite reformed yet and therefore difficult to work with. I should work with the 'Amaoti Youth Initiative' instead, with whom the councillor would bring me into contact.

I had by then thought out a possible solution to the issue of the value of research which would involve me and my University of Natal assistants collaborating in Amaoti with a group of local young people. We would employ and train them as local assistants and they would receive money and a certificate of learning if they agreed to carry out specified research tasks. I had also thought that if the focus of the research within the area was worked out in collaboration with, for example, 'Save the Youth', and their members acted as local assistants, we might be able to do something which would at the same time help them on their way as an organisation.

So what we set out to do was to form a working group consisting of three 'Save the Youth' and three 'Youth Initiative' people, with both young men and young women in it. The brief for the working group would be 1) to prepare an initial workshop for youth in Amaoti where the design, scope and focus of a questionnaire survey on 'The Social Situation, Self-Perception and Cultural Activities of Youth in Amaoti' would be discussed and worked out; 2) to participate in the preparation of the questionnaire which would be used in the survey; 3) to take the questionnaires around to the agreed sample and collect the responses; 4) to help organise a second workshop where an initial report on the survey would be presented by me. If all this worked out well, we might agree to continue our collaboration and the young people's employment by carrying out focus group and life story interviews that would follow up on the questionnaire survey. In this way, we would have both 'organised' and 'dropped-out' youth represented, could draw on the contacts and local knowledge of both and have the research reflect their different perspectives.

From the first meeting, the bringing together of the two groups turned out to be explosive, mostly because 'Save the Youth' did not want to 'share' me as a potential resource with a competing group and saw this initiative as yet another attempt by those in local power to frustrate them and their modest attempts at organisation. So in spite of my efforts, my project became another resource to be fought over bitterly and I got a first-hand demonstration of how envy, jealousy and anger related to apparently quite minor things could lead to confrontations of a passionate nature.

Eventually, however, after much negotiation, we got the working group together and into gear, organising the first workshop. A list of groups and organisations through which invitations would be channelled was prepared, using the contacts of both sides, and the 'Save the Youth' contingent had the invitations printed and taken around. We also arranged for lunch to be served to participants; I had wanted cokes and sandwiches, but the group were keen to have a *braai* with *pap*, vegetables and all the works. Mrs Phewa let us rent her pots and pans for a small fee. At the end of the workshop, there would be a cultural show at which different dance groups and choirs from Amaoti would demonstrate their skills. The whole thing would start in the morning and be over by mid-afternoon. It all appeared very promising.

The workshop was held at Amandhletu Secondary School in Amaoti on 10 October 1998 with around seventy people attending and started out successfully. An opening plenary meeting was chaired by Sabatha from the working group, addressed by me, and by Thulani Ncwane, the chairman of the Inanda Development Forum and a veteran youth activist from the struggle, who gave his support to the research and his view of its usefulness. Then Innocent Nojiyeza spoke on behalf of the KwaZulu–Natal Youth Council and linked the research to the youth policies of Government. After this people split into groups to discuss, 1) how 'youth' should be defined and delimited, 2) important distinctions and groupings among youth and 3) what would be important questions to ask of youth and concerning youth.

Both the plenary and the group sessions were conducted in Zulu, and since Mfanafuti, who had been appointed my interpreter, appeared to be fully occupied with the preparations for lunch, Sabatha had to both chair the plenary session and interpret for me. My daughter, Lotte, was tape-recording the plenary sessions, but as the groups came back from their discussions to report, she had suddenly disappeared, so the first part of the reporting was not taped. It turned out she had left the school with Mfanafuti and fifteen minutes later they emerged from a home in the neighbourhood, carrying a complete stereo set and loudspeakers which would be needed for the cultural activities in the afternoon. The group reports were in fact extremely interesting and were later reconstructed, translated and transcribed from the tapes by Sabatha. This turned out to be an excellent background for the design of the questionnaire and for deciding on the identity of the sample which became 160 people between the ages of 16 and 30, divided into quotas which were assumed to reflect roughly the composition of the actual youth population in Amaoti: 50 per cent women, 50 per cent men; 50 per cent in employment or paid-up, full-time students, 50 per cent unemployed; 50 per cent between 16 and 22, 50 per cent between 23 and 30. The survey thus turned out to be very close in its focus and sample to part of the research for Paul Richards's book on Sierra Leone (which I did not know at the time), though his sample was somewhat larger (Richards, 1996: 106).

After the last plenary, the atmosphere changed a bit, as lunch was not ready. By 3 pm, people were getting both hungry and bored. It also turned out that, against our agreement, some of the male members of my working group had decided to spend part of the lunch money on beer. Drinking was going on in nooks and crannies of the school, and some participants were beginning to be not only bleary-eyed and noisy, but slightly aggressive. Several 'trompie' connections of the 'Save the Youth' contingent came up to me to inquire about possibilities for paid employment with my project (which in view of the scale of the lunch preparations they thought, must be an extremely wealthy one). One particular well-known 'trompie' came to ask Innocent Nojiyeza and myself, if we were not afraid to move around in Amaoti, since it was known to be a very dangerous place where numerous visitors had been mugged and lost their cars. I told him that I felt protected by the good network of contacts I had in Amaoti, which he seemed to think was an excellent joke.

At one point, Sabatha, the leading 'Youth Initiative' representative in my working group, an old Amaoti activist and usually a very skilful mediator, left the school, having been threatened by the camp of 'trompie' followers, who were now also getting more seriously interested in the girls attending. We went to check with a red-eyed Mfanafuti on the preparations for the cultural programme. This seemed to have been transformed into a disco arranged in a class room on the first floor of the school with the equipment that he and Lotte had organised. There was an accident in the kitchen and the floor suffered some burn damage, but late in the afternoon, food was finally served. At this point, councillor Phewa and his wife also joined us. Having quickly munched a lamb chop and some *pap* it was a relief to escape the place before dark in my car with Lotte and the KwaZulu-Natal Youth Council representative. At this point he said he did not like the situation and later turned down an invitation to attend a second workshop at the end of February 1999. Responsibility for wrapping up the workshop was left with councillor Phewa.

The workshop thus ended somewhat chaotically; the school had suffered minor damages, and the key to its gate was missing. (We were not able to use it again as a venue). Some participants found it difficult to stop the drinking, and next morning, a Sunday, they with some friends came to the home of Mpume – the 'Youth Initiative' woman in my working group. She had been administering the kitty for the workshop lunch and the youth wanted money from her. They threatened her, banging on the door and walls of her mother's shack, claiming she had received more from me than she had let on. I have not been told exactly how events developed after this, but a week later Mfanafuti was arrested for assault. I was told he had taken on a job to collect a bad debt on behalf of a taxi operator and the business had become violent. This meant that he was no longer able to participate in the working group. He stayed in prison awaiting trial for several months, and when he came out on bail got involved in another bad situation where, in his presence, one of his friends killed a young man at Angola, next door to the Civic Association and the 'Save the Youth' office. He was then beaten up – this time not by the punishing elders of Lusaka, but by local residents of 'modernist' Angola – and subsequently disappeared and went into hiding outside Amaoti.

Meanwhile work on the questionnaire survey went on and the collection of responses was completed by early February 1999. I prepared the preliminary report, and on 27 February we had a second workshop to discuss it, this time at the Civic Association office in Angola. The second workshop was a bit of a flop: only 12 people showed up. I am not quite sure why; the date was the last Saturday in the month when people had money and perhaps preferred to go to town to shop. But there was a rumour also that the remaining 'Save the Youth' members of my working group had not taken the invitations around as they had agreed to, and had instead encouraged their contacts not to attend. They did not come to the workshop themselves and I did not see much of them after that. They never answered my request for an explanation of what had happened, but I think they may have felt that there was by now too little money involved in the work for them to be interested. Since Mfanafuti's disappearance, all thought of using the survey to consolidate the 'Save the Youth' project seemed to have been abandoned. However, they were keen to be given the certificates which had been printed out nicely on University of Natal stationery.

The remaining parts of the field research were carried out with the assistance of the 'Youth Initiative' members. On 24 March 1999, I presented the preliminary survey report to a meeting of the Amaoti Development Forum, chaired by councillor Phewa and held at the Amaoti Police Station, which had also been the regular meeting place of our working group. The meeting brought some valuable response and made up for the modest feed-back at the second workshop, although the response was generally from older people – the parents of those whose situation and views we were looking at. Following this, life story and focus group interviews were carried out with representatives of the different groups in the survey's sample. The field research was thus concluded successfully and the experience gained through having worked with the local assistants more than made up for the hiccups encountered.

Let us now step back and look at some of the central issues brought out, both in the process and the outcomes of the research.

Identities

Because of the ways in which apartheid policies were aimed at stimulating and manipulating ethnicity, there has been a tendency in studies of identity and politics in South Africa to regard ethnic identities as primarily the outcome of such manipulation, and to look instead for markers of class as indicative of more 'real' or 'objective' identifications: 'Of greater importance than ethnicity in daily life is the phenomenon of class, a pervasive feature of social interaction, especially in urban areas' (de Haas and Zulu, 1994: 441).

In young people's experience in Amaoti, it is obvious that class, social situation and economic position are major factors in determining identity and that an overruling circumstance is one of poverty and unemployment. If, as in the survey and in the CASE study *'Growing Up Tough'* (Everatt and Orkin, 1993), – we define youth as the age group between 16 and 30, it must be concluded that the unemployment which affects around 60 per cent of the group is the most urgent and desperate problem they face and a condition against which they measure and define their notions of self.[6]

Closely related to this are issues of education and being educated, with expectations of education leading to regular paid employment and career possibilities clashing sharply with experiences of actual employment among young people who have passed matric successfully or even done tertiary degrees. The Amaoti survey confirms that in the experience of all the groups contained in the sample 'unemployment constitutes the gravest and most urgent challenge that young people are faced with' and that they 'identify closely chances of getting employment with possibilities of access to education' (Kaarsholm, 1999b: 17).

Such notions of employment and education are closely tied to understandings of progress, modernisation and 'inclusion', of moving away from a situation of marginalisation which apartheid is seen to have systematically upheld, and which the new post-apartheid Africa has been expected to dismantle.

Markers of ethnic identity in terms of language and networks of 'home' also figure prominently, both in the self-perception of groups of young people and in their identification of 'others' within the community. This can sometimes find expression in quite stereotyped prejudice, as in the following statement from a young man:

> We have some people here who don't speak Zulu well, and they are the ones who are causing problems. They don't want this place to develop. These are the people who came here to cut sugar cane, and who now don't want to go back to their places of birth. They delay development. The thing is that Zulus here are in the minority, and the Pondos are in the majority. Pondos know that they are filthy, and that – when this place has been developed – they will have difficulty adjusting to it. Most of them don't work, they spend most of their time playing cards. Most of the Zulus here have good

[6] In the National Youth Commission Act of 1996 and other studies (for example, Jennings, Everatt, Lyle and Budlender, 1997), youth is alternatively defined as comprising the age group from 14 to 35. It is argued that because of anti-apartheid struggle, a generation of youth has been forced to stay young for longer than would otherwise have been considered normal. This widened definition, however, also makes it easier to control and 'dilute' expressions of youthfulness, and on the whole seems to obscure what is special about experiences of being young.

houses and are working... [while] the Pondos are the ones who are not well educated... when there is someone who pushes development, they kill him. Because the Pondos are not working, when good houses become available, they will have to pay, and where will they get the money? They will have to pay for water, telephones and electricity. They know they can't afford that, and as soon as a person talks about development, they quickly kill him... the people from Transkei are also the ones who bring *dagga* here (interview V-14, 23 May 1998).

In another interview, an older man who was born in South Africa, but whose family has a Malawian background describes how he would experience ethnic teasing and discrimination when he was growing up in Amaoti:

We were called Nyasas, others were called Pondos ... Our father was originally a Muslim ... Here in South Africa, if you said you were a Muslim, they usually said you were talking nonsense – Muslims are Indians ...When I told that I am a Muslim, they said there is no such thing here – Muslims are coolies, and this is an African school ... We became open about our being Muslim in 1987 ... I was not circumcised, so my father told me to go a doctor to be circumcised. I then went to the Islamic Centre and became fully a Muslim ... When you say you are from Malawi, people say you are from Zanzibar, but Malawi is where we are from ... It is my father who is from Malawi. I don't know where the place is. I only know it from the maps in the atlas, but some of my family members know the place. We all know the language of Malawi, even my mother who is a MaShezi, a Zulu, knows the language ... My father was proud of his Nyasa nationality, so he taught my mother the language, and in turn she taught him Zulu ... When we moved here [in 1964], and people called us Nyasas, we were embarrassed, and it was like being insulted, but now we are proud of being Nyasas ...

Today, there are some elements of democracy here – in this place the councillor [Phewa] is trying very hard – but there is also what I may call tribalism. People still say things like 'you are a Nyasa', 'you are a Zulu', 'you are a Pondo', so what can you tell? ... [Tribalism] used to make me feel inferior, like at school – when I arrived – they asked me what my nationality was ... and said that I should go to a school for Nyasas since this was a school for Zulus ... when I laughed, they would say things like, 'We are talking and laughing, and here is this Nyasa laughing – why don't you go and laugh with your own people?' ... When I did well and came first, they would say, 'We understand your case, Banda – you people are Nyasas so you have *muti* and use it to pass at school' ... At the end of one year when I had done quite well in terms of the results, they said to me, 'Now since you have done so well, how many people are you going to slaughter, since you Nyasas slaughter people when you are happy? People are going to be in trouble because you people are happy, and we would be good food for your people if we were your neighbours.' Such are the things they used to say (interview J-13, 25 September 1999).

No doubt such straightforward and 'essentialist' ethnic identifications became more prominent in the 1980s, when on the one hand the KwaZulu government would make rights of settlement, housing and employment in areas they controlled dependent on 'national' Zulu identity, and on the other, in areas like Amaoti, where controls were more informal, networks of language and origin could provide access to livelihoods.

It is also obvious that such identifications could easily play into and mix with political identifications of being either Inkatha/IFP or UDF/ANC, but with the effective banishment of Inkatha/IFP as a political identity in Amaoti from 1989-90, the rationalities and functionings of ethnic identification began to show themselves in a different light. Whereas before then, one level of difference in political discourse between the two parties had been one of 'old' versus 'young', of attitudes of 'respect', 'tradition' and 'moral rearmament based on customary cultural values' versus 'individualism', 'modernisation' and 'meritocracy', these two conflicting discourses now had to be contained and interact within a unified political ambit.

Ironically, this could be described as a movement 'back' from 'political tribalism' to 'moral ethnicity', in the sense introduced by John Lonsdale his discussion of the development of political thought (Lonsdale, 1992: 466 and 1994: 136-42). But it can also, and perhaps more adequately be seen as an opposition between what James Ferguson has called 'cosmopolitan' and 'localist' cultural styles (Ferguson, 1999: 82-122).

In this scenario, the politics of everyday life are not necessarily bound up symmetrically with the politics of parties and instead act themselves out in contestations between groupings and discourses that differ on the moral issues regulating the relationships between older and younger people and between men and women. When looked at in this way, the oppositions no longer appear as distinctions between ethnic groups, but rather as much more significant contrasts between attitudes, positions and styles of 'conservatism' and 'modernism' that cut across such boundaries in the context of a society like Amaoti.

In the questionnaire responses and interviews, the identity of youth and the idea of being young are being talked about in such moral and 'stylistic' terms, and it is clear that respondents have very different opinions about them. In this sense, youth in Amaoti stand out as a much more differentiated group than, for example, the image Paul Richards paints of youth in Sierra Leone who, in spite of the differentiation between RUF and *kamajo* militias towards the end of the book, appear much more like a unified example of 'Africa's rising generation' (Richards, 1996: 114).

The differing attitudes of Amaoti youth come out, for example, in their attitudes towards the paying of bride price (*lobola*) and the conducting of virginity tests. The background to the responses is a generally shared understanding of crisis in the community – of unemployment leading to crime being on the rise and undermining the quality of everyday life, of insecurity and fear in the face of the AIDS epidemic and of local society not having arrived at a stable mode of functioning after the long period of 'ungovernability' and the overturning of the social order imposed by the apartheid state.

In the 'conservative' set of responses, the moral and social crisis is linked to the decay of 'respect', to the fact too many people, both youngsters and parents, no longer uphold the codes of behaviour and obligations which used to exist in 'our culture'.[7] The remedy would thus seem to be a resurrection of 'respect' and values, and the preservation of institutions such as *lobola* would help to further this. Similarly, virginity tests would encourage parents to appreciate the value of their daughters and would therefore help protect these against teenage pregnancies and rapes. In this sense, a reconsolidation of a weakened patriarchy, whether it is styled in Zulu, Xhosa, Chewa or otherwise, would present a possible solution to the decay and dissolution which people experience.

On the 'modernist' side, the sense of social crisis is linked to the fact that expectations placed with the overturning of apartheid exploitation and racial discrimination have not been fulfilled. Also, young people have lost the position

---

[7] The Zulu word for 'culture' in this meaning of 'customs' is *amasiko* (de Haas and Zulu 1994: 440).

of power and influence they had during the anti-apartheid struggle, especially after the banishment of Inkatha in 1989-90. From this point of view, the reconsolidation of patriarchy is not a solution but part of the problem; *lobola* and virginity tests are associated with the past and with life in the rural areas, but in modern and urban conditions 'violate the basic human rights of women and are unconstitutional' (Kaarsholm, 1999b: 7).

In the survey responses, however, such 'pure' positions of 'conservatism' or 'modernism' are untypical and most responses represent blends of attitudes that appear not so much attempts at reconciling the extremes as expressions of identity in their own right. In the responses of young men, for example, it is common that opposition to the dominance of elders go hand in hand with positive attitudes towards *lobola* and virginity testing and that the alternative wished for would therefore rather be one of a reformed patriarchy than of egalitarianism between males and females. Similarly, in the questionnaires filled in by female respondents there is, especially in the younger groups in the sample, a surprisingly large proportion of positive responses vis-a-vis virginity testing which, while limiting some freedoms might enhance others and help young women to create a defensive space of their own against invasions from aggressive male sexuality.

In such negotiation of 'conservatism' and 'modernism', virginity tests may, for example, be cut loose from connotations of 'tradition' and conducted without any cultural festivities as just a system of parents' control over daughters and an AIDS prevention measure. This was the approach which was being contemplated in Amaoti by Mrs Phewa, the councillor's wife, and a group of her fellow health workers (interviews with Jane Chiwambere Phewa, Amaoti, 26 November 1999). It would keep 'unmodern' attitudes at bay but would also generally strengthen elders in the contestation between generations. (Interestingly, in the question-naire survey, some respondents referred to virginity testing as something which was 'the right of parents', without apparent concern for the rights of those subjected to the tests).

It is also typical that strongly patriarchal attitudes can be combined with otherwise radically 'modernist' positions among young men. This would apply to both members of the SACP-oriented organised youth (including members of the 'Youth Initiative') – some of whom demonstrated very contradictory attitudes concerning the rights and position of women in politics and in everyday life – and also to more marginalised groups and 'drop-outs'. Among the girls with whom I discussed this in Amaoti, the idea of the 'Save the Youth' group organising a virginity testing function (which never materialised) was a joke, because the group and its past were associated with responsibility for rape, forced sex and teenage pregnancies – central issues which the resurrection of 'traditional' testing and respect is intended to counteract.

Importantly, in spite of references to 'our culture' and 'our tradition', identity stands out in the research as something which young people construct out of the forms of association, discourses and styles that are available to them. To be 'something' or to be 'nothing' is dependent on what you do, and how you get organised or not. In a social situation where unemployment is such an over-whelming fact of life, the regulation of everyday life through self-help, cultural activity, the living of popular styles and association membership stand in for the identification normally offered by a working life. In spite of the high rate of unemployment – even among those who have had many years of education – hopes and expectations are still placed with education as the road out of exclusion from the world of modernity which the 'other' South Africa that the world of whites and their living standards represents.

Unemployment is still seen as part of a temporary crisis that the transition from apartheid has brought about and not yet as a symptom of a more permanent exclusion linked to the economic functionings of globalisation. The 'modernist' educated youth of Amaoti are therefore a long way removed from the desperation of 'excluded intellectuals' that Paul Richards found among the youth of Sierra Leone or the 'cosmopolitanism pressed to the wall' that James Ferguson describes among unemployed urbanites on the Zambian Copperbelt (Ferguson, 1999: 250). Such desperation seems to be more common among less educated and more marginalised groups of youngsters who are less organised, or whose forms of self-organisation are more radically at odds with local society, such as the 'trompies' and similar gangs.

Being organised also means acting in accordance with a rationality that is shared with other people. In this sense, there can be said to be rationality involved in the organised activities of 'gangster' groups like the 'trompies' whose views are only vaguely articulated in the responses dug out by the research, and which for the majority of respondents represent a threat to their endeavours at having a meaningful and peaceful social life in Amaoti. Violence as represented by 'criminal' groups and deeds in Amaoti may therefore not be 'irrational' and 'meaningless', in the same sense as Paul Richards points to the atrocities of RUF teenage boys in Sierra Leone as being governed by their own matrices of rationality. We are still faced, then, with a problem of conflicting rationalities and of how such conflicts over what represents meaningfulness to different groups of people and modes of organising might be reconciled within a more overall framework of order – of an agreed rationality at a higher level.

Violence and Popular Culture

Violence in South Africa and more specifically in KwaZulu-Natal has been studied extensively in the context of the 1980s and early 1990s (see Hughes, 1987; Minnaar, 1991 and 1992; Hindson and Morris, 1994; Ainslie and de Haas, 1995; Freund, 1996). Most of these studies have focused on political violence, with some of the studies paying greatest attention to the role of apartheid state and 'third force' interventions in instigating the violence (like Ainslie and de Haas, 1995), and others looking more at the internal power dynamics of local settlements as providing explanations (like Hindson and Morris, 1994 and Freund, 1996).

The 'meaningfulness' of political violence has thus been pointed out convincingly, given different interpretations (some of which I have drawn on above) and links between political and criminal violence have also been established. It is not difficult to see how the instrumental rationalities of certain forms of crime relating to the control over specific areas can interact closely with rationalities of political advance.

What has been less studied and explained are more recent examples of criminal violence perpetrated by youth whose 'rationality', beyond a very short-sighted one of enrichment or immediate sexual gratification, seems to be more difficult to work out. I am referring here, not so much to crime carried out 'externally' and directed against more affluent and privileged groups, but rather to crime and violence aimed at neighbours and the local communities where the actors themselves reside.

In the Amaoti survey and interviews, there is a general complaint by young people that they are victimised by crime, and that crime seriously and negatively affects the quality of their lives. Their movement is restricted; girls in particular are worried about moving outside their homes at night. Prospects of attaining some small degree of affluence – of having a bicycle, a stereo set, a video machine, a sewing machine – are brought to nothing by thefts and burglaries. Young women's lives are crippled by forced sex and rape; relatives are wounded or killed through violent assaults; you cannot have meetings or entertainments at night, because it is not safe to go outside. The grievances are endless. In the responses there is general agreement about a broad explanation which links the high levels of local crime to unemployment and school drop-outs, and also to a proliferation of hand guns in the wake of the anti-apartheid struggle. Similarly, there is widespread unhappiness with the performance and efficiency of the police who are often pointed out as accomplices in crime, as corrupt and partly responsible for the easy availability of guns. This is acknowledged even by some police representatives, such as the commissioner at Amaoti Police Station, where we had most of our working group meetings (interview, 1 December 2000).

There are very few statements by people who stand up for their involvement with crime except the occasional 'I have no problem with crime – I eat from it' or 'the police is continuing the oppression we were used to, and we have to fight them.' To many of the respondents, however, it seems clear that criminal activity, violence and the preoccupation with guns are linked to the influence of popular cultural media and to life styles associated with them. Among such influences and styles frequently mentioned are 'ghetto culture', *gangsta rap* and the admiration for cult figures within this world like Tupac Shakur. Similarly, respondents claim that criminals draw inspiration from violent genres of foreign movies, which have widespread circulation as videos shown in homes or in video parlours attached to shebeens. Among such films, *First Blood* and the *Rambo* series, whose impact and use as an 'educative' text Paul Richards analyses extensively in the context of Sierra Leone (Richards 1996: 57-9), figure prominently alongside other genre movies such as Jean-Claude van Damme's and *kung fu* or *ninja* fighting films.

What is interesting in the survey response relating to popular cultural preferences, however, is that these paradings of a macho and violent style of behaviour and of fighting back against an evil system of authority are popular more or less across the board among the sub-groups in the sample, among females as well as among males. They are combined with very diverse types of other expressions in the listings of preferences. Exactly as in Paul Richards' survey, the *Rambo* series in some responses appears alongside *Macbeth* or other Shakespeare plays which people have certainly read in school and may thus take up the role of an 'educative' text in the minds of readers. Given the variety and richness of combinations of readings in the survey, however, it is clear that very different moral and political lessons are being drawn from it. Certainly, among young marginalised, 'drop-out' males, icons such as Rambo and Tupac Shakur provide meaningful identifications with a role as 'ghetto martyr' and of being forced into a position of ghettoisation where violence appears as the logical response, and the only possible road to social catharsis. At the same time, in other responses the moral extracted seems to be rather one of distancing oneself, of opting instead for more traditional respectability strategies and ways to protect self-respect and identity: through education, religious activity, cultural group involvement, or political work, different varieties of 'being organised' from that of the rebel *gangsta* band, or youth gang are found.

My field work results and experience from Amaoti tell us about the coexistence of such different outlooks among youth, and situates violence – its meaning or meaninglessness – in the context of their interaction. On the one hand, it points to understandings of violence that see it as symbolically rational in terms of being an outcry *in extremis*, as in the case of the Sierra Leonean rebels studied by Paul Richards, who demonstrate unbrokenness and masculinity in the face of marginalisation and disempowerment and speak to the world through the violent languages of global popular cultural media. On the other hand, the weakness and defeat of such strategies of crying out is revealed when no response or dialogue ensue from them. Their symbolic rationality dissolves to be replaced by the prosaic humiliations of self-destruction with which townships and urban informal settlements have a long historical acquaintance. The attempt to break out of *gangsta* life-styles and into respectability by the Amaoti 'Save the Youth' group seemed to illustrate this. The failure of the organisation and the eventual social deroute and exclusion of its members from Amaoti testify to the difficulties of their project. Comparatively, in this case story from KwaZulu-Natal, the more 'traditional' respectability strategies of other types of self-organisation among youth – as represented by the members in my working group from the Amaoti 'Youth Initiative' – appeared to continue to be of resilience and to offer their subscribers a functioning framework of resistance against the onslaught of unemployment and meaninglessness.

References

Ainslie, Roy and Mary de Haas (1995) 'Bhambayi: The "Third Force" in Action', unpublished paper, University of Natal, Durban.

Blose, Stanley and Christopher Hurst (1998) 'Bhambayi Video Translation' [English translation of text on sound track of video recording of 'Bhambayi Celebrates Peace and Development', October 1997].

de Haas, Mary and Paulus Zulu (1994) 'Ethnicity and Federalism: The Case of KwaZulu/Natal', *Journal of Southern African Studies* 20(3): 433-46.

Everatt, David and Mark Orkin (1993), *'Growing Up Tough': A National Survey of South African Youth*, Johannesburg: CASE.

Ferguson, James (1999) *Expectations of Modernity: Myths and Meanings of Urban Life on the Zambian Copperbelt*, Berkeley and Los Angeles: University of Calfornia Press.

Freund, Bill (1996) 'The Violence in Natal 1985-1990' in R. Morrell (eds) *Political Economy and Identities in KwaZulu-Natal: Historical and Social Perspectives*, Durban: Indicator Press, pp. 179-95.

Hemson, David (1996) '"For Sure You are Going to Die!": Political Participation and the Comrade Movement in Inanda, KwaZulu-Natal', *Social Dynamics* 22(2): 74-104.

Hindson, Doug and Mike Morris (1994) 'Power Relations in Informal Settlements' in Doug Hindson and Jeff McCarthy (eds) *Here to Stay: Informal Settlements in Kwa-Zulu-Natal*, Durban: Indicator Press.

Hughes, Heather (1985) 'Imijondolo' in Omar Badsha, *Imijondolo: A Photographic Essay on Forced Removals in the Inanda District of South Africa*, Durban: Afrapix, pp. 2-10.

Hughes, Heather (1987) 'Violence in Inanda, August 1985', *Journal of Southern African Studies* 13(3): 331-54.

Hughes, Heather (1998) 'Travel Notes' for tour of Inanda for workshop on 'Popular Culture and Democracy, 18 November 1998', unpublished mimeograph, University of Natal, Durban.

Jennings, Ross, David Everatt, Arnold Lyle and Debbie Budlender (1997) *The Situation of Youth in South Africa*, Johannesburg: National Youth Commission/CASE.

Kaarsholm, Preben (1999a) 'Gangsta Rap y Pruebas de Virginidad: Cultura Popular en Sudáfrica del Post-Apartheid' in Fiona Wilson (ed.) *Violencia y Espacio Social: Estudios sobre Conflicto y Recuperaçion*, Huancayo: Universidad Nacional del Centro del Peru, pp. 89-117.

Kaarsholm, Preben (1999b) 'Preliminary Report on Questionnaire Survey to Investigate 'The Social Situation, Self-Perception and Cultural Activities of Youth in Amaoti', Durban: Department of History, University of Natal.

Kaarsholm, Preben (2000) 'Obituary', *Journal of Southern African Studies* 26(2): v. Special issue on 'Popular Culture and Democracy'.

Kaarsholm, Preben (2005) 'Moral Panic and Cultural Mobilization: Responses to Transition, Crime and HIV/AIDS in KwaZulu-Natal', *Development and Change* 36(1): 133-56.

Kaplan, Robert D. (1994), 'The Coming Anarchy: How Scarcity, Crime, Overpopulation and Disease are Rapidly Destroying the Social Fabric of Our Planet', *Atlantic Monthly* February: 44-76.

Lonsdale, John (1992) 'The Moral Economy of Mau Mau: Wealth, Poverty and Civic Virtue in Kikuyu Political Thought' in B. Berman and J. Lonsdale, *Unhappy Valley: Conflict in Kenya & Africa*, Book Two: *Violence & Ethnicity*, Oxford: James Currey, pp. 315-504.

Lonsdale, John (1994) 'Moral Ethnicity and Political Tribalism' in J. Hultin and P. Kaarsholm (eds) *Inventions and Boundaries: Historical and Anthropological Approaches to the Study of Ethnicity and Nationalism*, Roskilde: International Development Studies, pp. 131-50.

Marks, Shula (2004) '"The Dog That Did Not Bark, or Why Natal Did Not Take Off": Ethnicity and Democratization in South Africa', in Bruce Berman, Dickson Eyoh and Will Kymlicka (eds), *Ethnicity and Democracy in Africa*, Oxford: James Currey, pp. 183-99.

Minnaar, Anthony de Villiers (ed.) (1991) *Conflict and Violence in Natal/KwaZulu: Historical Perspectives*, Pretoria: HSRC.

Minnaar, Anthony de Villiers (ed.) (1992) *Patterns of Violence: Case Studies of Conflict in Natal*, Pretoria: HSRC

Project Vote (1996) *Local Government Elections. KwaZulu-Natal. 1996 Results at a Glance*, Cape Town: Project Vote.

Richards, Paul (1996) *Fighting for the Rain Forest: War, Youth and Resources in Sierra Leone*, Oxford: James Currey.

Richards, Paul (2000) 'Guerra dei giovani in Sierra Leone: Pacificare un Mostro?' in Marco Buttino, Maria Cristina Ercolessi and Alessandro Triulzi (eds) *Uomini in armi: Costruzioni etniche e violenza politica*, Naples: L'ancora del mediterraneo, pp. 189-99.

Vlassenroot, Koen (2000) 'Identitá e insicurezza: La costruzione dell'emergenza etnica nel Kivu meridionale', in Marco Buttino, Maria Cristina Ercolessi and Alessandro Triulzi (eds) *Uomini in armi: Costruzioni etniche e violenza politica*, Naples: L'ancora del mediterraneo, pp. 129-56.

9

War, Violence & Videotapes
Media & Localised Ideoscapes of the Liberian Civil War

MATS UTAS

'We are all one,' Doe pleads. A boy puts a pistol against his head. Swirling voices accuse him of murder and corruption. 'Let me tell you something,' he gasps, 'whatever happened was ordained by God.' 'Cut the man's ears off,' Johnson orders, and two boys hold the screaming president while another saws his left ear off with his field knife and tosses it into his lap. 'I say cut the man's ear!' Johnson says. Doe struggles wildly, howling, as they take off his the second ear. The boy with the pistol rests his foot on the president's bowed neck. Suddenly the power dies. The generators cease, the TV screen goes blank. The insects whir all over the compound, and then the throb of the generators masks the jungle sounds as they come on again. But the TV isn't working. (Johnson, 1990: 220)

This text is about media in Liberia. Quite a lot has been written about how the civil wars in Liberia and Sierra Leone have been conceived in the international news media. Paul Richards has written a forceful critique of the prevalent ideas in the media of what he calls 'new barbarism' and neo-Malthusian approaches, arguing that such ideas obstruct rather than aim at getting a proper understanding of the conflicts (Richards, 1996). In a more recent critique Rosalind Shaw has talked about *juju* journalism in the Liberia/Sierra Leone wars where 'the mingling of "modern" technologies such as AK 47s with "magical" techniques has been taken at best as a sign of "deep weirdness" and at worst as evidence that processes of counter-evolution are at work in the collapse of African states' (Shaw, 2003: 81-2). I have myself pointed out that news media reports often depict the Liberian civil war as a doomsday carnival, thus equally preventing ordinary Westerners from obtaining any commendable understanding through our media (Utas, 2000). These accounts form part of a larger anthropological critique of international news media reports on war and violent conflict as inherently different from 'our' rational wars (Allen, 1999; Pedelty, 1993).

With the exception of Paul Richards' piece on local radio as means for conflict moderation in Sierra Leone (Richards, 2000), his work on video imagery (Richards, 1994) and to a limited extent Louise Bourgault's work on radio in pre-war Liberia (Bourgault, 1995) little has been done to understand the interplay between media and local ideoscapes in times of conflict in the West African sub-region. Talking about local ideoscapes I aim at describing unbounded political landscapes of the everyday, local ideologies and counter-ideologies, interconnected with and to some extent generating the macro ideoscapes that Arjun Appadurai describes (Appadurai, 1996: 35ff). By looking at media in relation to local ideoscapes it becomes obvious that Liberians are not passive receivers of media but rather, as Debra Spitulnik reminds us, that 'people use mass media' as 'active participants in ongoing communication processes' (Spitulnik, 2000: 145). To prove this point I shall analyse a video clip of the torture of the late president Samuel Doe. I do so by (re)inserting the video clip in its proper social context, that is, the setting where it was shot and the audience it was intended for, thus highlighting local ideoscapes. In a contextually displaced form this particular video clip has been used by international media to pinpoint the barbarity of the Liberian civil war and the primitivity of the Liberian people. In order to give an alternative reading of the Doe clip I will compare it with fictional films produced and viewed in West Africa. By doing so I am able to contextualise issues of morality, magic, or the occult, issues available for the viewer of the clip but not readily understandable if not seen as part of the ideoscape. In Ghanaian fiction, these powers of the occult are thoroughly visualised (see Meyer, 2003a; 2003b). Such a comparison is thus based on similar idiosyncratic readings. I do so by looking at morality, religion and witchcraft in the light of modernity, as well as at 'visual truth' in the framework of transparency and conspiracy – forming part of global ideoscapes thriving on related sets of human uncertainties as proposed by the various contributors to the volume *Transparency and Conspiracy* (West and Sanders, 2003). West and Sanders talk about 'occult cosmologies' as what is hidden to the eye, as a second realm of power (2003: 6). In this text we shall see that the abstraction of an 'occult cosmology' will be eclipsed and be unravelled when confronted with a more direct, yet equally hidden, 'economy of occult objects and practices' in what is filmed and subsequently screened as a documentary film.

To contextualise the film, a short background to the Liberian civil war is given, followed by an outline of the access to and use of media in Liberia during the civil war. I shall argue that radio has played a major role, but that visual media, mainly in the shape of the VCR have established themselves as objective readings of war events while radio broadcasts have come to be seen as manipulations of the Liberian public.

A Compact War History

The Liberian civil war began on Christmas Eve 1989, when a group of roughly 150 ill-equipped rebel soldiers, supported by Libya and Burkina Faso (Ellis, 1999), crossed into Nimba County, Liberia from neighbouring Côte d'Ivoire. This group, which became known as the National Patriotic Front of Liberia (NPFL), initially enjoyed massive popular support, with many young men and women joining the NPFL, armed only with single barrelled guns and at times sticks. The government forces, the Armed Forces of Liberia (AFL), were soon driven out of Nimba County. Later, following an internal struggle, the NPFL split into two factions: the NPFL, as led by Charles Taylor, and the Independent National Patriotic Front of Liberia (INPFL) under Prince Y. Johnson. Taking different routes and at times fighting each other, both defeated the AFL and reached the Atlantic coast and Monrovia in July 1990. In August, a West African peacekeeping force (ECOMOG), was created under the leadership of Nigeria and sent to take control of the situation in Monrovia (see for example, Adebajo, 2002; Magyar and Conteh-Morgan, 1998; Olonisakin, 1997; 2000). Prince Y. Johnson seemingly struck a deal with the peacekeepers and lured President Doe into a trap, capturing him, torturing him in front of a video camera and eventually killing him. The struggle that at the outset had been viewed as a popular rebellion by the Gio and Mano ethnic groups in Nimba County, in due course turned the whole of Liberia into a war zone, where young rebel fighters not only fought each other, but terrorised, looted and committed gruesome atrocities against the entire civilian population.

After the killing of President Doe, the INPFL continued playing an active role in Monrovian politics until Johnson was brought into exile in Nigeria in late 1992. Meanwhile, several other rebel factions appeared. The United Liberation Movement of Liberia (ULIMO) was formed in Freetown, Sierra Leone, with assistance from the Sierra Leonean government. Soon ULIMO itself split into two: ULIMO-J and ULIMO-K. The Liberian army, AFL, continued fighting and was later aided by another faction, the Liberian Peace Council (LPC) originating in the south-east of the country. Other factions, often enjoying localised regional support, came and went, such as the Lofa Defence Force (LDF) and the Congo Defence Force (CDF). The main incentive to continue the war was, however, financial. Soldiers fought to obtain instant booty, whilst warlords aimed at gaining control over productive geographic areas, especially those with gold and diamond deposits, as well as timber and rubber, coffee and cocoa plantations. Rebel movements kept some amount of popular support alive by feigning the protection of the interests of particular regions and ethnic groupings. These were further politicised by the war itself (Atkinson, 1999). In reality, the brutality of combatants towards the very people they claimed to serve kept civilians submissive. Shady international businessmen, conglomerates of West African states and at times foreign departments of powerful Western states all supported the warlords (Keen, 1998; Reno, 1996).

After seven years, the war finally came to a halt, culminating in democratic elections in 1997. Ironically, in what Jimmy Carter, ex-president of the USA, and other international observers saw as 'free and transparent elections', Charles Taylor and his National Patriotic Party (NPP) – formed out of the NPFL – won a landslide victory and thus succeeded in achieving what they had not been able to accomplish through warfare. (On Taylor's political career see Harris, 1999.) The war had by then caused between 60,000 and 200,000 deaths. Without relying on uncertain statistics, it is true to say that during the course of the war most Liberians were displaced at some time. Areas across the borders in Sierra Leone, Guinea, and the Ivory Coast were at times flooded with refugees (Utas, 1997). Internally displaced persons (IDPs) moved up and down between temporary safe havens in search of the protection of some form of authority. The coastal cities of Monrovia and Buchanan, zones guarded by the peacekeepers, received most IDPs and up to this day, Monrovia, for instance, has twice the number of inhabitants than before the onset of the war.

During 1998 and 1999, the security situation in Liberia remained uncertain. Parts of Liberia experienced moments of unrest verging on war with heavy shooting and civilians fleeing helter-skelter. Even so, most observers regarded the war as a closed case. Yet in late 1999, Upper Lofa County experienced the first of a series of armed incursions. By mid-2000, groups of subversive soldiers were entering from neighbouring Guinea on a regular basis. Liberians saw the birth and growth of a new rebel movement, ironically named Liberians United for Reconciliation and Democracy (LURD). Since that time LURD rebels have operated in Lofa County, on occasion advancing towards Monrovia. During the first half of 2002, LURD made a series of successful raids in Bong, Bomi and Montserrado Counties, temporarily taking control of the major towns, Gbarnga, Tubmanburg and Klay Junction, before troops loyal to the government were able to recapture them. In mid-May, an attack on President Taylor's native town of Arthington, less than 20 kilometres from Monrovia, caused panic in Monrovia.

The tide changed, and during the autumn of 2002 LURD was forcibly driven back. However a new advance followed in the spring of 2003 that during the summer months brought the rebel faction all the way to Monrovia. With a core of soldiers recruited from among Liberian exiles in Guinea, LURD was also to enlist young people from within Liberia, yet still relied heavily on volunteers from Sierra Leone and Guinea. Various governmental security forces and pro-governmental paramilitaries, currently called GOL (Government of Liberia) also succeeded in drawing fresh support and recruitment among young Liberians, mainly from Monrovia and surrounding counties. In April 2003 LURD split into two along old ULIMO-J/ULIMO-K lines: LURD, with continued presence in the north, and MODEL (Movement for Democracy in Liberia) operating in the south. Rapid advances by both movements towards Monrovia and a unified inter-national pressure on the government forced Taylor to leave office and go into exile in Nigeria. In February 2004 an interim government was established and a UN force of approximately 8,000 soldiers was introduced to keep troops at bay. Yet still sporadic fighting continued in the rural areas of the country, with Nimba being a specifically troublesome area due to the presence of GOL, LURD and MODEL.*

Even though forced conscription took place in Liberia, most combatants, despite their age, joined of free will. At the outset of the war, as noted above, the people in Nimba County viewed the war as a rebellion designed to free them from a repressive government, seen as anti-Nimbadian. Parents sent their children off to fight in what was seen as a righteous war. However, young people also saw it as a youth revolution, a possibility to get rid of an elitist urban leadership made up of autocrats (Clapham, 1976; 1988; Liebenow, 1987), as well as a rural gerontocracy (Bellman, 1984; Murphy, 1980). In the eyes of the young, both groups gravely misused their powers over the younger generations of Liberians. In this way, the war was fought to a large extent by marginalised people, pre-dominantly youth, who saw the war economy as possibly the only opportunity for them to experience mobility from the margins into the centre of socio-politics.

The war changed its shape and, as rebel groups increased their terror against civilians and as looting excursions increasingly became the *raison d'être* for war, the grounds for joining as combatants also changed. Many young excombatants that I interviewed during my Liberian fieldwork in 1998 admit that it was the possibility of personal advantage that caused them to join the war. These advantages also worked both ways: certainly in direct gains, but also in escaping the disadvantages of being a civilian. Advantages included loot from raids, bribes paid during security assignments and payoffs received from protecting locals. A direct advantage would also be the acquisition of power in local communities.

The leap from being a powerless young boy, under the authority of parents and elders, to being a commander with a gun is tremendous. Being a soldier would also imply having girlfriends, often several at a time, quite an attraction for young men who were practically excluded from having relationships with girls. On the other hand, escaping the disadvantages of being a civilian would primarily involve preventing other rebel soldiers from harassing oneself and one's family. During the war it was crucial for every family to have someone – a son, a daughter, an uncle, or another close relative – in the rebel army in control of the area; otherwise, family members would be constantly harassed and farms and property looted. Finally, young Liberians would at times join the rebel forces in order to avenge family members killed by other rebel factions. During the early stages of our relationship, my informants would state that a desire for vengeance had been a main motive for their joining the war. But, as our relationship evolved, vengeance motives often disappeared behind other objectives. Most Liberians lost close relatives in the war, but very few of them took up arms for that reason.

Liberian Media and the War

For almost 200 years, Liberians have been able to read printed news. The first issue of *Liberia Herald* was issued in 1820 (Bourgault, 1995: 154). By and large, newspapers have been issued for an urban readership, with the exception of a rural effort in 1963 (ibid.: 173). During the Liberian civil war (1990-6), a handful of daily tabloid newspapers, varying in quality and regularity were published. However, in 2002, according to the US Department of State, as many as eighteen newspapers were published in Liberia. Monrovians often pointed out that the Liberian newspapers were far from objective news sources. This was due to three reasons: first, many newspapers were owned or supported by the Liberian government or supported by other political interests. Second, political interest groups bought (and continue to buy) large sections of the papers to distribute their messages. Interest groups ranging from a few individual politicians to large corporations and even INGOs bought articles – in most cases there was nothing to indicate what was 'bought' news and what was 'normal' journalistic work. Third, it was widely known that thugs, and/or units of police or security were attacking newspapers and individual journalists who were too forthright in their reporting. Individual journalists were arrested and threatened; thus in many cases they dared not to criticise the government. With these restrictions, printed news was viewed with a sound share of scepticism. Throughout the history of printed news it also appears that Liberian newspapers, in line with most other West African newspapers (see Bastian, 2003 on Nigeria), has been a constant source of rumour, conspicuous fantasies about magic and witchcraft – such as infectious stories of heart men (or heart doctors) operating in urban spaces, kidnapping and killing children to use their body organs for sacrifice in order to empower politicians and wealthy people – linking up with rich discourses of the economies of the occult (see Comaroff and Comaroff, 1999; Meyer, 2003a; West and Sanders, 2003).

Prior to the civil war, Liberia was an important place for radio transmissions. *Voice of America* (VOA) and the Christian *Eternal Love Winning Africa* (ELWA) both had large transmitters in the vicinity of Monrovia, covering West Africa and further afield. ELWA also broadcast on shortwave in several Liberian vernaculars. The state-run *Liberian Broadcasting Service* generally lent itself to outright state propaganda and the wishes of the President (Bourgault, 1995: 94, 98). Liberia also had its share of community radio projects sponsored by the larger INGOs, broadcasting 'developmentalist discourses', such as *Liberian Rural Communications Network* (NRCN) (Bourgault, 1995: 92-9, 232-3).

Richard Fardon and Graham Furniss have noted that

> [I]n situations of crisis, radio comes to the fore as an informational medium; but interpreting its statements and silences, knowing how to combine different radio accounts with street knowledge and background expectations to triangulate some – at least for a moment – credible account of what may be happening only a short distance away, belongs with all those other local capacities that outsiders have to learn by participation (Fardon and Furniss, 2000).

During the war, Liberian radio was by and large limited to urban microcasting, with privately owned stations transmitting on FM in Monrovia, such as Charles Taylor's *Liberia Communications Network* (LCN), including the popular *Radio Kiss*. In addition the Swiss NGO *Foundation Hirondelle* ran *Star Radio*: being too outspoken in its critique of the Taylor government it was closed in 1998, temporarily reopened in 1999 and then closed permanently in 2000. *Radio Veritas* was operated under the Catholic Archdiocese, also broadcasting in shortwave, reaching countrywide. Despite these channels, Liberians agreed that they could only rely on one radio channel: the BBC.

Several times a day, the BBC transmits *Focus on Africa*. In for instance a refugee setting such as Danane in Côte d'Ivoire, in addition to tuning in to the *radio trottoir* – translated as 'pavement' radio by Stephen Ellis (1989) – or the rural 'bush radio' of traders and occasional visitors from Liberia, the BBC was the only channel connecting them to the daily events in Liberia. In the late afternoon it used to be a fascinating experience to walk through Danane, where about half of the population were Liberians, and hear *Focus on Africa* from inside the compounds, echoing in the streets. People took a break from the regular activities and men especially crowded around the radios for the latest Liberian updates. The BBC's impact in the refugee settings as well as in the interior was massive.

During the initial years of the civil war, the BBC had access to the war scene mainly through one reporter: Elizabeth Blunt. She was taken to mythical heights in the Liberian imaginary and is by many believed to have been present at all important locations at all crucial moments. I would argue here that when her presence is claimed by local interlocutors, it is a way of objectifying the event discussed. She is generally imagined to have been close to both Charles Taylor and Prince Johnson simultaneously, and was frequently portrayed as the girlfriend of both warlords. Blunt has herself pointed out that there is no truth in these rumours. However, it highlights both the importance of BBC as a prime news source for Liberians during the war as well as the importance of Blunt as moulder of opinion, which depended on her connections with the two rebel movements.

Exercising control over media and/or to pitch correctly into existing mediascapes have become of increasing importance for success in current warfare. Today, news media play central roles in all types of warfare. Governments at war and guerrilla factions in civil wars have developed a wide range of techniques to manipulate media for their particular needs. Charles Taylor, as well as the other faction leaders in the Liberian civil war, were all highly aware of the importance of the BBC. The former used his influence with the BBC and so did the other rebel leaders. George Boley, the leader of the LPC faction, former minister of education and presidential secretary, and Alhaji Kromah, leader of the ULIMO-K, a former deputy minister of information, both had a strategic knowledge of how media worked and thus tried to bend public opinion their way through its manipulation. The BBC was their main target. A peculiarity in the reporting of the BBC on the Liberian civil war has been the extreme willingness of the rebel leaders to go live on *Focus on Africa*. During my stay in Danane (spring 1996) I heard them repeatedly on radio – at the time something rare for leaders of African rebel groups. From satellite phones in bush camps or from their mansions in Monrovia, they called the BBC hoping to get important airtime to present themselves and their movements as affably as possible, always suggesting intimacy by using the reporter's first name. In the five o'clock edition, they always appeared to be great chums with the studio reporter, Robin White, saying 'you know, Robin,' and then quickly, not to waste costly media time, moved on to paint their opponents in the worst possible light.

Television has been available in Liberia since the mid-1960s (Bourgault, 1995: 104). During most of the war years, broadcasts from only two channels could be picked up by Monrovians. The LCN, owned by Charles Taylor, and *Ducor Broadcasting Corporation*, privately owned but with close commercial ties with Taylor. Both mainly showed movies and entertainment and thus played an insignificant political role. The channels paid limited attention to screening rights as they often broadcast movies aimed at the American market and not thought of as having export potential. Very few Liberians had access to satellite television; satellite dishes mainly indicated the whereabouts of restaurants and hotels. The commonplace use of television in Liberia is in combination with the VCR. Video is mainly an entertainment media but it is employed for other purposes as well. Due to the straightforward and relatively cheap technology of video, the production and circulation of private videos from weddings, funerals and other important family occasions has become an important means of communication over short and long distances (cf. Meyer, 2003a: 208) and one way of linking imagined Liberian communities together. Videos from family occasions in, for instance, the USA are widely circulated in Liberia and vice versa. In this fashion, the video media is clearly signalling both modernity and connection with the Western world. To some extent video is also used for channelling news, and due to the absolute objectivity associated with the visual, Liberians – as well as many others – pay great attention to its contents. In this sense, circulating videos should be included in the 'small media' that people all around the world use 'to establish alternative spheres of communication, especially challenging state power' (Spitulnik, 2002: 177).

The Video Media

In addition to radio, the daily papers and the continuous flow of rumour, video recordings rose to be an important media in the Liberian civil war. Video proved to be a useful media for war propaganda and video cassettes were circulated throughout the country and among the refugee diaspora. Screening possibilities were many in Monrovia and the larger Liberian towns. In Gbarnga, Bong County, for instance, they had five video parlours running day and night during the early parts of the war (Richards, 1996: 102). Paul Richards (1994; 1996) has also noted that mobile video 'theatres' are found in the Sierra Leonean forest region bordering Liberia. Young entrepreneurs carry generators, VCRs and TV sets on their backs, bringing visual images to the most remote villages. I have not encountered similar business activities in Liberia but one of the main reasons to get a generator in a village is to watch video. Video recordings have been accessible to a large part of the Liberian population.

In the refugee setting of Danane during 1996 there were several video clubs that appealed to a Liberian crowd, that is, the films they showed were generally not dubbed into French. The films were mainly American action, Asian *kung-fu*, Indian films, Nigerian and Ghanaian low-budget films. A common denominator was a high content of violence, and/or a high content of magic. The film clubs generally had their first show at eight o'clock in the morning and ran the last show at midnight. Even during the day, they drew quite a crowd. The visitors were in general below thirty, predominantly men, but young mothers often brought their kids to see a show. As the videos were watched with vivid enthusiasm it was not uncommon to hear a young mother yell, 'Kill that motherfucker'. In this sense, we find striking resemblance with the reception of moviegoers in Accra, as studied by Birgit Meyer (2003b: 26). Meyer points out that it is often women who watch and urge their male partners to buy Ghanaian-produced films (ibid.: 24). Among Liberians, West-African films and the even more popular Indian movies, certainly draw a predominantly female crowd, but action films are popular among women as well.

Film media, quite obviously, influence people in various ways. Gillespie has pointed out, in a rather different context, that people use films 'to negotiate, argue, and agree about a wide range of customs, traditions, values, and beliefs' (1993: 158). The negotiation ground becomes even more immediate and psycho-socially important if images originate from or draw on an individual's own cultural context. The popularity of Nigerian and Ghanaian films can be explained by the familiarity of its imaginary. Frames from one's own backyard have greater authority in stipulating reality, good or bad, than those from afar, and thus play an important role in discussing, promoting and contesting local ideoscapes. Birgit Meyer's studies of the popular reception of Ghanaian cinema are instructive in this respect. Based on Christian values, Ghanaian films (and most Nigerian productions as well) have clear moral messages; people in Meyer's study say that these films are 'teaching morals' (2003b: 25). In Ghanaian movies, there is generally a clear dividing line between good and bad people, moral and immoral behaviour being articulated through the pious Christian character in sharp contrast to the ungodly character using magic powers and access to the economy of the occult. Meyer proposes that magic, based on a Christian dualism of God and the Devil, in these films is 'being constructed by a cinematic-Pentecostal mode of representation' (Meyer, 2003a: 202). Spectators state that the films 'reveal what was really going on in life' (Meyer, 2003b: 25) thus buying into the Christian message – Pentecostalism being a dominant discourse in south Ghana. Liberian ideoscapes are similarly filled with Christian values and political discourse (Gifford, 1993 has pointed to the great importance of Christianity in

Liberia) making the success of Nigerian and Ghanaian films understandable. It is also in this light I believe we should see the storyline of the Doe torture.

Video cassettes as a source of news with images from the civil war were widely circulated in Liberia and in the diaspora (both in refugee camps in neighbouring West African countries and in the wider diaspora, primarily in the USA). The demand for cassettes from the civil war was huge in all these settings. Available all over Liberia to the civilian population, they were also used in the training of newly recruited soldiers. When the films were introduced in video clubs in Danane they met with instant success among Liberian refugees as well as an Ivorian audience, even when the spectators were charged as much as ten times the usual entrance fee. The clubs were packed on such nights. At some time during the spring of 1995, films containing material from the Liberian civil war were banned in the Ivory Coast by the authorities. The reason for this, it is said, was that the government was afraid that these films might influence subversive elements in the Ivory Coast. The ban meant that the films were not shown in video clubs anymore, but cassettes still circulated privately.

What is shown in the videos and why were they so popular? There is an abundance of different compilations, most often produced in Nigeria. In general the films are based on more or less the same footage. A lot of the material is cut from reportage originating in Western news media covering the Liberian conflict. It is mixed up with footage shot by amateur filmmakers with home-video equipment. These amateur clips show fighting sequences, troop movements, military parades and hordes of refugees leaving war zones. To have these videotapes distributed to Liberians and others was a strategic move by leaders of the rebel movements (the NPFL and the INPFL, in particular), in order to present motion pictures from the front, the camp, and so on. Both are ways of manufacturing war heroes and produce proof of rebel success – a point I shall return to below. Even if certain tapes intend to follow a linear time perspective, the final products tend to become rather surrealist montages transposing time and space. Certain clips appear to exist only in the imaginary world, for example one showing the assassination of Dr Yekeson, Vice-Chancellor Emeritus of the University of Liberia. He was brutally manhandled and killed during the war, yet there is nothing to prove that this was actually filmed.

The Video of Samuel Doe's Torture

The cover of the video *La Guerre Civile Liberienne* (the French version) bears resemblance to covers of comic war movies of the *Kelly's Heroes* type. It is a tasteless collage – tasteless at least from an outsider's point of view – of images from the film. The happy 'heroes' Charles Taylor and Prince Johnson are planted among RPGs, Delta bombers, among fighters dressed in women's clothes, or in lion masks. Dead bodies are ruthlessly deframed from their filmed context and in the right corner there are two pictures of the late president Doe, coloured in red. An English version, popular in the United States, has been given the highly ironic name *Samuel K Doe (1980-1990) From Hero to Zero*. My analysis below is mainly based on this film. It begins with a reportage of British origin, dated soon after the 1980 coup (see Schröder and Korte, 1986 for a thorough study of the 1980 coup). It relays the well-known pictures from the executions of the

Tolbert government at the beachfront (nicknamed 'Liberian Beach Party') and continues with a report on Liberia under the new Doe government. As propaganda the reportage works brilliantly. It legitimises the coup against the Tolbert regime, but simultaneously reveals a large portion of doubt as to whether Doe has the potential to rule Liberia. The scepticism in the reportage is primarily directed towards his low education, some early indications of an emerging personal cult, and regionalism – or ethnic factionalism. The use of this media clip shows how international media can be used to impose authority in a totally different context than that intended. Without any outright visual manipulation it sets a tone of objectivity.

The British reportage is followed by the amateur filmed account of the torture of Samuel Doe. This particular clip is found on more or less every compilation. Doe was captured by the INPFL, under the leadership of Prince Johnson and in much of the footage, it is Johnson himself who plays the leading part (Ellis, 1995; Huband, 1998; see Youboty, 1993, for a background to the capture of Doe). In the eyes of my informants what is taking place on the screen is an *interrogation* (which coincides with what Prince Johnson calls it). However, with President Samuel Doe on the floor, his arms *tabaved* (elbows tied together on the back) and a sequence in which a soldier cuts of his ears, it is hard for a non-Liberian viewer not to see it as torture.

This second clip starts with Johnson and his INPFL soldiers entering the ECOMOG base on 9 September 1990. For reasons still not definitely understood, ECOMOG, a peace force established by the West African ECOWAS countries, had informed INPFL of Doe's visit, allowing it free passage to enter their base at the Freeport, Monrovia. Prince Johnson has been fighting for the past nine months with a single goal in mind: to topple the President of Liberia, Samuel Doe. When Johnson enters the base singing a Jim Reeves gospel tune (Reno, 1996: 211), he knows that Doe has been lured into a trap that will end his days as Liberian President. This is what the narrative of the video wants us to believe. However, according to Huband (1998: 193), the scene was shot earlier in the day at a different location (Island Clinic). The scene changes abruptly; we are now indoors. Of the battle that took place when INPFL entered Freeport we see nothing. Doe is already on the floor *tabaved*. Around him we see Johnson's men in triumph. Behind a desk sits Johnson, himself, sipping imported beer and giving commands on his communication radio. One cannot hear the conversation too clearly. The quality of the tape is low after several rounds of copying from a poor original. The spectacle proceeds. Once in a while Johnson's questions come out clearly: 'What happened to the people's money?' 'Why did you kill this person?' asks Johnson. The camera is moving unsteadily from Johnson to Doe. Doe, who has been shot in one leg, is obviously in pain. He pleads with Johnson to loosen the rope *tabaving* his arms on his back. Johnson answers: 'No, you might disappear.' Everyone is sweating profusely. The only female soldier present is wiping the sweat off Johnson's forehead once in a while. Then Johnson gives the order to cut off Doe's ears. Both ears are gone in less than a minute. The wounds bleed surprisingly little and Doe shows an enormous strength by still sitting up, and continuing to beg for mercy.

After about twenty minutes of questioning, the setting again changes. We are now outside. Doe has been taken to Johnson's base in Caldwell. Johnson has departed and his deputy Samuel Varney has taken over. But the same questions are asked repeatedly. 'What have you done with the people's money?' 'Give us your bank account number' and so forth. The sequence is long and tiresome. Nothing is really happening except that Doe is floating more and more into unconsciousness. The soldiers pour water over his head. After nearly forty minutes the images stop and the viewers are left in the dark.

What happened to Doe when the camera was turned off? It is not known for sure, but the version given by Johnson himself is that Doe later died at Johnson's mansion, in a bathroom, from loss of blood (Huband, 1998: 194; Johnson, 1990: 221). Rumour among Western journalists suggests that the entire process, until Doe finally dies, has been filmed. This appears to be without substance, as the remaining part of the Doe killing would then have appeared on the market long ago. That Doe should have been forced to eat his ears as suggested by Daniels (1991: 17) and Buch (1995: 13) is also mere rumour. It was hardly created and communicated in a socio-cultural void; rather it links up with popular notions of cannibalistic consumption as an issue in essence tied up with use and abuse of political power. As the most powerful person in Liberia, Samuel Doe was also viewed as the foremost consumer of occult powers – a function that included consumption of human body parts. The conspiracy between Doe and the powers of the occult unfolds in front of the video consumer thus further strengthening their belief that Doe sustained his power through magic and the economy of the occult. Over ten years of presidency, Doe created an image of himself as an omnipotent leader – or an enigma to use one refugee's (see p. 172) term – with tremendous powers aided by a loyal military force committing violence and dirty warfare, and using magic practices, including rituals rumoured to involve cannibalism (cf. Ellis, 1999: 25). Could Doe be toppled at all? Most Liberians doubted this possibility and wanted to see it with their own eyes. That was part of the reason why films containing this material attracted such a crowd of spectators.

If to a Western audience the video simply demonstrates African barbarism (see e.g. Buch, 1995; Daniels, 1991; Johnson, 1990), to Liberians it communicates a whole set of meanings. It deals with cultural and political issues of contemporary Liberia and is as such an important piece of war history for Liberians. The cover of the VCR is in itself loaded with symbolism. Johnson and Charles Taylor are depicted as two folk heroes who have proved more powerful than the President. Yet it is quite misleading to find the image of Taylor on the cover, as he is not present in the film. However, as Johnson ceased playing any important role in the civil war and left the Liberian scene quite early in the war history, the Taylor rebel side incorporated the film into the legacy of the NPFL movement, much as they had incorporated the bulk of INPFL soldiers. The film is intended as legitimation of the civil war and a moral justification of the INPFL incursion – in that vein it sets out to justify Doe's death. The answer is given in part already in the British clip, pointing to corruption, regional favouritism of Doe's southern home county and a growing personality cult. This is highlighted in the interroga- tions led by Johnson and Varney with their repeated accusations of Doe emptying the state finances, extracting money for his own personal accounts and their pointing out of his guilt in killing specific Liberian citizens. Johnson, on the other hand, is depicted as a modern man who, in contrast to Doe, draws power from righteousness. He is also a man of the people who is out to regain what was stolen from the Liberian state, to avenge suffering and re-establish pride in

Liberian citizenship. He is 'the chosen one' who is able to unravel the conspiracy of the Doe elite (West and Sanders, 2003: 19). Even though he is ordering the brutal manhandling of Doe, we learn that this is a precaution taken so that Doe will not be able to use his magic powers. In that sense the video's scenario does mimic popular Ghanaian films but more importantly plays on prevailing Christian ideas within a local ideoscape.

(V)ideoscapes

How was the video conceptualised in such a setting? How was the video justified? How was Samuel Doe depicted? Some young male refugees residing in Danane gave the following accounts, answering the questions of what brought them to go and watch the film:

> Oliver: Doe was like an enigma – like a restraint – Doe was like all powerful – Doe was like I can't come near this guy. He built a reputation of himself. He has built a concrete wall around himself that was too powerful. He brought fright in the citizens. And if they see this they know that he is definitely not alive ....
>
> Dao: They heard so much of Samuel Doe. They feared that he was a man that could not easily be toppled. He was a great man – a very strong man who could stand many coup d'états. He also made people believe that no man could kill him except God, or natural death. And how coming to see him die by bullet was something very much amazing.
>
> Doegolia: It was the first time for a president to be arrested by rebels, assassinated by rebels, besides that the President being a strong man, a strong African to be arrested by another strong African fighter, you know. I wanted to see some of the miraculous things that happened before the arrest.

It is obvious from the accounts that Doe, and the state machinery he acted through, were experienced with much dread by Liberians in general and Liberians from Nimba County – from where most people in Danane originated – in particular. They simply wanted to see him dead. But in these accounts it is equally clear that the powers bestowed on him are not only open or transparent powers but also concealed and magic. Thus Liberian people's wish to see the video is linked with the wish to unravel an occult cosmology of Liberian leadership personified by the Liberian president.

Prince Johnson is putting up a visual show full of other symbolic messages for the audience. When he first enters the frame in the first three minutes, playing guitar and singing, 'kicking around' with his soldiers, he appears to be no more than one of the lads. He is also himself in a later sequence (8:20, ie 8 mins. 20 secs.), pointing out that he is 'a great humanitarian'. He is not losing any opportunity to portray himself as an agent on the side of the good. At this point it is hard to believe that he is a brutal field marshal, and leader of the infamous INPFL faction. Simultaneously, he clearly wants to portray INPFL as a well-equipped army. This message is effectively given to the spectators through images of high-tech weapons and soldiers in brand new camouflage uniforms. The image is also stating that the INPFL is an army of grown men. This creates an alternative representation of INPFL, as the rebel faction had a reputation of being a poorly equipped, rag-tag army largely comprising under-age soldiers without military training.

If we jump to the indoor sequence after Doe has been shot in the leg, we find Johnson is sitting comfortably behind a large desk, symbolically superior to Doe who is sitting naked and humiliated on the floor. Even the INPFL soldiers are prone to show their new-found power over the president as they repeatedly pat Doe on his head as if he were a child (5:10). Johnson demonstrates his power by indifferently giving orders on his communication radio. Further, he is drinking imported beer. Radio and imported beer help portray Johnson as modern, not backward. He announces his victory to the world, with the camera as witness, by officially stating that he has toppled Doe and taken power on behalf of the Liberian people to protect them from the unjustifiable crimes committed by Doe. The ultimate proof of Johnson's power is when he orders his men to cut Doe's body, disjoining the ears from the head (19:30). His men then pose, triumphantly, like hunters over an animal they have brought down (20:40). Rather than just paying attention to the violent deed itself, I believe we must see it as a moral story. Violence is in this case merely opening up the muted discourses of magic and the occult. This is the moment of truth where Doe has to pay for his immorality and his deal with the devil. Thus the Doe clip shows, just as in the Ghanaian films studied by Meyer, that 'rather than celebrating these embodiments of punishments, films should show that evil deeds would have consequences for the life of the person committing them and that they would eventually be judged by God' (Meyer, 2003a: 215). Doe is punished by an agonising death.

Furthermore, we have to recognise that the film is prime evidence that Prince Johnson was the one who managed to topple Doe. To Johnson it was a matter of great prestige that he, and not his prime rival Taylor, managed to rid Liberia of Doe. In one sequence of the film (7:20) Johnson is addressing the NPFL leader and subsequently the US embassy on the communication radio. At the time, the United States was seen to have close to divine powers in Liberia. It is also said (as usual without verification) that Prince Johnson later personally handed over the film to Charles Taylor as proof. After Doe had been killed, a power struggle began over who was to take office at the presidential mansion. Taylor and General Nimley, commander of Doe's bodyguard, as well as Johnson declared themselves the president of Liberia (Van den Boom, 1995: 22). Johnson used the videotape, ultimately without final success, to prove that he was the legitimate leader of the country.

If we backtrack in the video plot somewhat: at the ECOMOG camp, Doe and his bodyguard were supposed to have been in a meeting with ECOMOG staff when the INPFL soldiers caught them by surprise, burst into the room and shot them all down. According to the legend, when the gunfire subsided, Doe had disappeared. It was suspected that he had used 'witchcraft' to disappear, although later he was found wounded under the dead bodies of his bodyguard. In an early sequence of the film (3:40) a young man is holding up a bunch of amulets (*seke*, *juju*, or 'African science') taken from Doe. *Seke* are objects containing supernatural powers. Most fighters in the civil war had been wearing several such to protect themselves from misfortunes. The most popular *seke* made its bearer bullet-proof; another *seke* protected him or her from discovery by enemies; and a third offered disappearance. Most Liberian people put great trust in such magic, thus the capture of Doe's *seke* signified Doe's loss of power and simultaneously that the men in the INPFL possessed powers exceeding those of

Doe. When Doe pleads with the soldiers to loosen the ties on his hands, he is refused by Johnson who says that he might disappear (12:50). This comment suggests that, even though Doe's magical powers had been stripped away, Johnson and his men were still anxious about Doe's ability to vanish.

Even if the INPFL side try to fit the image of being godly rather than accessing power through magic and the occult, it is obvious that they too draw power from the non-Christian world. The magic potency of the INPFL fighters is signalled for instance by soldiers having plaited hair (see e.g. 17:26), a characteristic of pre-colonial warriors among the Gio or Mano peoples, who plaited medicine into their hair for protection. However, such references should not be seen as direct contradiction, for magic of various kinds is often synthesised with a Christian belief system. Such an amalgamation is obvious from a statement, in the *Inquirer* newspaper (31 August 1998), given by Joshua Milton Blayee, who was at the time pastor of the Soul Winning Evangelist Ministry but also the legendary fighter, General Butt Naked, once active in the ULIMO-J. Writing in his post-war guise as a godly man, Blayee warns President Charles Taylor against using medicine-men, or partaking in the economy of the occult, while adding that Taylor cannot challenge him in the field of 'medicine' as Blayee is himself a chief medicine-man (chief *Zo*).

In the eyes and minds of the typical Liberian viewer, the Doe clip is a spectacle aimed at opening up hidden discourses of the cosmology of the occult in order to unravel a conspiracy. To borrow from Misty Bastian, to watch the Doe video is 'to know the spectacular "truth" of conspiracy' (2003: 67). Bastian deals with an isolated media story from Nigeria in which, as in Liberia, people are convinced that a trade in magic linked up with a trade in human body parts is part and parcel of the powers of the political and economic elite. In 1996, the filming by a local news team of local police arresting a young man for transporting a severed head immediately received country-wide attention in Nigeria. It was identified as that of a small boy who had gone missing, and was found in the boot of a rented car in Owerri, the capital of Imo state. Even if many children go missing in Nigerian cities and many people claim to have seen mutilated bodies,

> nothing had quite the immediacy of this image of Innocent Ekeanyanwu and his 'prize'; nothing else lent the horrific idea of 'ritual murder' for personal profit such 'concrete form.' The image was fantastic ... as well as galvanizing; what it wrought in the Nigerian socio-political landscape – as well as in its 'mediascape' – was more than a nine days wonder (Bastian, 2003: 67-8).

The media spectacle was followed by riots, where people in particularly targeted shops, the estates of wealthy business men, the palace of the chairman of the Imo state council and two evangelical churches. Ordinary people targeted the wealthy establishment because they believed its members to be the prime consumers in the economy of the occult, together with certain churches. In Liberia we find the same tropes of thought as the omnipotence of generations of presidents has been viewed as upheld by their magic powers (Ellis, 1995: 192; Utas, 2003: 155-6). If we see the video of the Doe torture in this light, we might conclude that its popularity was due to its exposure of the closed shrine of the occult, the revelation of all its secrets to a Liberian public. This sudden blow of transparency was used by Prince Johnson to put himself forward as a Liberian saviour.

What is more affirming than the presence of Elizabeth Blunt, the BBC reporter, at the site where Doe was caught and tortured? Although she is not seen in frame, that was the word on the street. It was widely believed that she went under the table with Doe when he was first shot. Whether she was there or not is beside the point; the rumour of her presence, tied up with the British reportage, powerfully asserts that what is screened is the *pure truth*. The technology of television and the VCR in itself supports the authenticity of the war clips.

The Objectivity of Technology

The first time we get an idea of who filmed the Doe torture-scene is when we see a man with a mid-size tape recorder and a simple plug-in microphone recording the sound (11:30). The man is of Middle Eastern origin, indicating that this is one of the many Lebanese tradesmen who maintained good relations with the warlord. My informants all state that the 'film team' was of Lebanese origin, yet some claim that it was a professional TV team. The fashion in which the film is shot shows without doubt that it was the work of an amateur. Huband (1998: 193) claims that a Lebanese trader by the name of Tahseen who had joined Johnson at that time shot the film, yet ex-fighters of the INPFL say it was shot by a young man named Moral, a Lebanese diamond trader who was still active in Liberia during my fieldwork in 1998. Indeed it could be the same man, but the mere presence of Lebanese gives an impression of objectivity. Sadly, Liberians are generally extra-suspicious of the authenticity of any work carried out by their own nationals. The question of who shot the film is taking us into a broader discussion of technology and technological access. An interesting issue is that many Liberians with whom I have spoken believe that films from the civil war were shot from satellites. It is widely thought that satellites circling around the globe are registering everything going on in Liberia. At one point during my stay in Danane a young man bombarded me with questions about what would happen in Liberia in the near future. I replied that he, as a Liberian, could probably foresee better than me what would happen. This answer made him even more upset, since 'we' (that is, Westerners) could watch the state of affairs in Liberia via satellite. Armed with the knowledge from satellite pictures we had the choice to stop the war anytime we wished, but we had chosen to stand aside and watch Liberians kill each other.

It is mainly the US government that Liberians condemn for political manipulation as well as lack of conflict-solving initiatives during the war. Monrovians have been able to watch large military carriers of US origin lie at anchor during the heights of the conflict in 1990, 1992, 1996 and 2003 without unloading any significant number of troops. Such action, or lack thereof, nurtured the popular idea that the US government was in control of the conflict but simply wanted it to take its own course. The bitterness harboured in Liberian civilians in relation to their 'big patron' grew quite intense during the civil war, only adding further to the plethora of conspiracy theories already at work in the country. It fed into afro-pessimistic ideas of an African disconnection from the 'modern' Western world (see e.g. Diawara, 1998; Ferguson, 1999; 2002). There is a growing gap between high-tech and low-tech wars, as Mbembe, among others, has pointed out (Mbembe, 2003: 30). If Western parties were really interested in Liberian affairs, they could bring in advanced reconnaissance equipment such as the SPAACE camera, the Hawkeye radar or the remote piloted 'Scout' (Virilio, 1989: 87, 89), to keep a closer watch on the current situation. Yet what the discussion highlighted for me was how abstract the ideas of high-tech equipment such as satellite technology are.

Popular thought harbours ideas that through technology everything not only becomes possible but also objectified, not unlike what Vertov proclaims in his famous film *Man with Movie Camera* (Vertov, 1929 [2000]):

> I am the camera's eye: I am the machine which shows you the world as I alone see it. Starting from today, I am forever free of human immobility. I am in perpetual movement. I approach and draw away from things – I crawl under them – I climb them – I am on the head of a galloping horse – I burst at full speed into a crowd – I run before running soldiers – I throw myself down on my back – I rise up with the aeroplanes – I fall and I fly at one with the bodies falling or rising through the air (quoted in Virilio, 1989: 20).

Even if many people believe at first that shooting the films from the civil war involved high-tech equipment such as satellites, when they ponder it more carefully most realise that it is rather unlikely:

> Doegolia: Done by satellite and brave journalists... Really what happened; the one I saw I don't think it was done by satellite. I want to believe that it was done by some amateur – because it was not clear. Satellite is very clear – explicit, you see every activity.
>
> Dao: I from an initial stage, I particularly thought it was a satellite stationed up the thing, but from viewing the whole frame ... There are pictures taken from the ground, on the ground level, and a majority of the pictures are taken from the back of the frame.
>
> John: Satellite, we would consider that too. So journalists went closer and did their filming and the satellite was able to pick it up and get a copy.

Cinema is generally not viewed as an objective source of information but is indisputably an object for simultaneous collective experience (Benjamin, 1969: 234). Viewing documentary films in cinemas combines the idea of the objective with the collective. I would argue that viewing documentaries from the Liberian civil war in a video club in Danane together with other exiled Liberians is an experience beyond that. In a direct sense the video club audience experiences a transgression of the private and the public, as the public realm leaps into the private when 'actors' on the public video screen merge with 'actors' of their own private realms of life. Thus the audience identification with the actor is no longer only mediated by the camera as pointed out by Benjamin (1969 [1961]: 228), but also forms part of a lived experience. Dao stresses this point:

> Showing the film did a lot to the people, showing the film excited the people. Because people who could not fight saw their brother or immediate friend in those frames and they were fighting, were rejoicing and after some time seeing their friends looting and commanding people. For those people it motivated some of them to go and be part of the whole system.

Dao recognises people in the Doe video:

> Oh yes, many – old schoolmates, friends, footballers. A personal friend of mine I can talk about is Moyu. I saw him and another friend Prince [common first name in Liberia]. They stand there in the cutting of Samuel Doe's ears. With an AK 47 in their hands talking to other boys; commanding men.

Who distributed the videos from the Liberian civil war? What did popular opinion say about it? According to the Liberians in Danane, businessmen or fighters of the NPFL brought video-cassettes from the civil war into town. One source suggested that fighters brought them along in order to show how well they fought, as a method of generating public support. When asked why the films were shot, the typical answer was that someone in the group had a special interest, or that journalists made them in order to make money. It was extremely rare that my interviewees expressed any ideas on these films being produced for the sake of outright propaganda, even if some agreed that the films were premeditated. Such expressions were partly dependent on the fact that through-out the war Danane was 'NPFL territory'. Even if people were not outright afraid of being critical of Taylor and the NPFL in general, they were certainly careful in giving official statements to outsiders. Indeed there were numerous stories of how NPFL personnel operated in Danane, threatening or even incarcerating political opponents. Even if the people in Danane hesitated to call the film propaganda, it is quite clear that this was what Johnson had in mind when he ordered it to be made back in 1990. Soon after the death of Doe, the film was screened to specially invited Western journalists at Johnson's Caldwell base (see accounts in Huband, 1998; Johnson, 1990). This was the official media launch of the film. At the time, neither Johnson nor anybody else could anticipate the popularity and importance of the film.

Conclusion

In this chapter, we have discussed the use of local media in relation to local ideoscapes. Radio was the primary media in Liberia during the civil war, but I would argue that an increased apprehension concerning the objectivity of the media, as well as ideas of the visual as being more objective, have created space for the circulation of video clips containing 'news' from the civil war. Visual technology not only signals objectivity but also modernity. If we set up a simple model, it could be stated that high-tech, modernity, Christianity and moral transparency are categorised in opposition to low-tech, backwardness (rather than traditionalism), powers of the occult and conspiracy. Yet we need to observe that such an opposition is frequently and easily transgressed without this necessarily being viewed as a systematic contradiction. As Peter Pels points out 'modernity not only constitutes magic as its counterpoint but also produces its own forms of magic' (Pels, 2003: 3). The pairing of technology and objectivity is thus in itself a sort of magic.

The video clip of the torture of President Samuel Doe has been the main focus of this chapter. What has been attempted here is an alternative reading to that of international news media. My aim has been to contextualise the video properly; to read it as part of a local ideoscape (to borrow from Appadurai, 1996). By doing so, we can see how the popularity of the video in Liberia and among Liberians in exile stems not from a general interest in violence and public vengeance, but rather from the fact that the video is communicating a different set of meanings to a Liberian public. I have used the notion of 'occult cosmology', as discussed by West and Sanders (2003), to show that Liberian video watchers see the video in the objective light of media technology as uncovering hidden powers originating from the economy of the occult. In one sense the unravelling of elite conspiracies aims at transparency, yet at the same time we have to accept that the dismantling of Doe's ritual powers is effected through the use of other ritual powers. This ambiguity is highlighted in the statement of Reverend Blayee aka General Butt Naked discussed on p. 174. Hidden power is fought with hidden power (James Scott in West and Sanders, 2003: 17). The opening up of the invisible is part of occult power as, in the words of Mariane Ferme, '[t]he skill to see beyond the visible phenomenon and to interpret deeper meanings is, then, a culturally valued and highly contested activity, because on it are predicated all social and political actions and different forms of wealth' (2001: 4). The visible world is dominated by invisible forces. And we continue the reading of Meyer:

> In this sense, here the camera is magic's fiercest enemy: following witches into their secret machinations and making their actions visible on the screen, the camera engages in a modern, mediated form of witch hunt, through which the guilt of the witch is established beyond doubt. In so doing, however, the camera also is very much complicit with occult forces, such as witches, because it confirms, and even proves, their existence. Indeed, the relationship between magic and the camera in popular film is paradoxical in that the latter confirms the existence of occult forces and defeats them at the same time (Meyer, 2003a: 218).

Furthermore, we have been able to observe the correspondence between the Doe clip and Ghanaian and Nigerian fiction films. We observe the close relationship between the mediascapes in this region. Meyer (2003a&b) describes the Pentecostal plots found in most films from Ghana where storylines are constructed around the battle between good and bad. Magic and powers of the occult are present in the films she discusses and are confronted by the Christian faith of the main characters. It is the moral of the films that the main characters, aided by their strong belief, thwart the success of the dark powers. The Doe clip draws on a similar imaginary and what we see is the final battle between good and bad, where Prince Johnson with his high morality and bravery is able to cast down Doe, literally cutting off his occult potency by hacking off his ears. Prince Johnson plays the 'man of the people' character who has set out to regain pride and esteem on behalf of the Liberian people. Simultaneously, he exposes the concealed powers of the political elite.

Prince Johnson is today a born-again Christian – what could be more natural?

---

* Since October 2003 a UN force, UNMIL, has maintained peace in Liberia. In January 2006 this force comprised 16,000 uniformed troops under Nigerian command. In November 2005 Ellen Johnson-Sirleaf was elected president after a close battle with popular footballer George Weah. To many of the young combatants in the civil war the appointment of the elderly Johnson-Sirleaf, instead of the youthful Weah, was seen as another defeat in the face of Liberia's gerontocratic establishment. Yet Johnson-Sirleaf's longstanding political experience and her connections within the international community and the UN system may well add to the country's post-war stability.

References

Adebajo, Adekaye (2002) *Liberia's Civil War: Nigeria, ECOMOG, and Regional Security in West Africa*, Boulder, CO: Lynne Rienner.

Allen, Tim (1999) 'Perceiving Contemporary Wars', in Tim Allen and Jean Seaton (eds) *The Media of Conflict: War Reporting and Representations of Ethnic Violence*, London: Zed Books, pp. 11-42.

Appadurai, Arjun (1996) *Modernity at Large: Cultural Dimensions of Globalization*, Minneapolis, MN: University of Minnesota Press.

Atkinson, Philippa (1999) 'Deconstructing Media Mythologies of Ethnic War in Liberia', in Tim Allen and Jean Seaton (eds) *The Media of Conflict: War Reporting and Representations of Ethnic Violence*, London: Zed Books, pp. 199-218.

Bastian, Misty L. (2003) '"Diabolic Realities": Narratives of Conspiracy, Transparency, and "Ritual Murder" in the Nigerian Popular Print and Electronic Media', in Harry G. West and Todd Sanders (eds) *Transparency and Conspiracy: Ethnographies of Suspicion in the New World Order*, Durham, NC: Duke University Press, pp. 65-91.

Bellman, Beryl (1984) *The Language of Secrecy: Symbols and Metaphors in Poro Ritual*, New Brunswick, NJ: Rutgers University Press.

Benjamin, Walter (1969 [1961]) *Illuminations: Essays and Reflections*, New York: Schocken Books.

Bourgault, Louise M. (1995) *Mass Media in Sub-Saharan Africa*, Bloomington, IN: Indiana University Press.

Brown, David (1982) 'On the Category "Civilised" in Liberia and Elsewhere', *Journal of Modern African Studies* 20(2): 287-303.

Buch, Hans C. (1995) 'Entfesselt zum Morden', *Die Zeit*, 12 May 1995.

Clapham, Christopher (1976) *Liberia and Sierra Leone: An Essay in Comparative Politics*, Cambridge and New York: Cambridge University Press.

Clapham, Christopher (1988) 'The Politics of Failure: Clientilism, Political Instability and National Integration in Liberia and Sierra Leone', in C. Clapham (ed.) *Private Patronage and Public Power: Political Clientilism in the Modern State*, New York: St. Martins Press.

Comaroff, John and Jean Comaroff (1999) 'Alien-Nation: Zombies, Immigrants and Millenial Capitalism', *CODESRIA Bulletin* 3-4: 17-28.

Daniels, Anthony (1991) 'Heart of Darkness', *National Review* 10 June 1991: 17-18.

David, Sonia M. (1992) '"To be Kwii is Good": A Personal Account of Research in a Kpelle Village', *Liberian Studies Journal* xvii(2): 203-15.

Diawara, Manthia (1998) *In Search of Africa*, Cambridge, MA: Harvard University Press.

Ellis, Stephen (1989) 'Turning to pavement radio', *African Affairs* 88: 321-30.

Ellis, Stephen (1995) 'Liberia 1989-1994: A Study of Ethnic and Spiritual Violence', *African Affairs* (94): 165-97.

Ellis, Stephen (1999) *The Mask of Anarchy: The Destruction of Liberia and the Religious Dimension of an African Civil War*, New York: New York University Press.

Fardon, Richard and Graham Furniss (2000) 'African Broadcast Cultures', in R. Fardon and G. Furniss (eds) *African Broadcast Cultures*, Oxford: James Currey, pp. 1-20.

Ferguson, James (1999) *Expectations of Modernity: Myths and Meanings of Urban Life on the Zambian Copperbelt*, Berkeley, CA: University of California Press.

Ferguson, James (2002) 'Of Mimicry and Membership: Africans and the "New World Society"'. *Cultural Anthropology* 17(4): 551-69.

Ferme, Mariane C. (2001) *The Underneath of Things: Violence, History, and the Everyday in Sierra Leone*, Berkeley, CA: University of California Press.

Gifford, Paul (1993) *Christianity and Politics in Doe's Liberia*, Cambridge and New York: Cambridge University Press.

Gillespie, Marie (1993) 'Technology and Tradition – Audio-visual Culture among South Asian Families in West London', in Ann Gray and Jim McGuigan (eds) *Studying Culture: An Introductory Reader*, London: Edward Arnold, pp. 147-60.

Harris, David (1999) 'From "Warlord" to "Democratic" President: How Charles Taylor Won the 1997 Liberian Elections', *The Journal of Modern African Stuides* 37(3): 431-55.

Huband, Mark (1998) *The Liberian Civil War*, London and Portland, OR: Frank Cass.

Johnson, Dennis (1990) 'The Civil War in Hell', *Esquiere* December: 43-6: 219-21.

Keen, David (1998) *The Economic Functions of Violence in Civil Wars*, Oxford and New York: Oxford

University Press for the International Institute for Strategic Studies.

Liebenow, J. Gus (1987) *Liberia: The Quest for Democracy*, Bloomington, IN: Indiana University Press.

Magyar, Karl P. and Earl Conteh Morgan (1998) *Peacekeeping in Africa: ECOMOG in Liberia*, Houndmills, Basingstoke: Macmillan Press and New York: St. Martin's Press.

Mbembe, Achille (2003) 'Necropolitics', *Public Culture* 15(1): 11-40.

Meyer, Birgit (2003a) 'Ghanaian Popular Cinema and the Magic of the Film', in Birgit Meyer and Peter Pels (eds) *Magic and Modernity: Interfaces of Revelation and Concealment*, Stanford, CA: Stanford University Press, pp. 200-22.

Meyer, Birgit (2003b) 'Visions of Blood, Sex and Money: Fantasy Spaces in Popular Ghanaian Cinema', *Visual Anthropology* 16: 15-41.

Murphy, William (1980) 'Secret Knowledge as Property and Power in Kpelle Society: Elders versus Youth', *Africa* 50: 193-207.

Olonisakin, Funmi (1997) 'African "Homemade" Peacekeeping Initiatives', *Armed Forces and Society* 23(3): 349-72.

Pedelty, Mark H. (1993) *An Ethnographic Study of the Salvadoran Foreign Press Corps Association (SPECA)*.

Pels, Peter (2003) 'Introduction: Magic and Modernity', in Birgit Meyer and Peter Pels (eds) *Magic and Modernity: Interfaces of Revelation and Concealment*. Stanford, CA: Stanford University Press, pp. 1-38.

Reno, William (1996) 'The Business of War in Liberia', *Current History*, May 1996: 211-5.

Richards, Paul (1994) 'Videos and Violence on the Periphery: Rambo and the War in the Forests of the Sierra Leone-Liberia Border', *IDS Bulletin* 25(2): 88-93.

Richards, Paul (1996) *Fighting for the Rain Forest: War, Youth and Resources in Sierra Leone*, Oxford: James Currey.

Richards, Paul (2000) 'Local Radio Conflict Moderation: The Case of Sierra Leone', in Richard Fardon and Graham Furniss (eds) *African Broadcast Cultures: Radio in Transition*, Oxford: James Currey.

Schröder, Günther and Werner Korte (1986) 'Samuel K. Doe, the People's Redemption Council and Power: Preliminary Remarks on the Anatomy and Social Psychology of a Coup d'État', *Liberia Forum* 2(3): 3-25.

Shaw, Rosalind (2003) 'Robert Kaplan and "Juju Journalism" in Sierra Leone's Rebel War', in Birgit Meyer and Peter Pels (eds) *Magic and Modernity: Interfaces of Revelation and Concealment*, Stanford, CA: Stanford University Press, pp. 81-102.

Spitulnik, Deborah (2000) 'Documenting Radio Culture as Lived Experience', in Richard Fardon and Graham Furniss (eds) *African Broadcast Cultures: Radio in Transition*, Oxford: James Currey, pp. 144-63.

Spitulnik, Deborah (2002) 'Alternative Small Media and Communicative Spaces', in Göran Hydén, Michael Leslie, and Folu F. Ogundimu (eds) *Media and Democracy in Africa*, Uppsala: The Nordic Afrika Institute, pp. 177-206.

Utas, Mats (1997) *Assiduous Exile: Strategies of Work and Integration among Liberian Refugees in Danane, the Ivory Coast*. Uppsala: Department of Cultural Anthropology.

Utas, Mats (2000) 'Liberian Doomsday Carnival: Western Media on War in Africa', *Antropologiska Studier* 66-67: 74-84.

Van den Boom, Dirk (1995) *Bürger Krieg in Liberia*, Münster: Lit.

Vertov, Dziga (2000 [1929]) *Man with Movie Camera*, DVD, London: British Film Institute.

Virilio, Paul (1989) *War and Cinema: the Logistics of Perception*, London and New York: Verso.

West, Harry G. and Todd Sanders, eds (2003) *Transparency and Conspiracy: Ethnographies of Suspicion in the New World Order*, Durham, NC: Duke University Press.

Youboty, James (1993) *Liberian Civil War: A Graphic Account*, Philadelphia, PA: Parkside Impressions Enterprises.

10

Forced Labour & Civil War
Agrarian Underpinnngs of the Sierra Leone Conflict*

PAUL RICHARDS

Introduction

Civil wars in Africa and the former Soviet sphere since c. 1990 have been termed 'New War' (Kaldor, 1999), to differentiate them from the ideological conflicts of the Cold War era. Cultural essentialism and biological instinct have reappeared by way of explanation (Huntington, 1999; Kaplan, 1996). Hannerz (2002) wonders why the response of anthropologists to the revival of these long-abandoned theories has been so muted. One answer is that necessary work on the institutional underpinnings of new forms of armed conflict has been neglected. A focus on the phenomenology of violence tends to crowd out the organisational analysis necessary to answer the proponents of New Barbarism or Clash of Cultures. Durkheimian studies have long linked violence, institutions and collective action and it is to this tradition that I propose to revert, in attempting to grasp some of the factors underlying the war of the Revolutionary United Front (1991-2001) in Sierra Leone. This conflict was infamous for its apparently mindless cruelty. The significance of the fact that a common agricultural implement – the farm cutlass – was a major tool of war seems to have been ignored. The conflict, I shall argue, has agrarian roots. The violence can be related to coercive forms of labour exploitation once associated with domestic slavery. The chapter revives some of Durkheim's arguments about the connections between forced labour, fatalism, violence and civil war.

Dazzled by Violence?

A benchmark for recent anthropological debate about violence was set by David Riches. Riches (1986) backgrounds war, a major cause of violence, in considering it 'simply as violence that is subject to a certain level of organization' (ibid.: 24). His words appear carefully chosen. He is not claiming war is (and only is) violence, but that it is a matter of analytical convenience, in a book on the anthropology of violence, to focus only on those aspects of war that amount to organised violence. Riches' main purpose – to argue in favour of the rationality of violence – provoked considerable reaction. Dialectically, much subsequent work in anthropology shifted the emphasis towards expressive, emotional and experiential aspects of violence (Kapferer, 1998 [1988]; Daniel, 1997; Nordstrom, 1997; Arce and Long, 2000). But thereby important institutional aspects of violent conflict remain overshadowed.

This can be illustrated by reference to two recent surveys of the anthropology of violent conflict picked more or less at random. Stewart and Strathern's *Violence: Theory and Ethnography* (2002) adjudicates between the rationalistic and expressive perspectives, advocating practice theory as a suitable standpoint from which to articulate rival approaches (see Chapter 8). But war – the context for much of the violence they discuss – appears in the index of the book only twice (and only then as 'warfare', that is, the practice of waging war), compared to seven mentions of massacres, nine of sacrifice and fourteen of revenge. A second offering – a set of essays edited by Schmidt and Schroeder (2001) – more explicitly tackles war (a word well represented in the index). But the layout and focus of the editorial overview suggests a focus on violence not dissimilar to Stewart and Strathern. Consider the sub-headings of the six sections into which the introductory chapter is divided. These are 'violent practice', 'comparing violence', 'violent imaginaries', 'the phenomenology of violence', 'theoretical approaches', and 'an anthropological approach to violence'. Schmidt and Schroeder explicitly rule out the analytical separation of war and violence. Their aim, they state, is '[the] understanding of violence as a total social fact' (Schmidt and Schroeder, 2001: 2). 'Total', here, seems to imply the view that war *is* violence. In anthropology, violence risks becoming a metonym for war, to the detriment of other analytical concerns.

Rites and Riots: The Durkheimian Approach to Violent Conflict

As the sustained and coordinated use of physical force by groups against other groups for political ends war both depends on forging social solidarity and upon breaking down the social solidarity of the enemy. An implication is that any theory of war depends on how we envisage the creation and breakdown of social solidarity. The focusing of mutual attention through the rite (a discrete, non-utilitarian, sequence of formalised, coordinated human actions evoking shared emotions, frequently but not exclusively found in forms of behaviour labelled 'religious' worship) is a basic mechanism in the Durkheimian explanation of social solidarity. The rite involves commitment, sacrifice and pooling of resources. It leads (through symbolic associations) to the fixing of collective representations. Ritual does not depend (as some anthropological accounts require) on positing the existence of spirit forces, or on following a programme.[1] 'Abstinences and

---

[1] Rappaport (1999) treats ritual as a signaling system, co-evolved with language, and like Durkheim, regards it as a 'basic social act'. He grants that in communication terms ritual can be both self-referential (i.e. it says something about the performers directly) and canonical (i.e. it operates according to liturgical precedent). Durkheim is less concerned with liturgy, placing more stress on the rite as a coordinated expression of the will, and thus allows more scope for improvisation. One way to express the difference is to say that Rappaport's analysis is oriented more to 'textual' aspects and Durkheim's more to 'musical' aspects. On the influence of Schopenhauer on Durkheim, see Mestrovic (1992), and on music in biocultural evolution, see Cross (2003).

blood-letting stop famines and cure sicknesses, *acting on their own*' (Durkheim, 1995 [1912]: 410, my emphasis). 'It is always the cult that is efficacious ... *we must act*, and we ... must repeat the necessary acts as often as is necessary to renew their effects.' (Durkheim, 1995 [1912]: 420, my emphasis). In short, ritual is first and foremost a group-based expression of the will. The Durkheimian approach to war takes shape accordingly. To understand the organisation and meanings of war (undoubtedly a group-based expression of the will) we must also understand war-as-ritual.

In the *Elementary Forms of Religious Life* (1995 [1912]) Durkheim often dwells on large-scale public rites such as the Australian *corroboree*, or the events of the National Assembly initiating the French Revolution. He stresses the unstable, open-ended and potentially violent nature of such events. Tumultuous out-pouring of emotions may lead both to acts of great heroism and bloody terror. Within the category of the piacular rite (a rite expressive of group feeling con-ducted on the occasion of death, misfortune or collective crisis) Durkheim includes both the vendetta and the acts of reckless self-harm sometimes associated with mourning rituals. In labelling ritually induced collective excitement 'effervescence' Durkheim instances both the St Bartholomew massacres and the Crusades. Modern commentators have continued usefully to mine this Durkheimian seam in seeking to understand massacre and genocide (cf. Stone, 2004).

In the micro-sociological development of the Durkheimian approach found in Goffman the rite must be thought of in terms of the myriad stylised exchanges through which everyday life is constituted. Goffman (1967) conceives social life as a constantly activated and re-activated web of minor ritual interactions – a ritual 'chain reaction' ('interaction ritual chains', cf. Collins, 2004). The small-scale rites of everyday life are made up of the same elements found in the cults – coordination and commitment, non-utilitarian gesture, focusing of attention, and engagement of the emotional intelligence. Satisfactory exchanges accumu-late over time in such a way as to fix, renew, add to or change meanings.

Over a number of years Randall Collins has both developed the potential of interaction ritual chain theories of social interaction and also sought rapproche-ment with macro-sociological theory. In developing a ritual-based theory of coercion and war he usefully pays attention to both micro-sociological factors and geo-politics in accounting for the ways in which imperial armies both expand into peripheries and are subject to sudden collapse (Collins, 1988). Armies are maintained by what he terms coercive coalitions. In his account of battle he focuses on the way an attacker may seek to undermine the ritually sustained forms of solidarity giving an opposing army its collective sense of well-being. Commanders struggle to counteract disorderly advance as well as panic-induced retreat. In both cases the regular firing of ritual chain reactions through which order is maintained is threatened; as a result freelance actions proliferate, including desertion and atrocity. Troops must be rallied and incipient collapse avoided by timely symbolic action – raising the flag or sounding the alarm. Beating a retreat is more than music-while-you-work. It supplies the essential rhythm through which an armed group preserves the temporal coherence of collective action in moments of confusion and crisis.

There is much in this suggestive re-working of Durkheimian theory that could be applied to understanding of patterns of atrocity generated by the war in Sierra Leone. Research conditions are currently rather unfavourable. Ex-combatants can be accessed, but few are yet ready to talk about atrocities due to fear of prosecution by the Special Court for war crimes. Precise analysis of predisposing and triggering factors will have to be postponed. But new data are available on the background of the combatants, their attitudes, and the social milieu from which they came (Humphreys and Weinstein, 2004; Richards, Archibald, Bah and Vincent, 2003). So what I intend to do in this chapter is turn the Durkheimian focus upon contextual problems of social cohesion and social exclusion upon which the war in Sierra Leone fed.

The war in Sierra Leone is often presented as a disaster falling upon a peace-loving country from 'out of the blue'. Outsiders are blamed (notably the Liberian faction leader Charles Taylor), and the question posed 'why did he attack us?' It was often claimed that the protagonists of the rebellion (members of the Revolutionary United Front, henceforth RUF) were 'Liberians', 'Burkinabes' or even non-human forces ('devils'). The RUF was allied with Taylor's insurgency in Liberia (both groups were trained by Colonel Qadaffi in Benghazi) and Taylor lent some of his 'special forces' to help the RUF establish itself in eastern Sierra Leone in 1991-2. But these troops were soon withdrawn (I have traced the identity of one – a Gio teenager, Nixon Gaye, who later led a Taylor-linked youth militia based in the rubber plantation at Salala in Margibi County, Liberia). Subsequently, it came to be argued that the RUF was a motley collection of urbanised drop-outs and petty criminals (Abdullah, 1997). This also 'external-ised' the problem. The criminals were no longer foreigners, but excluded from decent society. Only recently has it become possible to debate the war in Sierra Leone in terms of disordered institutions and incipient social collapse.

Seventy thousand fighters were demobilised from the war in 2000-2001, of which about one third belonged to the rebel RUF (Humphreys and Weinstein, 2004). What has now been established beyond doubt is that the great majority of these were both Sierra Leoneans, and from rural areas (mainly from the regions bordering Liberia). Few if any could be described as criminal in background, though many were (in fact) displaced, living as fugitives from a system of 'cus-tomary' courts specialising in extraction of young people's labour. A large number of the RUF intake (over 80 per cent) was conscripted, though in fact many abduct-ees developed a firm sense of commitment to the movement. Abductees were often prominent in committing atrocities, sometimes directed at their own families.

So a different question has now to be posed. Why did so many rural young people identify with the RUF and why did they then feel impelled to attack even their families? What caused such a huge inter-generational rift in rural Sierra Leone? I asked the Nigerian President, Olusegun Obasanjo, in a public meeting at the Clingendael Institute in The Hague, what his country had learnt from its involvement in peace-keeping in Sierra Leone. He thought for a moment, and mused 'I know a country in which children kill their parents', and added 'I used to think the problem in Africa was poverty, but now I know it is poverty allied to injustice.' The formulation is a good one. What accounts for this burning sense of injustice, capable of sustaining such levels of horror and atrocity, aimed so intimately at those who once considered themselves kith and kin? In attempting to answer the question I will return to Durkheimian theory concerning the roots of collectivity (and why a sense of collectivity might fail).

Durkheim is indeed a micro-sociologist, his account of collectivity beginning in the domestic setting. Solidarity between partners in a marriage entails work.

The marriage contract finds its expression in the sharing and allocation of household tasks. The everyday life of the household is a chain of minor rituals of sacrifice and affection, sustaining a positive sense of cohesion 'which unites the members of a family in accordance with the division of domestic labour' (Durkheim, 1964 [1893]: 122). This he then applies on a larger scale. The key to understanding modern society is the division of labour as embodied in contract ('the juridical expression of co-operation', Durkheim, 1964 [1893]: 123). A web of solidarity-enhancing ritualised exchanges, conventions and courtesies is protected beneath the wings of civil law.

As is well known, Durkheim then analyses two rather distinct forms through which everyday complementarities of working life are expressed – mechanical and organic solidarity. Mechanical solidarity – his presumed basis for the earliest forms of social life – depends on similarity. Humans cooperate around shared pursuits and concerns. Those who stand out from the crowd are perceived as a threat to the group. The institutions associated with mechanical solidarity are distinctive. Rotational labour gangs, for example, are recurrent manifestations in African village life. They enhance labour productivity in hoe agriculture, but depend on everyone planting the same crops in essentially the same way. The institutional culture of the labour gang centres upon how to maintain group unity and uniformity of output. Officials spend much time checking the ability of would-be members to keep up with the group, or weeding out slackers. The modality is durable. I have followed labour gangs in rural central Sierra Leone for twenty years (Richards, 1986; Richards, Bah and Vincent, 2004). Drawn into civil defence under wartime conditions, they quickly resumed farm labour functions in the post-war world. A good deal of the military effectiveness of lightly armed militia groups in bush conditions in African wars reflects this legacy of mechanical solidarity. Disabling such solidarities was a prime concern for rival militias. Physical mutilation – amputation of hands, feet or limbs – immediately marked off victims as incapable of contributing to the group.

Solidarity is also apprehended through an opposite principle: specialist contribution. Durkheim meant all specialisms, not just those rewarded with wages in a capitalist economy. Cohesion emerges through the many different kinds of activities human beings undertake, and a general recognition that human welfare rests upon the complementarity and interdependence of these activities. We respect others not because they perform exactly like us, but because they perform differently, whether in a team or as individuals. They possess skills to complement our own. The institutions associated with organic solidarity protect differences in skill, such as labour markets, the law of contract and educational systems based on respect for aptitude. The development of organic solidarity finds its eventual ritual expression in the emergence of what Durkheim terms 'the cult of the individual' (respect for a rights bearing person protected by law). In effect, this doctrine of the sacrosanct nature of the individual anticipates what would now be thought of as 'justiciable' human rights, that is, human rights enforceable in a national or international court of law.

Less well known is the last part of Durkheim's argument about the division of labour. Book Three of *Division* deals with the conditions under which social cohesion fails to form. 'Though normally the division of labour produces social solidarity, it sometimes happens that it has different, and even contrary results' (Durkheim, 1964 [1893]: 353), in which the worker 'lose[s] sight of ...

collaborators' (ibid.: 372) and a sense of 'serving something' larger (ibid. 372). These are the *abnormal forms*. The two most relevant to the war in Sierra Leone are the *anomic* and the *forced* divisions of labour (the third he characterises as a lack of coherence or continuity in work due to insufficient regulation). An *anomic* division of labour occurs where intensity of interaction is too low to generate a sense of regular and recurrent social interdependency. Groups and individuals exchange goods and services only intermittently and retreat into isolation. A *forced* division of labour occurs where a class or faction is so able to control the activity of another group that its members lack opportunity to express their ability. Any such society would lack 'the spontaneous consensus of parts' (ibid.: 360). Thus 'for the division of labor to produce solidarity, it is not sufficient... that each have his [her] task; it is still necessary that this task be fitting...' (ibid.: 375).   Inability to forge a sense of 'serving something', grounded in mutual respect for aptitude, ultimately manifests itself in the vulnerability of slave-based societies to violent uprisings.

A (Durkheimian) Labour Theory of Civil War

A society held together not by positive solidarity but by force sustains dangerous alienation in the minds of those unable to find their place through skilled accomplishments. One option to cope is fatalistic acquiescence – quietism, or myriad acts of petty sabotage, documented by historians of slave societies. But Durkheim offers another option – civil war. In fact he begins his chapter on the forced division:

> It is not sufficient that there be rules ... for sometimes the rules are the source of evil ... no longer being satisfied with the role that has been devolved upon them from custom ... [the lower classes] aspire to functions which are closed to them and seek to dispossess those who are exercising these functions ... thus civil wars arise which are due to the manner in which labor is distributed (ibid.: 374).

Durkheim's theory of civil war remains a tantalising suggestion, rather than a fully elaborated scheme. Commentators have tended to emphasise fatalistic acquiescence as the main product of a forced division of labour. Durkheim's suggestion that frustrations over labour might also lead to war deserves closer attention. *Civil* war implies the coming apart of a once shared (if defective) institutional framework. If we are to follow the logic underlying Durkheim's arguments concerning suicide (and homicide, as recently and ingeniously pieced together by DiCristina, 2004) we might suspect the existence of types of civil war varying according to the kinds of institutional frameworks shared. Just as mechanical and organic solidarity embody different ways of recognising common interest, so we might detect, in patterns of warfare, the distinctive features associated with collapse or destruction of distinctive solidarities. This (in a nutshell) is the analytic I propose to apply to the war in Sierra Leone.

In *Suicide*, Durkheim (1952 [1897]) demonstrates, from analysis of rates among different groups, that suicide is more than a question of an unbalanced state of mind; it responds to collective influences. Different social solidarities generate different patterns of suicide. Egoistic suicides result from too little group attachment; altruistic suicides from over-strong commitment to the group;

anomic suicides from inability to realise ambitions. Then, in a tantalising foot-note, Durkheim sketches the missing quadrant of a fourfold scheme.[2] This offers a space to 'a type of suicide the opposite of anomic suicide, just as egoistic and altruistic suicides are opposite' deriving 'from excessive regulation ... of persons with futures pitilessly blocked and passions violently choked by oppressive discipline' (Durkheim, 1952 [1887]: 239). For completeness sake, therefore, 'we should set up a fourth suicidal type', even if examples seem hard to find. Citing work on the slave societies of the French Caribbean [Corre, *Le crime en pays créole*], Durkheim notes that 'the suicide of slaves, said to be frequent under certain conditions, belong to [a] type ... attributable to excessive physical or moral despotism.' The type, he concludes, ought to be called *fatalistic* suicide.

We might (following this scheme) regard types of civil war as self-inflicted violence on society, much as suicide (in the Durkheimian view) is not just a private matter but violence against the social person. Durkheim's recognition that defective division of labour yields distinctive social pathologies (apparently anticipating the scheme in *Suicide*) suggests that the labour theory of civil wars should encompass three or four distinctive kinds of conflict. A struggle between rival hierarchies, such as that between King and Parliament in the English civil war, might be considered an instance of altruistic civil war (i.e. a war of political or religious principle). Conflicts dubbed to be 'greed, not grievance' might take up the space allocated to 'egoistic' civil war (wars fought with an excess of individualism). The kind of revolt of the underclass resulting in a maroon 'enclave' might be taken as an instance of anomic civil war. The Dream of Return (as among New World slave communities) is a desire that cannot be satisfied, except the plantation is abandoned and life begun anew in the forest. Is there then a fourth kind of civil war, corresponding to the tantalising footnote in *Suicide*, completing the scheme – viz. fatalistic civil war?

It seems an odd idea. Why would fatalists ever mobilise? But Durkheim has already pointed to the possibility of fatalistic suicide as a condition sometimes met within slave society. Suicide requires action. He thus allows that fatalism can under certain circumstances be more than acquiescence. Perhaps there is a kind of civil war in which the intended outcome is not escape, but group transcendence, via extreme, apocalyptical destructiveness. Durkheim's theory of ritual as the trigger of emotional energy and shaper of collective representations (the performative thread linking will and idea, cf. Mestrovic, 1992) seems to support just such a possibility. The piacular rite kick-starts the heart beat of collective action, even where it causes great harm (Durkheim, 1995 [1912]). Sacrifice of the group, or its enemies, may be necessary for the Rapture to commence.

The idea of such a civil war might be clarified by invoking first the notion of anomic revolt – insurgency fuelled by impractical or unrealisable desire. The result of such violence is not social reform (as eventuated from the French Revolution), but exodus and a search for the Promised Land. The notion has been brilliantly developed by Mary Douglas (1993) in her account of the politics of the enclave. The category of enclave fits the circumstances of the major rebellions of the Caribbean and South American slave plantation economies (Genovese,

---

[2] This is in effect the origin of the grid-group analytic scheme proposed by Douglas (1996 [1970]) and further developed by Thompson et al. (1990), justifying the designation of the Douglas 'school' of cultural theory as neo-Durkheimian.

1976). Slaves greatly outnumbered the planters. Caribbean slave groups failed to reproduce themselves (due to the harshness of the regime). The slave barracks was a social world constantly reinforced by fresh recruits from Africa, and the 'impossible' dream (of return to Africa) constantly refreshed. Where a slave uprising was successful it indeed resulted in such a 'return', but in practical rather than geographical terms; Caribbean maroon communities reinvented the African village in the neo-tropical forests.

But consider, now, the very different social conditions of slavery in the southern United States (Genovese, 1976). Here, slaves lived in much smaller groups, often physically integrated into the slave-owner's homestead. Recruitment from Africa died out by the early years of the nineteenth century, and there was no nearby neo-tropical forest to beckon. Southern slave owners were proud of their paternalism – believing their kind of slave-holding to be more benign than that of the Caribbean planters. But it also rendered the intimate social worlds in which slaves and slave owners lived more transparent to slave critique. The 'reading' by slaves of the social rules of this domestic society resulted in two (religion-based, ritualised) reactions – fatalistic acceptance of God's yoke, and (equally fatalistic) attempts at violent (millenarian) transcendence.

There are African precedents for fatalistic acceptance of slavery as a fixed and legitimate condition of social existence. Baldus (1977) describes the distinctive world of the *machube* – children rescued by Fulbe from native Batombe populations in Borgou (northern Benin), who would otherwise have put their children to death because their upper teeth appeared first, something locally reckoned an abomination. Living in small groups scattered in Fulbe encampments, *machube* did not contest the right of the Fulbe, with whom they were domestically intimate, to have made them slaves, even if this acceptance was accompanied by considerable intra-*machube* violence. The slaves knew that without Fulbe intervention they would have died at the hands of their own people. It is clear from Baldus' account that *machube* envisaged no alternative to the forced division of labour that (literally) allowed them life. It was the fixed criterion of *machube* social existence.

But these were very special conditions. It was otherwise in the American South. Slaves were not rescued, but bought and sold. And yet they lived in conditions of domestic intimacy with slave owners. Paternalism – in an agrarian economy with larger horizons than the pastoral Fulbe camp – was the Achilles heel of Southern slavery. As Genovese (1976) puts it: 'Southern paternalism ... unwittingly invited its victims to fashion their own interpretations of the social order it was intended to justify' (ibid.: 7). Undoubtedly, a key factor was shared religion. Although no African haven beckoned on the other side of the mountains there was a promised land beyond death where social marginality could and would be reversed. In the hands of a skilled Christian preacher this might take on a more forceful and tangible realisation. The most famous of the small slave revolts of the United States – at Jerusalem, Southampton County, Virginia in 1831 – was led by a preacher, Nat Turner.

Turner himself looked for signs and received guidance in visions. In an account he gave shortly before his execution he suggests the 'plan' lay in the extreme violence of the early stages of the revolt (in which no woman or child was to be spared). The terror was a calculated gamble to mobilise sufficient social energy among the slaves to deter all thoughts of backsliding or opposition.

The killing was to have been abated once the uprising had gained sufficient momentum.

The apparent lack of strategic acumen in Turner's rebellion has attracted puzzled comment. Eric Sundquist writes 'without question one of the most difficult misconceptions to overcome about Turner's revolt is its purported lack of a goal...' (Sundquist, 1993: 68). Numbers were tiny, resources non-existent, and a path of strategic retreat was lacking. Yet Turner was known from his youth as a careful strategist and was consulted by thieves and raiders because of his careful, calculating brain. There seems little room for doubt he fully appreciated the enormous risks involved. He was not mad, but nevertheless went ahead.

Seemingly, it was not escape that Turner had in mind. Extreme violence, divinely mandated, would serve both to rally the oppressed and unmask domestic slavery's false intimations of social solidarity. Either the venture succeeded in initiating, at a stroke, a millennial social world, or the rebels would perish in the attempt. Turner and his followers sought not Exodus but Apocalypse. They would make one last resounding, shocking dent in an unbearable and dishonest system of intimate relations. Thoughts of escape were transmuted to a fatalistic embrace of communal death.

War in Sierra Leone in Durkheimian Perspective

The war in Sierra Leone fell into four clearly distinct phases. Two small groups of RUF fighters crossed the Liberian border in 1991 and at first fought a conventional guerrilla campaign, seeking to control territory and rural populations in the border districts. Pushed into northern Kailahun District by army counter-attacks the leadership sought refuge in Sandeyalu, a village on the border of Luawa and Kissi Teng chiefdoms, where it came under pressure of air raids by Nigerian air force Alpha jets. It was then decided (c. November 1993) to abandon vehicles, heavy weapons and control of settlements, and build a series of sequestered camps in the network of forest reserves fanning out from the Liberian border towards the centre of the country. This launched the Phase Two campaign, during which the movement (increasingly cut off from contact with wider society) began to develop introverted, sectarian features (Richards, 1996). With difficulty, the leadership was extricated from the forest to take part in peace negotiations launched by the military regime in 1995. These were continued by a newly incumbent democratic administration, based on a general cease-fire agreement of 23 April 1996. By now the government side was being assisted by counter-insurgency experts from the former South African Defence Forces, invited into the country initially to protect mining installations. The South Africans conducted radio intercepts and flew helicopter gunship missions against RUF camps. This put pressure on the Abidjan peace agreement (30 November 1996) even before it was signed.

Sections of the sidelined national army mutinied in May 1997, deposing the democratic regime; the RUF was invited to vacate its camps and join a power sharing regime (Phase Three of the war). Short-lived and unstable, this army–RUF junta was displaced by Nigerian peace keeping troops in February 1998, and the RUF retreated to some of its strong points along the Liberian border (notably Buedu base), from where it was strengthened and rearmed by international mining and security interests. It then expanded (Phase Four) into the adjacent Kono diamond fields and took over a tract of land in the centre of the country (as far westwards as Makeni), once again trying to control territory and administer settlements. A raid was launched on Freetown in a failed bid to rescue its imprisoned leader, Foday Sankoh, in January 1999, after which the movement held the Makeni-Kono axis through protracted and unsatisfactory peace agreements (the Lomé process) and the deployment of a large UN peace-keeping force (supplemented by British military engagement) until a final negotiated end of hostilities based on the Abuja Accords of November 2000. Demobilisation took place throughout 2001 and the war was finally declared at an end early in 2002.

To what extent does it help to consider the rebellion in Sierra Leone in terms of the fourfold Durkheimian scheme outlined above? At the outset the RUF had high (if unrealistic) hopes of political reform (Phase One, war as an altruistic commitment). Post-war interviews confirm that the young radicals who took the movement into the bush had a clear agenda of political reforms in mind (RUF/SL, 1995; Richards, Archibald, Bah and Vincent, 2003), however feeble their grasp of revolutionary theory (Abdullah, 1997). This aspect was watered down by events – some ideologues withdrew at an early stage and others were eliminated in internal power struggles (Abdullah and Muana, 1998). Foday Sankoh – an army corporal once imprisoned for involvement in a coup attempt against Siaka Stevens in the 1970s – came to the fore as movement leader. Increasingly made up of youthful abductees, the RUF was by now incarcerated within thick forests in the east and centre of the country. Lack of surrender options (neither govern-ment troops nor the South African mercenaries took many prisoners) made exit impossible. The anomie of the radical volunteers built a maroon forest social world (Phase Two, Richards, 2005).

Hopes for reintegration rose in 1996 as the Abidjan negotiations got under way. But the deal was abortive. The South Africans were determined to destroy the RUF forest camps, despite cease-fire agreements (Hooper, 2003), and Sankoh was unable to sell the agreement to his scattered and traumatised followers. Escape from the bush, after the government army mutinied in May 1997, inviting the RUF leadership to accept an invitation to join the regime, was short-lived. Driven back into the east (March 1998) the cadres became increasingly paranoid and unstable. Return to forest obscurity seemed to unhinge the movement. Acts of atrocity took hold, apparently perpetrated in particular by abductees (Humphreys, personal communication). Some RUF cadres courted an apocalyptic recklessness ('Operation Destroy All Living Things'). Others were animated by more personal thoughts of revenge. Children sought out and butchered parents and guardians of whom they had expected better support. They were intent on making a terrible mark on a society that had demeaned and disregarded them. The bush knife rather than the gun became the instrument of vengeance to hand.[3]

Although the colony of Sierra Leone was established (at the end of the eighteenth century) as a home for freed slaves, in connection with British efforts

---

[3] In the 1970s I interviewed a group of elderly former slave owners in the Mabole valley (in Bombali District, northern Sierra Leone) and asked how they would have prevented runaways. They answered by posing for a photograph, reappearing with rusty nineteenth-century cutlasses which they proceeded to wave aloft.

to abolish the slave trade, domestic slavery in the protectorate was not finally ended until 1 January 1928. The reason for its legal longevity is inextricably bound up with war. Mende chiefs rose against the British in 1898, on the rumour that the newly extended British protectorate would free their slaves (Mende: *nduwanga*). Although the Protectorate Ordinance of 1896 made it illegal to acquire new slaves, the colonial authorities, shocked by the 1898 uprising, decided to press reform no further. The owners were left with their existing slaves. Any further episodes of rebellion might have fatally damaged British rule at a moment of maximum penetration of the West African interior. So the matter of the large number of people still living under domestic slavery was quietly shelved, until the government was eventually prodded into taking action by the League of Nations in the 1920s.

Since from 1896 it was no longer lawful to enslave people, the British assumed they could leave the institution to die a natural death. This was to underestimate the continuing importance of slave labour in the changing colonial agricultural economy of Sierra Leone. The historian John Grace remarks on the importance of the institution to the Mende people of the forested south and east, the country's main cash crop region. At the end of the nineteenth century slaves were estimated to comprise fifty per cent of the Mende population. Thirty years later an average figure of fifteen per cent hid considerable regional variation. As the Liberian border was approached, that is, in Pujehun and Mano River Districts, more than half the population in some chiefdoms remained slaves at abolition in 1928 (Grace, 1977: 429; cf. Holsoe, 1977).

Typically *nduwanga* did most of the heavy work of land clearing, while the children of chiefs and slave owners were increasingly free to seek Western education. A senior official once explained to me how he and his brothers had been sent through school and university on the profits from a large plantation developed for his father by several hundred domestic slaves in the 1920s. That the institution was actively maintained is evident from official papers, showing District Commissioners spending 'much time on cases involving slaves, especially runaways, and disputes over redemptions and ownership'. In Pujehun in 1919 and 1920 'no less than 82 [legal] cases [out of 352] were concerned with slavery, mostly with runaways and redemptions' (Grace, 1977: 427). Grace adds that after abolition slavery remained important to the Mende even if 'in a variety of thinly disguised forms'.

It is now known that perhaps 70-80 per cent of the cadres of the RUF were Mende-speakers. Most of those who volunteered for the movement originated in the Gola Forest region and adjacent parts of Kailahun and Pujehun Districts – precisely the chiefdoms where domestic slavery lasted longest, and slaves were most numerous in forming agrarian capital (Richards, Archibald, Bah and Vincent, 2003). In more accessible districts it was easier for slaves to change their status by running away. They found employment in Freetown, or in the more vibrant interior towns along the railway (for example, Bo and Makeni). But in 'deep rural' districts there were fewer options. After emancipation, older freed slaves settled into semi-subsistence rice farming. Their children were at times dependent on the patronage of one-time slave owners to gain a foothold on the lower rungs of the educational ladder. From the early 1950s many of these young people with a background in impoverished, ex-slave families moved into the alluvial diamond mining sector, hoping to find wealth and social respect.

But exactly how free were young people to find their social worth through selling their skills on a free labour market in independent Sierra Leone? Diamond mining is highly exploitative of the labour of diggers (Zack-Williams, 1995). Diggers have little idea of the true value of stones and nearly all the profit accrues to land owners, dealers and state officials who connive at smuggling (OTI, 2000). According to a report commissioned by the USAID Office of Transitional Initiatives, 'most diggers are the poorest of the poor, doing body breaking work with no certainty of finding stones' (OTI, 2000: 3). Nor does education level the playing. Village schools are often weak and badly supported (rural teachers were last in line for salaries when government finances collapsed in the 1980s) and impoverished rural families found it very hard to forego their children's farm labour and support them through school. Rural Sierra Leoneans at times bitterly deplore the hunger, lack of books, uniform or writing implements, as reasons for their lack of education. Some remain grateful to the patrons who helped them (including charitable school feeding programmes in the 1960s). Others are bitter about parents or families who might have done more.

In 1987 the IMF closed its wallet against the corrupt one-party regime of Joseph Saidu Momoh, and a cash-strapped president informed young people that education was 'a privilege not a right' (Richards, 1996). Thereafter much pent-up bitterness was trained on the government itself – the ultimate educational patron, apparently no longer interested in helping young people to acquire the skills to develop their social identity within a free labour market. Combatants from both sides of the war speak angrily about their sense of alienation caused by lack of education or jobs. One Civil Defence fighter summed up the mood among the RUF:

> most of the rebels are students, the majority are students ... After an attack, they write a message and drop it. These are the reasons why they are fighting ... The government doesn't give any encouragement ... to get land or go to school. When you come from poor families, but with talent to be educated, there is no financial support. The government doesn't [help] ... They are only bothered about themselves. (Peters and Richards, 1998).

Humphreys and Weinstein (2004) have established (from a random sampling of over 1000 ex-combatants in 2003) that forty-three per cent of the intake of the RUF were pupils (mainly from rural primary schools).

At the level of basic education the problem was structural – many rural children failed to receive education because teachers were unpaid or schools had collapsed. Where schooling continued (mainly in the capital and regional centres), the frustrations of pupils were intensified by corruption within the system. Skills of reading, writing and computation are more or less objective. It is clear whether a child is getting on because of aptitude, and resentment on an inter-personal level is held in check. The system was much harder to fathom at higher levels. Favouritism became a major issue. Those who failed exams suspected they were cheated, or that in some way they had displeased a teacher or sponsor. Qualified candidates failed to receive invitations for job or scholarship interviews, 'lost in the mail'. Jobs or overseas study opportunities were at times more or less auctioned to the highest bidder. Grades or certificates were handed out for sexual favours or bribes. Corruption destroyed discernible relationships between natural ability, hard work and achievement. A trainee recalls Foday Sankoh, when in charge of ideology training for the RUF at Pendembu base in

1992, describing Sierra Leone as a country in which 'people with no qualifications had jobs, and people with qualifications had no jobs' (Richards, Abdullah, Amara, Muana, Stanley and Vincent, 1997). Humphreys and Weinstein (2004) found a small but significant proportion of RUF intake (six to eight per cent) had secondary education. This group included students from the teacher training college in the eastern borderlands at Bunumbu (a major RUF base). Some of these Bunumbu ideologues shaped the RUF's food security strategy during the war (Richards, Archibald, Bah and Vincent, 2003).

The situation was compounded by the failure of successive post-independence governments to reshape citizenship legislation better to fit the circumstances of a modern economy and labour market (Fanthorpe, 2001). Young people in rural areas have full citizenship rights only in their chiefdoms of birth; elsewhere they are 'strangers' in their own nation (cf. Mamdani, 1996). This has proved an important issue in an economy dependent on migrant labour to run the alluvial diamond mining industry. Diamond land still belongs to lineages. To mine legally an artisanal tributor needs a government licence and the permission of landowners (Zack-Williams, 1995). This requires links to the rural landed elite. The majority of diggers did no more than supply labour. They were the so-called 'sand-sand' boys. Some joined diamond rushes in forest reserves, hoping to become a tributor in their own right. But the strategy was fraught with risks, one of which was abduction into the RUF (Richards, 1996).

Recruits more often state that they entered the war as renegades from a rural justice system still dominated by chiefly land-owning families. ('Even if you have a minor problem [the chiefs] exaggerate it ... taking it to a district chief, then you the young man cannot handle the case ... and you have to run away ... I was accused, so I ran away and hid .... ' [Archibald and Richards, 2002]). To some commentators vagrancy and criminality are connected (Smillie, Gberie and Hazleton, 2000). A Durkheimian orientation encourages us to consider the issue from the perspective of social organisation. Where institutional development is incomplete, or imperfect, notions of deviance are highly contested.

Many Sierra Leoneans dubbed the rebels *rare* (literally 'street people'). To be considered 'footloose' conjures up the image of a young 'runaway', a term as evocative of slavery as *fakai*, a name sometimes applied to the rebel camps in the bush. According to Grace (1977) *fakai* originally denoted a farm outpost manned by slaves (Grace, 1977). Current *fakai* dwellers are, in their own eyes, not fugitives from justice, but refugees from injustice. Trumped-up charges in a chiefdom court, or the collapse of childhood educational plans, are frequently cited as reasons for opting for militia membership ('[The chiefs] levy high fines on the youth, if you are sent to do a job and you refuse ... Most ... young men and women were suffering' [Archibald and Richards, 2002]). The war was seen by its perpetrators as a chance to 'take apart' a system seen to work only in arbitrary and unpredictable ways ('our chiefs and some elders were doing wrong to our young people ... some preferred to go and join the RUF, either to take revenge or to protect themselves' (Archibald and Richards, 2002). The RUF used the slogan 'no more master, no more slave'.

It puzzled many commentators that some of the worst atrocities took place in non-diamond rural districts. Here RUF violence against the rural poor seemed especially gratuitous. But these are the districts in which attitudes and practices formed under conditions of domestic slavery (prior to 1928) continued to resonate within the local social system. Chiefs and big men continue to extract unpaid labour from youths, if now by ruse rather than resorting to the stocks and lash. One means, widely admitted, was through manipulation of the offence of 'woman damage'. One of the marks of a 'big man' in the countryside is to be polygynously married. Poor families continue to send young girls to elders as wives in order to cement ties of clientage. Young men are often too poor to marry. 'Big men' in their fifties or sixties married to several young women in their teenage or twenties in a village with large numbers of unmarried young men is a recipe for frequent extra-marital liaisons. Elders tolerate these liaisons – they will claim any offspring as their own – but monitor the movements of wives and lovers closely. As a result, a young man might find himself working on an elder's farm without pay, or facing a steep fine in the chiefdom court.

Work in diamond pits is back-breaking, but young labourers are less under the thumb of traditional authority, and free to find their own partners and found families (Richards, 1996).[4] One young RUF conscript contrasted the situation in these terms:

> [In the village] elders ... force young men to marry ... as soon as we harvest our first ... palm fruits. If you refuse they cause more problems than being in the bush as a rebel. They charge you to court for smiling at a girl ... But the bride price is not reasonable. You will be required to do all sorts of physical jobs for the bride's family, like brushing and making a farm for the family ... sharing the proceeds of your own labour, harvest or business ... You will be forced to give them seventy per cent [of your drum of palm oil], or you will lose your wife and be taken to court ... Most of us ... avoid the scene ... here [in Tongo Field, the interview site] you can ... marry a woman of your choice. Marriage [in the village] is the same as slavery.

Exploitation of young men in non-diamond districts intensified as a consequence of state recession and collapse. The downturn in government fortunes in the 1980s meant the lowest levels of administration in non-diamond rural areas became more than usually strapped for cash. In consulting with villagers about the causes of the war, stories of village headmen and court chairmen who 'paid themselves' through arbitrary and excessive fines and exactions on young people were often encountered (Archibald and Richards, 2002). At times a charge was trumped up, because the elder needed labour, or a young man was known to have acquired some money by trading or growing a cash crop. Elders sometimes talked openly about 'squeezing dry' this or that young man for *fitiyai* ('arrogance'), resorting to some minor or imagined infringement of the customary (and unwritten) code. The fault might not be 'woman damage', but simply dressing too well, or having resources deemed inappropriate to junior status. Inflation in the 1970s and 1980s rendered the scale of prescribed fines meaningless. Frequently the fine fitted – as if by magic – whatever sum the accused young man happened to have in his pocket. Given the option of paying a fine through forced agricultural labour, many young men preferred the diamond fields.

The problem has outlived the war. A. was a 'ground [local] commander' of civil defence forces. I first knew A. as a member of a labour gang in 1983. Today, he leads the same gang and (aged forty-five) remains a 'youth'. He was among a group of CDF fighters that recovered terrain from the RUF in 1997, opening the

---

[4] The British government aid programme has funded, post-war, the rebuilding, by community labour, of houses to re-settle displaced Paramount Chiefs. Some young people see this as 'forced labour' to atone for the war.

way for civilians to return after two years of 'occupation'. With the war in final retreat in 2000, it was safe enough for representatives of the local administration to resume their work. The chiefdom court convened in September 2000. Shortly thereafter A. was involved in a drunken brawl with another ex-combatant. A few days later he received a neatly hand-written official summons to attend court accused of public affray. Having borrowed Le 30,000 (about $15) to buy seed to plant a 1.5 ha. rice farm cleared of the war-time growth of trees he knew the court planned to find him guilty and fine him the money he needed to plant his farm. He thinks that if this were to happen his wife would leave him. His only option – as he sees it – is to become a fugitive from justice.[5] He plans to go back to the diamond fields, where he once spent time mining. Familiar with the tactics of war, and knowing how to handle a semi-automatic weapon, he might in future think about fighting for a rebel group. He asks for help. I scribble a note to be presented in court, stating that he repents his brawl, and requesting that his case to be treated with the consideration due to a war veteran. I might as well have saved the paper. The fine was raised to Le 100,000 [$50.00 US]). But A. had meanwhile heard that long delayed demobilisation benefits might now be paid. This offered a life-line and he postponed vagrancy to another day.

The story is typical. Too many young people in rural Sierra Leone 'float' on a sea of deprivation, uncertain of where they belong, and where they might one day find respect and eldership (Richards, Bah and Vincent, 2004). Their frustration is doubled by the sense that country is not poor and that others succeed through favouritism and corrupt access to diamond wealth. In a recent ethnography drawing on long-term work in northern Sierra Leone, Rosalind Shaw brings out the extent to which memories of slavery are threaded through the region's thickly intertwined familial cultures (Shaw, 2002). A local justice system resting upon fines extracted in labour risks drawing attention to such threads. The young remain impoverished and dangerously alienated. A Liberian youth interviewed in 2004 summed it up as follows:

> [The chiefs] fine us too much for any small thing. Because we are poor, we cannot pay. So somebody 'buys' our case, and then we have to work for that person, and for the chief. This means we cannot work for ourselves, so we get poorer, so some have to steal to survive and, when ... caught ... get fined again. We don't call this justice ... it [is] jungle justice ... the only outcome will be back to war (Richards, Archibald, Bruce, Modad, Mulbah, Varpilah and Vincent, 2005).

Bad memories reinforce social discontent. Nat Turner's rebellion reminds us that the worst slave revolts are sometimes those marked by the greatest domestic intimacy.

Conclusion

This chapter has argued that war in Sierra Leone had agrarian roots and that these roots can be usefully illuminated through elaboration of a Durkheimian category (the labour theory of civil war). A rebellion that began with revolu-

---

[5] In January 2003 the government, conscious of the problem of arbitrary fines, announced a new scale of permitted penalties for chiefdom courts. However, chronic understaffing meant that court inspection procedures remain minimal, allowing rural officials scope to continue to operate arbitrarily.

tionary intent eventuated in a forest-based 'maroon' society. When RUF forest camps were destroyed by South African mercenary interventions during a cease fire period in 1996, rebel fighters embarked on a frenzied outburst of revenge for which there are parallels in the annals of nineteenth-century North American slave revolts. These outbursts of exceptional violence jolted the conscience of the world. Military intervention (by UN and British forces) bought time to organise a negotiated cessation of violence followed by extensive demobilisation. Peace has returned to a troubled country, but in fact not much has changed for impoverished rural young people. Their marginalisation seems set to continue. The long-term defence against recurrence of this kind of war is to work towards a more open agrarian division of labour. Reform of land, marriage and rural justice is required. War is more than violence, and the anthropology of 'new war' in Africa would benefit from a return to institutional basics.

* I wish to thank Professor Perri 6 for helpful comments on the argument and many useful suggestions concerning recent Durkheim scholarship (cf. Stedman Jones, 2001; Collins, 2004).

References

Abdullah, Ibrahim (1997) 'Bush Path to Destruction: The Origin and Character of the Revolutionary United Front (RUF/SL)', *Africa Development* 22(3/4): 45-76 (Special Issue: *Lumpen Culture and Political Violence: the Sierra Leone Civil War*).

Abdullah, Ibrahim and Patrick K. Muana (1998) 'The Revolutionary United Front of Sierra Leone (RUF/SL): A Revolt of the Lumpenproletariat', in Christopher Clapham (ed.) *African Guerrillas* Oxford: James Currey.

Arce, Alberto and Norman Long (eds) (2000) *Anthropology, Development, and Modernities: Exploring Discourses, Counter-tendencies and Violence*, London: Routledge.

Archibald, Steven and Paul Richards (2002) 'Conversion to Human Rights? Popular Debate About War and Justice in Central Sierra Leone', *Africa* 72(3): 339-67.

Baldus, Bernd (1977) 'Responses to Dependence in a Servile Group: The Machube of Northern Benin', in Suzanne Miers and Igor Kopytoff (eds) *Slavery in Africa: Historical and Anthropological Perspectives*, Madison, WI: University of Wisconsin Press.

Collins, Randall (1988) 'The Micro Contribution to Macro Sociology', *Sociological Theory* 6(2): 242-53.

Collins, Randall (2004) *Interaction Ritual Chains*, Princeton and Oxford: Princeton University Press.

Cross, Ian (2003) 'Music and Biocultural Evolution', in Martin Clayton, Trevor Herbert, and Richard Middleton (eds) *The Cultural Study of Music: A Critical Introduction*, London: Routledge.

Daniel E. Valentine (1997) *Charred Lullabies: Chapters in an Anthropology of Violence*, Princeton, NJ: Princeton University Press.

DiCristina, Bruce (2004) 'Durkheim's Theory of Homicide and the Confusion of the Empirical Literature', *Theoretical Criminology* 8(1): 57-91.

Douglas, Mary (1996 [1970]) *Natural Symbols: Explorations in Cosmology*, London: Routledge.

Douglas, Mary (1993) *In the Wilderness: The Doctrine of Defilement in the Book of Numbers*, Sheffield: Sheffield Academic Press.

Durkheim, Emile (1964 [1893]) *The Division of Labor in Society*, trans. George Simpson, New York: Free Press.

Durkheim, Emile (1952 [1897]) *Suicide*, trans. John A. Spaulding and George Simpson, London: Routledge and Kegan Paul.

Durkheim, Emile (1995 [1912]) *The Elementary Forms of Religious Life*, trans. Karen E. Fields, New York: The Free Press.

Fanthorpe, R. (2001) 'Neither Citizen nor Subject? "Lumpen" Agency and the Legacy of Native Administration in Sierra Leone', *African Affairs* 100: 363-86.

Genovese, Eugene (1976) *Roll, Jordan, Roll: The World the Slaves Made*, New York: Vintage Books.

Goffman, Erving (1967) *Interaction Ritual*, New York: Doubleday.

Grace, John J. (1977) 'Slavery and Emancipation among the Mende in Sierra Leone', in Suzanne Miers and Igor Kopytoff (eds) *Slavery in Africa: Historical and Anthropological Perspectives*, Madison, WI: University of Wisconsin Press.

Hannerz, Ulf (2002) 'Macro-Scenarios: Anthropology and the Debate Over Contemporary and Future Worlds', The Munro Lecture, University of Edinburgh, 16 May 2002.

Holsoe, Svend E. (1977) 'Slavery and Economic Response among the Vai (Liberia and Sierra Leone)', in Suzanne Miers and Igor Kopytoff (eds) *Slavery in Africa: Historical and Anthropological Perspectives*, Madison, WI: University of Wisconsin Press.

Hooper, Jim (2003 [2002]) 'Appendix: Sierra Leone', in *Bloodsong! An Account of Executive Outcomes in Angola*, London: HarperCollins.

Huntington, Samuel P. (1997) *The Clash of Civilizations and the Remaking of the World Order*, London: Simon and Schuster.

Humphreys, Macarten and Jeremy Weinstein (2004) 'What the Fighters Say: A Survey of Ex-combatants in Sierra Leone, June-August 2003', unpublished Interim Report.

Kaldor, Mary (1999) *New and Old Wars: Organized Violence in a Global Era*, Cambridge: Polity Press.

Kapferer, Bruce (1998 [1988]) *Legends of People, Myths of State: Violence, Intolerance and Political Culture in Sri-Lanka and Australia*, Washington DC: Smithsonian Institution Press.

Kaplan, Robert D. (1996) *The Ends of the Earth: A Journey at the Dawn of the 21st Century*, New York: Random House.

Mamdani, Mahmood (1996) *Citizen and Subject: Contemporary Africa and the Legacy of Late Colonialism*, London: James Currey.

Mestrovic, Stjepan (1992) *Durkheim and Post-Modern Culture*, New York: Aldine de Gruyter.

Nordstrom, Carolyn (1997) *A Different Kind of War Story*, Philadelphia, PA: University of Pennsylvania Press.

OTI (2000) 'Diamonds and Armed Conflict in Sierra Leone: Proposal for Implementation of a New Diamond Policy and Operations', USAID Office of Transition Initiatives, Washington, working paper, http://www.usaid.gov/hum_response/oti/country/sleone/diamonds.html (August 2000).

Peters, Krijn and Paul Richards (1998) 'Why We Fight: Voices of Youth Ex-combatants in Sierra Leone', *Africa* 68(1): 183-210.

Rappaport, Roy A. (1999) *Ritual and Religion in the Making of Humanity*, Cambridge: Cambridge University Press.

Riches, David (ed.) (1986) *The Anthropology of Violence*, Oxford: Blackwell.

Richards, Paul (1986) *Coping with Hunger: Hazard and Experiment in an African Rice-farming System*, London: Allen and Unwin Publishers.

Richards, Paul (1996) *Fighting for the Rain Forest: War, Youth and Resources in Sierra Leone*, Oxford: James Currey (reprinted with additional material 1998).

Richards. Paul (2005) 'Green Book Millenarians? The Sierra Leone War within the Perspective of an Anthropology of Religion', in Niels Kastfelt (ed.) *Religion and Civil War in Africa*, London: C. Hurst.

Richards, Paul, Ibrahim Abdullah, Joseph Amara, Patrick Muana, Edward Stanley, and James Vincent (1997) 'Reintegration of War-Affected Youth and Ex-combatants: A Study of the Social and Economic Opportunity Structure in Sierra Leone', unpublished report, Freetown: Ministry of Relief, Rehabilitation and Reintegration.

Richards, Paul, Steven Archibald, Khadija Bah and James Vincent (2003) 'Where Have All the Young People Gone? Transitioning Ex-combatants Towards Community Reconstruction After the War in Sierra Leone', unpublished report submitted to the National Commission for Disarmament, Demobilization and Reintegration, Government of Sierra Leone.

Richards, Paul, Khadija Bah and James Vincent (2004) 'Social Capital and Survival: Prospects for Community-driven Development in Post-conflict Sierra Leone', *Social Development Papers: Conflict Prevention and Reconstruction*, Paper No. 12, April, Washington: The World Bank.

Richards, Paul, Steven Archibald, Beverlee Bruce, Wata Modad, Edward Mulbah, Tornorlah Varpilah and James Vincent (2005) 'Community Cohesion in Liberia: A Post-war Rapid Rural Assessment', *Social Development Papers: Conflict Prevention and Reconstruction* Paper No. 21, January, Washington: The World Bank.

RUF/SL (1995) *Footpaths to Democracy: Toward a New Sierra Leone*, No stated place of publication: The Revolutionary United Front of Sierra Leone.

Schmidt, Bettina E. and Ingo W. Schroeder (eds) (2001) *Anthropology of Violence and Conflict*, London: Routledge.

Shaw, Rosalind (2002) *Memories of the Slave Trade: Ritual and the Historical Imagination in Sierra Leone*, Chicago: Chicago University Press.

Smillie, Ian, Lans Gberie and Ralph Hazleton (2000) *The Heart of the Matter: Sierra Leone, Diamonds and Human Security*, Ottawa: Partnership Africa Canada.

Stedman Jones, Susan (2001) *Durkheim Reconsidered*, Cambridge: Polity Press.

Stewart, Pamela J. and Andrew Strathern (2002) *Violence: Theory and Ethnography*, London: Continuum Books.

Stone, Dan (2004) 'Genocide as Transgression', *European Journal of Social Theory* 7(1): 45-65.

Sundquist, Eric (1993) *To Wake the Nations: Race in the Making of American Literature*, Cambridge, MA: The Belknap Press.

Thompson, Michael, Richard Ellis and Aaron Wildavsky (1990) *Cultural Theory*, Boulder, CO: Westview.

Zack-Williams, Alfred B. (1995) *Tributors, Supporters and Merchant Capital: Mining and Underdevelopment in Sierra Leone*, Aldershot: Avebury Press.

Index

Abacha, Sani 35, 37-9, 41
Abbay, Alemseged 122, 126, 130n14
Abbink, Jon 18, 123, 124, 128, 129, 132n19, 136
Abdullah, Ibrahim 44, 184, 190, 193
Abiola, M.K.O. 38
Abraham, Arthur 43
Abugu, Uwakwe 34
Achebe, Chinua 2
Adams, Gani 33
Adebajo, Adekajo 163
Adhana, Adhana Haile 122n1, 126, 134
Afeworki, Isayas 128n11, 129, 131
Afghanistan 25, 45-6
African National Congress (ANC) 18, 30, 33, 139, 145-9, 154
Agbu. Osita 2
Agekameh, Dele 35-6, 40
Ainslie, Roy 144-6, 157
Ajayi, Jacob 39
Ajawin, Yoanes 102
Ajulo, Steve 33
Akayesu, Jean-Paul 67n2
Akhavan, Payam 67
Akparanta, Ben 37-8
Albert, Isaac 33, 36
Alexander, Jocelyn 9, 14, 16-17
al-Mahdi, Sadiq 94, 98
Almond, Gabriel 11
al-Turabi, Hassan 98
Amin, Idi 4
anarchy 7, 56, 139
Anayouchukwu, Arthur 37
Angola 2, 7, 147-8, 152
anomie 190
anthropology 11, 15, 19, 70, 161, 181-

2, 196,
apartheid 2, 7, 10, 18, 127, 139, 142-3, 153, 155-8
Appadurai, Arjun 14, 162, 177
arabism 96, 98, 101
Arendt, Hannah 68-9
Arkan 44
Armenia/Armenians 70-1, 74, 75n18, 76n25, 78
authoritarianism 10

Baldus, Bernd 188
bandits 27, 34, 59, 64, 95n2, 100
Bangladesh 78
barbarism 3, 18, 20, 51, 140-2, 161-2, 171, 181
Barkan, Joel 9
Barnett, Michael 84
Barre, Siad 8
Bartov, Omer 74n16, 77-8
Bashir, Omar 98-100
Bastian, Misty 165, 174
Battera, Federico 128
Bauer, Yehuda 67, 75n20, 76n26, 77
Baum, Gerhart 99
Baxter, Paul 122
Bayart, Jean-François 1, 5, 10, 12, 55
Bazenguissa-Ganga, Rémy 32
Belgium/Belgian colonial authorities 78, 80-3
Bell-Fialkoff, Andrew 81
Benjamin, Walter 176
Berg-Schlosser, Dirk 12
Berhane, Mekonnen 128
Berhe, Aregawi 130n14, 132n19, 133n21, 134

201